THE THIRTY YEARS WAR
J. V. POLIŠENSKÝ

J. V. POLISENSKY was educated at the universities of
Prague, London and Oxford. Now Professor of
Universal History at the Charles University of
Prague he is also a member of the Dutch Royal
Academy of Sciences and the sometime visiting pro-
fessor at the universities of California, Heidelberg,
Vienna, Budapest, Cologne and Santiago de Chile.
His publications in English include: ENGLAND
AND CZECHOSLOVAKIA (Prague, 1946); A
HISTORY OF CZECHOSLOVAKIA IN OUT-
LINE (Prague, 1948); THE BOHEMIAN WAR
AND ENGLISH POLICY (Prague, 1949) and
BRITAIN AND CZECHOSLOVAKIA (Prague,
1964).

Robert Evans, the translator, was educated at Jesus
College, Cambridge and is now research fellow in the
field of Hapsburg history at Brasenose College, Oxford. Dr. Evans is at present preparing for publication
a book on the Emperor Rudolf II.

The Thirty Years War

J. V. POLIŠENSKÝ

Professor of Universal History
at the Charles University of Prague

Translated by ROBERT EVANS
of Brasenose College, Oxford

NEW ENGLISH LIBRARY
TIMES MIRROR

First published in Great Britain by B. T. Batsford Ltd.
© Czechoslovakian edition, J. V. Polisensky 1970
© English translation, B. T. Batsford 1971

*

FIRST NEL PAPERBACK EDITION SEPTEMBER 1974

*

NEL Books are published by The New English Library Limited from Barnard's Inn, Holborn, London E.C.1. Made and printed in Great Britain by C. Nicholls & Company Ltd

450021882

CONTENTS

BOHEMIA AND MORAVIA
c.1618

—— Boundary of Holy Roman Empire

LUSATIA

Sagan

Mulde

Elbe

Dresden

Neisse

Bobr

SAXONY

Friedland

Ústí nad Labem

Teplitz

Litoměřice

Most

Hradiště

Jičín

Kadaň

Ohře

Žatec

Louny

Mladá Boleslav

Elbogen

Falkenau

Slany

Elbe

Podebrady

Eger

Rakovník

PRAGUE

Kouřim

Kolín

Berounka

Kuttenberg

Čáslav

Tachov

Pilsen

BOHEMIA

Sázava

Domažlice

Jankov

Klatovy

Vltava

Tábor

Jihlava

Bechyně

Vodňany

Hluboká

Třeboň

Danube

Budweis

BAVARIA

0   25
Miles

Passau

AUST

One

EUROPE IN A CENTURY OF CRISIS
AND REVOLUTION

THE year 1567 has traditionally been seen as the beginning of the
armed uprising of the Dutch Estates against Spanish government;
exactly a century later, in 1667, it was in Amsterdam that the
Moravian exile Jan Amos Comenius wrote the sorrowing pages
of his *Angel of Peace*, a political treatize designed to reconcile the
two great powers of the new commercial Europe, England and
Holland, and to terminate existing trade war between them. It
was England and Holland, but above all the latter, which
Comenius all his life regarded as models of a purposive ordering
of society and government; he thought it their task to crush the
"universal monarchy" of the Spanish and Austrian Habsburgs
and safeguard the European *corpus evangelicorum* in a united
and enlightened form. In them, and in Sweden whose links with
them were close, he placed his hopes for the resurrection of an
independent Czech state, that Bohemia which had been engulfed
by the Habsburg "Babylon" at the very beginning of the recent
great war, the "Thirty Years War" as contemporaries were
already coming to call it.

In the late 1650s the first historian of what we now call the
"English Revolution" of 1640–60, Cromwell's colleague John
Rushworth, likewise began to perceive the broad connection
between his own Civil War and the fateful events of 1618 in
central Europe. His close associate in the service of the English
Republic was Samuel Hartlib, a great friend of Comenius. Can
it be coincidence that Comenius, Rushworth and Hartlib were all
three capable, unlike historians of the Thirty Years War writing
in the nineteenth century, of seeing the wider European sig-

nificance in that conflict without being diverted by the distorting lens of nationalistic historiography?

The views of contemporaries were not of course readily adaptable to the liberal and chauvinistic models of thinking current in the last century, which looked down with a feeling of superiority on the "passions of religion" and with incomprehension on all phenomena transcending the purely national. Perhaps we, the generation of two world wars, can for this very reason penetrate more deeply than our predecessors into such 300-year-old problems. That is far from saying that we understand them. On the contrary it is correct to say, as Pierre Daix wrote recently: "Our knowledge of the seventeenth century, whether of France or of Europe as a whole, is minimal and vitiated by many constantly repeated errors; it is high time the whole position was changed." Daix seems also to be right in pointing out that historians of the social, economic and Marxist schools have been concerned primarily with the "more revolutionary" sixteenth and eighteenth centuries and have cast little light on the seventeenth. The latter appeared to display none of the vitality of the European late Renaissance and the age of overseas expansion, none of the economic stimulus of the "price revolution", still less the drama of the rise of the Western bourgeoisie under the influence of the Enlightenment, which led to the final struggle with the *ancien régime* in the French Revolution of 1789. But the superficiality of such an attitude has lately been stressed by several historians, among them Pierre Goubert, Robert Mandrou, Pierre Chaunu, B. F. Porshnev, N. A. Chistozvonov and M. A. Barg.

All accounts of the Thirty Years War have been influenced in some degree by the wider context of the whole evolution of European society and the importance of this within the narrowly political conflict, even where, as for example with S. H. Steinberg, they recognize only a war for continental hegemony which involved no changes in social structure. It has become fashionable today to speak of a "crisis" which overtook Europe roughly during the hundred years between 1560 and 1660. The notion derives particularly from a study by the English Marxist historian E. J. Hobsbawm which appeared in the review *Past and Present* in 1954 and put forward the view that the seventeenth century was an age of "general crisis". Hobsbawm's conception was adopted and carried over into the political field by H. R. Trevor-Roper in 1959, and both articles called forth a discussion with the French historian R. Mousnier and the English hispanicist

J. H. Elliott. Other contributions followed which drew parallels from Spain and Sweden (Michael Roberts), but the debate became concentrated increasingly on the crisis and its revolutionary outcome in Stuart England.

In 1965 the majority of these articles – though not all – were brought together in the book, *Crisis in Europe 1560–1660* with an introduction by Christopher Hill. Hill suggested that a number of conclusions could be inferred from the work done hitherto: 1. All western and central Europe witnessed in the seventeenth century an economic and political crisis; 2. this crisis manifested itself in different ways, and these merit individual attention; 3. the differences in the incidence of crisis must be explained by reference to social and political structures and to religious institutions and beliefs; 4. the results of the crisis in Holland and England, where political revolutions led to significant economic and social changes, were markedly different from the results in the rest of Europe, with France and Sweden occupying an intermediate position; 5. the history of Britain in this period can be clarified by comparison with the contemporary developments on the Continent, and *vice versa*, and in general sensible application of the comparative method by the historian is not only instructive but even approximates to the conditions of a laboratory experiment.

There is no doubt that the concept of a widespread European crisis, i.e. one within the very framework of feudal society, at least enriches our view of the past, and any historian of the seventeenth century must be grateful to Mousnier, Hobsbawm and Trevor-Roper for their attempts to cast light where till now so much has been darkness. But we must remember here that in the late 1940s the Soviet historian Vainshtein was already speaking of a "European crisis", while at the same time (1949) the present author summed up his standpoint thus:

The history of diplomacy (during the Thirty Years War) is unthinkable without an explanation of the given social structure: if we do not first observe that Jacobean England was a society in transition and on the brink of revolution, then its politics will necessarily appear hopelessly chaotic. However important and interesting the relation between Bohemia and Britain before 1618, its significance cannot match that of the Czech-Dutch connexion in those years. For it was not England and France, but the Netherlands on the one hand and the Vatican and the Spaniards on the other who were the motive spirits in

11

European politics in the years 1618–20. The example of the Dutch, relatively the most progressive contemporary state, illustrates most clearly the interrelation of European policy-making and its socio-economic foundations on the threshold of the Thirty Years War.

The weaknesses of the collection *Crisis in Europe 1560–1660* are obvious: its title makes a promise which the contents do not fulfil. In fact after the introductory generalizing study by Hobsbawm its discussion is exclusively of the seventeenth century and the period 1560–1600 is forgotten. It is anyway easy to find agreement that a "crisis" had in large measure overtaken Europe when no attempt is made to establish what the various authors understand by the word, or whether their definitions coincide. In this respect there may well be a repetition of the sad history of the "general crisis of feudalism", which was first canvassed in 1950 by R. H. Hilton as applicable to the fourteenth and parts of the fifteenth century, but which later, even in the works of Hilton himself (*viz.* his *A Mediaeval Society*, 1966) passed into oblivion.

There are certainly still historians who follow Hobsbawm's broad approach, according to which the crisis of the seventeenth century is the concluding and decisive phase of the transition from feudalism to capitalism, a transition whose beginnings Hobsbawm places in the thirteenth century, but which according to him was not completed in some parts of Europe until after 1800. The majority of historians however fear that such an interpretation of the notion of "crisis" is so nebulous that it is scarcely conducive to any fuller understanding of the past. It would only be a logical extension of this to cast the term in the rôle of *deus ex machina* for explaining any kind of phenomenon over a period of a full 500 years. Not only could the Italian Renaissance be viewed as the outcome of a "general European crisis", but the Hussite movement in Bohemia, the German and Swiss Reformations and even the Thirty Years War would qualify too.

Doubts about the Hobsbawm thesis have been expressed above all by Dutch historians, whose country has anyway been remarkably neglected in this general picture. With the single exception of the agrarian historian B. H. Slicher van Bath, they have doubted whether it is possible from the standpoint of the Netherlands, which were enjoying their "Golden Age" in the seventeenth century, to speak of any "general" crisis at that time. To this it may indeed be replied that the Dutch had already in the sixteenth century resolved their crisis by revolutionary means, and thus their history in the hundred years following was the exception which proved the rule, a new chapter in the passage from feudalism to capitalism.

In my own opinion however, any interpretation of the Dutch revolt and the English Civil War as "successful resolutions of a crisis of transition" presupposes that we have some clear idea what the crisis itself involved. Hill's conclusions seem to me thoroughly sound if we sum them up thus: a crisis is the culmination of ever-deepening internal conflicts within the infrastructure of a given society, which leads to a sudden collapse of existing economic, social, cultural and political relationships, and whose consequence will be either regression – regional or general – or on the other hand a powerful step forward in the development of that society. This means that there have existed, besides those crises which have issued in revolution, others, more restricted territorially, which proved to be abortive. To define crisis in this way as purely the culminating phase of a process, rules out applying it, at least in any precise sense, to the process itself; thus in practical terms we may speak of the period between the Dutch revolution of 1566–82 and the English revolution whose climax was in 1640–9 as characterized by crises limited both geographically to a single country, and socially to a single class. To yoke together, as does Ruggiero Romano in his book on the *European crisis of 1619–22*, (1962), a study of agricultural prices with far-reaching conclusions covering the whole of Europe, is an exceedingly risky proceeding.

A similar approach to Romano's is followed by the Polish historian J. Topolski in *The so-called economic crisis of the seventeenth century in Europe* (1962), who argues from the situation in Poland, where after the years around 1600 a stagnation of the economy can be observed, passing into a regression which lasts until the middle of the eighteenth century. Topolski's identification of crisis with stagnation and regression is methodologically unsound, since the latter are neither the only manifestations of crisis nor its necessary outcome, as M. Hroch and J. Petráň correctly observed in their critique of his book, published in the *Československý Časopis Historický* for 1964. Hroch and Petráň view the crisis as a direct result of the sharpening disparity between the development of factors of production and old productive relations, a disparity of European dimensions whose proportions are sufficient to destroy the existing *status quo* in one sector of society or another. On the basis of the same, hitherto available source material they reach the conclusion that the "general crisis of feudalism" can equally serve as a touchstone for evaluating developments in the Czech lands, whereas Topolski judged that there was no case for admitting any general weakening or slowing-down of economic advance in Europe as a whole. Topolski stresses rather the disproportions which already existed in social, economic and other spheres within individual countries, and which divided Europe into three camps: firstly, the lands with the greatest economic dynamic where the dissolution of feudal relations had proceeded furthest – England and the Netherlands; secondly, those where neither stagnation nor regression was observable – France, Scandinavia, Germany and the other countries of central and eastern Europe, including Bohemia but not Poland; and finally the areas of regression – Spain, Portugal, Italy and Poland. A. Wyczański and A. Mączak have attempted to test Topolski's findings, but no measure of agreement has been reached, either in Poland or elsewhere.

The only rational approach to the problem must surely be that of analysing concrete historical material in the light of a *theory* of feudalism which gives insight into the nature of the *crisis* of feudalism. Hitherto, researchers have all dilated on the crisis alone without explaining its own context. We may agree with Hroch and Petráň that the general crisis which announced the beginning of the collapse of the old order of society, without itself being its concluding chapter, is a misleading starting-point for meaningful parallels between the crisis of feudalism and the problems of the protracted supplanting of the old system by the new; at the same time it seems probable that their results will also be subject to the same sobering process which we have already observed with R. H. Hilton. Where they both judge that it is not necessary to introduce the term "general crisis of feudalism" we may readily agree; nevertheless it is clear that for at least some years to come we are likely to encounter more and more of such theories, extended to embrace the regions of eastern Europe, like Henry Kamen's "Reformation crisis" of the sixteenth century, Joel Hurstfield's trade cycle crisis of the years 1620–40 and Pierre Chaunu's *Civilization of Classical Europe* (1966).

The standpoint of Chaunu, who follows Mousnier's position to its logical conclusion, is worthy of attention. He is not only concerned with the crisis as a category of economic history, of "Europe in its second phase of development", the phase of falling prices, stagnation and consolidation, he regards as far more significant the positive achievement of these years in the history of thought. The "miraculous twenties" of the seventeenth century are for him the cradle of Classicism, by which he means "that short period when the resolution of tragic tensions on the foundation of the Baroque led to perfect harmony and equilibrium at least in the field of art".

> The Classicism of the seventeenth century is an art of revolution, the "mathematization" of the world in its celestial orbit, a world which had never before felt so great and majestic, a moment when the ordering of society coalesced with a whole cosmology. Viewed from the social point of view it could be said that Classicism is a short spell of great longing, the longing which seized the bourgeoisie, briefly diverted from its own, evolutionary struggle by its search for office in France and its slower advance in Holland in the year 1650–70.

It was perhaps because Chaunu's bold thesis appeared in a series under the title *Great civilizations* that the author made no attempt to explain what he understood by civilization, and indeed scarcely used the term in his text at all.

It appears to me however that, unless we wish to remain blindly amassing economic facts, we must at the very least elucidate the relation between society and civilization. The latter I take to mean broadly a given stage in the evolution of society, such as has been defined successively by Morgan and Engels, Lucien Fèbvre and H. Marrou. Civilization is a complex of many phenomena, each of whose parts reflects one aspect of human society, and whose whole is defined by the mutual relations of those parts. It is not a valid objection to Chaunu that his *Civilization of Classical Europe* is in fact the history of *l'Europe française* in the seventeenth and eighteenth centuries, and that for him French "hegemony" replaced that of Spain. The very notion of "hegemony" is of course a concept drawn from politics and "ideology": which is to say that the hegemony of France did not eliminate that of Spain through confrontation, but rather the absolutist Versailles of Louis XIV simply took over the function of the Castilian *peso politico de todo el mundo*, the political centre of gravity of the whole world. France was not a direct competitor to Spanish civilization, but a new form of society and state, such

15

as had been forged in the United Provinces during their Eighty Years War from 1568–1648, and it inherited the Dutch "model" thanks rather to the bankruptcy of the Dutch regent class in the middle of the seventeenth century than to the three wars between the Netherlands and the England of the Commonwealth and Restoration. Chaunu thus judges that it was France and England, or more correctly Great Britain, which divided world hegemony between them until the last years of the eighteenth century.

What caused the conflict between these two conceptions of civilization, these two approaches to the questions of life and death, society and the state, education and the processes of the mind? The answer is simple: the civilizations created their own ideologies, in other words there were developed in certain restricted areas (Spain and the Netherlands) conceptual attitudes which, while never embracing the whole breadth of those civilizations or even their most progressive aspects, became so far the support of certain forms of government that any attack on them was regarded as an attack on the state itself and its social framework. Within the given society these attitudes came to be placed before any other considerations, which were only allowed expression on condition that they remained subordinate to the ruling official doctrine. Thus it was the transformation of *civilizations* into *ideologies* which created the precondition for open conflict, and the danger of such a conflict was directly dependent on the stage which had been reached in the evolution of a "doctrine of state".

Most historians who, willingly or unwillingly, have faced the fact of the ideological confrontation of our own century and asked themselves whether we are not ourselves reliving the events of 300 years ago as witnesses of a new Thirty Years War, are agreed that the conflict possesses a new and unpalatable topicality. The majority accept the view that the changes undergone by European society in the crucial years between 1618 and 1648 brought to a close a period which the Renaissance civilization of the small Italian urban states had inaugurated, and ushered in through its series of crisis situations a "new age" which may only now be ending. Hill and Porshnev, R. Mandrou and A. Tenenti, J. H. Elliott and J. Topolski agree that the changes were not limited to the political sphere, but involved radical shifts in economic life, religious observance and questions of taste; in short, they affected the whole life of the 500 million or so people who were then living on the earth, and that of their descendants.

What you are about to read is an attempt at a new and different account of the Thirty Years War, seen as an example of two civilizations in ideological conflict. The clash of one conception, deriving from the legacy of Humanism, tinged with Protestantism and taking as its model the United Netherlands, with another, Catholic-Humanist one which followed the example of Spain, becomes thus the point of departure for the development of political fronts and coalitions of power. It would be a crass oversimplification to contend that the War was a collision between the champion of capitalism and the bourgeoisie on the one hand, and the representative of the "old régime" and feudal aristocracy on the other. These two models were merely the poles in a whole complex struggle, the centres around which were forged two powerful political camps, and the Netherlands played a leading rôle, always cautiously and as it were under compulsion, only until about 1630. Ten years after that the Spanish adversary had already for all practical purposes been eliminated, and England, while still looking to Holland as a model, was also beginning to see her as a potential rival. It belongs to the central theme of this book to examine how during the War new and modern prototypes were evolved by France and England, models for experiment both in parliamentary government and absolutism, economic advance and manufactory production, colonial expansion and unbridled repression of minorities at home, scientific progress, religious toleration and witchhunting. The traditional themes like the "war for European hegemony", the fate of "Europe divided", the relationship between Baroque and Classicism, will not be the centre of attention here, but this author considers that the present interpretation of the Thirty Years War can throw light on those problems too.

There is no need to stress that this is an endeavour which only takes as its starting-point the criticism of existing treatments of the War, above all the bold condensed account by C. V. Wedgwood which was published on the threshold of the Second World War. Although still being reprinted and widely acclaimed, Wedgwood's book presents the history of the Thirty Years War as a portrait gallery of rulers, statesmen, diplomats and generals, who according to the author themselves controlled the destinies of the nations of Europe. What I have attempted to do in more recent years has been to alter the emphasis, to reconsider the motives for the conflict in the light of what could be established about socio-economic changes in central Europe and elsewhere.

In this work there has been no question of a "revaluation", but rather a testing of thesis and hypothesis from an openly Marxist position in the light of unexpectedly rich source materials which languished until 1945 in the family archives of central Europe and have only since become available for the purposes of research. For there is no other way in which historical investigation can develop than by linking its theoretical reflections with the practice of the historian's trade, combining synthesis and analysis in the study of the more restricted, as of the most extensive, phenomena of the past.

Two

THE WORLD AT THE TURN
OF THE CENTURY

I wish to introduce to you the three protagonists in the story
which follows: the first is the whole population – perhaps 70
million – of the continent of Europe, at most an eighth of the
total on the globe. At a time when only one person in two survived to reach maturity and no-one could expect to live more than
45 or 50 years, this means that the War touched the fates of at
least 100 million individuals, since it was the exception for anyone already adult in 1618 to witness also the conclusion of
hostilities in 1648. Figures are revealing, but they never tell the
whole story, and the seventeenth century was anyway a pre-
statistical age; from this mass of Europeans we shall only be
able to distinguish and bring back to life a few "great individuals".
There are the same problems with the second protagonist, the
inhabitants of the Kingdom of Bohemia, that half-federal, half-
dynastic entity linking together Bohemia proper, Moravia,
Silesia and the Lusatian duchies. The Bohemian state had at the
beginning of the seventeenth century a population of approximately four millions, and this lent it in the context of its time
almost the status of a great power. It seems however that the
figure ceased to rise further during precisely this period, and signs
of economic, social and political tension began to be manifest at
the very moment when the fate of Bohemia and its people was
becoming one of the central questions in the complex nexus of
problems facing the diplomats of Europe. This "Europeanizing"
of the Bohemian crisis took place within a situation of great
delicacy and carried with it both unsuspected opportunities and
incalculable risks. Finally, there is our third protagonist: the

inhabitants, now to be numbered in tens of thousands only, of a smaller region in south-east Moravia, which was the birthplace of Comenius and scene of some of Wallenstein's activities; more concretely still, the thousand people who lived in one small country town and its immediate neighbourhood.

To survey this whole continental scene we must necessarily take up a point of vantage. Considering what has been said about the European dimensions of the "Bohemian question", and considering also the consensus among historians of culture that the Prague which was the residence of Rudolf II of Habsburg, Holy Roman Emperor and King of Bohemia, was at the same time one of the most notable cultural centres in Europe, I feel it justified to sketch in my subject from a Prague perspective.

PRAGUE AND EUROPE IN 1600

For the years around 1600 we possess at once three impressions of Prague, as seen both by local artists and more particularly by visitors from the Netherlands. From the flat top of the Letná hill, the Dutchman F. H. Hooghenberg depicted it in 1593 with the river Vltava winding through its narrow valley and caressing the ancient arches of the Charles bridge. His Renaissance landscape, drawn with true Venetian fidelity, shows the Imperial residence, the Hradschin, in profile only. The city of Prague, capital of Bohemia, *Regni Bohemiae Metropolis*, is cradled in the undulating folds of a typical Czech countryside, with the Little Town, Malá Strana, on the left bank, the district where most Italian, German and Dutch merchants lived, especially those *mercatores aulici* who supplied the court, and on the other side of the river the Old and New Towns. A woodcut view of Prague made by the Silesian Jan Willenberg in 1601 is taken from the Petřín scarp and shows the broad façade of the royal palace on the Hradschin together with the urban microcosm below. Finally, there is a large copper engraving dating from 1606, which was published by Aegidius Sadeler after a drawing by Filip van Bosche, cut by Jan Wechter and dedicated to the mayors, councillors and aldermen of all three towns of Prague. The three prospects are each enlivened with rafts on the river; Hooghenberg placed two citizens of Prague in his foreground, while his countrymen in 1606 drew in a crowd of small figures going about their business on the river and beside it, walking in the vineyards and gardens beneath the Petřín's "Hunger Wall", which had been built in an earlier age by the Emperor Charles iv to relieve unemployment and famine.

The towns of Prague represent a first and lowest level; the Hradschin and royal palace, inhabited by courtiers, nobles, foreign ambassadors and agents and their retainers, form a second one; while the heights of Pohořelec, Strahov and Petřín were symbols of a higher perspective which was probably hidden from the Emperor Rudolf and his ever-changing advisers and entourage. In the year 1600 Rudolf, the head of the Austrian branch of the House of Habsburg, the representative of the Holy Roman Empire of the German Nation, King of Bohemia and Hungary, and Archduke of Austria, could not gaze down on the town from the windows of his palace without a feeling of pride, or at the same time a sense of great unease.

He had finally migrated to Prague in 1583, when he was 31 years of age. The first third of that span of life he had spent with his father Maximilian ii and his mother Donna Maria, the daughter of Charles v (his parents were thus cousins, and some detect in this fact the cause of his neurosis and his state of psychical depression) in the hands of his Humanist educators, men like the botanist Clusius and the physician Crato. The second portion of his life till then had been passed at the sombre court of the "prudent monarch", *el rey prudente*, Philip ii. In contrast to his father, Rudolf was not accompanied there by a group of his own contemporaries who might have been able to take over at his court from those who had been with Maximilian in Spain and the courtiers of the "Spanish party". The consequences of this first became clear in 1584, the year after the Emperor moved to Prague, when on the initiative of the Papal nuncio Bonomi several representatives of the Catholic high nobility met together to discuss "by what means Prague and the whole of Bohemia might be brought back to the Catholic faith". This "Roman" faction derived support not only from the nuncio but from the Spanish ambassador, who was able besides to form a small "Spanish party" from admirers of his country's far from popular ideal of universal monarchy. The *facción española* rose to power only in 1599 when its leader, the "tall Hispan" Zdenek Vojtech Popel of Lobkovic, became Chancellor, the most influential if not the highest Bohemian office of state.

This however did not by any means signify that either the nuncio or the Spanish ambassador held decisive sway over

Rudolf's European policies. Lobkovic was of less importance than the Emperor's valets, and the nuncio Spinelli had to contend unsuccessfully for the soul of the monarch with the astronomer Tycho Brahe, the court *literati* like Typotius and Pontanus, and above all his artists, musicians and alchemists. This state of affairs was well-known to all Europe, and Barclay's *Satyricon*, (a scandalous *roman à clef* lampooning the relations of nuncios, Venetian and other agents) conveyed the message that Rudolf was more interested in the works of his artists: Sadeler, B. Spranger, J. Heintz, the Hoefnagels and the rest, than in disputes over religion or political prestige. Of course, his art collections and *ateliers* were not far removed from the political stage, indeed they played their own considerable rôle upon it. In a book, the one surviving copy of which belonged for a time to the Protestant Humanist Caspar Dornavius, we find described the works of art which were designed to glorify the essentially unheroic monarch who had brought with him from the court of Spain the gift of dissimulation and endless temporizing. It was for this reason that his attacks of "melancholy" sometimes coincided with times when he was called upon to make some unwelcome decision. That happened frequently enough: Rudolf was especially unwilling to enter into a marriage with the Infanta Isabella Clara Eugenia, the daughter of his uncle Philip II, until finally she became, at least in name, the wife of his brother Albert. This gave the Emperor a further reason for mistrusting Spanish policy, whose influence in central Europe he anyway regarded with disfavour. To the conflict in the Netherlands he remained neutral, and he refused to support the rather frivolous involvement of his young brother Matthias in the quarrel.

If however the Dutch question left him cold, to the frequent despair of the Spanish "orator" at his court, he displayed more concern for the Eastern question. The year 1593 saw the beginning of the fifteen-year war with the Turks in the districts of Upper Hungary, i.e. modern Slovakia. After some initial successes the imperial advance was brought to a halt by 1599, and thereafter the frontier could only be maintained with the help of Spain, which supplied both money and troops for the offensive. But whether it was the units of the Turkish *begs* or the Walloon mercenaries of the Prince of Mansfeld who brought the greater damage to the peoples of the contested territories is a difficult question to answer, one which still provides a source of argument among Czech and Slovak, Austrian and Hungarian historians.

In the view of Czech bourgeois publicists like the chronicler Daniel Veleslavín or his friend Kocín, a student of Bodin, what was required was a town militia to be organized against the Turks instead of the unreliable mercenaries; but the local brigades which were sent from Bohemia against the enemy scarcely distinguished themselves, and so the situation remained the same. One of the leaders of the Czech Brethren, Václav Budovec, a man well-known for his contacts with the centres of Calvinist culture in the West – Geneva, Basle, England, Holland and the French Huguenots, thought it necessary to put forward arguments against those who, according to him, had come to the false conclusion that the Christian powers were behaving worse than the Turks. Budovec employed the Ottoman threat as a weapon to urge all Christians to settle their differences. The Turkish "tyranny" was however to him only a little worse than the potential tyranny of Spanish "universal monarchy", and he found his ideal in a republic based on Estates.

The "Dutch question" and the "Turkish question" exemplify on the political plane the ever-aggravating confrontation around 1600 of three civilizations: the first the Islamic, the second the Mediterranean, Ibero-Italian and Catholic-Humanist, the third the maritime world of Protestant Humanism. According to the designs of Rudolf himself, his Imperial court in Prague was to realize the ideal, still mediaeval in conception, of a united and crusading Christendom. But his successes were negligible, and probably the most lasting of them was a purely military development. During the war with the Turks along the Upper Hungarian frontier there were evolved, besides the methods of warfare of the Spanish and Dutch as represented by Ambrogio Spinola and Maurice of Orange, the so-called "Hungarian tactics", which consisted in modifying the Spanish compact masses of soldiery because not enough men were available, and relying instead, perhaps influenced by the Dutch example, on towns and well-defended lines, and the cheap light cavalry raised by the *comitats*.

In other respects however the Prague court was an international meeting-place for artists and men of letters, not only from Italy and the Netherlands, but also the whole continent north of the Alps. There was room in Prague for many conditions of men: Giuseppe Arcimboldo from Milan, the Dutch artists de Vries and Hans von Aachen, the alchemists Kelley, Dee and Sendiwoj, Giordano Bruno and Johannes Kepler, Tycho Brahe and Jan Jessenius. Most of them were neither "Spanish" nor "Dutch" in their ideology, but seekers after new ways in philosophy, science, art, and not least politics. Towards questions of religion Rudolf revealed himself a pure agnostic, and he was quite openly resolved to play a rôle in politics. In this he hoped to realize a "third way", a balance of power in Europe, for only thus could effective resistance be organized against the Turks. The Prague admirers of Mannerist art stood close in matters of religion to Erasmus of Rotterdam, while in their politics they were eclectic, and we can find among them students of Jean Bodin as of Justus Lipsius. In 1600 such hopes of a "third way" in central Europe could still be considered respectable; succeeding decades were to sweep them totally aside.

But no-one could yet know this at the turn of the century. In the very year 1600 Prague welcomed an embassy from the Persian Shah, the prince of potentates, which included the English adventurer Anthony Sherley, the later renegade Don Juan de Persia and representatives from Muscovy, seeking support against the Porte or the Empire of Poland-Lithuania. The city was full of foreigners, and from England alone there were present at one time three groups of secret agents: one the "official" envoys of Cecil, another the "Essexmen", and a third the Scots from the court of James VI. In the Jesuit colleges of Bohemia there were active Spaniards, Dutchmen and even Englishmen – one of these the same Edmund Campion who was later put to death in London. Beside the agents were foreign merchants: by 1600 a powerful group of Dutch and Italian traders had settled in Prague, not to speak of Germans and native Czechs, as well as the occasional Englishman or Frenchman.

Notwithstanding the thesis of R. Schreiber that the trade of Bohemia inclined at this time towards the north and only became reorientated southwards during the course of the war, there is no evidence that a dominant rôle was played either by the route along the Elbe and the road to Lusatia on the one hand, or by commerce with Passau and Linz on the other. As far as customs revenues were concerned the most important through routes for merchandise were from the south-west to the north-east, and from the north-west to the south-east: in practical terms, from Nuremberg via Prague to Breslau and Danzig, and from Leipzig via Prague to Vienna. But the Czech and Silesian linen industry was reinforced by merchants and factors from the Netherlands and Westphalia, and financial dealings were conducted through Nuremberg as well as Leipzig and later Frankfurt.

Thus at this time, people from all corners of the continent could find their way to Prague, and the heretical views of Raymond Lull, Giordano Bruno, Calvinists and Cryptocalvinists, Catholic and non-Catholic statesmen, all found disciples and readers in the Bohemian capital. From this imaginary third and highest level of the Prague reality we must now proceed to some characterization of the actual situation in Europe. It will probably be best to employ a technique of separate but overlapping perspectives, embracing details of economic, social, cultural and not least political conditions.

An economic map of the continent in 1600 betrays, as has already been observed, many patches of white, and even the facts which we possess are far from being wholly reliable. In the area of south-central Europe, i.e. the lands of what was then the state of Bohemia and the Austrian and Hungarian territories which surrounded it, all of them ruled over by Rudolf II, we can gain a reasonably clear picture of the situation. Here as elsewhere there were signs of the general conflict between factors of production and productive relations which was already reaching crisis-point in some parts of Europe. This conflict was of course one of long standing, and dated back at least to the fourteenth century. We can say broadly that its roots lay in the opposition between the ever-increasing application of the law of value consequent on growing flexibility in the means of exchange, and the system of feudal rent which was maintained in conditions where the authorities could bring non-economic pressure to bear. The "price revolution" of the sixteenth century, whose very extent bears witness to the deep roots which transactions in money had already struck in Europe, affected regions where feudal relations were by then in an advanced state of decay, just as it affected other areas where the overlordship of the feudal ruling class remained substantially unquestioned. In this respect central Europe offered no uniform pattern, since the development of productive forces and the decline of feudalism had proceeded there in unequal measure, and thus the manifestations of crisis were varied. The feudal nobility, and this is particularly characteristic of the lands of central Europe, sought to exploit the revolution in prices, the new opportunities of the market and the means of exchange. Their intervention, especially in the making of prices, was wholly reactionary in its effects and revealed itself by the extension of feudal obligations in the capital and labour markets. Thus, far from freeing labour as a factor of production, they contributed to the strengthening of serfdom. All this reinforced the class of feudal proprietors and brought a sharpening of social tensions, especially where the towns were concerned, and severe political crises. At the same time it would be wrong to say that the reversal of development had already become decisive by the beginning of the seventeenth century in central Europe; that point was only reached during the War, which thus represented a fateful turning-point for this part of the Continent.

The War was less conclusive for the lands of eastern and northern Germany and Poland, where there were clear signs of regression by the turn of the century. These regions had been regularly exporting grain during the sixteenth century to the urbanized areas of western Europe, particularly the Netherlands and England, but also to the less advanced Spain and Italy. The historian Hausherr, as we now know, was overstating his case when he claimed that the import of grain into England and Holland was necessary because the swift rise of industrial capitalism in those countries had involved a neglect of agriculture. Dutch agricultural techniques stood on a very high level, but productive capacity could not keep pace with the growing consumer demand, and the traditional remedy for this was to bring in supplies from the east and the north-east of Europe. There were at the same time great differences in the character of land use between the various parts of England and Holland, as in the contrast between the south and the north of England, or that between the provinces of Holland proper and West Friesland on the one hand and the provinces which bordered Germany on the other.

In northern Germany and Poland a spread of the money economy took place, bringing with it the expansion of western European financial capital into regions where the feudal economic system was still untouched. These areas hence became dependent on England and Holland, countries with advanced methods of production, ever more dominated by the forces of commercial and financial capitalism. In such a situation the feudal landowner had ample opportunity to exploit the growing demand for larger-scale production and increased credit. Polish and German studies have demonstrated that the great feudal estates were not maintained by higher productivity, or new techniques of manufacture and productivity, but by the application of brute force.

At the other end of Europe, in Castile and the south of Italy, we encounter a crisis whose roots were apparently demographic. The regions ruled by the Turks were distinguished economically by a fairly well-organized commercial network and the development of some artisan trades, while their agriculture showed a neglect of cereals balanced by a spread of market-gardening and the introduction of a number of experimental crops. To compare either of these areas with the rest of Europe is extremely difficult in the present state of our knowledge.

If we turn now to trace the social ordering of the continent we find ourselves faced with the same problems, and the picture we can build up will of necessity be somewhat analogous. We can again use as indicators the towns and the level of urbanization, the strength of the "middle classes", i.e. the bourgeosie, and their economic and political significance as measured by their degree of commercial gain and their share in effective power. Both Topolski's and Hobsbawm's classifications are concerned with "Christian" Europe, and since the Ottoman Empire played only a small part in the Thirty Years War, and that part a passive one, I shall ignore it here. According to L. Barkan it was just during this period that Turkish society took on a feudal character – adapting itself to the European lands which it bordered – and this of course contributed to its decline.

The traditional commercial centre of Europe, the Mediterranean, was indeed, as Braudel showed in the late 1940s, unable from the time of the "collapse of the Borghesie" to halt the shift of the economic centre of gravity towards the north-west, the shores of the Atlantic. Until about 1580 merchants in Flanders continued to use Italian systems of accounting; after that time they were replaced by more modern methods of Dutch invention. This was a qualitative change which clearly reflected another, quantitative one. The earlier sudden rise of the city states of the Italian Renaissance had fallen away in the fourteenth and fifteenth centuries, and when Florence passed to Spain in 1531 the hispanicized peninsula had become an area whose people saw their only release in emigration. The thesis of Guglielmo Ferrero that Italy committed a subtle form of suicide by the voyages of Cabot, Columbus and Vespucci, cannot be sustained in this simple form: Machiavelli in his major work was writing simply as a politician seeking vainly to discover the cure for an urban civilization in premature dissolution. The findings of modern Iberian historians and the English writer J. H. Elliott, ascribe the "decline of Spain" to similar causes. All around the Mediterranean the towns were being subjugated, with the single exception of Venice, and even there the situation was growing steadily worse under the pressure of the Turks, the pirates and advancing rival *entrepôts*.

In the year 1600 some Czech travellers in Italy saw with amazement a Dutch ship anchored off the port of Leghorn. The Dutch were becoming the carriers of Europe, and they exercised with the English Merchant Adventurers a monopoly in the coastal trade of north-west Europe against which the remnants of the Hanseatic League could not compete. By contrast with the "Mediterranean" type of refeudalized civilization it was the "maritime" lands which were consolidating their superiority: England, the United Provinces, parts of Scandinavia and north-west Germany. Further east the state of Poland-Lithuania, threatened on its flanks by the Turks and dependent economically on the maritime powers, fully justified its title of "Spain of the North" by its social composition, especially the powerful position of its magnates. Conditions were to some extent similar in parts of Upper Hungary, where cattle and wine took the place of the grain staple. But the Hungarian situation was particularly complicated and no clear picture has yet emerged, even after the recent work of P. Zsigmond Pach and T. Wittman. The remainder of Europe, stretching from the Pyrenees to the Arctic ocean, cannot be fitted either economically or socially into the first or the second of our patterns. France, the greater part of Germany, the southern half of central Europe, the kingdoms of Denmark-Norway and Sweden were all regions where the direction had not yet been decided. Power was in the hands neither of a regent or other bourgeois class nor of large feudal proprietors.

I have suggested that the reflection in the cultural sphere of our two polarized "civilizations" is represented by two offshoots of European Humanism, the Catholic and the Protestant. The first of these found its ideological support in the Jesuit order, especially in the second generation of its members, who made complete surrender of their reason and subordinated their intellectual powers to the higher interest of discipline. It was precisely the end of the sixteenth century which saw the triumph within the Society of Jesus of a cult of the irrational and a monolithic authority, with the subordination of the personality in the service of a monstrous organism. This pressure was only to a limited extent moderated by the opposition of other orders – notably the Capuchins and a few individuals like Paolo Sarpi – and by the ranks of the secular clergy. Yet it is fair to remember that besides the Inquisitors the

Catholic Church produced also Las Casas and Vitoria, Juan de Mariana and Ribadeneira. Hispanicized Italy and Italianate Castille were always the focus of unbounded cultural interest, and it would be senseless to argue the relative merits of the Spanish late Renaissance as against the English. Impending danger came only when civilization was identified with ideology, when dialogue was replaced by terror of the insidious advance of Inquisition and Index.

We may now superimpose on the outlines of the European continent the shapes most familiar to us from our historical atlases: the map of political relations. From the chaotic fragmentation of central Europe and the Italian regions beyond the Alps we shall however only seek to grasp what the brightly coloured mosaic but rarely reveals – the real interactions and antagonisms.

The first point of tension was the Turkish question, which affected directly the immediate neighbours of the Ottoman Empire: Poland, Transylvania, the Habsburg federation of states, Venice and Spain. The Porte was still in political isolation, and the struggle with it was still concentrated in the Mediterranean despite the decades which had passed since the destruction of the Turkish fleet at Lepanto in 1571. At the same time however it was not only France, but also England and Holland who now maintained contact with the ostracized Turks, as the Venetians had always done. The Christian *cordon sanitaire*, designed to divide Islam from Europe, had already been abandoned, and in Prague negotiations were proceeding with the Shah of Persia who was no Christian, but might be able to divert Turkish forces usefully in far-away Mesopotamia.

The second antagonism was provided by the Dutch question, that cancerous growth which had been draining the life-blood of Spain since 1566 and had been the root cause of Spanish bankruptcies in 1557, 1575 and 1596, as it was to be again in 1607. During the last years of Charles V they had already begun debating at the court in Valladolid whether it was more important for Spain and its rulers to hold the Netherlands or Italy. Italy meant primarily Milan and the control of the Alpine passes, which carried with it the ability to maintain a dominating position in Germany and central Europe as a whole. Federico Chabod and Fernand Braudel seem to be correct in stressing that Charles V and the *rois catholiques* were basically at one in their preparedness nevertheless to abandon Italy if the very worst should befall them. In the event, of course, such a choice was not necessary; Philip II could apparently strengthen his hold on Italy and on America, and his empire was in reality an Atlantic *Imperium* which depended on the silver of the New World. But he could not subjugate the Low Countries, and a cloud had begun to hang over his Atlantic realms since the defeat of the invincible Armada in 1588.

The liberated Netherlands had already become, by the end of the old century, the potential organizer of an opposition to the Habsburgs since their political and economic interest were diametrically at odds with those of Spain. By 1598, the year which saw the end of Spanish intervention in France with the Peace of Vervins, the Dutch problem was the major consideration in European politics, and Henry of Navarre, like Elizabeth of England, entered the lists on behalf of the United Provinces. But the Dutch themselves had meanwhile established relations with Venice, the Swiss cantons, the Wittelsbachs of the Rhenish Palatinate and the kingdoms of Denmark and Sweden. They were logically the supporters of any action which might divert the weight of the Spanish *tercios* from the borders of the southern Rhineland. The two strongly fortified lines of defence in this region left neither Spinola nor Maurice of Orange with room to manoeuvre, and hence came the concern of both sides to extend the conflict beyond Wesel into the Empire, then further afield to the valley of the upper Danube and beyond.

It would clearly be quite false to imagine that the United Netherlands were backed diplomatically by any firm coalition of powers. But this was no more true of the other side: Madrid and Prague, like Vienna and Valladolid before them, were united only by the ties of blood, and the spider's web of their contacts also embraced Brussels, where Albert and Isabella began their joint rule in 1599, and Graz in Styria, where the Archduke Ferdinand was waiting for his hour. The stronger partner was clearly the Spanish branch of Habsburgs – without their assistance neither defence against the Turks nor hegemony within the Empire was conceivable. Spain had its problems in Italy and with the "barbarians" of North Africa, but she still held Portugal, and the fate of the Iberian *flota* still engaged (every autumn) the attention of men over the length and breadth of Europe.

Beside these two fundamental oppositions the smaller antagonisms recede into the background: the constant tensions between Polish and Swedish Vasas, Sweden and Denmark, English merchants and the Hanseatic League, Polish-Lithuanian magnates and Muscovite Russia. In the more restricted world of Germany there was the latent conflict between the Calvinism of the Palatinate and the orthodox Lutheranism of Saxony, and between Protestants and Catholics. If we add to all this the further contradictions between the nobility and the towns, the different levels of the aristocracy, and the real international struggle between classes, we have the picture of a Europe divided.

However great the dangers of generalization, this is the message which all the maps of 1600 convey; a Europe riven within itself as it enters the new century. The liberated Netherlands on the one hand, the Spaniards on the other, had become the two focuses for a gathering of forces which affected the whole of the continent, saving only that part which had fallen to the Turks. From the Atlantic to central Europe stretched an area where the different kinds of geographical frontier most frequently overlapped. Here the "Dutch" and "Turkish" questions were only a distant source of action and a political protext; and since a solution of the conflicts had become too hazardous where there were lines of direct confrontation, the sphere of involvement stretched increasingly to the upper Rhine, the Danube and the Elbe. This should be more evident when after a consideration of Europe as a whole we proceed to a discussion of the "Bohemian question".

BOHEMIA AND HER NEIGHBOURS: ECONOMY, SOCIETY, CIVILIZATION
The Hussite revolution was the first movement in Europe to fling open the gates which had prevented the masses of the people from receiving proper education and from playing a part in all departments of public life. With the fall of exclusive scholasticism went a widening of mental and physical horizons among all sections of the population. The ferment of ideas and the emergence of the free critical reason in matters of religion which took their origins from the fifteenth century Hussites had an influence far beyond the borders of Bohemia, throughout the whole of central Europe, and even in more western lands. The neighbouring German territories, which were in permanent, if fluctuating, contact with the Czech state and with the economic concerns of its inhabitants, had especially to come to terms with Hussite thought and its consequences both for the affairs of state, the life of society as a whole and the mutual relations of its various constituent groupings. What was most significant for further political developments within Bohemia, as for the relations of the latter with its German neighbours was the basic fact that a unified and centrally govern-

ed Czech state pursuing its own independent policies now stood alongside the fragmentation and disorder of the Empire.

The successes of the Czech religious reformation, which remained quite isolated in comparison with the other nations of Europe and yet were upheld through the fifteenth century despite the strong pressure of Rome and the Catholic powers of Germany and Poland, provided the new generation growing up after 1500 with a sure base for further peaceful evolution. The fact of religious tolerance and its consequences for society had become so characteristic of life in the Czech lands, and were so rooted in all sections of the population, that even the changes which followed the linking of the Bohemian state with the Alpine lands of the Habsburgs left the new ruler no opportunity to upset the balance, at least in the first years of his reign. The political, economic and social cooperation of Catholic and Utraquist groups which had emerged during the course of two or three generations in Bohemia became uniformly accepted by the beginning of the sixteenth century and was a firm foundation, granted the terms of a late feudal system, for the maintenance of religious peace and the calm furthering of domestic affairs of state.

Such a situation depended of course to a large extent on the relationship between the two main constitutional powers in the feudal Czech constitution, the monarch and the Estates. The beginning of the sixteenth century saw a certain consolidation of their joint rôle in public affairs. These two pillars of the existing social order created a platform for further political development in Bohemia which had consequences for all central Europe and helped to define the character of future relations between the east and the west of the continent.

The election of Ferdinand I to the Bohemian throne meant not only a great strengthening of the power of the Habsburg family in Europe, giving it more scope against its French rival by guaranteering the solidity of its eastern front, but was also the express result of a serious political decision on the part of the Czechs, for with it they brought the leading central European state into harness with the mightiest continental power. Marshalled against the mounting Turkish pressure, which certainly had its influence in this decision, there thus arose a highly effective and stable rampart, a well-organized Western political block in the heart of Europe.

It may be asked to what extent the choice of the new monarch was governed by the relationship of Bohemia to her German neighbours. Here it is clear that by rejecting the candidature of one of the princes of the Empire, be he from Bavaria, Saxony, Brandenburg or Liegnitz, the Bohemian Estates were showing their unwillingness to link the political development of their state with that of any of the far weaker German lands, which were less than wholly independent, and their determination to seek a partner of equal rank among the leading European powers. Any realistic assessment of the European situation at the time made it obvious that none of the German states could stand comparison as to resources or population with Bohemia, while the social disorders within the Empire, where the great revolt of the peasants had erupted just before 1526, argued strongly against any Czech alliance in that direction. On a wider international view it was equally clear that a dynastic alliance with France, which had just been forced into large concessions to Charles V after its defeat at Padua, would have dragged Bohemia into the bitter conflict of the two great powers, and that at a time when the overall situation in central Europe was extremely delicate with the threat of a further Turkish advance across the plains of Hungary. The course of the war between France and Spain during the succeeding decades amply justified the caution of the Czech political leaders.

All calculations about the suitability of a Habsburg for the throne of Bohemia had to take into account the character of the young Emperor Charles V, Ferdinand's brother, and here the prospects for the Czechs were less favourable. Charles had already revealed his basic position at the Diet of Worms in 1521: "in Germany there must be one ruler only, not many"; and this uncompromising attitude showed Czech politicians that the advent of a new sovereign had materially altered the balance of power on their western frontier. The strength of the Bohemian Estates gave reason to hope that the problems of Germany, where the structure of society was different, would not directly affect the Bohemian lands. The implementation of a new conception of the state and its administration on the Spanish model, a model foreign both to Germany and Bohemia, occupied the new emperor so thoroughly and for so long that he had little chance to interfere in Czech affairs, even indirectly through his brother Ferdinand.

It has often been suggested in the literature on the subject that Ferdinand's electoral success was largely the result of the corruption of the Czech political leaders. But although this kind of practice was standard in those days (the recent election of the new emperor had been effectively secured by the financial activities of the house of Fugger) it would be wrong to interpret every mention of transactions involving money before the election of Ferdinand as bribery of the Bohemian Estates. The payments which were agreed upon during the campaign were for the most part not gifts, but rather the first settlement of existing crown debts, and it was from this standpoint that the first delegation proceeded in December 1526 to negotiate with the new ruler on behalf of the Bohemian diet. The promise which Ferdinand gave to recognize the standing financial obligations of the state was a step which helped considerably to maintain the credit of the nation, placed under the severest strain during the last year of the Jagellon dynasty.

With the accession of a new king and a powerful new dynasty, Bohemia was carried into a new political and cultural orbit. She entered a world dominated by the might of the Spanish monarchy but which through the rivalry of other nation-states, France and England, with exclusive political and religious ideologies, was exposed to recurrent and far-reaching crises. We have already spoken of the profound changes in the spiritual life of Europe, the great economic expansion and growth in population, and the unprecedented strengthening of the machinery of state which took place at the beginning of the sixteenth century. All these factors, interacting with one another to a greater or lesser degree, produced stresses in the various European countries and frequently led to violent confrontations between old and new forms of thought and action. From such conflicts, which involved vitally important areas of spiritual and economic life, there developed protracted and deep-seated crises, manifesting themselves in acute and chronic forms throughout the continent despite the varied underlying historical patterns. At the same time the changes which were brought about in one country affected the life of other states, although not necessarily with the same intensity, or in the same fields of public, economic and cultural affairs. It was precisely this varying impact of critical situations on the life of organic societies, with the spur it gave to the encouragement of sympathetic and the repression of antipathetic tendencies within those societies, which lend the history of the sixteenth century its dramatic and tragic character.

The first shock of these great social and ideological conflicts came in the early years of the century with the German peasants' revolt and the beginnings of the Lutheran Reformation, which were linked to the stern power-struggle between the Emperor and the princes of the *Reich*. Neither brought any significant change in the Bohemian situation: the peasant opposition which was felt in a few parts of the country had no serious repercussions, while the religious tolerance which had a long and stable tradition in the Czech lands was able to ride out without major trouble the first waves of Lutheranism. In the field of internal politics the firm resistance of the Estates frustrated attempts by the king to concentrate the administration of all state finances in the newly created Royal Bohemian Exchequer, organized in 1527 according to west-European models, and the highest executive organ of state remained the Bohemian Chancery, under the direct control of the representatives of the Estates. At the same time certain separatist tendencies which had appeared in Moravia and Silesia during the election of the new monarch were not allowed to become established.

While the power of the king, operating through his Viennese officials, was improved and extended to cover all realms of public life, the party of the Estates had firm support not only in the national Diets, which decided on all matters of state taxation, and hence on the main source of central finance, but also through its departmental representatives, who could ensure that taxation policy in practice reflected no bias in favour of the royal authority. This vindication by the Estates of their old rights and methods of administration showed success in the 1530s when an attempt by the crown to extend the competence of the Exchequer was forced to yield to their protests and confirm the existing wide field of activity of the Chancery; for many years after this the Estates were able to guarantee their interests through the person of the Chancellor.

The Estates thus carefully observed the workings of each and every part of the administration, and rightly believing that their most important public duty was the maintainance of good relations between the king and his subjects, they laid great stress on this in their contacts with the monarchy. They were well able to adapt their methods to the needs of any given situation. After Jan of Pernstein had openly but unavailingly warned the king in 1539 that he was in danger of losing the confidence of the country, they did not hesitate to resort to the most resolute expedients. A firm protest from the Diet against the royal initiative in introducing new principles of administrative practice unfavourable to the Estates culminated in their rejection of the king's proposals and the dissolution of the assembly. The solid front presented by the Estates was the foundation of their political strength and the essence of their statecraft. This resolve did not weaken in the years that followed, and it soon afterwards survived the first serious international crisis of the year 1547.

Thus the political community of the Bohemian Estates withstood the competition of the monarchy throughout the first half of the sixteenth century. The spring and summer of 1547, when a political and religious crisis which originated in Germany penetrated deeply into the Bohemian situation, brought an especially severe test, and the leaders of the Estates were able to surmount it only with resolve and fortitude. The self-assurance of the victorious Charles V, who saw before him the realization of all his plans, acted as a spur to his younger brother Ferdinand, the King of Bohemia, and the latter began to elaborate considerably more far-reaching aims than those which, in the event, he succeeded in implementing. The strengthening of state finances by placing further burdens on the towns was only one point in the programme suggested by his advisers. But thanks to the military strength of the Estates of the nobility, who even after the imperial victory in Germany refused to disband their forces, and to the energetic and incisive leadership of Jan of Pernstein and others, the old, familiar structure of state was maintained in Bohemia and the Estates continued to play an unrestricted part in the means of government.

The period from 1547 to 1552, when the victorious Habsburg camp could contemplate the limiting of Protestantism in Bohemia, was shortlived and gave way to a renewed equilibrium between the monarch and the Estates. Besides the entrenched position of the Bohemian Estates which we have already mentioned, a large part in this was played by the brusque change of political fortunes inside Germany, where the protracted efforts of the Emperor Charles V to achieve a monopoly of power ended after thirty years of warfare in a victory of the electors, the princes and the towns. The lengthy, bitter bouts of conflict between the old feudal conception of government and the new encroachments of an absolutist ideology, together with the growing influence of the Lutheran Reformation, destroyed the inner foundations of imperial political power, while Charles's complicated international involvements – especially his war with France – exhausted both the financial resources of Spain and the practical energy of both Habsburg brothers. All these intricate factors were also restraints on the Bohemian king, allowing him no base from which to assay any similar alteration of domestic arrangements within the Czech lands. The measure of stability achieved between king and Estates in Bohemia was assisted by the retreat of the Catholic Emperor before the demands of the Protestant princes and Estates, and the conclusion of the religious peace of Augsburg in 1555. This created a new balance of forces within the Empire, and its indirect effects were soon felt in Bohemia, particularly through changes in the structure of the Church and the character of religious observance.

By the middle of the sixteenth century, profound and notable developments had thus affected the face of the Bohemian state and its society, penetrating its internal structure and organization, the social and economic conditions of all its Estates and classes, and the nature of its finance and commerce. While the beginning of the century had found the order of society much as the Hussite revolution had left it, the rich economic advance which followed, coupled with the political and religious changes proceeding from the 1540s, brought a rising ferment and modified the life of every single citizen. To this the sharpening conflict between king and Estates over the interpretation of the polity of state and its domestic and international obligations, added an important channel through which the existing foundations of feudalism were amended.

Here is the place to consider more closely the main constituent parts of Bohemian feudal society at the stage which it had reached by the end of the sixteenth century. The collective appellation "Estates", encountered so frequently in historical literature, embraced in fact various layers of society with quite different economic hues. First came the two classes of lords and knights, whose possessions represented the greater part of all landed property in the country. By 1500 the arrangement of land holdings which the Hussite period had brought into being was taken on final form. For a majority of the third and fourth generation members of these lordly and knightly families, the landed estates, inherited from their predecessors, guaranteed a regular standard of life commensurate with their status in society, while certain enterprising individuals were already beginning to build the foundations of the large-scale *latifundia* familiar from the end of the century. The outstanding examples of this kind of economic rise are the knightly families of Trčka of Lípa and Smiřický of Smiřice. The tax registers of 1544 provide a very clear and detailed insight into the economic affairs of the Trčkas, and indeed of all the knights in the three provinces of Central Bohemia. The Trčkas, whose property was already by the mid-sixteenth century some of the most substantial, not only among the knights but even the greatest magnates, succeeded by the beginning of the seventeenth century in creating an extensive and concentrated territorial block in the east of the country sufficient to rival the five large domains which the crown possessed in the most fertile part of the Elbe valley.

The general economic expansion which took place in the Czech lands during the second half of the sixteenth century was thus turned to advantage not only by traditional magnate families like the Rožmberk (Rosenberg) and Pernstein, but also by such as the Veitmils, Schlick and Smiřický. These came to represent the highest form of economic concentration, underpinning their own agricultural production with finishing and direct marketing of their output. By improving methods on their estates, other less significant families appeared among the successful entrepreneurs in such branches of agriculture. Berka of Dubá, Vartenberk, Černín of Chudenice, Gersdorf, Hodějovský of Hodějov, Hrzán of Harasov: members of these and other families brought into being within two or three generations during the sixteenth century large landed complexes which provided a firm basis for their political aspirations and whose economic scope was sufficient to influence the course of national developments.

Within this group of leading landed proprietors the whole sixteenth century was a time of economic progress rather than decline. The only major casualty during these years was the Pernstein family, which fell tragically from grace during the space of three generations after having had in Vojtech of Pernstein one of the most important politicians and successful entrepreneurs of the early years of the century. The reason for the fall of the Pernsteins was extravagant living and heavy outlays both on their own court and on maintaining their position with the king. Such a mode of life and such unconcern for the management of their estates were not to be found among other families in this extreme form; rather the reverse, for at the very time when the Pernsteins were obliged to forfeit Pardubice, which their ancestor Vojtech had earlier made into a model of wise administration, the Trčkas, Smiřickýs and other lordly and knightly families were reaching the zenith of an economic advance based on personal participation in the running of the estates which they controlled.

Thus there arose during the sixteenth century on the lands of the nobility a new type of successful, large agricultural and industrial enterprise which lent a characteristic impress to the Bohemian national economy. It was not however restricted to the aristocratic sector. The extensive estates of the free towns became in each individual province competitors almost equal in rank with the properties of the high nobility, differing from them but little in the nature of their production and in their social and economic relation towards the peasantry. Here too husbandry was directed primarily towards the crops and livestock which could best be sold in local markets (wheat, beer, fish, cattle), and there is no sign that any propertied town-dwellers selected estates of such a complexion as to yield raw materials such as wood or wool, or semi-finished products such as cloth or iron, which could be worked in specialized urban *ateliers*.

In this direction the corporations of the free towns had great opportunities, but they failed to take advantage of them. The very extent of their land holdings bears witness to this. In the province of Hradec the properties held by the towns represented in 1544 a value of 84,867 Bohemian marks, in Litoměřice 70,049, and in Žatec as much as 153,834. If we compare these figures with those for the real property of the two aristocratic estates it emerges that in Hradec six free towns had 22,000 marks more than the lords in that province, and almost a quarter as much as the knights. In Litoměřice three towns possessed nearly half as much property as either lords or knights, while in Žatec four free towns had real wealth which was only marginally below that of the lords and exceeded that of the knights. When we look more closely at individual towns we discover that in Hradec alone the common holdings of the town of Hradec Králové (Königgrätz) with their 63,576 marks were worth almost as much as the estates of the magnate Jan Trčka of Lípa and Lichtenburg (66,875) and only the property of the heirs of Mikuláš Trška of Lípa was significantly greater at 82,753 marks. In the province of Litoměřice the town of Litoměřice had wealth amounting to 50,105 marks, which was over half as much again as the possessions of the two largest lordly landowners, Václav of Vartemberk and the brothers Šlejnic. In Žatec the economic importance of the towns was higher still: the town of Žatec with its 61,561 marks stood only just below the richest man in the province, Sebastian of Veitmil, while the property of Louny at 44,650 marks was equal to that of Jeronym Schlick.

It is clear from this that a number of free towns must be included among the richest landed proprietors in Bohemia, and that state of economic affairs goes far towards explaining the accord which is frequently to be seen between towns and nobility in their attitude towards questions of land taxation. We have already mentioned that the urban communities followed the same guiding lines of economic policy as the aristocratic magnates, and there is no evidence that they were prepared to seek out new ways of advancing artisan crafts and trades in the towns by their own intervention in the markets for raw and semi-finished materials. In total, their economic management was a curious combination of two systems: the flexible methods which were being developed on the lands of the nobility and the old, inelastic framework of the guilds of traders and artisans. The traditional and reliable ways of marketing their finished goods, a major concentration of their means of finance and investment, and the chance to give greater initiative to small artisan undertakings; all these provided the corporations of the free towns with wide opportunities to improve and accelerate the development of urban economies – but they were not utilized. New impetus and lasting initiative was brought to the economic life of the sixteenth century rather by the domain towns and townships* where basic trades and forms of commerce were developed unencumbered by guild regulations and unhindered by the attempts of the free towns to create their own monopolies. These will engage our attention more fully later.

Among the feudal *latifundia* in Bohemia, the royal domains occupied a special position. A limited block of them, comprising Dobříš and Křivoklát, were based on large-scale forest management and entered into provincial and national economic life effectively only by limiting the resources of timber. Against these the complex of five extensive central- and east-Bohemian estates: Lysá, Brandeis on the Elbe, Podebrady, Chlumec on the Cidlina and Pardubice, came by the second half of the sixteenth century to play an important rôle in the economy of the broad, fertile basin of the Elbe, as in more distant trading with Prague and other Bohemian towns, both in the growing of crops and in the rearing of livestock, especially fish and cattle.

The economic administration of these domains differed from that of the other large landed properties, most particularly in being centrally controlled from Prague by the Bohemian Ex-

*"unfree" towns on the lands of the crown or the nobility (trans.)

chequer. This direct subordination to the financial department of state, which was primarily concerned with other matters, brought with it frequent difficulties for the managers of the estates and their many individual enterprises. The clumsy, often ill-informed decisions of the Exchequer restricted the provision of necessary investment and left insufficient freedom of initiative to the bailiffs or wardens of the several branches of production: breweries, fisheries, forests and the rest. Similarly the pressure of the high financial demands of the monarch affected adversely the maintenance of a very large number of buildings on the crown lands and squandered too great a proportion of their income on the wholly unremunerative purposes of the court. The pledging of all proceeds from the crown estates to the banking house of Fugger, to which recourse had to be made in the 1560s, put a complete brake on the expansion of all their activities for a number of years, especially those sectors which elsewhere were proving the chief foundation of prosperity, i.e. breweries, fisheries and animal husbandry.

To the list of forms of estate management which landed proprietors in Bohemia practised and amended during the sixteenth century the lands of the Exchequer added one which had previously been unknown: the mortgaging of a whole domain. Besides the traditional *rentier* type of landlord who relied, beyond the yield of his staple products, mainly on the regular financial, and to a lesser degree natural, payments from his serfs (for example the Trčkas, Rožmberks and Smiřickýs and later Albrecht Wallenstein), there stood others more progressive and enterprising, who were extending the most lucrative branches of production and seeking new sources of income. Against both these models the crown lands were distinguished by being less efficient and less well-organized, while the experiments and numerous suggestions of various commissions charged by the court to investigate ways of improving the situation brought little change during the 1570s or 1580s.

The internal workings of the very largest estates, whose most outstanding representatives in the early years of the sixteenth century were the Rožmberks as traditional feudal lords and the Pernsteins as exemplars of more modern techniques, came to be characterized (from the decades immediately before 1500) by attempts to fully utilize two particular branches of husbandry: brewing and fisheries. Beer, like grains and livestock, was sent for sale to local markets, but the fish also found its way abroad to trading centres in Germany and Austria. The continuing successes of these two sectors of agriculture induced the owners of less extensive estates to construct fishponds and to improve their facilities for brewing. The result of that general tendency was a shift in the returns accruing from the various sources of profit on estates large and small. The yield from these two branches of production came to substantially exceed that from the regular feudal dues of the peasantry, which remained unchanged at the levels fixed by ancient tenancy agreements. The high returns, easy availability of raw materials and above all the regular yield throughout the year, combined to attract the attention of all estates both in town and village to the brewing of beer, and the results of this revealed themselves increasingly during the sixteenth century in a major change in economic priorities through the whole country. While before 1550 breweries were to be found only on estates which embraced at least five to seven villages, production of beer had so expanded by the beginning of the following century that many smaller country properties had become self-sufficient in this respect. The taxation returns for 1620, which draw a line under the economic ledger of independent Bohemia, afford a detailed picture of the technical structure of the average estate, and they reveal clearly that even those so small as to include only nine or ten peasant settlements were actively and successfully involved in this branch of production.

Czech economic development in the sixteenth century was not of course just the rosy picture whose main contours we have just outlined. It too had its times of crisis, both personal and regional, and periods of regression touched all levels of society. These misfortunes affected most deeply the owners of smaller settlements in the country who belonged to the ranks of the poorer knights and the peasantry, as well as the weaker artisan crafts in the towns. At times of harvest failure, fluctuation in price and market conditions, serious losses of livestock and dislocations in transport, it was the smaller economic units which felt the pressure much more directly than the great landowners, whose wide-ranging productive activities and easier access to credit facilities could cushion the effects of any crisis. The preponderance of lesser landlords came from the ranks of the knights of the provinces.

It would be worth a separate, detailed study to follow the evolution of these smaller estates through the sixteenth century, which marked the climax of their importance for the national economy and for social and cultural life in Bohemia at large. The private fates of many of these knightly families, which taken as a whole formed one of the pillars of the established social order, were closely linked with changes in economic life and political and religious developments at home and abroad. The continual division of smaller estates among members of one family, which in three or four generations could lead to serious fragmentation of the property, had brought, by the beginning of the seventeenth century, a great increase in the smallest holdings of land, and such ill-equipped units could not guarantee their owners a standard of living appropriate to their social claims. Thus many scions of impoverished knightly families were obliged to seek a living elsewhere.

The taxation registers for the sixteenth century illustrate this trend in detail, both for the knightage as a whole and for its individual families. The full returns for 1544 from among those whose income lay between 100 and 300 mark show that in the provinces of Žatec, Litoměřice and Hradec (the latter being the province *par excellence* of the lesser knightage) many of the knightly estate were already working with holdings whose value was no higher than that of two or three prosperous peasant farmers. In subsequent decades the tendency was strengthened, so that by 1620 every province had large numbers of knights with land holdings of ten settlements and less. The findings of the severe confiscation tribunals after the battle of the White Mountain reveal not only a broad stratum of knights with so little property that their living standards were indistinguishable from those of the well-to-do peasant, but also a large number who were saved from prosecution because even thorough investigation could not prove that they held any property whatever.

The economic activities and importance of this numerous order of society have so far received little serious attention in historical literature. But even a superficial study of five tax registers (those for 1544, 1557, 1603 1615 and 1620), together with the frequent mentions in the literature of some few dozen knightly estates, make it clear that it was an active and significant social class, controlling perhaps a third of all the land holdings in Bohemia. Their estates were both well equipped, especially in the provision of smaller utensils, and undertook a wide range of agricultural and manufacturing activities, e.g. brewing, milling, sheep-farming, etc. There is ample proof that the knight in his castle was not restricted to maintaining the traditional tenant-plough-man, but could also be a landlord of initiative and industry, taking his part in producing the whole range of commodities which could be sold in the flourishing domestic market. This general striving of the knightly Estate to contribute to all departments of economic life was the ground-swell on which a few daring and successful entrepreneurs could ride – the Trčkas and Smiřickýs are the best-known of them – and amass fortunes exceeding those of the richest magnates.

The economic and social importance of the middle stratum of feudal society was not however limited to material and proprietorial considerations and the personal part they played in agricultural production. If we follow developments in the administration of the *latifundia* of the crown and the great magnates we can see that it was members of the Estate of knights who by the first years of the sixteenth century already filled the majority of supervisory posts, both as bailiffs of whole domains, estate accountants and managers of the various productive enterprises. Thus on the royal lands of central Bohemia, as on the lands of Trčka and Smiřický, the burgraves and bailiffs, chief clerks and masters of the fisheries and forests, even in many cases the foremen of the common ploughing-teams, were all knights. Neither can we pass by without any mention the part played by this class in the culture of the century: its best-known figures are the travellers Kryštof Harant of Polžice and Václav Vratislav of Mitrovice, and the diarist Mikuláš Dačický.

When we pursue the differences between the economic position of the free towns and that of the nobility it becomes clear that the question of the ownership of land is only part of a more complicated problem. It would be false to suggest that the royal free boroughs, which formed the third estate of feudal society, were the only ones belonging in the category of centres of nonagricultural production and commerce. From the beginning of the sixteenth century, but more especially in the years between 1550 and 1600, a large number of domain towns and townships had sprung up, thanks to the swift growth in population and the more sophisticated needs of both lord and peasant. The everyday requirements of maintainance and new investment in larger undertakings like plough-teams, breweries, mills and the bigger peasant farms, as well as things of a more personal character such as shoes, clothes, table-ware, were to be bought more easily, quickly, and above all more cheaply, in a domain town which was near at hand than in a distant free one. While the network of free boroughs remained substantially unchanged throughout the sixteenth century there were many estates both large and small which obtained the permission of the government to create their own urban communities. The registers of the Bohemian Exchequer from the second half of the century contain many references to the growth of new craft and trading centres. This wave of changes in the organization of non-agricultural production and commerce was a significant factor in the development of the domestic Bohemian market and the economic life of the country as a whole on the eve of the 1618 revolt.

Besides these external and territorial changes the sixteenth century also saw major alterations in the internal structure of the municipalities. The first attack by non-urban consumers on the monopoly position of the free towns, led of course within the limits of the existing feudal order by the aristocratic landowners, was waged, as we have seen, over the brewing of beer, and thus over a commodity which provided both a seller's market and also, given the guarantee of local raw materials, a very high rate of profit. Even though the boroughs' monopoly in this direction was limited in 1517, this did nothing to destroy their economic resources either as a community or through the undertakings of individual citizens. The taxation figures for 1544 bear witness to the flourishing state of communal property in the towns.

Throughout the sixteenth century prosperous members of the urban patriciate had considerable success in acquiring estates in the country, and cases of rich burghers gaining a foothold in the lesser nobility were far from unknown. Affluent townsmen played an important part in financial dealings, both by offering credit to private traders and artisans, and by providing greater loans to corporations, members of the nobility or the state itself. Although Bohemian conditions gave no opportunity for the rise of banking houses like the Fuggers and Welsers, there were enough financiers to provide facilities for the country's internal needs.

After the temporary regression which followed the events of the year 1547 the free towns blossomed forth again, and by the end of the century their total holdings of land almost equalled those of the knights' Estate. The craft guilds and traders enjoyed many years of untroubled development, so different from their neighbours in Germany where the *Reichsstädte* underwent at the beginning of the century a tempestuous social and economic crisis, the result of the struggles of the artisan class against the patricians and a growing burden of taxation.

Yet the upsurge of the free boroughs was not without its upsets and hindrances. These stemmed essentially from two factors: the growing competition of the domain towns, and the severe demands of state taxation. The lasting cooperation and interdependence of country towns, primarily those subject to a feudal lord, and the surrounding agrarian villages led increasingly to economic groupings which could effectively challenge the products of the free towns. In this they were greatly helped by the nature of prices for non-agricultural products, which were markedly lower with craftsmen and traders in the country than in the free towns. These price scissors were a prime factor in reducing levels of profit among enterprises in the latter and holding down the wages of employees, which in turn led to frequent and at times quite serious manifestations of social discontent. The domain towns, on the other hand, whose artisans operated with cheaper labour and had access to less-expensive sources both of raw materials and the essentials of life, could market their products at a more favourable price. They could also cut costs by selling directly to consumers in their neighbourhood, while the prosperity of medium-sized and larger peasant settlements and the rising wages of agricultural day-workers provided a reliable basis for high turnover of a large variety of goods. The great increase in domain towns throughout the sixteenth century (and accelerating towards its end) proves that this form of partnership with village communities was advantageous to both sides and speeded the economic development of each. The result for the free boroughs, especially the small producers in them, was naturally a pressure which made itself felt most severely when coupled with increasing tax demands from the state, and resistance against these sometimes grew into political disaffection, as in 1534 and again in 1543.

The influence of the domain towns and townships was not limited to the conditions of production and movements in the price level. The small number of concerns in these towns provided insufficient scope for the formation of guilds, and hence complete freedom from the obligations which the latter entailed, and which were anyway no longer appropriate now that manufacture was so much extended in scale and variety. Stagnation of output and slowness in introducing new methods of production became thus as important a factor in increasing social tensions among craftsmen and workers in the free towns as were the unfavourable shifts in prices. For their part the domain towns which possessed a rich hinterland of potential customers could sometimes exploit these favourable conditions and attain to free status themselves.

The progressive expansion of production, relaxation of guild restrictions and improvement in the supplying of domestic markets were not achieved solely through the agency of the domain towns. There were also spheres of production which lay completely beyond the limits of urban organization. The massive output of cloth in the villages, especially those of the hilly districts in the north and east of Bohemia, glass-making, iron-founding and the working of other ores, all developed in an essentially independent way, albeit within the terms of the feudal land system, and thus remained outside the territorial competence of the town communities and the supervision of their guilds. With their direct access to markets throughout the country such enterprises therefore contributed much to a loosening of the general encumbrances on trade. At the same time middlemen from the villages became active through the whole of central Bohemia (they showed especial initiative on some of the crown lands along the Elbe) and played their part in throwing off the old guild shackles in favour of freer commerce. The large and well-organized mining companies attracted both domestic and foreign workers and their liberal employment policy was instrumental in accelerating labour mobility. The whole great edifice of feudal obligation, both personal and occupational, was thus being undermined by a series of pressures which tended in their different ways to liberate production from its fetters.

The relation of lord to peasant is another of the chapters in the history of Czech economic life in the sixteenth century, and any definitive solution to this complicated question will reveal the structure of society at that time in all its intricacy and variety. The relationship between the Estates of the nobility and towns and the peasants who formed the largest section of the population was governed basically by old tenurial agreements. While these ancient contracts ensured tolerable conditions for the better-to-do and propertied peasants, and allowed them to develop agricultural production both for their own needs and for the market, the lowest layers of rural society, landless and lacking the necessary chattels and livestock, were thrown to a great extent onto earnings from hired labour. This was a source of great trouble. On smaller estates, in most cases those owned by knights or burghers from the towns, the peasants whose holdings were insufficient for subsistence could not maintain their families from that source alone, while the limited extent of their land-lords' property left no available land on which to found any new settlement. The wage labour which might have compensated for the deficiency in natural produce was little in demand on such small estates, and it was mainly seasonal work, especially at harvest time. Neither the maintenance of their lord's private lands nor the provision of new investment could give the chance of permanent occupation. From this class of men came the majority of migrant workers who sought a living in the towns; while their employment there could only be as unskilled assistants, there was at least the prospect of keeping body and soul together.

On the great *latifundia* of the kind we have been describing, however, there were much better opportunities for founding settlements and increasing the peasant's return from his own small plot. The land-registers of the large crown estates, notably Pardubice, and the Trčka lands around Opočno, as well as other sources of an economic character demonstrate that from the first half of the sixteenth century until the White Mountain this broad and fertile belt of the Elbe valley from the foothills of the Orlice mountains (Adlergebirge) to the Silesian border witnessed a lively and continuous process of colonization. Not only did existing settlers take part in it as a means of extending their own holdings, but also, and more significantly, many landless immi-grants found in it a new home and means of livelihood. The area was rich and extensive enough to assimilate for decade after decade the increase in population which came especially from the weakest sections of peasant society and give it a secure economic foundation.

At the same time the largest estates could offer the under-privileged inhabitants of both village and town the prospect of all kinds of financial rewards. Many of their undertakings, from the plough-teams through the breweries, water- and saw mills and fisheries to forestry work, were run with a limited number of permanent employees and could only pursue longer-term and large-scale activities by taking on hired labour. Thus much of the arable land on the estates of the Smiřickýs, which produced large quantities of corn, employed a great number of peasants throughout the winter to mill the grain and work in the forests, while sowing and harvesting could also only be carried out with their help. On estates where methods of production were ad-vanced a chronic shortage of workers came to be felt. In such circumstances the small farmer with his own limited holding could with advantage eke out the poor returns which this provided with paid labour on a large estate. The acute problem of how to guarantee the required number of workers and their efficiency was resolved by landlords not through an increase in the *robot* (*corvée*) but by raising the wages of labourers. There is no sign in the records of any unilateral raising of the *robot* without a corresponding extension of the peasant's own holding, but the precise accounts which survive from the Smiřický lands show quite clearly that wages paid to agricultural workers formed between 40–50 per cent of the expenses incurred by their arable farming, and that in the years from 1609–1616 these wage rates rose, with allowance made for local variation, by between 20 and 50 per cent. To judge by the relatively peaceful state of society during the second half of the sixteenth century and the years to 1620 it would seem that a similar situation must also have obtained elsewhere.

The prosperous peasant farmer devoted more time to his own interests, while his relation to his landlord was more complex. The returns from his own farming were often increased still further by the common practice of commuting the *robot* into a money payment, which left most if not all his working day free for private concerns. The commutation of this feudal obligation occurred of course only on those estates which had already achieved more advanced, almost modern methods of production, based on a market valuation of all the factors with which they dealt. Even where the peasants fulfilled their *robot* obligation *in natura* it presented no great hardship. The averages for the year 1609–18 as they emerge from the precise Smiřický records show that those peasant farms which owned a plough-team gave rather less than one day's service in the year, while those which did not provided between one and two days.

It was however a different story on many other estates whose owners sought to raise a labour force and expand production by increasing the *robot*, especially for those of their tenants who possessed plough-teams. These claims of the landed proprietors, unjustified in common law and offering no compensation, led to many disputes. The peasantry whom they affected resorted to active opposition and defended tooth and nail the rights to which they were entitled by tradition and sometimes even by written contract. If it came to open conflict with their masters the peasants relied on the support of the authorities, the courts and the central government. The proceedings of the State Council of Bohemia for the years 1602–10 give ample proof that the government was making a concerted attempt to ensure the inviolability of the ancient rights of the peasantry, and in cases of contention between lord and servant was insisting on due respect for the law, thus preventing the landed proprietors from any arbitrary or oppressive measures. This standpoint had been a fundamental principle of government in Bohemia since the beginning of the sixteenth century. As one example of many we may cite the attitude of the celebrated Zdenek Lev of Rožmitál who in the late 1520s, when the struggle of the peasant classes in Germany was at its height, insisted on the need to maintain order in the Czech lands by firm respect for the rights of the subject. Almost one hundred years later in 1609, the same spirit governed the deliberations of the highest officers of state, at a time when the country was in a position of severe political tension.

The resolute stand of the central authorities in this direction provided an ever-present reminder to the peasant classes, and by convincing them that their legal rights would be protected at the highest level it was one of the chief guarantors of social peace in the land. It is a fundamental characteristic of social evolution in sixteenth century Bohemia that even where conflict between the peasants and their masters was lasting and took on acute forms, there were no armed risings. There was no general worsening of the economic and social conditions of the lowest classes through the direct oppression of their landlords.

This brief survey of the main orders of Bohemian society and their economic development during the sixteenth century has shown the central importance of economic considerations in the political activities and ambitions of each state, but they were never alone in determining the course of constitutional evolution. Questions of religion and nationality, which were already becoming more acute during the first half of the sixteenth century, began in the years after 1550 to play a permanent and characteristic rôle in the counsels of state. It speaks well for the conduct of politics in Bohemia at this time that in two matters of the highest importance the rights of all citizens were calmly and consistently mentioned without regard to estate or class: in religious tolerance, and in justice for the non-Czech minorities. The very composition of the Bohemian state pointed to the necessity of preserving good relations between the mother country and the associated territories with a predominantly German population, i.e. Silesia and the two Lusatias. Contacts between all the lands of the Bohemian crowd developed from the late fifteenth century in an atmosphere of mutual understanding, and the Czech officials sent to operate in Silesia and Upper and Lower Lusatia contributed to this, both in their day-to-day dealings and their political activity. The Czech nobility and towns, especially the richest of them, were in close touch with German citizens in these associated lands and the Empire. In addition to this the studies of young Czechs from the noble classes and bourgeoisie at foreign universities, notably those in Italy and the German Protestant foundations, strengthened contacts between the races, above all in the cultural sphere, while the commercial links between Bohemia and all the territories of the Empire operated in the same direction.

The accession of the Habsburgs to the Bohemian throne introduced new factors into the nationality question which did not always work to the advantage of the Czechs. The growing numbers of Germans, mainly members of the lesser nobility from the Austrian lands and the Empire, who settled permanently in Bohemia in the service of the king, brought changes in the character of many branches of administration; among the officials of the Exchequer we encounter many names of recognizably German origin both in Prague and the dependent branches in the provinces – collecting tolls and administering mines, forests or crown lands. They helped to bring the German language into more frequent use in written and verbal dealings throughout the country, a tendency which was strengthened by the trading connection between Bohemia and many parts of the Empire and by the students, who brought back with them not only the language of their foreign hosts but also an intimate knowledge of their problems.

The result of all this was on the one hand a large and increasing overlap of societies throughout the Czech lands, on the other the regular forging of ties of marriage with German families from Silesia, the Lusatias and the Empire; the latter affected particularly the high nobility and the town, helping to create and sustain an atmosphere of mutual tolerance during succeeding generations. From the second half of the sixteenth century the development proceeded apace, thanks to the growing power of Lutheran ideas and the permanent settlement of the Emperor Rudolf's court in Prague, which brought with it an army of officials and retainers of German origin. Since however the Czech language maintained its dominance as the chief means of communication of all Estates and classes, public and private, so the state of Bohemia grew to be

51

a notable representative of the kind of racial and confessional toleration which is regarded as the achievement of the age of Enlightenment, two centuries later. The first signs of strain appeared in the language ordinance of 1615, by which the two senior Estates sought to protect themselves against the incursions of a foreign, primarily German, element ignorant of the Czech language. Popular opinion in the towns was stirred up against the Germans particularly as a reaction to the firebrand oratory of some Lutheran preachers.

The generally favourable conditions of economic development in Bohemia found their reflection too in the field of culture. Printers disseminated not only the religious literature which by the end of the sixteenth century had penetrated to the very lowest levels of society as a vehicle for polemic and public agitation, but were also active in reporting the events of the moment, providing technical books, especially in the sphere of agriculture, and feeding the popular demand for travellers' tales and folk songs. The most outstanding success in confessional literature and the cultivation of the Czech language was achieved by the Czech Brethren. The Czech grammar of Jan Blahoslav and the collective translation of the Scriptures which was published in 1579–88 as the Bible of Králice established themselves as lasting models and exemplars for their purity of style. Inexpensive editions of books of entertainment and improvement sustained the interest of the broadest sections of the population in their national literature long after the disaster of the White Mountain.

The desire to know foreign lands and an interest in all the manifestations of nature, both so typical of the European Renaissance, bore fruit in Bohemia in the writings of travellers (Oldřich Prefát of Vlkanov and Krištof Harant are best remembered) and in the specialized scientific literature of botanists, astronomers and physicians. Much of this was practical guidance, designed particularly to improve farming methods, and proprietors of estates could find useful instruction in the rearing of animals, particularly breeding of horses, the culture of fish, the production of beer and other commodities, and the cultivation of market-gardens and forests. In the field of history there were editions of chroniclers like Václav Hájek, as well as original works describing events of the time, among which Sixt of Ottersdorf's account of the troubles of 1547 was the most important politically. Among the major material contributions of the age (together with much continued building in the late Gothic style) were some proud Renaissance additions to the royal castle in Prague, notably the tennis-court and Belvedere, and Italianate rebuilding of the seats of some of the great magnates – Pardubice, Litomyšl, Opočno. Besides Prague a number of the domain towns were largely rebuilt in the Renaissance style, among them Pardubice and Nové Mesto on the Metuje.

The year 1547, which saw the first major internal crisis of Bohemian society and challenge to its Estates, was a moment of significant change throughout Europe. With the deaths of Henry VIII of England on January 28, and Francois I of Valois on March 31, the Emperor Charles V and his brother Ferdinand suddenly found their hands free for decisive action in Germany. The agreement in 1551 over the Imperial succession brought the Habsburgs to the summit of their prestige, but the unexpected *volte face* of the following year and the creation of a stable and organized Protestant block led by Maurice of Saxony materially weakened the imperial drive towards re-Catholicization and the religious peace of Augsburg, in 1555, a shattering blow to Charles's self-confidence, was a direct cause of his abdication. This stormy series of events was followed with lively interest in the Czech lands, but their own peace was not disturbed; the king of Bohemia, occupied more and more by the affairs of the Empire, had neither the time nor the courage to reinforce his position against the broad front of the Estates' resistance.

In an international situation characterized by the crystallizing into religious forms of the warring political ideologies and spheres of interest of the great powers, the Churches in Bohemia remained within the framework which had emerged from their unhindered evolution during the previous half-century. Bohemia was the only state in central Europe where the principle of toleration was upheld both in public and in private, and the ideative legacy of Hussitism, founded on a personal interpretation of Scripture which departed from the official theses of Rome, was the leaven encouraging the spread of confessional freedom and the Christian life, most clearly in the teachings of the Union of Czech Brethren. The co-existence between Catholic minority and Utraquist majority remained undisturbed by the first onset of the Lutheran Reformation in nearby Germany. It came to belong organically among the guiding principles which underlay Czech society, allowing free transition between the various Estates of the feudal order and giving scope to individual initiative in cultural and economic life.

The years after 1555 in Germany demonstrated the bankruptcy of imperial policies as a solution either to religious or constitutional problems. The Protestant princes of the Empire, well-organized politically and buttressed by weapons of culture, were able to defend themselves successfully against penetration from east and west at a time when the reviving Catholic world, given clear dogmatic orientation by the Council of Trent, was beginning to reform its ranks in Italy and Spain. The introduction of the Jesuits into Bohemia in 1556 was the first tentative step towards Counter-Reformation, bringing as it did an order whose organization – already comprised of 13 provinces – bore signs of an embracing international mission. But it came at a moment when Protestantism, which controlled most of central Germany, was putting down firm roots both in Bohemia proper and the surrounding lands of the Czech crown, and neither this royal initiative nor the others which soon followed it (the filling of the vacant archbishopric of Prague and the Papal dispensation of 1564 allowing communion in both kinds in Bohemia) had the expected effect of halting the Lutheran advance.

We have already seen what stage had been reached during the first half of the sixteenth century in the relation between king and Estates and its reflection in the organization of politics, culture and the economy. The entrenched positions of the Estates in internal questions were maintained after 1550, despite the ever-increasing and insidious incursions of the political and financial organs of the central administration. The Bohemian Chancery, which executed all government decisions and supervised the different levels of civil administration throughout the lands of the Czech crown, remained a strong unifying force and retained its powers quite unimpeded until the great reform of 1611. The royal Exchequer, however, underwent numerous alterations to its original competence, which had embraced all the crown estates in the Czech lands, most especially that which by the middle of the century had removed from it all business in Silesia. This development gradually led the Silesian Estates to believe that they could with advantage to themselves extend their existing partial autonomy from the restricted sphere of royal finances to the administration of public affairs in general. Their success in carrying through a measure of devolution for the crown finances in Silesia encouraged the authorities in Vienna to try similar tactics in Bohemia, but such attempts were met by the Estates there with a firm refusal to cooperate, and the series of disputes in which the

Exchequer became involved brought important repercussions in the climate of public opinion and the negotiations of the Diet. The Estates' stiff resistance was instrumental in upholding the Bohemian Chancery as the *de facto* central executive organ of state, and its wide powers were modified only in 1611, when a general reorganization of administration took place.

The actions of the government in Vienna lent support to separatist tendencies which threatened to disrupt the structure of the Czech state and its administrative procedures. The origins of the political dilemma with which the country was faced in an increasingly unmistakable way could be traced back as far as 1527. The Czech assumption that Ferdinand would make the Bohemian kingdom the centre of his realm was soon seen to have been unrealistic, and the centralizing attempts of Vienna came to be directed towards splitting up the Czech lands into smaller units for the purpose of ruling them directly. Thus, in contrast to the marked tendency towards centralization in unified states which was proceeding in Spain during the first half of the sixteenth century and took a strong grip in France and England after 1550, Bohemia and with it all central Europe stood at a parting of the ways.

Within Bohemia the struggle between the two forces was a complex one: the broad stand of the Estates against monarchical assaults on their prerogatives was carried through within the framework of a united kingdom, yet the differing interests of the individual lands did not allow any permanent political alliance of all the nobility and towns. Lack of agreement on basic issues was already evident during the election of 1526, while in 1547 and on later occasions during the century it reemerged in stronger forms which spread into many spheres of public life. During times of peace such diversity of opinion within the Estates was not dangerous, at least so long as their standpoint was similar in broad outline. But the threat became acute as soon as a new political ideology and the militant Catholic Counter-Reformation created lines of opposition which crossed the frontiers of individual territories and brought wholly divergent views into positions of power and potential repression.

Two fundamental problems dominated internal politics in Bohemia in the second half of the sixteenth century: one was the pressure on economic activity of the continuing expense of defending Hungary against the Turk; the other was the development of religious antagonisms in Europe as a whole and in central Europe in particular. The unsuccessful eleven-year war against the Porte placed higher taxation burdens on the Czech lands, and the crushing annual tribute of 30,000 gold pieces which was stipulated by the Peace of Constantinople in 1562 shook the military and political prestige of the Habsburg dynasty. Thus on the death of Ferdinand I in 1564 the Estates were able to put strong pressure on the new King Maximilian II and to achieve two important concessions: a change in the system of taxation from a poll-tax to a tax on hearths, and a relaxation in the policy of re-Catholization. By a Maxmilian's recognition of the Bohemian Confession (*Confessio Bohemica*) in 1575 the way was opened towards a stable and unified organization covering all the non-Catholic creeds and a barrier set up against the sharpest assaults of the radical Papal wing and its supporters among the high nobility. Similar concessions by the Emperor in the Alpine lands and Hungary gave the Bohemian Estates a sense of security and strengthened the common front between the Protestants of Bohemia and their Austrian co-religionists.

Yet this success of the Czech Protestant Churches was achieved at the very time when the forces of revitalized Catholicism were beginning to reorganize themselves on a broader and sounder base, both internationally and within the domestic political scene in Bohemia. The bitter conflicts in western Europe and their blend of religious and political animosities formed a sombre backcloth to Bohemia's peaceful evolution. The four civil wars in France, the attempt at Catholic restoration in England and its ruthless suppression, the successful struggle of the Dutch against Spanish counter-reforming attempts; all showed how the burning issues of Church and State were moulding the destiny of European society and drawing ever-wider circles of humanity into their bloody embrace. Czech religious tolerance found itself faced from the 1580s onward by an uncompromising Catholic offensive in which the interests of the Church of Rome were joined with a new absolutist ideology of State, and the Habsburg striving after total monarchy was underpinned by the moral and material support of the Church Militant. The Council of Trent had given dogmatic and organizational content to this Catholic onslaught, and from the 1570s the Papal divisions engaged on a planned assault of the broadest dimensions against every brand of Protestantism. The main force of the Tridentine armoury was turned against the entrenched Protestants of Germany; but Bohemia which stood a little to one side of this line of attack, was nevertheless itself soon to feel the consequences of the new disposition of ideologies and powers.

There was no relaxation of the tense situation in Europe with the beginning of the seventeenth century, when religion and politics in Bohemia were reaching an important turning-point in their hitherto undisturbed evolution. The prelude to this was the dynastic crisis within the House of Habsburg which early in 1608 threatened to bring open hostilities between the Bohemian and Silesian Estates on one hand and the Moravians on the other. The Spanish party, backed by the Papal nuncio and Philip III's ambassador, sought to seize the opportunity to call in question all the religious and political prerogatives of the Estates, but the latter's determined stand under the leadership of Matthias Thurn and Václav Budovec and their readiness if necessary to resort to arms in their own defence frustrated the manoeuvre. With the year 1609 and Rudolf's grant of the celebrated "Letter of Majesty" the whole series of developments in Bohemia since the arrival of the Habsburb dynasty reached their culmination, and Czech Protestants and their national leaders were finally assured, after many uncertainties and tribulations, of a dominating rôle in all sectors of public life.

At this critical time the representatives of the non-Catholic Churches in Bohemia were able to agree on a common programme (the negotiations over the "Letter of Majesty" were a compromise between Budovec and J. A. Schlick) and their solidarity brought them both legal and political guarantees for their religious communities. This of itself entailed a strengthening of the influence of the Estates in all affairs of state. The rights of the "defensors"* as guaranteed by the Letter of Majesty included the permission to summon the non-Catholic Estates without the authority of the crown, and this clause could have opened the way to a regeneration of the old Diet of the Estates, whose provincial organs had long formed effective guarantees of local autonomies until abolished by Ferdinand I.

Such a promising development in the sphere of religion pointed the self-sufficiency and maturity of Czech political life, and in the spirit of a tradition of enlightened religious toleration the fabric of Czech society, private and public, ecclesiastical and cultural, gained added strength. The fact should also be underlined that through the whole of the sixteenth century and beyond until

---

*30 "defenders" or guardians of Protestant rights, who were to be chosen equally from among members of all three Estates. (trans.)

1620, at a time when in nearby Germany religion was becoming entirely a matter of pressure from above and Luther's reasoning was carried to its logical political conclusion by princes, Estates and towns alike; at such a time the leaders of Czech public life, who themselves belonged mostly to the Protestant camp, were able to maintain that tolerance of faith and individual conscience which alone is the foundation of any religious morality. In this aspect of its spiritual life Bohemia anticipated by almost two centuries the course of events in the rest of central Europe, where at the time the celebrated German historian Troeltsch rightly sees only a late stage of the intolerance of the mediaeval world.

Freedom of faith and religious conviction was but one side of a broad and liberal spiritual evolution. The extensive foreign connections of leading Czech political figures and the endeavours of intellectuals and men of letters maintained extremely high cultural standards throughout the country. Thanks to the frequent tours of study in Germany, the Netherlands, France, Italy and Spain by young Czechs from the nobility and towns, both Catholic and Protestant circles at home became acquainted with all currents of European thinking. Good examples from among many are the two leading statesmen of the early years of the seventeenth century, Karel Žerotín on the one hand and Zdenek Lobkovic on the other.

These important successes of the Czech Protestant community at home and abroad were not however an unqualified benefit. The free development of religious life brought with it a great diversity of churches and sects. Besides the Hussites or Old Utraquists there were New Utraquists, Lutherans, Calvinists and Czech Brethren, and their internecine feuds could easily pass from the theological or liturgical sphere to wider matters of public life and individual relationships. A tense and involved situation was thus created by the end of the sixteenth century which allowed the rigorous organization of the Catholic Church an easy *point d'appui* for its campaign to achieve influence in the apparatus of state and the cultural life of the country. It was with the appointment of Lobkovic to the office of Bohemian Chancellor in 1599 and his assiduity in all departments of public life that the pro-Spanish Catholic group of Czech politicians gained a notable access of strength. This body of men, still few in number but disciplined and united in direction, stood thereafter at the nerve-centre of the whole administration of Bohemia and could exercise a permanent influence in all affairs of state.

Such domestic political changes came at a time when the general central European picture was already undergoing a marked alteration. Fateful developments were taking place at the turn of the sixteenth and seventeenth centuries, especially in the lands which bordered the Southern provinces of Bohemia. Archduke Ferdinand of Styria, fresh from his studies at the Jesuit college of Ingolstadt, began his reign in 1595 with a series of militant anti-Protestant measures. His abrupt disturbance of the peace within Austria for the first time in 70 years gave the clear warning that no sympathy for religious toleration could be expected from the rising generation of the House of Habsburg. Similar policies in Bavaria, instigated by the energetic Duke Maximilian, another former pupil of Ingolstadt, were finally crowned in 1609 by the formation of a League of Catholic princes. With the founding of the League (a project conceived earlier but only now accomplished) the whole western and southern frontier of the Czech lands stood open to the ideology of a Catholicism uncompromised at home and uncompromising abroad.

THE MICROCOSM: THE HOMELAND OF COMENIUS

On Monday, 22 January 1567 Marc'Antonio Varotta, once a painter of standards, now a weaver, stood before the Venetian Inquisition to face the charge that on his travels in Hungary, Poland, Moravia, Austria and Geneva he had fallen into heresy. Varotta submitted to the Holy Office, renounced his heretical opinions, and revealed details of the apostates with whom he had had dealings, especially those of Italian origin, and where he had met them. At that time it seems, the Church of Rome was being deserted *en masse* by large numbers of artists, architects and masons, while some of the settlements of craftsmen were serving as cells of Italian Protestantism. The interest of the Inquisitors was directed particularly towards Varotta's reports about citizens or natives of Venice. Among these one name stood out: Master Nicolò Paruta, living in Moravia, "where there are many Anabaptists and other sects" in the town of Slavkov (*Austerlici, terra di Moravia*). Paruta had a wife, houses and vineyards there (and evidently in Brno and Olomouc too), as well as a remarkable library full of heretical literature both in Latin and *in volgare*. "And in Nocolò Paruta's house Bernardino Occhino died, a man first Calvanist and later an Arian"; in fact earlier still Occhino had been a Capuchin, General of the whole Capuchin order, a famous and popular preacher, then the head of the Waldensian circle and a pillar of the Italian Reformation (1487–1564).

Twenty-nine years later, in 1596, another Italian, far more significant than Varotta, travelled through Moravia to Poland: the Roman aristocrat and Papal nuncio Cardinal Caetani. The official diary of this legation has survived in his family archive, and in it we read that after crossing the Moravian frontier at Mikulov and being entertained there by the Dietrichstein family Caetani and his companions stopped in the small town of "Slofcuf *alias* Austerlitz, a place full of so many and various heresies and sects that some say in the same house the father could believe one and his son another. There the wife could be of one persuasion in matters of faith and her husband of another, so it was not surprising that 64, perhaps even 70 kinds of heresy could be found. But of Catholics there was not a single one."

Three years earlier, in 1593, the English traveller Fynes Moryson passed in the reverse direction, from Poland to Italy, and noted his impressions in his *Itinerary* published in 1617. Moryson was not particularly interested in religious matters, but observed rather that the language of the Moravians was little different from that of the Bohemians, their land was pleasant and fertile with many towns and villages, their markets were cheap and their people welcoming. He recorded that the northern part of the country was largely given over to rich cornfields and pastures, while the south was covered with vineyards.

Moryson was right in pointing to the prosperity of Moravia, which stood in economic and political importance second among the lands of the Bohemian crown. But the Italian visitors were also justified, for it was a country open to people of all confessions, from the Hussites, through the Bohemian Brethren and Anabaptists to the Socinians and other outspoken foes of the Roman Curia and the Inquisition. Besides the Italian heretics there were fugitives from Switzerland and the Netherlands and large numbers of German Anabaptists. The highest officer of state, the Moravian *hejtman* Václav Ludanic had already warned King Ferdinand early in the sixteenth century that his country would sooner lie in ashes than suffer the destruction of its religious liberties.

Moravia was not on the periphery of European affairs. It lay on the very borders of Hungary, separated by only a few miles from the outer confines of the Ottoman Empire. It was crossed by the important trading route which led from the bridges over the Danube on the outskirts of Vienna to Mikulov (Nikolsburg), then via Slavkov or Brno to Vyškov, where it split into two, one branch passing through Ostrava to Cracow, the other through Olomouc (Olmütz) to Breslau in Silesia. Moravia had, it is true, only three quarters of a million inhabitants at most, against more than twice as many in Bohemia, where the total may have reached two million, but the structure of its society and economy were similar to that which we have already examined for Bohemia. Approximately one person in a thousand belonged to the feudal ruling class of the nobility. The number of serf-owning landed proprietors fluctuated between 2,000 and 1,600, with a tendency to decrease, and thus there were constant additions to the ranks of those lords and knights who owned very few serfs or none at all and made their living either as officials and administrators on the great estates, as functionaries of the crown or the church, or by finding work in the towns. In Moravia also there were two observable directions of economic evolution: the tendency to base the management of an estate on the forced labour of the *robot*, as did the bishops of Olomou, the Žerotíns and the Manriques; or else to do without the *robot* altogether. The latter course involved either counting on the money rents of the subject peasantry, or deriving the utmost productive advantage from its payments in kind. Moravian wines from the neighbouring towns of Mikulov and Breclav, for instance, could be found competing against each other in the taverns on the Old Town Square in Prague.

Towards the south-eastern corner of this land, a little to one side of the main lines of communication, but in the region where Jan Amos Comenius was born in 1592 and which was soon to feel the towering presence of Albrecht von Wallenstein, lies the "microcosm" which we shall now consider in rather greater depth: an estate more typical than outstanding whose centre was the little domain town of Zlín.* On Comenius's own map of Moravia, published in Amsterdam in 1627, Zlín does not appear as a place of any particular importance or wealth. It lies on the river Dřevnice which flows from the Carpathian mountins on the Eastern border of the country and issues finally into the Morava, the central axis of the land which bears its name. The Dřevnice was the focus of communications for the whole domain, which included besides Zlín the township of Grygov or Trávník and the

*Now the industrial town of Gottwaldov.

villages of Březnice and Mladcová, with parts of Želechovice Prštná, Přfluky and Lůžkovice. The Zlín estate contained in 1619, a total of 319 peasant families, and as such was outdone among the domains which immediately surrounded it only in Lukov, which had 471, but was rather numbered among the "Wallachian" * or upland estates where pasturage largely took the place of land under the plough. Lukov belonged at the beginning of the seventeenth century to the family of Neksch of Landek, whose widowed heiress Lady Lucrezia was married in May 1609 to her exact contemporary, Albrecht Wallenstein. More important estates were to be found further north, on the eastern edge of the fertile valley of the Haná (Holešov), or to the south, in the plain of the Olšava (Nový Svetlov, Uherský Brod and Uherský Ostroh). These latter three all had some connection with the ancestors and family of Comenius. The writer's forbears had probably migrated from Hungary to the lands of Nový Svetlov, where they acquired the property of hereditary village bailiff in Komná, the name which they assumed – as Komenský – when they moved elsewhere. Comenius's father evidently lived in Nivnice, on the estate of Ostroh, and died in Uherský Brod, for Jan Amos himself acknowledged Nivnice as his birthplace. The two valleys of the Olšava and the Dřevnice had no geographical barrier between them, and the sixteenth century saw continual attempts to unite them within the bounds of a single great *latifundium*.

The first to try this were members of the family of Tetour of Tetov. Their ancestor, Vilém Tetour of Tetov had begun his career in the early fifteenth century, at the time of the Hussite wars, as Rožmberk's commander in South Bohemia. He then passed into the mercenary army of the Hungarian king Matthias Corvinus and became one of the leaders of the famous "black company" of Czechs and Moravians, receiving as his reward a title of nobility and the grant of some estates which had been ravaged in the fighting. Among these was the domain of Zlín, whose central point, the little town itself, the Tetours had entirely to rebuild. The family lost its lands in Hungary during the course of the sixteenth century and acquired as compensation a few small estates in east Bohemia, where it sought to ensure its future livelihood by merging itself and its coat-of-arms with the less eminent but affluent knightly family of Vchynský of Vchynice,

---

*So-called from the "Vlach" peoples of Latin descent who had colonized some of the hillier areas of the Moravian-Slovakian frontier. (trans.)

which was later to change its name to the more international form
"Kinský". About the year 1570 the Tetours reached the height
of their power in south-east Moravia and their territories stretched from the river Morava to the borders of Upper Hungary (the
modern Slovakia). The grandfather of Jan Amos Comenius, Jan
Sekeš, bailiff in Komná, was thus a servant of this same family
which was also ruling in Zlín.

But in 1571 the Tetours sold Zlín to Jan Kropáč of Nevedómí,
lord of Hranice, Drahotuše and Rataje. This Jan Kropáč was
another *arriviste* in the ranks of the high nobility, but an influential and rich one. He had been an adviser and confidant of King
Ferdinand I and his sister, Mary, Queen of Bohemia and Hungary, famous in history for her correspondence with Eramus of
Rotterdam and as the heroine of Brantôme's *Vies des femmes
galantes.* When Jan Kropáč came to Zlín, where he immediately
ordered the castle to be rebuilt in the Renaissance style, he was
already sixty-eight years old but not yet at the end of his career.
In the sixteenth century, however, the passage from life to death
could be one of apocalyptic swiftness, both for individuals and
for whole families, and within a year some nameless epidemic laid
low Kropáč and all his kin, saving only his daughter Anna who
was married to her relative (probably a cousin) Jan of Kunovic.
The latter was educated and tolerant, had studied at Wittenberg,
was the patron of the Czech Brethren, in Zlín and Uherský Brod,
and was popularly expected to rise high in the world of diplomacy. Kunovic was one of the group of Czech and Moravian
nobles who accompanied Archduke Matthias, brother of the
Emperor Rudolf, on his ill-fated mission to the Netherlands in
the autumn of 1577 following an invitation from the party of
Dutch "moderates" led by William of Orange. Matthias's secret
acceptance of this call was equally displeasing to Rudolf and to
his cousin Philip of Spain, because both they and other informed
Habsburg sources realized that it was the Archduke's thirst for
the independent exercise of power, at least as some kind of
Lieutenant-Governor in the Low Countries, which had led him
to interfere.

Jan of Kunovic did not survive to see Matthias's miserable
homecoming in 1581: he had died sometime during the winter of
1578–9 and only his mortal remains were brought back to
Moravia for burial. His death frustrated all plans to create a solid
block of Kunovic territory stretching from the Olšava to the
Dřevnice. He left two young children, Anna Marie and Jan

Jetřich, and his widow Anna (née Kropáč) who immediately re-married and took as her second husband another Moravian magnate, Jan the Younger of Žerotin. In the early years of the 1580s they administered jointly the estates of Zlín and the neighbouring Vizovice and Hranice, but by 1585 they too were in their graves, and after this brief and abortive Žerotín intervention the lands were divided up. Zlín passed to the aunt of Kunovic's two orphaned children, Bohunka of Žerotín, whose own son Zdenek later married his cousin Anna Marie. And thus was born another attempt to make the little town into the focus of a large feudal land complex.

All this changed again in 1589 when Zlín was sold to Jan Cedlar the younger of Hof, known as Pačlavský. Cedlar was no lord like his predecessors, but a member of the knightage whose wealth however – thanks to careful mangaement of his estates – exceeded that of more than one magnate. We know that he frequently lent considerable sums of money and that it was he who financed the diplomatic mission of the bishop of Olomouc, Stanislav Pavlovský, to Poland in 1587 to defend Habsburg interests against the supporters of Sigismund Vasa. In addition to Zlín Jan Cedlar purchased the estate of Velký Ořechov, so that at the beginning of the seventeenth century his lands stretched, like others' before him, to the gates of Uherský Brod, where Comenius's father, Martin, was active in the service of the Church of the Czech Brethren. Cedlar had originally been an adherent of the Brethren, who in the time of the lords of Kunovic were turning increasingly towards Calvinism and seeking to strengthen the organization of their Church; but in Zlín he came into conflict with Jan Brotan, the administrator of the Brethren's congregation there, and he and his children Krištof and Anna grew more and more Lutheran in sentiment. Cedlar and his family spent most of their time either in Zlín itself or in their town house at Olomouc.

The Tetours, Kropáčes, Kunovices, Žerotíns, Cedlars: these families, whether old-established, *parvenu* or merely of the knights' Estate, formed the ruling class in Zlín and its environs. Of course their "rule" was not felt directly, and their will was executed by a band of officials who themselves played a very important rôle. These were for the most part members of the impoverished petty nobility who were forced to eke out the modest returns from their miniature holdings or free tenancies with some salaried occupation. Sometimes they enriched themselves further by other less illicit means, taking advantage of the privileges which went with their position: buying plots of land cheap and selling dear, profiting from the trade concessions of their masters, managing their employers' mills to their own benefit, lending money on credit and accepting mortgages. In Zlín they came and went very frequently, since each new proprietor usually brought his own trusted officials. One man who probably grew reasonably prosperous in the service of the lords of Kunovic was the same Martin Komenský or Comenius of Uherský Brod whom we have already encountered more than once.

The castle of the landed proprietor was the centre of all administration on his estates, including taxation, military business and the maintenance of public order, since the lord's domain or patrimonium was the smallest unit of local government. The town was also an autonomous community, as it was the seat of all trading and commercial activity and all manufactured goods. The domain town of Zlín around the year 1600 consisted of a central market square surrounded by twenty or so of the most expensive and distinguished houses, the separate township of Grygov or Trávník, the upper settlement around the church with its four streets and about forty dwellings, and finally the two streets called Dlouhá and Čepkov. In all there may have been 200 houses inhabited by between 1,400 and 1,500 people, comprising perhaps two thirds of the total population of the estate. In the whole of south-east Moravia Zlín was exceeded in size only by the towns of Strážnice and Uherský Brod (with nearly 300 houses each), Hradiště with 250, Velká and Kunovice.

As elsewhere in the length and breadth of feudal Christendom the life of this little domain town was centred on the church, dedicated to St Philip and St James, and the market, the townhall and the castle. The chapel of Saint Barbara, whose dedication points to a foundation in the fifteenth century at the time of the Tetours, lay in the suburb of Grygov, which probably also had its own magistrate. The townhall which still stands in the main square was rebuilt in 1581. The whole town was surrounded by a fence and there may have been a gate at the entrance to the urban enclave thus bounded. But the strongest building beside the castle, securely defended by its moat, was the church tower, and it was this to which the population turned in times of trouble.

What was the livelihood of this town and the inhabitants of the estate of Zlín? The major activity of course was work on the land, and here as elsewhere the leading traders in foodstuffs were the butchers, whose guild was also one of the most powerful. Two other artisan guilds, the clothiers and the shoemakers, had an importance which extended far beyond the confines of the town itself. Both sold their products mainly at the regular annual fairs (*Jahrmarkts*) which were held in spring and autumn. This was probably also where most of the local wine was consumed. But some craftsmen went as far as Hradište, Kremsier, Holešov and Uherský Brod to market their goods, while raw materials for Zlín found their way from even further afield: wool from the whole of eastern Moravia, leather from the towns of Banská Bystrica and Trencsén in Slovakia. Greater sums of ready cash were necessary for this kind of trading, and thus the artisans of Zlín were frequently in debt to Jewish money-lenders in Uherský Brod, Ostroh and Holešov. There were a number of economic institutions serving the community at large: two mills on the Dřevnice, one of which belonged to the lord, another on its own race and a fourth turned by the wind; two breweries, one belonging to the estate and the other the town; the lord's malthouse; a washhouse and dyeworks for cloth beside the river, which also had frames for drying. The butchers of Zlín possessed their own shambles and meat-store, while behind the church was a brick-works "in the claypits" and on the river stood a certain Matthew's bathhouse

Trading and production in the town were underpinned by urban privileges. The foremost of these was the right to hold two annual fairs, each of eight days' duration. From the beginning of the sixteenth century the town patriciate, i.e. those who lived in houses round the market squares paid an annual contribution of 60 gold pieces in lieu of their *robot* obligation, and in 1592 the other citizens of Zlín also commuted this to a money payment. In addition the town possessed the powers of *escheat*, considerable legal autonomy, and the guarantee, though only to the patricians, that their orphans would not be carried off "at the lord's whim and pleasure", but rather they and all the property of any deceased would be guarded by the whole town corporation. Around the year 1600 therefore every citizen of Zlín was liable to three separate payments: one the dues to his lord, which as we have seen were of various kinds; another the national and Imperial taxes; the last his municipal rates. The clearest general tendency was for the feudal authorities to attempt to replace ancient payments and obligations by regular contributions, and in this way the differences between the position of townsmen and villagers were gradually eliminated. The lords of Zlín did not themselves begin to enter into the processes of economic production during the sixteenth century, but remained content to squeeze every available penny from all those who lived on their lands. They allowed the town to take over control of the marketing of meat, soap and wine, and Jan Cedlar even sold his monopoly right, at least for as long as he saw fit, over the trade in wine. The citizens' freedom to brew their own beer had never been contested.

Senior among the officers of the town were the members of the council and the "sworn and elected magistrate" who held the reins of justice and audited the municipal accounts which were maintained by a town clerk and survive from the middle of the century. The highest dignitary was the mayor, to whom aldermen and councillors were subordinated, and whose term of office was approximately one year. To the aldermen fell the task of overseeing the administration of communal property and municipal finances and (managing the hospital, while they, together with the mayor and councillors, formed a court of appeal, beyond which it was still possible to refer to the provincial tribunal of Uherské Hradiště. The feudal authorities were not concerned with administration, but intervened in questions of property, chiding the feckless householder and punishing the offending one, permitting newcomers from the villages to settle in the town and disposing of any vacant dwellings, gifting, letting or selling all abandoned smallholdings. The lord had two properties of his own in Zlín itself, but neither was extensive. No *robot* was required on them, and the inhabitants of newly founded village settlements were sent to work on the distant fields of Zbožensko. The lord also legally owned all forests on his lands, and thus the peasants had to pay for *estovers* and *pannage*.

The total income derived from this feudal estate in the years around 1600 is unknown. The proprietors of Zlín clearly realized at an early date that the readiest source of revenue to them was their serfs, particularly the artisans, and they naturally lost no opportunity in using them to the full. Thus they supported the economic activity of the domain town by granting it privileges, a procedure which was also being followed on other estates in Bohemia and Moravia by feudal authorities seeking to threaten the hitherto dominant position of the free towns. But it is not likely that Zlín was ever any serious competitor to the royal town of Hradiště or the bishop's residential town of Kremsier, not to speak of Olomouc. All that the Cedlars conveyed to Olomouc were their essential provisions (until they bought a holding of their own on the outskirts of the city) and a certain number of cattle driven from the Zlín estate for slaughter. There are no recorded sales of corn there, so we may presume that this was passed on directly to middlemen in Zlín.

By the end of the sixteenth century it seems that the agriculture of the lands of Zlín had begun to encounter difficulties, both of a natural and demographic kind. The estate lay in the central part of the valley of the Dřevnice where the soil was least fertile, and in an assessment of about 1650 only one-sixth of its arable land was designated as of even average quality, while the rest was classified as poor. On top of this the area available for cultivation was plainly being outstripped by the rise in population, and it thus became necessary to have recourse to newly assarted land in the hills. Hence there grew up in the years before 1600 two settlements, Jaroslavice and Kudlov, on sites recently cleared of their age-old covering of timber.

The movements of population and prices, set against a background of natural and climatic influences, were factors which affected long-term economic tendencies, and lent a greater or lesser degree of stability to them. If we now consider a further category of historical agents, the conflicts within society, religion and culture, we must ask the yet more intractable question how those 1,400 people of Zlín lived out their lives between castle and church, municipal hall and feudal court. Although the well-to-do clothiers of the market square and the indigent settlers of the outskirts were united in viewing with wary mistrust the actions of the feudal lord and his servants, they had little else in common. For centuries the whole structure of the town community had been conditioned by a guild organization which scarcely altered with the years, and the man who was not a craftsman and affiliated to one of these brotherhoods was only an inhabitant, not a citizen of the town. Indeed the administration of Zlín was carried on largely by members of the three senior guilds: the butchers, shoemakers and clothiers.

The fact that people migrated to Zlín both from the immediately surrounding districts and further afield is sure proof of the town's prosperity. In the middle of the sixteenth century there was a stream of settlers from Bohemia, probably refugees who belonged to the Czech Brethren; later the predominant immigrant group came from south and east Moravia. Those speaking a language other than Czech were rare, and were usually speedily assimilated to the local community. This can be seen from settlers bearing the name "German", "Italian", "Hungarian" and so forth, though such names provide no real clue to ethnic origins since wandering individuals could take on new ones at different periods of their lives. In fact, the development of family names among the lower classes in Bohemia at this time observed certain definite rules, and the commonest class was of those which had originally been sobriquets, followed, apparently in this order, by those derived from Christian names, from places of origin and from occupations. But in a small domain town it is difficult to follow the individual immigrant. In conditions where long-term loans could easily be contracted citizens were not inclined to remain for long in the same house or smallholding, but moved frequently to a better one, and many of them were probably as little committed to their chosen occupation. It is noteworthy too that nearly all the artisans in the town (with exceptions among the butchers, clothiers and shoemakers, and perhaps also some of the potters, weavers and tailors) were peasant farmers at the same time.

The great majority of Zlíners were Protestant, and indeed there is no mention of Catholics at all for the later years of the sixteenth century. The old "Hussite" faith of the Utraquists was transformed during the rule of the lords of Kunovic into a Lutheranism which still embraced reverence for the person of Hus as father of the Czech Reformation. This confession was known officially as "Evangelical Utraquism". The vicar of Zlín, Samuel Sytinský or Syčinský, had become a firm adherent to the Lutheran faith while serving as a deacon in Uherský Brod. He received subsistence from the so-called ecclesiastical payment of two cottages in the Church Street, together with an annual tithe of two chickens and a hen and two days of "clerical" *robot*. These obligations to their vicar must be added to the sum of feudal dues owed by the peasantry of Zlín, but they could have meant no great hardship: the Church in the Reformation era was not a burdensome overlord.

When the tenets of Calvinism began to spread among the Utraquists of South-east Moravia it is clear that both the authorities and the peasantry of Zlín remained true to their Lutheran creed. The town of course contained a congregation of Czech Brethren, but it was too small even to occupy its own building, and priests and faithful of this community were buried in the churchyard of St Barbara. The dominant confession remained the "New Utraquism" with its strongly Lutheran overtones, and the dogmas of Wittenberg can be seen in the rules of the literary fellowship of Zlín which was founded in 1593. The members of this society were concerned primarily with Church music and singing, and they were required to be able to read. The latter skill, at least, could be acquired in the unpretentious municipal school, though it is difficult to believe that such an institution for the "teaching of children in the literary arts" would have imparted much more than a bare grounding in reading, writing and arithmetic. The schoolteacher was also the cantor and choirmaster in the church; from the mid-sixteenth century the two offices in Zlín seem to have been filled mainly by members of the family of Kantor-Přerovský. Besides this figure the town clerk was also necessarily a man of some education, though sometimes teacher and clerk were one and the same person. The final social service we must mention was one of no little practical importance: the municipal hospital in Castle Street, extended and underwritten by the town council during the sixteenth century, and benefiting from the legacies of a whole series of individuals.

Thus life went on within the microcosm of a small town and a single estate, a life pursued from the cradle to the grave in the shadow of religious faith, according to the calendar of nature and the seasons of the Church. Neither Zlín nor Moravia as a whole was an idyllic place around the year 1600, but the private tragedies of individuals had yet to coalesce into the public destruction of entire generations. This microcosm itself experienced at least the reflection of great European events, and the inhabitants of Zlín were themselves involved, more than they might have realized, in the travels of their feudal masters to glamorous courts and learned academies abroad. The noble family and its immediate circle brought tidings of the monarch and the Diet which was held every year in Olomouc or Brno. The distant Netherlands, Lutheran Germany, turbulent Hungary, the "graveyard of Europe", ever demanding soldiers and money for defence against the Turk; these were all battlefields whose cannon made only muffled thunder in the streets of Zlín. Yet by 1600 the same kind of tension was beginning to be built up within Moravian and Czech society, and gradually came to affect the fabric of central Europe as a whole. Conflict was turning into crisis: the sharpening conflict of nobility and towns, lords and peasants, monarch and Estates, Catholic offensive and Protestant retrenchment.

Only a few hours travelling separated Zlín from Holešov, the seat of the magnate Ladislav Popel of Lobkovic, brother of the young and militant Romanizing Chancellor Zdenek, and himself one of the two leaders of the Moravian Catholics. The other was the Cardinal-Bishop of Olomouc, František Dietrichstein, a man born in Spain and not yet thirty years of age, who felt himself a foreigner in his own country, and, whether he spent his time on the family property of Mikulov or his palaces of Vyškov or Kremsier, always surrounded himself with Italians and Spaniards and the literature of the Mediterranean lands. Olomouc did not attract him with its patriciate, largely German in language and Lutheran in sentiment, and he went there only for the most important Church festivals and the sessions of the Diet. But Olomouc contained other people who stood much closer to him: the members of the Jesuit College which had been founded in 1566. Among them were Spaniards, successors of the first rector Hurtado Pérez, Englishmen, Dutchmen and Czechs. The first generation of the Society of Jesus had made an attempt to combine Humanism with Catholic revival, but this spirit was now dying and being replaced by active propagandists of the faith, disciples of the *Collegium Nordicum* in Rome, who sought by their missionary endeavour to recover the whole of the north and east of Europe for the universal Church. The students at the College were a mixed collection of Czechs, Germans, Poles, Ukrainians, Swedes, Danes and Norwegians, and in all Olomouc was not the least important strategic base for powerful Papal nuncios like Possevino, Caetani and Spinelli.

To travel from Zlín to Olomouc it was not however necessary to pass through Kremsier. The other road led through Přerov, and there the Czech Brethren, supported by the local overlord Karel Žerotín, were seeking to create a Protestant school high enough in standard to prepare its pupils for study at the best Calvinist universities abroad. Jan Amos Comenius went to Přerov for a time, like many another of the devout Protestant Moravians of his generation. Thus we can see in Olomouc and Přerov the two poles of educational reform, but beneath this the representatives of a much profounder cultural clash. Moravia in 1600 was no contented, peaceful backwater, even if the free flow of its traditional way of life had not yet been openly disturbed. This was all to change with the advent of the new century, when nobles, burghers and peasants, both in the country at large as in the limited world of Zlín, were suddenly and dramatically enveloped in a political crisis which grew out of the struggle of two social groups for dominant power in the state.

Three

THE END OF EQUILIBRIUM AND FIRST
ATTEMPTS TO RESOLVE THE CRISIS

BROTHERLY HATRED IN THE HOUSE OF HABSBURG

IN the early morning of May Day 1605 the first enemy troops for over a century crossed the borders of Moravia near Stráni. The invaders were light cavalry units of the Hungarian insurgents under the command of Stephen Bocskai, and although their night attack on the town of Uherský Brod was not successful, they took prisoners from among the inhabitants of more than one frontier village. Bocskai's forces aroused terror throughout south-eastern Moravia, and many people began to withdraw towards the centre of the country.

This terror did not stem from the unexpectedness of the attack. It was widely known that the halting of the anti-Turkish offensive in Hungary had brought the beginnings of opposition to the Habsburgs among the non-Catholic nobility there. At the same time the Emperor Rudolf, who had passed through a further mental crisis in 1600, was losing faith in himself and in his policy of equilibrium, and was abandoning his firm stand against the Turks. In Bohemia he exacerbated the religious antagonisms by opening the highest offices of state to members of the "Spanish party", led by the young Chancellor Zdenek Lobkovic and by choosing as his chief councillor Karl von Liechtenstein. Liechtenstein, although educated by the Czech Brethren at their school of Ivančice in Moravia, had forsaken his early religion, while by winning the hand of the wealthy heiress of the Lords of Boskovice he had moreover established himself as a creditor of the insolvent Emperor. His fellow pupil at Ivančice, Karel Žerotín, was relieved of his office, and in 1602 Rudolf even renewed the extreme

Mandate against the Brethren which had been issued a century before.

To this Protestant reaction was swift, and the leader of the opposition, Václav Budovec of Budov, sought to organize resistance by urging the Estates to refuse the payment of taxes until the government should come to terms. The scope of his appeal was however limited; he called only on the nobility – lords and knights – and neglected entirely to engage the support of the municipalities, which were already resentful towards Lobkovic for his policy of strict price control, both of raw materials and finished goods. Despite the insight of some contemporaries (like the authors of the tract signed by "a number of honest patriots") that the towns were the key to any genuinely popular movement throughout the country, the attitude towards the urban estate of Catholics and non-Catholics alike remained cold and hostile.

This aloofness was not the only miscalculation of Lobkovic and his colleagues Martinic and Slavata, Liechtenstein and Dietrichstein. Like the militant Jiří Lobkovic only a few years earlier, they were induced by the sudden capture of power to overplay their hand, and to draw exaggerated confidence from the promises of support by the nuncio and the Spanish ambassador, by Duke Maximilian of Bavaria and the Archdukes Ferdinand of Styria and Leopold, Bishop of Passau. They found a welcome opportunity in the call from Catholic prelates and landed magnates in Hungary that Imperial forces should be used against the Protestant opposition in Upper Hungary, and they urged this course of action on Rudolf. Thus the Emperor's commander-in-chief, Bastian Belgiojoso, who had already proved himself a disastrous failure against the Turks, instigated in 1603 an indiscriminate campaign against the towns of eastern Slovakia and the county of Zips (Szepes). The Estates interpreted this action of Rudolf's as the treacherous and inexplicable breaking of an established agreement. In fact the roots of the policy were not religious, the Emperor cared nothing at all for one confession or the other, but rather a final attempt to revive Imperial sovereignty in Hungary, crush the Turks, and assert the supremacy of Habsburg power in Europe.

The resistance of the Protestant Estates in Hungary soon received backing from the new Prince of Transylvania, Stephen Bocskai, who under the protection of the Turks was maintaining a certain independence of political action. At the beginning of 1605 Bockai moved with the approval of the Porte towards central Slovakia and the regions along the Danube, then with the help of his *hajducks*, a fierce crew of herdsmen and peasants from the valley of the Tisza, and some light units of Turks and Tartars carried his offensive as far as the borders of Moravia. Having arrived at Pressburg he issued a summons for all non-Catholics in Moravia to join his standard. As the provincial government was in the hands of the Liechtensteins and a small oligarchy of incapable Catholic magnates Bocskai could expect no success there; but the opposition led by Karel Žerotín had no intention of joining him either. To them the Transylvanian was a rebel, and the Protestant Estates thought as yet only in terms of voicing their grievances at the Diet. Moreover he was in alliance with the Ottoman, the scourge of Christendom. And thus the Moravian Estates, called to meet early in March 1605 at Vyškov, agreed to recruit troops against Bocskai. The defence of the country was entrusted to individual local governors, but neither at Vyškov nor at the full Diet in Brno towards the end of April was any real method introduced into those arrangements: Instead of calling out the provincial militia the Moravians simply turned to the rest of the Bohemian lands with a request for help.

By the end of April four regiments had been collected together, but the most organized of these, the one commanded by a Protestant, Kryštof Dykart, was still somewhere in the middle of the country, and thus neither the passes across the Little Carpathians, nor the fords across the River Morava were defended on the first of May. Resistance was offered only by a few estates near the frontier, like that of Karel Žerotín's cousin, Ladislav Velen, who owned the domains of Břeclav and Moravská Třebová. In Břeclav the man charged with defence was the bailiff, Jan Urban of Domanín, whose brother Elias was a freeholder in Zlín, both men of peasant stock, but educated and well-advanced in the service of a series of Protestant landowners.

This first attack served to demonstrate that Bocskai and his forces could not be halted by the natural obstacles of hills and river, or by the little fortified towns along the line of the Morava: Břeclav, Strážnice, Ostroh, Veselí, Uherské Hradšite and further east through Uherský Brod and Nový Svetlov to Brumov. By 5 May the invaders had already taken Strážnice and the land surrounding Břeclav, and those inhabitants who were not killed or burned alive in their homes were dragged off into Hungary to Skalice and Senice. One punitive raid now succeeded another and within a week fighting along the Morava had reached

Dřevnice. A high representative of government, Jiří Hodický of Hodice, the "Supreme Lieutenant of the Margravate of Moravia" and second only to the *hejtman* Liechtenstein, was now dispatched to the battlefront and joined with Jan Urban in defending the crossing of the Morava. This was at last successful, and the ford at Kopčany stemmed the Hungarian advance until the end of May. In the middle of the month Colonel Dykart even ventured a counter-attack and penetrated Hungarian territory as far as Skalice, but was there repulsed and mortally wounded. His troops, who had been obliged to leave the body of their leader where it fell, were united with those of Hodický and the defence now received further reinforcements with the volunteers of Ladislav Lobkovic of Holešov and even a troop of infantry recruited by the brother of the *hejtman*, Maximilian Liechtenstein.

In the latter part of the month the Hungarians interrupted their attacks while their commander, Mihály Czobor, sent missives to the Moravian Estates, and to Karel Žerotín as the leader of the Protestant opposition, calling them to join in an offensive military alliance; but this initiative was abortive. Around Hradiště the Moravian militia was gathering a force of about seven units of foot-soldiers, perhaps 2,500 men, strengthened with 500 mounted arquebusiers and a few "cossacks", who were mercenaries hired in Poland. The local nobility had also come together for firmer action: it placed defence in the hands of the *hejtman* and a committee of twelve, and called for positive assistance from Prague and Breslau.

Meanwhile the troops of Bocskai had arrived in Zlín on 10 May (probably on their return from Holešov). The trustworthy author of the *Lamentations of the Land of Moravia* writes: "they found the people that day thronged together in the Church . . . and the young Lord Pačlavský they took with his steward in the castle." The little town, surrounded at most by a fence, had evidently made no defence – for the Hungarians were, after all, of the same faith as they. Kryštof Cedlar of Hof "called Pačlavský" (like his father), who had probably succeeded to Zlín in 1604, was anyway no warrior. He had been born about 1585, and was thus scarcely more than twenty years of age, and in his house on the market square of Olomouc he had a library of books. Even though there is now no trace of his "portrait in an interior room", we know that he was a man of learning, a convinced Lutheran, and probably infirm in body, since there are records of a physician-in-attendance for this period, and Pačlavský died when he was barely thirty-five.

In the year 1605 a relative of Pačlavský's, probably his uncle, George Martinkovský was the senior official of the knight's Estate in the province of Hradiste, and thus the new captive was a rich picking for Bocskai's men, one for whom a rich ransom might be demanded. How many Zlíners were carried off with him and his steward is hard to estimate, especially since this incursion was not the only one which took place during 1605. From the end of May Hungarian attacks were renewed: the cossacks were seriously defeated near Brumov and detachments from Skalice came to reoccupy the valley of the Dřevnice which included Zlín. At the same time another offensive was launched across the Austrian Marchfeld to attack Břeclav from the rear, and Hodický had to withdraw some of his forces from Kopčany to defend it.

On 31 May Bocskai's forces reached Holešov again, and as they returned through Zlín they took prisoner the brother of Jan Urban, Elias Domanský. The feebleness of the whole Moravian defence at the end of May was indeed scandalous, and although the *hejtman* began to screw his energies to the task he could achieve no more with existing forces than the protection of the Austrian border and the line of the Morava. In June the Hungarians made three assaults: at the beginning of the month they burned Kyjov but suffered serious losses, and an attempt to seize Břeclav was firmly resisted at the Lake of Nesyto by the infantry of Hodický and the cavalry of Colonel Teufel. On the tenth of the month both these units were engaged again with the enemy near Uherský Brod. Then Czobor launched one more attack on Břeclav, but by now the initiative was gradually changing sides and the Moravians were able to make a raid on Skalice, part of which they left in ashes. The *hejtman* Liechtenstein however soon withdrew again and returned to Hradiště where the feudal levy of the Bishop of Olomouc and 4,000 men from Silesia were already assembled, while a further reinforcement of 10,000 Bohemians under Adam Sternberg was expected.

Yet despite this Bocskai reasserted his ascendancy during July and was able to launch a series of indiscriminate punitive forays, burning Bzenec, Bojkovice and a number of settlements around them. Once again Liechtenstein was nowhere to be seen, and was now being publicly accused of treachery. It was clear that there could be no end to the incursions until Bocskai's strongholds in western Slovakia and the valley of the lower Vág had been reduced. His unfortunate tactics of sudden raids and bloodshed had of course frustrated any hope of creating a Protestant coalition of Hungarian, Moravian and Bohemian Estates: and it was only in the more distant Bohemia that his actions had any favourable response, in the form of a variant of an old Hussite song, which now circulated as *the Ballad of the famous Lord Bocskai of Slovakia, sent hither to us out of Hungary*.

The fight against Bocskai called forth both Catholics and Protestants, both supporters and opponents of the Habsburgs. Among the new recruits was the young Bohemian noble Albrecht Waldstein (Valdštejn) who, returning from travels in Germany and Italy, had joined the Imperial army in Hungary and been sent back to court at the beginning of 1605. In February 1605 a certain Václav Valdštejn was entered among the students of the Jesuit college in Olomouc; whether this was the same Albrecht Václav Eusebius has not been proved, and it is anyway clear that Wallenstein's main schooling was the battlefield. Another military noble with similar experiences of travel and the Turkish wars was also among the Bohemian detachments: Heinrich Matthias von Thurn, a man fifteen years older than Waldstein* (he was born in 1568). The armies, now united in Moravia, forced the Hungarian commanders Dengeleghi and Rédai to retreat to Nagyszombat (Tyrnau), but dissatisfaction with Liechtenstein led to his replacement by Cardinal Dietrichstein. In this state of stalemate both sides were satisfied when offers of mediation were made by the High Sheriff of Trencsén, Stephen Illésházy, and by September a truce already seemed near enough for the Bohemian contingent to be released and the hastily assembled recruits to be disbanded. Among those who returned home was Jan Urban of Domanín, and it was a looted and empty house which awaited him in Strážnice. During the Tartar raid his wife and young daughter had been captured, and had then perished while being forced to cross the Morava. His estate had been laid waste, and the only crumb of comfort was probably his elevation into the Estate of knights. He seems to have found consolation in his *Diary*, a sober and factual account of the cowardice of the magnates, the sufferings of the common people

---

*The regular name of the family to which the great general belonged is Waldstein (German) or Valdštejn (Czech). In the present narrative the popularized form "Wallenstein" is only employed from the time he attained international prominence. (trans.)

and the fortitude of simple men during that fierce, bloody year of 1605. Equally bitter were the testimonies of the town clerk of Brno, George Hovorius and the anonymous author of the *Lamentation*, a rancourous indictment of the lords of Moravia. The *Lamentation* discloses the vast gulf which separated the people from the small clique of nobility at court and the Estates party. It is a critique of men who "rob their serfs, raise their dues, increase their *robot*, expropriate their orphans, permit only their own wines and beers to be sold, refuse to honour any fair obligation", who "see it a shame of weakness to speak to their serfs", who "will stoop to any injustice or cruelty"; the Estates are condemned whether Catholic, Utraquist or Bohemian Brethren, Karel Žerotín as much as Karl Liechtenstein.

Still more eloquent than these chronicles is an analysis of the state of things in Zlín in 1606, at the time when Kryštof Cedlar returned from his imprisonment under Bocskai. In the town registers we find a stereotyped entry that "so-and-so lost his money in 1605 and 1606" or a moratorium was declared. The raids left full two-thirds of the houses and plots unoccupied, especially the best of them around the market and church. A number remained vacant for years as burnt-out shells, despite attempts by the authorities to dispose of them. Kryštof Cedlar was evidently attached to Zlín, for he sold off his two more distant estates, Pačlavice and Velký Ořechov, and acquired instead another one near at hand. Besides this he owned two houses within Olomouc and two freeholds on its outskirts, the estate of Paskov near Místek and vineyards at Lipov, Blatnice and Bečov. In Blatnice his vines grew beside the more modest holding of "orphan John", the son of the recently deceased burgher of Brod, Martin Komenský. Comenius had lost almost everything he possessed in 1605, and went to live with his sister in Strážnice where he began school. Only in 1608 did he receive some money "to educate himself" and this allowed him to go to the school of the Brethren in Přerov which stood under the patronage of Karel Žerotín, and thence to university in Germany three years later. Although his writings reveal only indirect memories of that terrifying spring of 1605 (they are clearest in the early pages of the *Labyrinth of the World*) – these must nevertheless have remained with him vividly.

In the period that followed there is again little news of Zlín. Cedlar evidently divided his time between Zlín and Olomouc, but his poor health seems to have kept him from active participation in public life. He devoted himself rather to the management of his estates and this brought him success. As far as we can judge, his incomes from Zlín were between 100–120,000 Moravian florins, and thus about a half of the total which was estimated at 230,000 florins, not including ready cash and promissory notes. Against this revenue he could set expenses which ran at a tolerable level of about 140,000.

None the less, Cedlar seems to have been a man of personal integrity who looked after his servants with generosity. His religious and political convictions emerge from a document of 1 July 1613, when he granted the town of Zlín and the village of Želechovice powers of advowson over their local parishes, provided they installed "a suitable priest of the Wittenberg Observance according to the Augsburg Confession". Among the witnesses we find representatives of the whole Protestant nobility of south-east Moravia: the lords of Žerotín from Strážnice, the lords of Kunovic, and a number of knights who were to reappear in 1619–20 as radical members of the Estates' opposition. Cedlar's officials came mostly from impoverished landed families, especially in the region of Troppau, but some were directly recruited (a novel step) from among the burghers of Zlín. Thus his ownership of the town saw the rise of among others, Daniel Přerovský, later the civic cantor, and the mayor Kundrát Bavorský. Cedlar established around himself a miniature court, made up of several families of minor freeholding nobility.

This grant of liberty to Cedlar's Lutheran subjects stands on the threshold of a new period when toleration in Moravia was beginning to yield to intolerance. One cause was the violent development of the conflict between Rudolf and his brother Matthias, the *Bruderzwist in Habsburg*. Peace was only concluded with Bocskai in Vienna in 1606. This was followed in November 1606 by a treaty with the Turks at Zsitva, near Komárom, and both these initiatives were led by Matthias. For Rudolf the end of the Ottoman War and the concessions to the Hungarians meant a clear and final collapse of his far-reaching political plans, which had always depended on a triumph along the eastern front. What had been the purpose of employing for many years leading European sculptors and painters to depict him in their works as victor laureate over the Turk? What use had been all the many pamphlets defending his preservation of the balance of power in the West and his concentration of forces in Hungary for an advance into the Balkans? It is not surprising that he was embittered, and moreover saw the actions of his brother, who had spent years of obscurity in Linz and Vienna since his early escapade in the Netherlands, as a deliberate attempt to deprive him of his throne. He could not appreciate that the inhabitants of Hungary and the Austrian lands, like the Moravian estates, had already suffered too many disillusionments for them to let this dispute between Archdukes leave them exposed to Turkish attack.

The simplest explanation of Rudolf's reaction is that he had become insane. And thus Catholics and non-Catholics alike, members of the court circle as much as the opposition, began to isolate themselves from him. In Moravia Albrecht Waldstein found himself moving closer to Karel Žerotín. The latter, who in 1605 came before Rudolf to defend his opinions, had in August 1604 married Katerina Anna Valdštejn, the sister of Albrecht. The bride died soon afterwards, but the brothers-in-law remained in fairly close contact, despite the fact that Waldstein was at this time following the example of Slavata and Liechtenstein in forsaking the Brethren and becoming a convert to Catholicism. Žerotín was also drawing nearer to Cardinal Dietrichstein, his former rival, but his general mood was sombre. He lamented the return of the apostate Liechtenstein to the Imperial court, and did not conceal, in his so-called *Apologia or Defence to Mylord Jirík of Hodice*, his presentiment that God "is preparing the downfall of Moravia, and has shaken its pillars and splintered its defences so that he may at last lay it bare and overturn it". In a letter to Amandus Polanus in Basle he wrote that everything around him was bringing nearer the collapse of Empire and Kingdom: oppression of men's faith, lack of respect for the law, the decline of mutual trust, the flood of foreigners, the destruction of freedoms and the abandonment of age-old customs.

Waldstein, whom the Peace of Vienna had deprived of the chance to distinguish himself in Hungary, began to side with Matthias in the struggle – and he was not alone. In August 1607 Rudolf named as *Lieutenant-Hejtman* Ladislav Berka, an untalented member of the Catholic court party, well-known for his confessional intransigence. But the Moravian Estates were understandably roused by the successes of the Hungarian Protestants, who had won recognition of their religious and political freedoms, and Žerotín, like Peter Vok of Rožmberk in south Bohemia, developed during 1607 his contacts with a series of opposition leaders: Georg Erasmus Tschernembl and Richard Starhemberg in Austria, the Margrave of Jägerndorf Johann Georg of Hohenzollern and the Hungarian magnate Stephen Illésházy. Having been disappointed by Rudolf, Žerotín set his hopes on the younger brother, Matthias, and another to do the same was the learned physician Jan Jessenius who had already attempted, with the help of Tycho Brahe, to make a career at court as Imperial historiographer and pamphleteer.

By the end of 1607 the German Protestants were taking an interest in the situation, and Christian of Anhalt, the adviser of the young Count Palatine Frederick v, began to extend his influence on Rožmberk, and through him on Žerotín, Tschernembl and Starhemberg. At the same time Rudolf broke with Liechtenstein who returned from Prague to Moravia firmly set on revenge. In December a secret meeting was held between the Austrian leaders and the Žerotín group at the latter's castle of Rosice, and on 1 February 1608 Archduke Matthias came to an agreement with the Estates of Austria and Hungary which was openly directed against Rudolf. At the beginning of March Liechtenstein pressed the Moravian Estates assembled in Vyškov into calling a Diet for the following month at Ivančice. The Diet ousted the Catholic clique headed by Berka; while Žerotín, Waldstein, Jessenius and a Moravian contingent joined the march of the allied army from Austria and Hungary towards Prague.

But a united front of the opposition in all the Habsburg lands was beyond even Žerotín's powers. The Bohemian Estates, and with them the Silesians, preferred to negotiate directly with the Emperor. Shortly after the Hungarians, Austrians and Moravians had strengthened their confederation by signing (at Šterboholy near Prague) a treaty based on earlier agreements, the Bohemians and Silesians came together in the same way, and efforts to unite the two camps were abortive. By the Treaty of Libeň (Lieben) of 25 June 1608 Matthias became sovereign in Austria, Hungary and Moravia, while Rudolf retained Bohemia and Silesia.

Matthias had now to honour his obligation, and he gave, in the words of the chronicler Pavel Urbanides, "such freedom of religion that anyone could be anything", while Žerotín was appointed Moravian *hejtman*. His co-religionists of Bohemia, led by Budovec and Thurn, extracted the same kind of guarantee from Rudolf by the celebrated *Letter of Majesty* of July 1609, though only after resorting to the threat of civil war. But this was not the end of unrest in either land. In 1611 Rudolf enlisted the aid of the mercenary troops of his nephew Leopold of Passau to turn his fortunes, and the exploit only ended in fiasco after the invaders had fought their way into Prague and the other confederate armies were on the march to deliver battle against them. The small "Roman" and pro-Spanish party at court was suspected of involvement in this episode and it redounded to its discredit, although most of them, still in the cautious spirit of the Spanish ambassadors San Clemente and his successor Baltazar Zuñiga, regarded the affair as a catastrophe. Zdenek Lobkovic was accused of secret dealings with the Passauers, but it was eventually only Rudolf's confidant Tengnagel who was proceeded against.

The events of 1608–9 strengthened the position of the Estates majority and temporarily restored the balance of forces, but it soon became clear that little had changed. The Prague Spanish Party, the ambassadors and nuncios, withdrew with Matthias' court to Vienna and now the Viennese Bishop, Cardinal Khlesl became the dominating personality. The struggle by Protestants to unseat him proved vain, and in 1615 it cost Žerotín his post as Moravian *hejtman*, while at about the same time Budovec, Thurn and Wenzel Ruppa (Václav of Roupov) were being forced once again into the background in Bohemia. The Catholic minority paid as little attention to the *Letter of Majesty* as to the glib promises of Matthias, and the chronicler of Holešov recorded with anguish the arrival of the "Jesuitical oppressors" in his small town, with their orders on the authority of the Lobkovices to force the population into apostasy from its Utraquist faith. The learned doctor Joseph Securius of Moravské Budejovice recorded in his diaries supernatural portents which "betoken new tribulations and the outbreak of a great storm", and few people in the Moravia of the years after 1610 can have doubted that a judgment was imminent. Another who observed the signs of the times was the young scholar from Herborn and Heidelberg, Brother Jan Amos who returned home in 1614, and taught for two years at the school in Přerov where he had been a pupil. He complained of the "feebleness of the Czechs", kept close contact with Žerotín, and in about 1617 contributed to a volume written by a group of Brethren priests called *A salve against Antichrist and all his Wiles*, an extensive work which although unpublished was widely copied. Comenius observed "that the clouds of persecution were gathering, and that lightning always flashes before it strikes".

THE CRISIS OF OLD BOHEMIA

All the warning signs of the worsening situation in central Europe failed to call forth from the circles of Czech Protestantism the necessary counter-measures. This unsettled time showed very clearly that the lack of unity between Bohemia and the lands associated with it gravely prejudiced the actions of the Czech state both at home and abroad, and made easier the manoeuvres of the Habsburg government. The long-standing attempts of Moravia to follow a clear line of action independent of its Bohemian neighbour emerged again with the negotiations over the *Letter of Majesty*. For while Bohemians and Silesians gained the recognition of their religious freedom by written legal agreement with the Emperor, the Moravians, led by Žerotín, were satisfied with the verbal promise of Matthias, and Catholic propaganda was not slow to exploit this difference. It was again Žerotín's reticence which prevented full advantage being taken of the dynasty's embarrassment over the Passau invasion of 1611. By 1613 Matthias' government in Vienna was already displaying by its actions (like Khlesl's firm repressions in Brno and Olomouc) that it was inclining increasingly towards the radical Catholic wing and counting on division in the ranks of the Estates to further its violent ends.

Against this steadily increasing Catholic pressure, continually reinforced and organized by the great power of Spain, the leaders of the non-Catholic opposition sought to retrench behind the position they had won in internal politics and to call on a united defensive front from all the component lands of the Habsburg Monarchy. We have seen how the idea of a confederation had been partially realized during the crisis of 1608–9, though it was still split into two factions, dominated by Žerotín and Christian of Anhalt. The objective remained, and discussions continued on the lines which Anhalt, Rožmberk and Tschernembl had initiated, but vital opportunities were wasted. The confusion of the Catholics in 1611 showed clearly that the opposition must use such political tension to intervene at both national and international level in its own vital interests, and it was a grave blow to the Estates that the general diet of that year, from which so much was expected, failed to press home their advantage. For a broad-based alliance of anti-Habsburg forces: the Netherlands, Switzerland, Venice, the Hanseatic towns, the international situation was not yet ripe, and the necessary state of organization and personal contact which could allow the realization of such a far-sighted and even revolutionary aim had still not been achieved. Lack of territorial unity and diversity of aims were obstacles difficult to surmount.

When Matthias became king of Bohemia he and his agile Catholic advisers were able to deflect further these dangerous designs by making shrewd concessions to localist sentiment in the provinces which resented overdependence on the administration in Prague. The government gave ground over taxes and the management of official business and thus diverted attention from more serious matters. At this time the Imperial court strengthened its economic position and the influence of the Catholic Church in the Silesian principalities of Troppau and Jägerndorf, but soon new expenditure on military preparations against the Turk brought a further shift, and the Estates were able to insist on the recalling of the general Diet. Matthias counter-attacked by summoning representatives of all his lands to a meeting at Linz in 1614, and the differing demands of Bohemian, Austrian and Hungarian spokesmen again frustrated the hope of a broad confederation of the Estates opposition. The Prague Diet which met in 1615 was then pressed to permit a higher rate of taxation for five years and to assume three million thalers of state debts, a clear mandate to the régime to continue its offensive throughout every field of public life.

Political pressure was accompanied by cultural pressure. The educational system of the Jesuits with its expertly planned instruction was expressly directed to achieve the long-term incorporation of Bohemia, especially its younger generation, in the intellectual world of Spain and the Papacy. The Jesuits were the forward troops of the Catholic camp, the ideative inspiration of its propaganda, and as such they became in the years of crisis the focus of non-Catholic retaliation. It was especially the Order's college in the Old Town of Prague which organized the mission of the Spanish party among the Bohemian nobility; and its success in gaining a number of young aristocrats, by contrast with the rarity of this kind of convert in the Rhineland, gave its activity a firm basis in the highest political circles, a link with the executive power of state. The Jesuit headquarters in Prague and later in Vienna came to be controlled by the Papal nuncios, first established in 1560 and increasingly the leading representatives of Rome in central Europe, who held together a network of agents to spread the ideological and political message of the Counter-Reformation. We should not overlook the great influence of the new dogmas elaborated by the Catholic Church on the basis of the Council of Trent and used as a multiform weapon of propaganda at all levels of society. The interrelation between this hierarchical principal of ecclesiastical organization and the fundamental ideas of the absolutist theory of government proved, despite intermittent disputes between Pope and Emperor, a notable unifying factor along the whole European anti-Protestant front.

The favourable conditions for Catholic advance were created in part by its opponents. The whole of Protestant Germany, especially its western territories where Calvinism derived strength from the proximity of the Netherlands, saw increasingly violent squabbles between Lutherans and Calvinists which weakened the resistance of large sections of the population, above all in the towns, to Catholic overtures. These quarrels passed over into Bohemia, and brought unease and dissention to the richly diversified religious life there. The Lutherans particularly were split into several factions which vilified each other with more prejudice and passion than the Catholics.

Yet it is a significant insight into the strength of traditional Czech Estates democracy that the rigorous movement of Catholic renewal which sacrificed the old and proved methods of religious tolerance in the interests of a militant Spanish-inspired ideology, could not completely eliminate the Catholic adherents of moderation, even in the critical years around 1609. This still numerous group led by Adam Sternberg the High Burgrave sought a peaceful accommodation in the decisive summer of 1609 between the Protestants and the Imperial faction which would respect the long-established tradition of Bohemian political life – that the Estates and their organs, above all the Diet, were partners on an equal legal footing with the sovereign. Sternberg's words at the session of the Royal Council on 5 March 1609 deserve to be quoted: "I propose that His Imperial Majesty be pleased to appoint certain persons instructed to treat with the Utraquist party, to the end that this matter be brought to agreement in a peaceable fashion."

We have here in a nutshell the main precept of Bohemian politics, which informed the country's government throughout the sixteenth century: negotiation, based on respect for the demands of each party, as the best guarantee for ensuring concord in administration and undisturbed political evolution. This principle, expressing itself in religious issues as the tolerance of other confessions, penetrated deeply into the personal relationships within the families of the nobility. In many cases members of the same house, even the same family, belonged to different churches and this religious diversity was no hindrance either in private life or public activity. Adam Sternberg the High Burgrave and his brother Wenceslas themselves had another brother Stephen George who was a Lutheran. The position of the leading moderates was assailed not only by fervent Catholics of the circle around the Spanish ambassador Zuñiga: Lobkovic, Vilém Slavata and Jaroslav Bořita of Martinic, but also by the intolerant Lutheran camp, whose leaders, principally Kaspar Schlick and Jan of Sezimovo Ústí, raised political and religious demands which could only heighten the existing tension. The fierce attacks both of Bohemian and foreign preachers – the latter mainly from Saxony – were directed with great vehemence against the Czech Brethren, and placed the uncommitted majority of the population between two fires, a situation of strain, uncertainty and dispute which could easily lead to violence.

These complex and frequently dramatic political developments both within Bohemia and abroad were accompanied by an economic advance among all orders of society which was itself a complicating factor by the beginning of the seventeenth century. The rural population which formed the overwhelming majority of the nation was still (whether living on estates belonging to nobles or to free towns) bound for the most part to traditional forms of natural economy, but an increasing amount both of crops and animal production from the holdings of the larger peasant farmers was finding its way onto the competitive market. Hence this considerable section of the subject population saw a rise in its own family standard of living and the level of its agricultural techniques. This was to some extent reflected in an extension of the area of land under the plough, and the early seventeenth century saw continuance of the intensive colonization of waste whose beginnings we have already noted. A particularly important fact here is that even where feudal payments on new lands were pushed up by the general rise in prices to a level above that of the old, original fields, these peasant entrepreneurs did not lose their initiative. We can observe such pioneer work both by cottagers and by well-to-do farmers not only in the fertile valleys of Bohemia but still more in the frontier districts, and it was especially the latter regions which were made by stubborn effort to yield new resources and increase the intensity of national economic evolution. These two factors: the extension of farmable land and improving techniques, were among the main causes of the continuing rise in general living conditions in Bohemian villages during the years before 1620.

New areas of ploughland and a still rising population helped to maintain into the seventeenth century the prosperity of the towns, especially the small domain towns which had grown markedly since about 1550. These came to form a dense network of market centres directed especially towards the needs of the agrarian community, and with them a powerful new class of rural artisans and traders entered the Bohemian social framework who could not be entirely absorbed within the rigid framework of the feudal order with its three privileged Estates and undifferentiated "subject" population. The economic function of the rural craftsmen and merchants was almost the same as that of the inhabitants of the free towns, yet they long remained in the same personal relation to their lords as the peasantry proper. At the same time it was in the interests of the authorities, especially the great landowners, to guarantee outlets for their produce, which could be sold more cheaply than those of the free towns, and the greater autonomy of their semi-urban communities made easier the organization of manufactures.

Thus the domain towns came to form an intermediate gradation of society between city and country, and by the early seventeenth century there were so many that competition was beginning between them for markets, while some sought to establish a monopoly position in their home territories. The towns best placed to achieve this were those on the large *latifundia*: Pardubice, Podberady, Jičín, Náchod, whose landlords gave support and counted on deriving their own advantage in higher urban rents and the rising purchasing power of the peasant consumer. Such domain towns did not restrict their activities to the immediate circle of settlements but penetrated with their wares within the economic orbits of the smaller estates, mostly owned by knights, which formed, as we saw in the last chapter, a substantial part both of the territory of the country and of its population. In the years before 1620 they were nearly as large a market as all the domains of the great landowners, and their many settlements invited exploitation by neighbouring towns, since most of the land units, which held on an average between three to six villages, were too small to develop their own artisanate. Hence the smaller estates became a field of fierce economic warfare between the products and crafts of various competing towns, and the provinces where there were many of them (especially Kouřim, Čáslav and Hradec) left the customer with much freedom of choice among different traders; this in return helped to loosen guild restrictions and local monopolies in the free boroughs and to check the tendency towards them in the domain towns.

All the above factors in the productive and commercial structure of the Bohemian economy supported a strong internal market. Rising agricultural output, both from the farms of the nobility and the peasant sector, meant not only the marketing of raw produce but also an increasing penetration of finished or semi-finished goods into the towns to take advantage of greater expertize and higher consumption there. Beer, malt, butter, poultry, eggs, cattle and oil established themselves as regular and powerful elements in urban trading. The strength of the domestic market was important for Bohemia as a whole since few commodities either agricultural or manufactured needed to take the difficult and expensive export routes. Demand in the larger towns, whether free like Prague, Pilsen and Hradec, or domain like Pardubice and Jičín, could accommodate most of the goods and thus guarantee the necessary maintenance of equipment and new investment in the agrarian sector. This domestic balance of forces in the Bohemian lands was strikingly different from conditions in neighbouring Poland, where much produce from the land (especially grain) found its way abroad. The lively home demand was not restricted to the ordinary run of articles for consumption and textiles. Furnishing and household luxuries made from glass or porcelain found a good market, primarily of course among the nobility and the patrician class, though the sumptuary legislation directed against the peasantry shows how the wealthier of its members were indulging more expensive tastes in dress and personal comfort.

These transactions within Bohemia called for extensive credit facilities. Borrowed money was a basic business need not only for the large-scale merchants in the free towns and on the *latifundia*, but also for local traders and even for many of the middlemen whose activities embraced only a single village. There was also a special market in real estate which involved primarily opulent members of the aristocracy and the major cities. With Rudolf's transfer of the Habsburg court to Prague credit dealings increased greatly in scope, taking on a more international character and becoming concentrated to a large extent in the hands of a few foreign financiers. These years saw the founding by Lazarus Henckel of his international banking house and the transactions of some wealthy magnates (Betengl, Smiřický) went beyond the frontiers of Bohemia, while the list of the greatest state creditors included names like that of Karl Liechtenstein. Private lending, backed usually by property or stores of goods, observed regular rules of trading practice and contributed to the development of local commerce, but the credit operations of the state caused more difficulties. These were a burden on all the more prosperous elements of society, especially since the financial administration was often unable to settle its obligations within the agreed period, while it frequently resorted to pledging whole sectors of public revenue as surety for foreign creditors. The profits of the state mines, customs, crown lands, and the poll tax had regularly to be put in the hands of foreign agents for a number of years and thus remunerative enterprises were held back, or even stagnated completely.

In this context a few words must be said about the question of American silver. Silver played an important and well-known part in the economic evolution of western Europe, based on the thriving Atlantic trade of the sixteenth century. For Bohemia it was much less significant, and this primarily because the kind of international finance and credit required to introduce large quantities of silver into the currency was not sufficiently strongly developed to affect materially the structure of the domestic economy. The Bohemian products which were carried abroad for export were limited to certain kinds of agricultural supply: fish, grain, wood, or artisan manufacture: textile and leather goods; and they were sold in the neighbouring areas of Austria and Germany without penetrating directly to the rich markets of western Europe which would have given added volume to the currency in circulation and stimulated its flow. On the contrary, much debased money entered Bohemia from the Empire and upset exchange relations within the country.

The positive aspects of national development were however accompanied by other less desirable ones which stemmed partly from the pressure of the government's indebtedness and partly from the influence of economic crises. The pomp of the Imperial court, and vast expense on the military defence of Hungary against the Turks swallowed up not only the returns from the crown's own enterprises and direct customs and excise revenues, but also raised the general level of taxation throughout the population. Both the Imperial and the Bohemian Exchequers had to resort to regular loans from individuals and corporations at home and abroad. The very accession of the Habsburgs to the throne had aggravated the debts inherited from the Jagellon dynasty, and under subsequent rulers the level of this burden, far from being reduced, rose to unprecedented heights. By the end of Rudolf's reign it stood at about 2,000,000 florins, a sum whose servicing, not to speak of amortization, called for new borrowing; and since a large part was owed to members of the nobility and the patrician class, the consequences of this financial weakness were felt throughout the land in the form of economic and social instability.

The effects of the periodic crises within the economy, whose roots lay both in natural calamities like harvest failures and floods, and in the particular structure of agricultural and artisan production, can be seen in governmental attempts at regulation, import and export control, and in the surviving records of large estates. Although the rise in living standards which continued into the seventeenth century was sufficient to absorb most of the higher output of commodities, imbalances could arise and we can follow the uncertainties of the years 1609–18 from the account books of the Smiřický lands. Here the most striking feature is the falling price of beer, albeit not evenly distributed, which was fraught with serious consequences both for the overall profitability of the estates and the permanent and temporary workers employed. The crisis was not restricted to the Smiřický *latifundia*, which stretched from Prague to the north-east borders of Bohemia, and if the Smiřický documentation is the fullest available, traces are not lacking in many governmental discussions of the same years. The regular negotiations of the Estates over the chronically crippled state finances are full of complaints about the decline in corn prices, the higher rate of interest on loans, the indebtedness of landowners, the serious results of collateral securities against government borrowing, and the economic difficulties of the peasantry.

Thus the threat of depression was joined in the second decade of the seventeenth century to the dangerous political development. The gradual but systematic progress of re-catholicization on the estates of the crown, clergy and some magnates, the militancy of the Jesuits, and the political deadlock which followed the Passau invasion up to the accession of Matthias and beyond held the country in a state of continual tension, while the background of sharpening international conflicts made the further continuance of peace appear increasingly unlikely. The opposition to the Habsburgs was hardening both within Bohemia and the Empire; by 1614 the plans of both Lutherans and Calvinists to replace them with a different dynasty were crystallized, the former looking to the Elector of Saxony, the latter to the Count Palatine with the expectation of support from England, whose prestige had risen greatly throughout Europe since her victorious wars with Spain.

The free hand which Vienna had gained from the general Diet of 1615 and the agreement between the Spanish, Austrian and Styrian branches of the Habsburg family on a common plan of action in central Europe allowed the government to prepare for a decisive assertion of its intentions in the uncertain climate of Bohemia by forcing the election as King of the Archduke Ferdinand. The debates of the Diet of June 1617 in Prague show clearly the dangerous extent of the gulf between this bigoted Catholic prince and the Protestant majority of the Estates, and the election itself was far from the formal acknowledgment which Ferdinand and his Catholic supporters had counted on. The opposition group, which included leaders of the lords (Budovec, Thurn, Schlick), knights (Kaspar Kaplíř) and burghers (Valentin Kochan) put up a spirited defence of its right of free choice. But the length of the negotiations and the personal adroitness of the Chancellor Lobkovic brought an eventual erosion of the union of the Protestants: only Thurn and Colonna von Fels stood out until the very end, and even Budovec, who was known to have the strongest objections to Ferdinand's candidature, was finally persuaded to accept him. This was the bloodless Catholic victory; and the Protestants were to learn within a year how much it had compromised their position for the bitter conflict which lay ahead.

EUROPEAN POLITICS AND THE DEEPENING CRISIS

The years 1608–9 saw the emergence in central Europe of formidable new power-groupings. On the one hand the Hungarian, Moravian and Austrian Estates faced the Bohemian-Silesian confederation; on the other the Union of Protestant, mainly

Calvinist princes and cities of the Empire, stood ranged against a league of Catholic rulers. The alliances within the Habsburg lands proper were however very loose: that which had brought Matthias into power was far from solid, especially its Hungarian elements, while differences soon arose between Bohemians and Silesians, largely over the position of Troppau and Jägerndorf. Christian of Anhalt and the Margrave of Jägerndorf, Johann Georg of Hohenzollern sought to win all the Estates over to the side of the German Union and privately made no secret of plans to dispossess the Habsburgs completely.

The chief spokesman of Protestant Moravia, Karel Žerotín, was forced from office for his moderation in 1615, the year of the general Diet in Prague; shortly before this he had a long discussion with his friend Hartwig von Stitten, the confidant of Johann Georg, about the whole state of Europe and the Habsburg dominions. The basic question which occupied them was the matter of the succession in the Empire. The Emperor Matthias was ageing and had no children; neither of his younger brothers, Archdukes Maximilian of Tyrol and Albert, the joint governor of the Spanish Netherlands, presented a better prospect. The Catholic camp urged two candidates, each one as bad as the other: either Philip III of Spain or the equally dangerous Ferdinand of Styria, notorious for his strong extirpation of the Reformation in Styria. Žerotín and Stitten had to consider the chances of eliminating Habsburg government in Germany as well as in Bohemia and Hungary and hence the probable attitude of the various Estates in central Europe if they were presented with a choice which would necessarily be contentious. Žerotín was well-informed about the political situation and did not conceal from Stitten his assessment of the real probability of foreign intervention on the Protestant side.

Žerotín, the representative of the Church of the Brethren which was more and more inclining to Calvinism, did not deny in principle the right of the Estates to rebel against their sovereign, but he allowed this possibility of resistance only when no other way remained to defend the cause of justice. But who could judge that such a situation was at hand? For Žerotín the answer hung on another basic question: that of whether the Bohemian crown was to be considered hereditary or elective. This he could never fully resolve, but we have seen that the Moravian tradition since 1526 had tended to the first alternative, and thus the decision to take arms against the dynasty could only be a more difficult one there than in Bohemia proper. A great practical problem which they considered at length was whether the Estates should join the German Protestant Union. Žerotín had no doubt that such a move would bring civil war within the Bohemian, Hungarian and Austrian lands, since the whole of Estates society was everywhere split both politically and religiously. Its Catholic leaders would certainly not abandon the Habsburg camp; failing this the most that the Union could expect from central European Protestants in the event of conflict within the Empire would be a benevolent neutrality.

Žerotín had no illusions either about the strength of the Union itself: it seemed to him to have neither money, nor troops, nor skilled diplomats. Against the combined might of the Austrian and Spanish Habsburgs it would avail little. The Prince of Transylvania Bethlen Gabor was aware of his own weakness and therefore inclined to negotiate with Vienna, while the Sultan, occupied with domestic interest and the Persian war, would not be eager to break his peace with the Emperor. Poland was negotiating an alliance with Vienna, preparatory to attacking Prussia if the Elector of Brandenburg should take any initiative there. Saxony and its Elector were, according to Žerotín, wholly unreliable. France would intervene on the Union's side only if a growth of Spanish power seemed to threaten. The English king could do little to help his son-in-law Frederick of the Palatinate, and even the greater prospect of support from the Estates General of the United Provinces was jeopardized by the latter's competition with Spain in the Atlantic and the southern Netherlands. Žerotín warned against underrating Spanish preparedness in Italy or the activity of Ferdinand in Styria. In all it was clear that he was not willing to recommend his Moravian friends to link their destinies with the Union, and did not regard the whole European situation as propitious for a fight to the death with the Habsburg house.

The events of the next three years proved him abundantly right. The general Diet of 1615 left the opposition in a more sober mood, since the Hungarian Estates did not appear at all, and the Bohemians and Austrians could not agree, while the Czechs showed themselves domineering towards the Moravians and Silesians. Žerotín stood out beside Dietrichstein against his Bohemian co-religionists whose political plans seemed to him too radical and unrealistic. Then, to his surprise, the Austrian and Spanish branches of the Habsburg family submerged their differences before the Diet of 1617 in the so-called Oñate Treaty and agreed to support the candidature of Ferdinand of Styria both in the Empire and Bohemia. Žerotín again joined Dietrichstein in leading the Moravian Estates who welcomed Ferdinand at Polná and accompanied him to the Diet of allegiance in Brno. The new monarch neither accepted nor rejected explicitly the claims for political and religious freedom; he was clearly little concerned to stress, in the spirit of their local traditions, that faith is a gift from God and a matter over which none can suffer compulsion.

With the coronation of Ferdinand completed, prospects of successful resistance to the Habsburgs became even more distant than before; Žerotín would no doubt have agreed with the judgment of Polyxena Lobkovic, wife of Zdenek, as recorded by the Chronicler Pavel Skála of Zhoře:

> Polyxena, born a Pernstein and wife of the Lord Chancellor of this Kingdom, a woman of high thinking and a strong Romanist was bold enough to say quite openly before certain persons that things were now swiftly coming to the pass where either the Papists would settle their score with the Evangelicals, or the Evangelicals with the Papists.

The same year 1609 when the opposition of the Estates in central Europe achieved undeniable success against the Habsburgs and the two power blocks in Germany were formed saw also the conclusion of a twelve year truce between Spain and the liberated northern Netherlands, mediated by France and England. Paris and London were to cooperate once again, in 1614, when they secured a compromise peace at Xanten to end the long-standing dispute over Jülich-Cleves, but their coalition was only temporary and soon showed signs of instability. Even in Holland there was already a sharp division between the pro-French party represented by the "Arminian" regents and the pro-English orientation of the *Stadholder*, Maurice of Orange.

Despite the truce, it was the "Netherlandish question", the conflict between Spain and Holland, which remained the key issue in international politics. There is no doubt that the vast majority of observers among the central European Estates regarded Spain, if not inimically, at least with a very critical eye. To the Protestant leaders, including Žerotín, Spain meant for all intents and purposes Castile, a rich land with an advanced culture and supported by the fabled hinterland of the "New

World". Thus she is described in the Czech edition of Münster's *Cosmographia* in the mid-sixteenth century; thus she is spoken of by Vilém Rožmberk, and Vratislav Pernstein; thus she emerges from the annual negotiations of Vienna and Prague about the subsidy from Madrid, and thus she drew to herself the attention of the various newsheets written in Venice, Antwerp, Rome, Lyons and Frankfurt. But there was another side to the picture, and tracts about a Spanish crisis soon began to spread through central Europe after 1588 – the defeat of the "invincible" Armada.

The notion of Spain was always understood to include the whole Spanish-American Imperium. As such it appears in the reports of Gamiz, agent of Ferdinand I and Mary of Hungary in Brussels, as early as the 1550s. The riches of America and their effects on European prices were interpreted by Czech and German Bodinists in an anti-Spanish sense, while Bohemian castle libraries preserve a variety of pamphlets from the other side: some vaunting the splendours of Castile and professing their faith in absolute monarchy, others (the writings of the *tratadistas*) calling for caution and economic revival. Which of these opinions had the greatest influence? It is unfortunately rare to be able to establish on the basis of such collections when and where their owner purchased the individual items and how much effect they had on him – though an exception is the Krumlov library of Johann Eggenberg, one of the leaders of the Viennese Spanish party. We must thus content ourselves with saying that the views of the Bohemian Estates on Spanish civilization were far from uniform, and that leading families like the Lobkovic and Pernstein were well aware of such things as the Iberian Protestants and the devolutionary forces which showed themselves especially in the revolt of Aragon in the 1590s. The central European "Hispanists" well knew (they also had their personal experiences to draw upon) that the Empire of Philip III was by no means united, that its government was much nearer polysynody than autocracy, and that the ties of the dynasty concealed what was really a loose federation between Castile, Aragon and Portugal. And it would be very difficult to discover any firm and clear formulation of a "Spanish programme" among the supporters of Philip either in Vienna or Prague, at least until 1617.

By 1617 it was clear that the Austrian Habsburgs could not continue without financial support from their cousins in Madrid, but neither the one branch nor the other had much grasp of the principles of economics. Most of the American silver was used up in maintaining the court, in the politics of the Holy Roman Empire and in military expeditions against the Turks. The twelve year truce was forced on Spain by the economic crisis in Castile. The seriousness of this situation was shown too by the inability of Castile to quell the bloody Araucanian revolt in Chile which from 1599 wiped out half the gains made earlier by Spain. The Araucanian campaign was much discussed in central Europe; it forced the Spaniards to proclaim, at least temporarily, the doctrine of a *defensive war*, and caused a transformation of society in colonial Chile where the existing militias of the great landowners had to be replaced by a regular army financed from Peru. But this brought only a few months of truce and in 1615 the prospect of peace had completely disappeared. By this time it was anyway becoming clear in Madrid that absence of hostilities was not bringing economic reform in Castile or the limiting of political ambitions. The leaders of the *partido militar* were trying to convince Philip III and his minister the Duke of Lerma that the truce with the Dutch heretics was only benefiting the enemy, and that since it was impossible to defeat Holland economically it would be better to crush it once and for all. Readers of the reports of the nuncio Bentivoglio, who prophesied a new war in the Netherlands and called for the elimination of the Dutch menace, were willing to risk renewed military conflict to recover Castilian prestige and hegemony in Europe. Bentivoglio had little difficulty in persuading such people that the axis of European politics was a line linking Brussels and the Hague.

The importance of Bohemia and the Empire was appreciated by Baltazar de Zuñiga, the former ambassador in Prague and Vienna, as well as by his successor Count Oñate. Oñate's colleague Diego de Zeelandre was agent of the court of the Archduke Albert and Isabella in Brussels, and these dual monarchs thoroughly shared the belligerent opinions of their generals, led by Ambrosio Spinola and Buquoy, who had large armies stationed along the fortified Dutch frontier of the southern Provinces. The "war party" was backed by the Spanish viceroys in the Milanese and Naples, the Dukes of Feria and Osuna, who were continually pointing out the threats to Madrid's traditional links with the Low Countries from the English and Dutch fleets on sea and from the hostility of Savoy on land. The Netherlands could only be held with the help of the Austrian Habsburgs and even then only if the latter were bearers of the Imperial crown. Thus any threat to the dynasty in Bohemia or Germany must mean danger to the whole edifice of Spanish interests. In all Italy there were no more than two smaller countries which stood against Madrid in 1617. One was Savoy-Piedmont whose Duke, Charles Emmanuel, was seeking to strengthen his position as buffer-state with the help of France, England and the Dutch and was openly at war with Spain over Vercelli. Eventually the Spaniards were satisfied to come to terms with him in October 1617 at Pavia through the mediation of the Pope and the French. The following spring Savoy even regained Vercelli and Charles Emmanuel was left with the problem of disposing of the mercenary troops which he had recruited. Among these was one foretaste of the future – a Swiss regiment of foot raised by Ernst von Mansfeld.

The other challenger within Italy was Venice. "The Queen of the Adriatic" was still one of the most important commercial and financial centres in the world, and her diplomats, her painters, her theatres, and her university at Padua were all models for the rest of Europe. But Venice was involved in too many places at the same time: in a war with the Uskoks, the pirates of the Dalmatian coast, a struggle with the Papal Curia and periodic skirmishes with the Neapolitans. In 1605 the *signoria* seized control of all landed property of the Church and a year later expelled the Jesuits from its territories, in addition to nominating the general of the Servite order, Paolo Sarpi, author of the famous anti-Papal *History of the Council of Trent*, as its chief adviser. By their very position the Venetians were natural allies of any who opposed the Habsburgs or Pope Paul v: not for nothing were they called "honorary Protestants", and co-operated with Henry iv of France, the Swiss cantons, the United Provinces and the German Calvinists.

In 1615 a dispute broke out between Venice and Ferdinand of Styria over the fortress of Gradisca. After the Jülich-Cleves crisis this was the second trial of strength which could have consequences for all Europe. Ferdinand's army included Baltazar Marradas (once the commander of Rudolf's guard in Prague castle), Dampierre, Montecuccoli, and the young Albrecht Waldstein, Lord of Lukov and Vsetín in eastern Moravia. In Venetian service there were Dutch detachments commanded by Jan Ernst of Nassau, a relative of the *Stadholder* Maurice. The Habsburg troops captured Gradisca, but here too French and Papal diplomacy managed to intervene in the interests of the existing balance of forces and peace was concluded at Paris in

1617. The following winter relations between Venice and Spain were again aggravated when the *signoria* took firm action against foreign *condottieri* who were preparing a violent revolution against it and claimed to be acting in concert with Osuna and the Spanish ambassador in Venice, Bedmar.

The Catholic League led by Maximilian of Bavaria wavered between straight allegiance to Spain and obedience to the dictates of Rome. The Pope sought to limit it to an alliance between Bavaria and the bishops of Würzburg and Bamberg, while Cardinal Khlesl, as the chief adviser of Matthias, wished it extended and buttressed with the support of the Lutheran princes, above all Saxony. But he had no success, and thus the League was in 1617 still a confessional organization which followed the Curia and the Jesuit order rather than the Habsburgs.

On the other side, the Evangelical Union was in no better shape. The Duke of Pfalz-Neuburg and the Elector of Brandenburg had both left it, the latter despite being a relative of the Palsgrave Frederick v. The Union was in fact largely a grouping of Protestant rulers from the south and west of Germany, led by Frederick and controlled by his politician, Christian of Anhalt-Bernburg, who had since 1595 been governor of the Upper Palatinate, the area immediately adjoining Bohemia to the west. Anhalt had been a friend of Henry IV of France and a regular correspondent of Protestants in central Europe: Peter Vok of Rožmberk, Karel Žerotín, Starhemberg and Tschernembl. It was he who had organized opposition to the Habsburgs at the Imperial Diets and arranged the marriage in 1613 between Frederick, who was the nephew of Maurice of Orange, and Elizabeth Stuart, the daughter of James I. It was he too who, helped by his Heidelberg colleagues Camerarius, the Dohna brothers, Buwinckhausen and others, was pressing the ambitious plan of underpinning the Union with support from England and Holland. But he could not shake the position among the Lutherans of John George of Saxony, another immediate neighbour of Bohemia. The view in Dresden was that Catholics were easier to deal with than Calvinists, and although the Union managed to gain the Dukes of Saxe-Weimar, descendants of the Senior Wettin line which had lost the electoral dignity in 1547, there was never any doubt that John George would rather join with the Emperor than with those who opposed the Habsburgs. When voices began to be raised in Germany arguing that after Matthias's death the Habsburgs should be deprived of their Imperial dignity and the Bohemian crown, Saxon diplomacy rejected any idea of cooperating with such "rebels".

Outside Italy and the Empire the Habsburg-Catholic front had only one ally: the state of Poland-Lithuania, the "Northern Spain". The Polish Vasas, represented in 1617 by King Sigismund III, were in permanent conflict with their Lutheran cousins who ruled in Sweden and Finland, and this confrontation stretched all along the Eastern shore of the Baltic. Charles IX of Sweden and his son Gustavus Adolphus had a series of realistic objectives, but these also brought them into dispute with their powerful fellow-Protestant neighbour, the Kingdom of Denmark-Norway which under Christian IV (1588–1648) was seeking to implement an ambitious programme both at home and abroad. The Jesuit-inspired plan for a union of Poland with Russia and a re-Catholization of northern Europe came to nothing in the years after 1605, but Smolensk and Livonia remained in Polish hands and the tension was not abated by 1617.

For all the internal strain between Papal and Habsburg policies, the two together had created a power block which stretched from Portugal and Spain, across most of Italy to the southern Netherlands, the German territories of the League, the lands of the Austrian Habsburgs and the Poland of the Vasas. It was a block whose unity was not monolithic, yet whose feudal Catholic programme answered the mood of the day, as was appreciated for example by the Venetian political writer Traiano Boccalini: "People have never loved a ruler whose religion was other than their own, and have rather hated him . . . since modern heresy has now become an affair of state, disputations and councils are no longer enough, and arms must decide the issue . . ."

The model for this whole campaign was a Spanish universalist ideal best seen in the popularized treatise by Campanella, the *Monarchia Hispanica*. Against it stood another Europe, an urbanized, bourgeois Europe of the Protestant Estates, whose model was the United Provinces of the Netherlands. Holland, like Switzerland, was an examplary confederation, a new variant of the Utopian dream to supersede the oligarchy of Venice. It was a model of government by Estates, of vital commerce, of newly established manufactures and workshops, of cartography and overseas expansion; the cradle of a new realistic art which suited the taste of a partly anonymous town audience; a land of literary fellowships and concern for vernacular language, whose publishing houses pushed those of Venice, Antwerp and Basle into the background. Its University of Leiden stood on the same eminence as the traditional citadels of Heidelberg, Oxford, Cambridge and Padua, and served as exemplar to smaller academies like Herborn and Altdorf. The army of Maurice of Orange was a training ground for young Protestant and Catholic nobles from almost the whole of Europe, and Dutch tactics, threatened by the powerful *tercios* of Spinola, evolved smaller and more mobile infantry units equipped with greater firing power, new techniques of siege-warfare and gunnery. Men like the Kinskys of Tetov and the Kaplíŕs of Sulevice saw service in Maurice's camps; others as eminent as Gustavus Adolphus and Oliver Cromwell were his pupils.

The twelve-year truce with Spain in 1609 had been signed by the seven insurgent provinces as a "virtual" sovereign republic. But this could deceive no-one. The truce had really been concluded on behalf of the social forces which ruled this new kind of state, a polity where – as Grotius wrote in 1610 – monarchy, aristocracy and democracy were mixed. The real author of the peace was the *advocate* of Holland Jan van Oldenbarneveldt, the spokesman of the patrician class of regents who were moderate in religion, and sought to guarantee their independence by an alliance with France. Against them stood Maurice of Orange as the natural head of a coalition embracing immigrants from the south, Calvinist preachers, soldiers, and adventurers who called for political *revanche* and wished to build on the success of the Dutch East India Company by founding a West Indian counterpart to provoke Spain into a decisive battle for colonies and control of the seas. This power struggle, revealing itself on the surface as a religious rift between the orthodox Calvinists (Gomarists) and the more tolerant Arminians, had grown by the winter of 1617–18 to a state of potential civil war. It was understandable that by now the links with England, the Union and other Habsburg opponents were becoming dominant, since only four years remained until the expiry of the agreement concluded in 1609.

France anyway threatened to be a doubtful support in the case of renewed warfare. Since 1610 the widow of Henry IV, Marie de' Medici had ruled the country. Her connections, not only with Tuscany but also with the Papal Curia, had steered France temporarily right into the Spanish camp through the marriage of her young son Louis XIII to the Infanta Anne of Austria. The constitutional opposition was silenced in 1614 with the dissolution of the Estates General, the last meeting of that body before the revolution of 1789. But this wavering resistance from the Provinces and the Huguenots was backed by a firmer front against Marie and her favourite, Concini, within the Council of State. In 1617 the latter was murdered with the certain connivance of Louis XIII, if not at his direct request, and his successor in the office of chief minister, Luynes, aimed at a policy of neutrality which kept equally distant both from Spain and Holland.

A similar conflict over constitutional principle was taking place in England where James I, the first King of Great Britain, sought rights which, according to his ideas of absolute sovereignty were no different from those his predecessor Elizabeth had enjoyed. But under Elizabeth the Speaker of the House of Commons had changed from being the representative of the crown to that of the Parliamentary majority, and thus the famous "Addled" Parliament of 1614 was symbolic of a split between the opposition and a ruler who had already been trying since 1604 to form an alliance with Spain, the sworn enemy of a whole generation of Englishmen. James imagined himself not only monarch of a Greater Britain (though his was really nothing but a personal union between England and Scotland), but arbiter of all Europe. His ambitious plan suffered from the disadvantage of being an open secret, while it was also well-known that the king lacked the power to accomplish it. The marriage of Princess Elizabeth to the Elector Palatine left a need to complete the symmetry of James's intentions: the betrothal of Charles, Prince of Wales to the Spanish Infanta.

England was thus only in a very loose alliance with Holland, the Protestant Union and Christian IV of Denmark, James's brother-in-law. In some places English and Dutch capital had the same interests, especially in the Baltic regions where they could combine to mitigate the rivalry between Denmark and Sweden. Elsewhere, at sea and further afield, things were more difficult. Here there were old disputes about English loans, as well as newer friction over fishing rights off the coasts of Scotland, Iceland, and Greenland, and even a full-scale blood-bath in the East Indies. During the winter of 1617–18 representatives of the Dutch States General were in London in an attempt to resolve these strains between the interests of their own bourgeoisie, which was already enjoying a Golden Age and held a position of power in the state, and those of the English merchant class whose struggle for political domination was just beginning.

These economic conflicts had already had their echo in Prague. During the winter of 1610–11 there were negotiations in the city between the Hanseatic League and the English Merchant Adventurers, who had been at loggerheads since Elizabeth's closure of the Hansa's London staple, the Steelyard, in 1599. The Hansa was represented by Rudolf's one-time confidant, Duke Heinrich Julius of Brunswick, and supported by the Spanish ambassador; the English sent Stephen Lesieur as emissary. The debates brought no result, and the participants were already thinking of transferring their sessions to Frankfurt when they were surprised by the invasion of the Passauers and the occupation of the Hradschin and the Kleinseite. Lesieur, by origin a French Huguenot and acquaintance of Žerotín, had nevertheless a number of friends among the Passau troops, although the latter had come as a tool of the court party and in the service of reaction. While attempting to smuggle out of the country the war-booty of his countryman, Colonel La Ramée, and Rudolf's emissary Tengnagel (the son-in-law of Tycho Brahe) Lesieur was arrested by a cavalry unit of the Estates and brought ingloriously back to Prague. This abject incident was significant not only as the end of his diplomatic career; it showed that even in 1611 religious issues were far from all-powerful, and that Bohemia entered into the calculations not only of the Dutch and the Spanish, but also of Jacobean England.

In 1611 the Emperor Rudolf at last disappeared from the European scene and with him the "Turkish question" too temporarily vanished. A second problem, which Rudolf had of course made no real attempt to resolve, the "Dutch question" was also provisionally in abeyance. Now a third matter began to occupy the minds of the European courts: the "Bohemian question", or what would happen in Central Europe when political control in the Czech lands should slip from the grasp of those who were seeking to maintain the existing order of things. It was this which took place in the spring of 1618.

Four

THE BOHEMIAN WAR: THE LOCAL
CONFLICT AND ITS WIDER IMPORTANCE

THE HISTORY OF THE WAR, 1618–20

THE political crisis within Bohemia reached its decisive phase with the forced closure of the Protestant Churches of Broumov and Hroby. Immediate reaction both from the Estates and government showed that the affair could not be limited. The Estates gathered from 5–11 March 1618 and under the leadership of the militant Thurn, issued a sharp protest against such a blatant breach of the *Letter of Majesty*. When the two *Statthalters*, Martinic and Slavata, dismissed this action, the Estates turned directly to the Emperor, but here the decision was also against them. Matthias's letter of 21 March went so far as to prohibit them from holding any further meetings, thus infringing one of Rudolf's fundamental guarantees. The reply of the Protestants, again impelled by Thurn, was to convoke a gathering in the Prague Carolinum, the main building of the University, on 21 May where their leading spokesmen drew up a list of all the grievances, both political and religious, which had long been vexing them. In the minds of the assembled Estates it was clear that the government was moving to a well-prepared offensive and that any further concessions to it would destroy the whole effectiveness of the *Letter of Majesty*.

At the same time the Estates were seeking to distinguish between the basic religious dispute and the immediate political issue. Thus their resolution stressed that they were opposing not the Emperor but the misconduct of his lieutenants in Prague. Had this thesis been accepted in Vienna it would have been possible to resolve the conflict, but the court wholeheartedly took the side of its representatives and was not prepared to treat the matter as a religious disagreement which could be referred to the *Letter of Majesty* and *Compromise* of 1609–10. Thus the confusion of political and legal argumentation obscured the real question which had gradually turned from the small-scale skirmishes of the later sixteenth century into an issue of critical importance, i.e. whether the ruling power in Bohemia was to be the old and tested local ideology of religious and political freedom, with all its consequences in private and public life, or a stiff and uncompromising system of absolutist power vested in a Catholic monarchy which did not regard itself as bound by the traditional laws of the land. The domestic principle of social and political organization which had guaranteed almost two hundred years of measured and peaceful evolution within a large central European realm was challenged by an ideology which had grown up on the soil of Italy, Spain, and France and was based on a different balance of forces. The notion of a powerful state and ruler, culminating in a Machiavellian theory of absolutism buttressed by religious exclusiveness and the intolerance of the revived Catholic Church, stood opposed to the policy of Bohemia which was founded on the recognition of free religious and political expression and applied in practice the principle of negotiation and compromise rather than dictation.

Tension did not lessen in Prague after 21 May 1618 and a meeting of the four most determined leaders of the Estates' radical wing brought a decisive turn in the situation. Václav Budovec, Matthias Thurn, Oldřich Kinsky, and Albrecht Jan Smiřický came together the following day in the latter's house on the Kleinseite and resolved on an outright condemnation of the *Statthalters* Martinic and Slavata, the two "disturbers of general order". The outcome – the celebrated Defenestration of 23 May showed clearly that the radicals, spurred on by Thurn, were entering into a final combat not only with their most hated individual foes like Lobkovic, Martinic and Slavata, but also with the régime which was seeking after decades of preparation to encompass its plan of deliberately destroying the Bohemian state and debauching the legal guarantees of its existence. They thus set in motion immediately after the Defenestration a wide propaganda programme to justify before opinion abroad, especially among other national Estates, the aims and motives of their opposition to the Habsburgs.

For this purpose a delegation met in the house of Bohuslav of Michalovice and elaborated a thorough analysis of documentary evidence which was then edited as the first *Apology* of the Bohemian Estates. Led as before by Matthias Thurn and Wenzel Ruppa this action aimed to elucidate the Prague events before an international audience and also to gain moral and perhaps material support from Protestant circles. Both *Apologies* (the first appeared in May and the second in December 1618) presented the initiative of the Estates as a defence against Catholic oppression, and the stress on resistance to pressure from Vienna was calculated to engage the especial sympathies of the Austrian and Hungarian Estates who had also long been threatened by the same agency. The leading Bohemian insurgents rightly saw this as a promising lever to solidarity within central European Protestantism. They were concerned to lay bare the broad, international implications of the conflict which was being waged in Bohemia and the difficulties of resolving it in any straightforward way. At the same time all sections of public opinion within the country emphasized from the outset that the extreme steps taken against the evil royal lieutenants had been undertaken in defence of legally guaranteed religious freedoms, not as a conscious gesture against the authority of the Emperor. This claim of the leaders of the revolt that no steps were intended against the sovereign was a powerful argument in the ears of many waverers.

The court in Vienna had been assessing developments in Bohemia under the influence of its successes at the general Diets of 1611 and 1615 and underestimated the extent and strength of the Estates' dissatisfaction. It accordingly made light of the tension in Prague and was caught unawares by the Defenestration. When the Imperial advisers met to consider the situation and the measures to be taken it soon became plain that there were large differences of opinion; only in July 1618 after the acknowledged Bohemian king Ferdinand had ordered the arrest of Cardinal Khlesl, who was working to negotiate an agreement, did the radical wing gain control and move to immediate military action. With Spanish help it established a small company of troops under Dampierre and soon afterwards gained the experienced general Buquoy as commander of the whole army.

Meanwhile inside Bohemia the Estates were taking steps to form a new government, reorganize the administration and begin collecting together their own army. Thirty-six Directors, among them the highest officers of state and other leading political figures, were elected on May 25 on the basis of the legislation of

1609, twelve from each of the Estates. The most important of the lords were Václav Budovec, Wenzel Ruppa and Joachim Andreas Schlick; the knights included Kaspar Kaplíř, Bohuslav of Michalovice and Peter Mylner of Mylhausen, while the leading burghers were Martin Früwein, Jan Theodor Sixt of Ottersdorf and Daniel Škréta of Závořice. The Chancellor of the Directorate took over the functions of the old Bohemian Chancery and its wide powers remained in the capable and experienced hands of Peter Mylner. Kryštof Harant of Polžice became head of the Exchequer, whose earlier conflicts of competence with the Chancery were thus eliminated since Harant was also a member of the Directorate.

These firm steps against the Habsburgs found widespread support among opinion at large. The Protestant clergy were especially appreciative of the prospect of improved religious conditions and their influence carried most of the citizens of the free towns. At the same time an important aspect of the opposition was that from the beginning the Protestant majority was joined by a number of Catholics like Diviš Černin of Chudenice, the wealthy members of the family Hrzán of Harasov, some of the Kavka Říčanskýs of Říčany, and even Jan Slavata of Chlum, a kinsman of Vilém Slavata. This fact was of course very useful to the propaganda of the Estates, since they could point to it as evidence that they were maintaining traditions of religious tolerance against the uncompromising military offensive of the Emperor and his absolute ideology. The international weight of the argument was however soon weakened by the social influence of the great Catholic families who had taken the Viennese side. And before long the latter began a counter-attack exploiting the reservations of moderate Catholic and old-Utraquist circles, especially among the Moravian nobility.

The unity of the Estates opposition was moreover gravely threatened from within as early as the end of 1618. The most serious source of open discontent was centred on a politician well-known from the time of Rudolf and Matthias, Adam Waldstein, whose associates included the head of the Trčka family Jan Rudolf Trčka of Lípa and others like Jan Jiří Bechyne of Lažany and the very active Václav Mágrle of Sobíško, an influential citizen of the Old Town of Prague. Although this group could not operate publicly after its decisive defeat at the Diet of August 1618, it had enough breadth of personal contact and material resources to undermine the morale and coordination of the majority. The more the government of the Directorate was forced to meddle in the economic and political arrangements of the land the more insistent became the voices of domestic dissent. A particularly serious issue was the disagreement among the Directors about the proper course of action towards those who sympathized with the Emperor. Thus Pavel Kavka of Říčany, himself a member of the government, did not agree with the expulsion of prominent Catholics and recommended accepting the Emperor's call for a delegation to be sent to settle the dispute; the same line of policy was advocated by Theodor Sixt of Ottersdorf. Others were playing a double game like Stephen George Sternberg, the brother of the Burgrave Adam, or Bedřich Švihovský of Rýzmburk. Another cause of friction was the opposition to the new régime from many townsmen, some of whom refused to take on the functions assigned to them by the Directorate, and the defiance of Pilsen and Budweis caused great difficulties, both political and military. Great animus was shown against Pilsen after Mansfeld's capture of the town in November 1618 and some called for its complete destruction; while Budweis in the south was a perpetual thorn in the operations of the Estates' army.

Within two months of the Defenestration, after the fall of Khlesl (July 20), the Imperialist troops under Dampierre began an offensive in southern Bohemia, but their attack on Jindřichův Hradec was warded off, and the hastily assembled army of the insurgents led by Thurn and Colonna von Fels was able to recover the whole region with the single exception of Budweis. These early defensive successes of the Estates were soon set at nought by the advance of a larger army under Buquoy through Moravia to the borders of eastern Bohemia. This was the first tragic consequence of the separatist policy of the Moravians who in June, under the influence of Karel Žerotín and Cardinal Dietrichstein, had announced their neutrality and now carried the anti-Bohemian attitude so far as to grant Buquoy free passage across their land. It was their unfriendliness to the leaders in Prague which made possible the Imperialist attack on the unprotected eastern frontiers of Bohemia and Buquoy's invasion as far as Čáslav in the heart of the country.

In this extremely critical situation, when it was clear that a small army of mercenaries could not maintain intact the defences of the realm, the Diet of August 1618 proclaimed after long debates (in which the energetic and militant Albrecht Jan

Smiřický was prominent) the formation of a national militia. Smiřický, head of one of the most famous Czech families, was militarily active in other ways too, using his great wealth to establish and maintain a regiment of 1,100 infantrymen. Beside him Peter of Švamberk contributed a smaller troop. On the recommendation of Matthias Thurn and Georg von Hohenlohe whom the Diet elected supreme commanders of the army, the militia was to be constituted by mobilizing every fifth citizen and every tenth peasant. Victualling of the army was entrusted to Nicholas of Gersdorf, and Pavel Kaplíř of Sulevice was appointed quartermaster-general. In the provinces government commissioners carried out the organizing of the militia, while a large part was played by the lower nobility both in personally commanding small units and in helping to provide weapons and supplies.

The quality of this new national armed force was very variable. Wealthy nobles and burghers could afford to equip their men adequately, but the recruits sent out from the smaller estates often had outmoded weapons (the shortage of effective firearms was most serious) and the lack of training, especially in formation manoeuvres, sharply reduced their military effectiveness. The smallest knights' estates which provided only two or three men (such landowners sometimes banded together for a common contribution) could not raise any potential officers even at the lowest level, and were sorely pressed to finance even this modest venture. All these drawbacks tended also to sap the morale of the troops, and the knowledge that they were worse prepared and paid than professional mercenaries and more exposed to personal risk, was a poor foundation for endurance on the field of battle. Financial backing for the political and military initiatives of the new government was another difficult task. Money for the army came of course mainly from taxes and these were paid very regularly in the main, though there were a few isolated voices of protest like that of Václav Záruba of Hustiřany. As expenses spiralled it was necessary to have additional recourse to credit operations which were in any case the regular means of raising funds for any major state undertakings. Loans for military purposes were provided by all sections of the Estates: the largest sums came from the rich nobility (Smiřický for example lent 50,000, Václav Šťastný Petipeský 57,000 and Adam Hrzán of Harasov as much as 303,600 marks) while many of the knights offered 2,000–4,000 crowns. A further source was the sale of silver and jewellery from the royal treasury as well as the disposal of confiscated Church lands. Munitions and weapons for the army had also to be financed by the Directorate out of loans. Although local production of arms, both light and heavy, flourished in many workshops in Prague and other large towns, decisive help came from Christoph Betengl the Younger of Neuenberg who acquired large stocks from Nuremberg.

At the same time as mobilizing their own troops the Directors, led by Smiřický, took steps to disarm Catholics who were known to be strong supporters of Ferdinand II and thus protected both Prague and the country at large against a possible diversionary attack mounted from within. In Prague and some other towns fervent Protestants took severe measures against the Catholics, even to the extent (as in Tachov or Prague itself) of exiling and dispossessing them.

As we have seen, the town of Čáslav was the furthest point reached by Buquoy during his invasion from Moravia in the autumn of 1618. After the arrival of reinforcements sent by Duke Charles Emmanuel of Savoy and of detachments from Silesia, the army of the Estates was able to assume the offensive and before the end of the year it forced Buquoy back beyond Budweis. Despite this measure of military success the Czechs could not fully gain the Moravians for their cause against the opposition of Žerotín, and Thurn's negotiations with the Austrian Estates brought no positive fruit. Mansfeld's capture of Pilsen in November had deprived the Imperialists of an important strategic centre and brought back the whole of the west of Bohemia into the insurgents' camp; but during the winter the Catholics strengthened their numbers with several thousand mercenaries raised in Flanders, among them a cavalry regiment under Waldstein.

In the early months of 1619 the Elector Palatine, the Dutch Estates and the King of England entered into protracted and involved diplomatic discussion, but their bargaining brought only some financial help to the Bohemians and no securing of their political position. The attempts at a peaceful resolution of the conflict with the Emperor were never more than an abortive political manoeuvre, and after the death of Matthias in March 1619 the issues involved in the "Bohemian question" became more brutally straightforward. Since there was no thought whatever of negotiating with Matthias's successor Ferdinand, the July Diet in Prague took the decisive step of confiscating the lands of the crown and the property both of leading enemies of the Estates and of Catholic institutions. Among the latter it was the monasteries which suffered worst; in the capital itself popular loathing of the Jesuits was intense and their college in the Old Town was generally regarded as the ideological centre of the Counter-Reformation offensive. The sale of sequestered estates provided the government with significant sums of money which could be put to military purposes, while the town saw an extensive turnover in ownership, with individuals and councils both bidding for forfeited ecclesiastical property.

Meanwhile the Directorate could point to a real achievement in Moravia where in May 1619 the anti-Imperialists came to power under the leadership of the energetic Ladislav Velen Žerotín. This event not only fortified the political and moral position of the insurgents, but buttressed the whole strategic block of the opposition, since Moravia could offer reinforcements for the army and act as a firm bridge linking Bohemia with Ferdinand's enemies in Hungary. The change in the situation immediately became evident, and before the end of May Thurn had begun a determined offensive which soon carried his united forces to the gates of Vienna – the very centre of Habsburg power. But this significant success could not be exploited because of events on the battlefield in Bohemia. There the six-month siege of Budweis by troops of the Estates under Hohenlohe ended in failure and left Buquoy controlling a large part of the south, while tactical mistakes by the leadership caused the isolation of Mansfeld who was then defeated at Záblatí. The engagement at Záblatí, the first important victory of the Imperialists, had far-reaching consequences: Thurn was forced to interrupt his attack on Vienna, and the whole south-eastern front, which had carried so many Protestant hopes, was at one stroke driven right back into Bohemia. The neutrals in Moravia, led by the now inactive Karel Žerotín were confirmed in their negative attitude; while the severe population losses on both sides of the Bohemian battle-line reduced the numbers of potential recruits and their stomach for further fighting.

Morevia's entry into the anti-Habsburg camp was the climax of protracted efforts by the Bohemian Estates, whose leaders were well aware from the outset of the conflict that Bohemia could not hope to stand alone without engaging the support of all its neighbours. Moravia understandably occupied first place in their calculations, but it took them a long time to reach their goal, for the Moravians, although extremely close to the Bohemians both racially and territorially, were very hesitant in their reactions to the rebellion. The prestige of Karel Žerotín had held a great proportion of the Moravian nobles in neutrality although their unhappy experiences in 1613 could have given them little confidence in the promises of the Viennese government; indeed Žerotín used his influence in August 1618 to have three regiments of the local militia handed over to the pro-Habsburg arch-Catholic Cardinal Dietrichstein. The threat which this attitude represented to Bohemian security was shown by Buquoy's campaign of September 1618, but at the Moravian Diet in December the delegates sent from Prague (among them Pavel of Říčany, Oldřich of Gersdorf and Smil of Michalovice) were still unable to press the Estates to take their side openly. Only with the withdrawal of Žerotín from public life in May 1619 could the anti-Imperialist faction take control and join forces with the Czech insurgents.

The Bohemian Estates were also acutely concerned from the spring of 1618 to extend the anti-Habsburg front to Silesia. The meeting of the Silesian princes and Estates in September of that year was however clearly influenced by the Moravian example and refused to declare an alliance with the Czechs, despite the concerted efforts of a delegation led by Joachim Schlick. Only the Margrave of Jägerndorf, Johann Georg, offered positive help. But in the spring of 1619 Silesia and both Lusatias, Upper and Lower, took up the rebel cause; at the same time the mission of Radslav Kinsky and Peter Mylner of Mylhausen succeeded in persuading the Estates of Upper Austria to enter into a confederation on 4 April.

Another matter which had occupied the Directors since their first discussions after the Defenestration was to ensure the security of the south-east frontiers of the Bohemian lands, and this meant coming to terms with Hungary. The lands of St. Stephen along the Danube had acquired during the sixteenth century an exceptional importance as the buffer territory through which the Turks exerted direct pressure on the Habsburg dynasty. Thus by the beginning of the seventeenth century the developments in international politics had brought guarantees there of equal rights for non-Catholics (the Peace of Vienna, 1606) and power relations within the country exhibited features similar to the Bohemian evolution. It was obvious that the Czechs would seek to mobilize the proven reserves of strength among the other Protestant Estates (the germ of a total central European confederation had been implicit in some of the initiatives at the general Diet of Linz in 1614) and Jan Jessenius was despatched as early as 21 June 1618 to Pressburg for negotiations with the Hungarians. This mission proved abortive, since the emissary was interned and detained for six months at the Emperor's pleasure. The failure did not deter the Directors from further efforts, but active military support was only forthcoming from Bethlen Gabor in September 1619.

Relations between the Bohemian Estates and Saxony had long been close both economically, culturally and socially. In order to secure the northern border and to defend Silesia and the Lusatias the Czechs had now to accomplish at least the neutrality of Dresden, although the fickle politics of the Elector John George gave little prospect of active backing from the leading German Lutheran state. Colonna von Fels was sent to treat with the Elector in June 1618 and was able to elicit a welcome promise of help, but it soon became clear that the Emperor could outbid the insurgents, offering financial and territorial gain to wean John George from a Bohemian alliance. The fact that material advantage thus triumphed over the considerations of freedom for co-religionists and resistance against the advance of Imperial absolutism was one of the main causes of the eventual failure of the Bohemian rising.

Elsewhere in Germany too the Directors were pressing their case with all the diplomatic resources at their disposal. They sent delegations to every territory which was Protestant and every prince who stood in the anti-Imperialist camp. Georg von Hohenlohe pursued discussions in Heidelberg with the Palsgrave and Christian of Anhalt while emissaries led by Maximilian Kolovrat left in July 1618 to negotiate with the Elector of Brandenburg, John Sigismund. At the same time the personal correspondence of leading directors with important nobles throughout the Empire was a further weapon in creating an understanding there of the Bohemian situation.

With the return of Thurn from Vienna and the arrival of a detachment of reinforcements from Holland the home front was consolidated during the autumn of 1619 both in Bohemia and in Moravia where the energetic Ladislav Velen Žerotín had cleared the whole country of Imperialist troops. All the lands of the Bohemian crown were now united under the ultimate authority of the Directorate in Prague and the second wave of the Habsburg offensive had been halted. But events had already shown that more extensive political and military measures would be necessary for any prolonged resistance to the growing forces of the Imperialist camp, backed as it was by Spanish money and steady arrivals of new recruits from Italy and the Netherlands. The crucial need was to stabilize the internal situation (and thus to yoke together more closely the different Bohemian lands) by resolving the problem of a new head of state and laying the foundations of a constitution in which real power should lie with the body of Estates. The months of July and August 1619 brought these matters to a head, at a time when international interest was itself concentrated on the question of electing a new Emperor to succeed Matthias.

The great diplomatic efforts of the Habsburgs, backed by bribes and promises, eventually succeeded in raising their candidate to the Imperial dignity and Ferdinand II was duly elected on 28 August; two days earlier he had been deposed by the Bohemian Estates General in favour of Frederick, the Elector Palatine. An especial irony of fate was that even the Palatine representative cast his vote for Ferdinand. From the standpoint of Habsburg dynastic policy, founded throughout the sixteenth century on the principles of legitimacy and inheritance, the election of Frederick was a stunning blow, a threat to the whole hegemony of the *Casa d'Austria* and a threat the more serious in that the Catholic parties in Bohemia and Austria had been seen as the vanguard in central Europe of the militant absolutist ideology of the family's Spanish branch.

But the election of Ferdinand as Emperor pointed a different moral: by guaranteeing the Habsburg power position in the *Reich* it heralded an immediate and concerted assault on the very forces which in Bohemia had just issued this challenge to the Counter-Reformation conception of state and religion. At the same time it demonstrated very clearly the want of unity within German Protestantism and the readiness of its leaders, the Saxon and Brandenburg Electors, to put material self-interest before the demands of a common front against the Habsburgs.

To the Lutherans the behaviour of John George of Saxony was galling above all things since they had placed their best hopes in him, and it showed how the influence from that quarter, far from providing active help, could even serve to threaten the unity of the Bohemian lands. The choice of Frederick had itself not been unanimous, the six votes of the group around Colonna von Fels being cast for the Saxon Elector, and signs of serious differences among the Lutherans were already visible. For John

George himself the victory in Bohemia of his personal rival exacerbated a long-standing hostility to Calvinism and now turned him decisively against the leaders of the Bohemian Estates. His natural loyalty to the Emperor was rendered the more congenial by ample promises of territorial gain.

The general Diet of 1619 brought not only a decision over the Bohemian crown; it earned a special importance in the history of domestic politics for its preparation of the new constitution of 23 July. This established the relation between monarch and Estates and laid the basis for peaceful evolution by granting religious freedom to all confessions, the Roman Catholic among them. The emphatic and triumphant assertion of these traditional cornerstones of Czech public life was the more valuable in that they were proclaimed anew at a moment when the intolerant power doctrines of Spanish absolutism and the Counter-Reformation were being brought together for a final uncompromising assault.

Bohemian resistance was now by September 1619 coordinated at home. Abroad, its chances were improved by the signing of a confederation with the Estates of Upper and Lower Austria, and then by the decision of Bethlen Gabor to renew his war with the Emperor. Pressure from Hungary caused Buquoy to withdraw most of his troops to Vienna and gave Thurn and Hohenlohe a new opportunity to advance on the Habsburg capital. This favourable turn of events coincided with the arrival of Frederick in Prague on 31 October. The presence of the king lent stability to the government while his coronation Diet voted taxes and approved concluding new loans for military purposes. The reception of the new monarch at Waldsassen was no empty diplomatic courtesy; the speech of Joachim Schlick by which the representatives of Bohemia accepted their new ruler reminded him that his coming was a bilateral agreement founded on the free choice of the Estates. As well as investing him with sovereign powers it imposed weighty duties towards the country and its political representatives. The ceremonial occasion must certainly have put the Czech participants in mind of similar events almost one hundred years before, when representatives of the Estates had received the first Habsburg king at Jihlava (1527). The experiences of the three or four generations of Bohemian politicians since then did not however give encouragement for the future.

In October and November the Bohemian army joined with Bethlen's troops and together they fought their way to the walls of Vienna; but then Polish cavalry recruited by Bethlen's enemy György Drugeth of Homonna threatened his bases in Hungary and he was forced to withdraw eastward. Thus the second offensive against Vienna again failed to bring the anticipated results and a golden chance to defeat the Emperor was frustrated. Bethlen's truce with Ferdinand, concluded on 4 February 1620, left the south-east front again exposed to attack, and this at a time when the new king had a promise that the Protestant Union would defend the Palatinate, but no positive military support for the Bohemian war. Within the country discord was again growing. Many Catholic members of the Estates had signed an oath of obedience to the new king, but at the same time reiterated their refusal to act in any way detrimental to their religion, and this declaration could only bring differing interpretations and new uncertainty. It was also disquietingly common knowledge that certain Catholics were in contact with emigrants in Passau and at the Imperial court.

By early 1620 Ferdinand's policy in the Empire and the consolidation of his armies were beginning to show results. By its treaty with Maximilian of Bavaria and with its financial subsidies from Spain the Viennese government was able to prepare for decisive action against Heidelberg and Prague and three armies were mobilized for the spring campaign. On top of this Imperial diplomacy scored a notable success at the end of March when the Elector of Saxony entered into an alliance and his example was followed by the rulers of several of the smaller German states. The full isolation of the Czech insurgents was encompassed by the treaty of Ulm in July, when the Protestant Union concluded an agreement with the League to neutralize the territories of the *Reich*. Thus Bohemia was cut off by an iron ring on almost every side: the antipathy of Poland and the hesitations of England and Holland had left her entirely without allies, since the desperate attempts begun at the April Diet in Prague to enlist Danish, Swedish or Venetian support had reached only a tentative stage. In Bethlen Gabor alone lay hopes of military assistance; despite the continuing efforts of Schlick and others the old link with Saxony was broken irretrievably.

The diplomatic abandonment of Bohemia by England, Holland and France (who were by the summer seeking mainly to defend the Palatinate on the Rhine) meant that help from this quarter shrank to an insignificant trickle. Nearer at hand the beleaguered Czech Directors gained some compensation in a promise of

7,000 men from the Hungarian Estates, but now the internal crisis was beginning to undermine all their efforts. The two-year war had already brought economic exhaustion and left the army short of equipment and supplies; the government found itself unable to remedy the situation either by political concessions to the burgher class or by further more resolute taxation of landed property. Steps to involve the peasantry more effectively in the struggle were not envisaged at all, though the shrewd mind of the Austrian Tschernembl rightly saw the great fighting potential of the rural masses.

Until the middle of 1620 stalemate remained and the periodic skirmishes in Upper Austria had no general effect on the positions of the two sides; in August however Maximilian began a serious advance which soon scattered the ill-led resistance of the Austrian units and marched into south Bohemia. Mansfeld still occupied Pilsen, and the Bavarians were thus committed to holding two fronts, the one directed south and the other west, but when Saxony initiated its campaign in Lusatia the Czechs found their resources stretched and the disastrous weaknesses of their army soon asserted themselves. Now they were without any major support from Hungary or Moravia, and the intrigues of Karel Žerotín again sapped morale at the moment of crisis. The outcome was the Battle of the White Mountain, a two-hour engagement whose significance lies far less in its military aspects than in its immediate consequences: the political incompetence and indecision of king and government and the personal cowardice of Frederick himself. His flight called forth, as a chain reaction, the violence of the victorious Imperialist mercenaries and confusion and despair among the crushed populace.

It can easily be seen why even contemporaries raised the question of what could have caused a disaster of such magnitude as the Battle of the White Mountain and it is a question still unresolved today. One suggested explanation is the lack of understanding which the broad mass of the Estates had for the struggle with the Habsburgs and their unwillingness to make sacrifices. But this does not stand examination. It was not only among the leading figures of the Protestant camp that the fight for political and religious freedom found supporters most eager for resolute measures against Ferdinand II; they were strongest of all among the knights and burghers. The most powerful testimony to this appears in the registers of the expropriations of the confiscation commissions after 1620 which make clear that thousands of the lower Estates played an active part in the rebellion, especially during 1619–1620 when it was affecting every aspect of the country's life. The well-known names like Albrecht Jan Smiřický, Matthias Thurn, and Linhart Colonna von Fels were simply models for countless others, notably among the gentry, who gave life and lands, however small, for the cause.

An analysis in religious terms of the disaster and its consequences emerges in the lament of Comenius that the Czech people were being cruelly punished for not living according to God's commandments. It is not surprising that the devout Comenius should seek guidance from his religious principles through the complexities of internal and foreign political factors; what is more striking is that Thurn, one of the Bohemian warleaders, also found the deepest meaning of the defeat in a feeling of religious guilt and the retribution of the Almighty. He makes no mention of the involved interplay of the European powers, the benightedness of a large part of the Protestant camp, especially in Germany, or the comparative economic and military strengths of the two sides. The judgments of some of the foreign commanders who played an important part in the events of 1619–20 lay stress on externals without touching the complex essence of the matter. Of this kind is Anhalt's assertion that the army failed at the crucial moment and Mansfeld's condemnation of the Estates' own selfishness. The most trenchant observations were Tschernembl's on the treachery of the German Protestants and the incompetence of the Bohemian government.

Our present state of historical knowledge allows a clearer analysis and evaluation of the events which led to the Battle of the White Mountain. Let us consider both the internal and the external political factors, together with the psychological motives which underlay developments in Bohemia from the middle of the sixteenth century. The struggle of the Estates for a share of power in the land, which they had pursued since the beginning of Habsburg rule, brought complete success and encouraged them in the conviction that the rights they had acquired must be fully respected both by the King himself and by every organ of state. This attitude, which formed the ideological substratum of all political activity, was indeed upheld by the courts and the civil administration, and the leading representatives of the Estates, the highest official dignitaries, defended it against the Emperor himself, in times of stress as in times of calm. The records of the Council of State for the early years of the seventeenth century, a period of growing tension, demonstrate this abundantly. It is highly probable that the leadership, which was well acquainted with the currents of contemporary political and theoretical literature, found backing in the propaganda against absolute sovereignty and the question, freely broached at the time, of the possible deposition of tyrants. Both from the standpoint of that given situation and as a point of principle, there can be no denying the moral justice of the Estates' fight to maintain forms of political life and social standards which had been tested by two hundred years of evolution. The structure of Bohemian society which the revolt sought to defend against Habsburg interference guaranteed all sections of the Estates acceptable conditions for economic, religious and cultural development, and even contained the seeds of a better life for the mass of the peasantry.

The unprecedented situation created by the Defenestration clearly called for extreme efforts by all sections of society and there is no doubt that the behaviour and ideas of the Directorate were not able to stir the subject masses into sufficient activity. The experience of the Hussite wars had shown that this class could lend incalculable weight to any cause, and a realization of the project to implement radical improvements in their living standards, as recommended by Tschernembl, would surely have strengthened the forces of the Estates both physically and morally. The continuing courageous resistance of peasants in several provinces of Bohemia and Moravia after the White Mountain, when they maintained their defiance despite the cruel reprisals of the Imperialists, shows what influence they could still exert on military events despite the technical advances which had been made since the Hussite era. We cannot of course place the whole blame on the leaders of the Estates for failing to transcend the horizons of thought common to their time and class: they had anyway too little practical opportunity in the anxious years of 1619–20 to turn economic and social life into entirely new channels, and the situation of the Bohemian peasants (far better than that of their German or Polish neighbours) did not call for sudden fundamental reforms.

Any examination of political developments within Bohemia at the beginning of the seventeenth century makes it very obvious that religious tensions called forth a general atmosphere of uncertainty, mutual distrust and lack of concern for the common good of the community, which dulled public reaction to the exhortations of the insurgents. The waverings of some well-known personalities and the strong reactions of opponents of the new régime hardened the populace, especially the townsmen, in their neutrality, while differences among members of the government hindered the elaboration of a consistent propaganda programme. The Bohemian public at large was disillusioned and embittered by the attitude of Moravia, whose long refusal to join the rebellion (at one stage it almost openly rejected it) crippled from the outset the organizational unity of the Estates' cause, as well as reducing its military effectiveness since the plans for a common offensive with the Hungarians could not be put into operation.

These domestic weaknesses were joined by serious international factors. The age of struggle for a European balance of power, which had lasted throughout the sixteenth century, had brought so many sudden changes of aim and allegiance within the two great power blocks, the Spanish-Austrian complex and its English, French and Dutch opponents, that the leaders of the Bohemian revolt could find a constant attitude only in the unrelenting antipathy of Spain. The Protestant camp was forever rent by disagreements and friction, most of all by the double-dealing and eventual treachery of the Elector of Saxony and the ostentatious unconcern of a majority of the German princes; the help it could offer was never likely to be either prompt or efficient and in the decisive military engagements of 1620 this proved a crucial determinant.

The compounded handicaps at home and abroad were instrumental in preventing the Estates' leadership from utilizing even the exceptionally favourable chance offered by Thurn's two advances to Vienna in 1618 and 1619. Such dramatic actions were not enough: the political and military initiative passed irrevocably to the Emperor's side and the weakened Czech front was forced onto the defensive. In this critical situation Bohemian isolation and the personal incompetence, indeed cowardice of Frederick and his government turned defeat into calamity: there was no single leader of the Estates who had the fortitude and authority to brace the rest for a defence of Prague and a continuation of the struggle.

Only the flight of the Winter King from his capital and the collapse of the government led to the loss of the city and confirmed the Imperialists' triumph. Disbanding of the provincial militias soon followed. Resistance continued at isolated points: the hired army of Christoph von Redern held out in Friedland at the end of the year, as did Johann Albin Schlick around Ellbogen (Loket), but these were insignificant exceptions. Even the year-long resistance of Tábor and the long endurance of the garrisons in Třeboň, Zvíkov and Orlík had no more than local importance. Mansfeld's troops hung on in the town of Tachov and the surrounding area until February 1621 and the last opposition in Falkenau and Elbogen was broken in March. In Moravia too all the efforts of Thurn and Ladislav Velen Žerotín could maintain only flickers of resistance, and power was regained by the loyalists under Karel Žerotín. In February and March 1621 the Silesian and Lusatian Estates capitulated and gave themselves into the hands of the Saxons.

TWO YEARS IN THE HISTORY OF A MORAVIAN TOWN

As we have seen, Moravia entered the war against the Habsburgs only belatedly, in the spring of 1619, and thus the rebellion there lasted scarcely two years. This is a ludicrously short period in the history of any community, and it is a justified question whether any traces at all can be found of what happened during that time in a small and remote domain town.

Zlín lay in 1619–20 far from the centre of political activity. It was in the nature of the Estates' revolt that its main participants were members of the upper classes, lords, knights and most of all the royal cities of Olomouc, Brno, Znojmo, Jihlava and, in the south-east of Moravia, Uherské Hradiště. The society of the Estates, the only section of the population which could assert itself politically within the traditional framework, was represented in Zlín by the landed proprietor and his noble officials, to whom could be added the lower gentry of the surrounding areas.

The table of grievances of the Moravian Protestants, presented evidently under the influence of events in Bohemia at the Brno Diet of December 1618, contains as its fourth article the complaint that Lady Anna Cedlar, sister of Kryštof Cedlar, had recently been deprived of her house in Olomouc because a Utraquist priest was preaching there on saints' days. This had presumably taken place the previous year when serious measures began to be taken against non-Catholics. Anna's brother Kryštof was of similar views and both belonged to the radical wing of the Estates' opposition. This we know from his decree on the amending of religious arrangements in Zlín, issued some time during 1619. In it Cedlar renewed the town's privilege of procuring its own priest, provided only that he should hold to the Confession of Augsburg and the doctrine of Wittenberg.

The demand for rigid Lutheranism was a complete innovation

in Zlín and Moravia as a whole. On the Zlín estate it indirectly excluded a whole group of subjects from full membership of the community. Since there were no Catholics in the town these must have been Czech Brethren. The uncompromising nature of the text may have been occasioned by the agitation of the time, a response to the attempts at re-catholicizing of which there is clear evidence in the immediate vicinity. Jesuit missionaries were beginning to oppress non-Catholics on the Lobkovic lands at Holšeov and were already taking steps to close the meeting houses of the Brethren. On the nearby estates of Lukov and Vsetín similar measures were enforced by the wife of Albrecht Waldstein, Lady Lucrezia Neksch of Landeck. They had been married in 1609, and whether or not it was directly arranged by the Jesuits of Olomouc, there is no doubt that it represented Waldstein's definite break with the Protestant environment in which he had been brought up. With it he immediately became joint-owner of his bride's extensive possessions and found himself in conflict with the family of her first husband, Arkleb of Víckov. The newly married couple were said to have deprived Lucrezia's nephew Jan Adam Víckov of the greater part of his inheritance, since he sold to them a portion worth at least 50,000 florins for only 8,000. Bohunka, the cousin of Jan Adam and Lucrezia, was not caught so easily; she fought a long legal action against Waldstein and his wife which did not end either with Lucrezia's death or with her own marriage to Václav Bítovský, lord of the manor of Bystřice pod Hostýnem.

The name of Waldstein must often have been on people's lips in Zlín. The marriage to Lucrezia provided him with a welcome opportunity to begin a career as military entrepreneur. As early as 1605 the Moravian Estates had charged him with preparing a new and more efficient way of paying their troops. In 1611 he was one of the three commanding officers sent to Bohemia to help against the Passau invasion, and by February he was already in Prague with Matthias's retinue as representative of the Moravian chief-of-staff. In 1612 he went to Italy and in August 1614 accompanied the Emperor to the Diet at Ratisbon. By that time he was already a widower since Lady Lucrezia, who had been ailing (though she was not older than her second husband, as some have suggested) died in the spring of 1614. Perhaps to express his debt to Lucrezia who had been a fervent convert to Rome, Waldstein continued to press the peasants on his lands to accept the Catholic missionaries. But the estates of Lukov and

Vsetín were especially obstinate; they had long possessed the right to bear arms (the area was mountainous and near the frontier) and were jealous of their "freedoms" even though these were basically only customs or contractual alterations of their feudal obligations. The *hejtman* Karel Žerotín refused to send military assistance to Waldstein and with time the latter's ardour for the enterprise cooled, especially after the death of his wife. He negotiated with the Jesuits over the founding of a college to be devoted primarily to missionary work, but when he thought their demands were growing excessive he broke off the project and in 1617 endowed instead a Carthusian monastery in Štíp, not far from Zlín, together with a Church in which he deposited the mortal remains of Lady Lucrezia. All in all Waldstein was not happy either in Lukov or Vsetín and he chose when in Moravia to live mostly on the smaller estate of Rymice near Holešov, the seat of the Catholic leader Ladislav Lobkovic. In 1615 he was recovering his health in Rymice, but by 1617 he was again in Italy near Gradisca at the head of a company of cavalry which he had raised at his own expense. During the winter of 1617–18 he returned to Moravia, and in May 1618 the provincial Diet named him commander of an infantry regiment of 300 men recruited as a surety for Moravian neutrality on the lines recommended by Waldstein's former brother-in-law Žerotín.

Waldstein began treating at the same time with Vienna and Count Buquoy, the new Imperialist commander-in-chief sent from the Spanish Netherlands, about recruiting a regiment of Walloon cuirassiers for the sum of 40,000 gulden. When Buquoy and Dampierre failed to take Prague in the autumn of 1618 Waldstein aided Dampierre in his retreat to Austria by sending supplies for his troops. His reward was to be nominated a colonel in the Imperialist army in March of the following year. A month later Thurn, his comrade-in-arms from Hungarian days, entered Moravian territory at the head of a Bohemian army and precipitated the *coup* which brought Moravia onto the side of the insurgents. Waldstein, now a colonel twice over, sought to engage his whole regiment, which was stationed near Olomouc, on the Imperial side, but when this failed he killed at least one of his officers and fled to Vienna with the land's treasury. This act however raised such a storm of indignation that Ferdinand handed back the treasure to the Moravian Estates and Buquoy did not accept Waldstein's offer to incite the Bohemian peasantry against the government of the Directorate.

The Moravians now exiled Waldstein as a traitor, confiscated his estates and gave them to a relative of his late wife, Jan Adam of Víckov. In him the Cedlars of Zlín acquired a new neighbour who was certainly more to their taste than Waldstein. Kryštof Cedlar took no personal part in the Moravian rebellion, but there is no doubt at all where his sympathies lay; he was anyway clearly ill, and died sometime towards the end of 1619. By his subjects he was remembered as a generous lord who sought the good of their town community and shared its faith, though his decree on religious freedom was not in the tolerant tradition of his country, nor in the spirit of the Bohemian *Letter of Majesty*. Jan Adam was a fervent supporter of the Estates: in 1620 he settled at Lukov and demanded the recall of all the weapons which had been confiscated from his peasantry (probably by his predecessor) and taken to Olomouc. As was soon to be shown, the new lord gained the favour and devotion of his subjects to such an extent that they were willing to go anywhere with him.

The same was true of other neighbours and acquaintances of the lords of Zlín. The Dóczys from Vizovice joined Waldstein in exile, but against them the two Ulersdorfers, Christoph and Wilhelm, of Nemčí seized some of the Waldstein lands in June 1619; Christoph even became a member of the Directorate as a representative of the knights and was named commissioner for the valuation of ecclesiastical estates. Here too we see the same unfortunate departure from earlier principles, for the proscription of opponents and confiscation of their property was an unfamiliar expedient and a dangerous precedent. The desire to improve their own position by expropriating political adversaries was no doubt forced on members of the nobility by economic circumstance, and was not therefore peculiar to one side or the other. As early as 23 April 1619 the emigrant Martinic was writing from Münich to Chancellor Lobkovic in Vienna: "Just as they . . . are beginning to behave with our estates, so may it please His Imperial Majesty to deal with them at a later time."

Christoph Ulersdorfer was also present in March 1620 at the torture and trial of Jan Sarkander, a deacon from Holešov accused of high treason. At the beginning of February an army of the so-called "scourges of the steppes", Cossacks recruited in Poland for Ferdinand II, had passed through the eastern half of Moravia. These Cossacks marched through Bystřice, which belonged to the Protestant Václav Bítovsky, and devastated it, while sparing the Lobkovic lands at Holešov. It was being said that Sarkander was responsible for this, as he had earlier been abroad, perhaps on a pilgrimage, perhaps, so people whispered, on a secret mission to Poland. What is most likely is that Sarkander, who died as a result of the torture, was a victim of the vengefulness of the Estates since his lord was immune from their wrath. The Cossacks did not reach Zlín; they hurried over into Austria instead. But the town helped in raising a national militia, an amalgam of cavalry and infantry, the former noble, the latter peasants and townsmen from the provinces of Hradiště and Olomouc. This militia then inflicted serious damage on the second influx of Cossacks which traversed the country in the summer of 1620 under the leadership of Jakuszewski.

After the death of Kryštof Cedlar his sister Anna became the heiress of Zlín but she did not live there. She preferred to stay in Olomouc or at the castle of Hranice which belonged to her fiancé Václav Mol, a member of the Moravian Directorate. When the government needed money for the army, Lady Anna lent it 11,423 florins, a very considerable sum. Her interests in Zlín she left to a bailiff, who may have been Peter Kopřic, whose father was also bailiff at Bystřice and had attended the trial of Jan Sarkander. Another Zlíner, Karel Vrochyne of Rept, the son of a small freeholder in the town, was bailiff of Lukov at the time of the revolt.

The militia was called out for a second time in August 1620 by the *hejtman* Ladislav Velen Žerotín. The patent authorizing this step explained the causes of the war and urged men to emulate the heroic deeds of Jan Žižka and Prokop the Bald during the Hussite struggle. But this time the cause was hopeless, and news of the defeat at the White Mountain, followed by the collapse of the Moravian government forestalled any action. At the crucial moment the energetic Ladislav Velen Žerotín and Václav Bítovský were in Breslau discussing how to organize the future prosecution of the war; in their absence moderate, even timid elements took over and resolved upon the capitulation of Moravia. Buquoy's army reached Brno around New Year's Day 1621; on 6 January it burned Bzenec and in the middle of the month it overcame Uherské Hradiště. The towns of southeast Moravia surrendered without a fight and their inhabitants fled into the woods or sought refuge in communities ruled by a Catholic lord.

There are however already reports of rapine before the end of 1620. It is possible that Waldstein who was holding certain towns in north Bohemia at the time of the White Mountain hurriedly sent detachments to seize his old estates in Moravia. However this may be, some of the houses in Zlín were destroyed during 1620. It was at the beginning of the following year that the town fell into a state of collapse. Imperialist forces which occupied the valley of the Dřevnice probably belonged to one of Spinelli's regiments and had been raised in Naples on the Spanish model and with Spanish money. These "Spaniards" clearly did not treat Zlín with any great delicacy. The town records are terse: "In the year of our Lord 1621 a force of troops came hither and took up station, such that the Wallachians, who are the local rabble, came down and attacked the said troops. As a result one house was seized by fire and perished." Other local chronicles substantiate this report that in January 1621 the Vlachs, who had been armed during the uprising to defend the frontier, invaded towns and villages occupied by the Imperialists. On 5 January Vlachs from the lands of Vsetín attacked the village of Malenovice "where they did most grievously wound the men of His Imperial Majesty", and on the 15th there were skirmishes in Zlín. There was not long to wait for the reaction of the soldiers. Reinforcements from Hradište and Holešov moved against the Vlachs on 30 January, burning Zlín and the villages around it. Clearly the whole town was not destroyed since there were Spanish troops quartered in part of it, so many of them indeed that it was necessary to deduct from the taxes the cost "of clearing up in the house of Plačkovský the disorder which the Spaniards have made there".

Thus at a moment when the chief rebels were fleeing either to the county of Glatz, where Ladislav Velen Žerotín and the younger Thurn were being joined in resistance by Johann Georg of Hohenzollern, or Hungary, or else went to ground nearer at hand (various officials disappeared from Zlín at this time and administration was taken over by the burgher Daniel Přerovský), the Habsburgs were suddenly threatened by an entirely new enemy. This was the pastoral people of the mountains, the Vlachs of Lukov, Vsetín and Zlín who felt themselves to be freer than their neighbours, the peasants who tilled the soil. It was above all the shepherds of Vsetín and Lukov who refused to be dictated to. We have already seen that they opposed Waldstein during the revolt and then came to terms with his successor Jan Adam of Víckov; initially only the armed Vlachs were involved, but their example soon drew other sections of the local population.

They directed their attacks first of all at the estates of Catholic authorities, especially Cardinal-Bishop František Dietrichstein. Dietrichstein had been interned at the beginning of the revolt, but he then escaped to Vienna and employed his talents persuading the Moravian Estates to spare his family property of Mikulov. His letters to his bailiff Henry Bruce, presumably a Scots Catholic, are full of concern lest Bruce should provoke the Moravian troops and thereby threaten the stores of wine in the castle cellars. Nevertheless the army of the Estates took Mikulov and drank up or destroyed bottles to the value of 30,000 gulden – the Cardinal was so incensed that he seriously thought of emigrating to Spain.

Waldstein, whose regiment of cuirassiers had distinguished itself against Mansfeld at the battle of Záblatí in south Bohemia, but had then suffered losses at Vestonice just a few miles from Mikulov, was in no mood to play second fiddle to this noncombatant prelate. Nevertheless it was Dietrichstein who was appointed Governor-General of Moravia in the winter of 1620–21, though his writ ran only as far as the Imperial armies could enforce it. As the chief representative of a detested régime it was he who became the target when Protestant lords were replaced on the battlefields by simple artisans, peasants and herdsmen. These were the people who suffered the first blows from the new conquerors, but they were also the first to reply in kind.

THE EUROPEAN SIGNIFICANCE OF THE WAR

Historians of an earlier age used to interpret the war of 1619–20 as a local conflict primarily about religion or control of the state, which proved to be the beginning of an ever-wider and increasingly worldly struggle. However, this traditional portrayal of the Bohemian revolt is false. From the point of view of Czech history the rising against the Habsburgs represented an attempt to resolve a chronic socio-political crisis which was common to all the territories of the old Bohemian state and parts of the Austrian lands.

From the Spanish standpoint the issue was a similar one. J. H. Elliott has shown conclusively that the question of Spanish "decline" was really a domestic economic and social problem within Castile: the crisis of an ever more impoverished and depopulated country, its relations with the other lands of Philip III and the inflation of silver imports from America. The decisive reason why Madrid was evidently unwilling to extend the twelve years truce with the United Provinces after April 1621 was the general conviction there that this *pax hispanica* was proving advantageous to the enemy. Don Fernando de Carillo, President of the Council of Finance, the *Consejo de Hacienda*, expressed in 1616 his feeling that the peace "is worse than if we had continued the war". The *damnosa haereditas* of the conflict in the Low Countries, the unresolved "Dutch question", dominated all Spain's policies.

The specialist economic writers, the *arbitristas* and the *procuradores* of the Cortes of Castile, were unanimous in urging that something must be done to change a situation where the import of American silver had shrunk within a single decade from two million ducats to less than one million and Castilian taxes from three to two *milliones*. At the beginning of 1618 a special committee of reform was created, the *Junta de Reformación*, while the Council of Castile was charged with preparing a report on the state of the country and suggesting what should be done. This report was ready by February 1619 but it contained nothing which the *arbitristas* had not written and put in print long before. The reform proposals were vague, especially where they touched the concrete problems of the Castilian economy, and it was by these that the monarchy would stand or fall.

The only other result of the reforming efforts was the palace revolution of 4 October 1618 in Madrid by which the Duke of Uceda ousted his father, Lerma, from the position of chief minister. Beyond this no changes took place, and thus it is possible to understand the contempt in which Philip III's government was held by the great proconsuls of the Spanish Imperium in Italy and the Netherlands – Count Fuentes, the Marquises of Bedmar and Villafranca, the Duke of Osuna, Archduke Albert and Ambrozio Spinola. These men had all been pursuing for years a line of aggression wholly unreconcilable with the moderate and pacific policies of Madrid. Osuna was indeed recalled in 1620, but Bedmar and the rest all stayed at their posts.

Whatever economies could have been achieved would anyway have been insignificant if war was to be resumed. The annual cost of the army in the Netherlands alone rose from two million to three and a half million ducats by the year 1621 and the expenses of the Atlantic fleet doubled to reach one million. The normal sources of income, the *regulares*, could not begin to bear this burden. On hearing the first anxious reports from Bohemia in August 1618 the Duke of Lerma demanded extraordinary subsidies for the armies in Germany and Italy, and received the reply from the President of the *Consejo de Hacienda*, Count Salazar, that "the royal finances cannot provide such sums at the present time. . . . The regular income and what remains from the royal treasury are pledged to an extent greater than their own value." But Philip III intervened on Lerma's side: "these measures are so urgent that the Council of Finance must find a way. Germany simply cannot be lost."

Money was indeed somehow forthcoming and contingents were raised in the Low Countries and Italy; these were moved during 1619 and 1620 into central Europe, while Spinola's army was prepared in the spring of 1620 for an attack on the Rhenish Palatinate. The first subsidies in fact came from the pockets of the Spanish ambassador in Vienna, Oñate, who put Dampierre's army at the disposal of Matthias early in 1618, and Archduke Albert, who sent Buquoy to Austria from the Netherlands. The League, Tuscany, and the Papal Curia all contributed, and it can be said that Spain, together with its proconsuls in Italy and the Netherlands, not only strengthened the will of the Habsburgs to fight in Bohemia but prevented the shipwreck of that will by lending prompt and substantial support. They quite simply proved themselves better able to mobilize resources at short notice.

What was the approximate size and composition of these resources? As early as June 1618 Oñate was calling for Madrid to recruit 10–12,000 men on behalf of the Austrian Habsburgs in Naples and the Low Countries. Madrid as we have seen was not enamoured of this plan, but Osuna backed it. Oñate eventually succeeded in acquiring (on his own account and with Albert's credit) the troops which had been raised in Friuli against the Venetians. When Buquoy arrived from Brussels to take over the command, he found an army of about 12,000 waiting for him; the soldiers had been partly paid by Oñate who complained that his debts on this score by September were already 130,000 florins. The cavalry regiment of Créange was largely composed of Spaniards.

The first reinforcements to be sent through the offices of Madrid appeared in the earlier half of 1619. These were Gauchier's troops of cavalry and 6,000 Walloon infantry, all of them recruited in the Spanish Netherlands. They were still too few, and it was therefore decided in the Council for Italy during June or July to raise more forces in the Neapolitan lands by using money from the sale of crown estates. The project was realized in August and 7,000 infantrymen under Carlo Spinelli and Guillermo Verdugo were prepared for embarkation in Naples. The following month they took ship to the port of Finale, thence passed through Milan and the Brenner pass into the Tyrol. Half these troops were originally intended for the Netherlands, but Oñate held them back. In addition he paid for a contingent of cuirassiers under Marradas, whose strength was raised to that of a full regiment, and another regiment of infantry from Germany. Thus from the winter of 1619–20 Dampierre, operating in Lower Austria, and Buquoy, hemmed in at Budweis, could both count on about 12,000 or 13,000 men, brought with Spanish money from Italy or present-day Belgium. To pay these forces it was necessary in the first months of 1620 to sell off estates in Naples worth 1,600,000 florins, and by the end of June more than half a million florins had passed through the hands of Oñate alone.

By July 1620, when Spinola attacked the Palatinate while at the same time the Spanish Viceroy in the Milanese opened the crucial Alpine pass of the Valtellina to Habsburg troops, the Imperialist coalition had already won a clear advantage. Its armies now joined with the 15,000 men of the Catholic League directed by Maximilian of Bavaria and Tilly, and it was possible to commence the "Bohemian campaign" which between July and 8 November 1620 led the newly combined forces to the battlefield of the White Mountain – within sight of the city of Prague.

Few Spanish troops were involved in the battle itself, although some regiments were in Spanish pay. There were Spaniards proper only in the seven infantry battalions of the Fuggers, some 2,000 men at most, and the eight companies of cuirassiers led by Areyzaga in Marradas's regiment, though of course many more Neapolitan and Walloon mercenaries were serving under Spanish officers. Verdugo and Spinelli commanded 31 battalions of foot from Naples, and this was one-fourth of all the Imperialist infantry. They formed the central *tercio* of the battle-line. Other *tercios* were made up, according to the Spanish model, of Walloons (45 battalions) and Germans (36 battalions), but it was the Neapolitans, together with the horsemen from Florence, who shed enough of the enemy's blood to open the road to Bohemia and Moravia for their lords and masters. Among the Spaniards and Walloons only four acquired lands as reward: Marradas in south Bohemia and Huerta in the valley of the Šumava, Verdugo at Doupov and Mašt'ov, and of course Buquoy, again in the south of the country. Italian families gained substantial properties, especially after 1634, and the names Caretto Millesimo, Thun (Tetschen), Collalto (Brtnice), Piccolomini (Náchod), Gallas (Friedland), and Colloredo (Opočno) were a lasting reminder of the triumph on the *Monte Bianco*.

Facing the Spanish and Italian lines on that fateful day were a certain number of Dutchmen. By the middle of 1620 Holland had provided 5–6,000 men as military assistance to the Bohemian Estates. Of the 700,000 gulden granted by the States General only about 550,000 actually reached its destination, the remainder was left unpaid. 1619 saw the arrival from the Netherlands of Frenck's infantry regiment, and its 1,500 men were stationed in south Bohemia, under the direction of Mansfeld. Mansfeld was also commanding his old regiment from Savoy (recruited in Switzerland) and the Anglo-Scottish troops of Gray, as well as 1,000 cavalrymen under Stirum, 1,500 infantrymen of the Duke of Saxe-Weimar and another 1,000 infantry led by Colonel Seton. Holland was the recruiting ground for the bodyguard of 300 men which accompanied Frederick wherever he went. Together these forces comprised between one-fifth and one-sixth of the Bohemian army. At the White Mountain Stirum's four companies of undisciplined riders played no worthwhile part in the fighting and the same was true of Hohenlohe's cavalry, originally raised in the Netherlands for the Union and now taken over by the Bohemian king. The seven battalions of infantry from Saxe-Weimar and the royal guard stayed in reserve; they were not involved in the battle, nor was Colonel Jan van Mario or the Venetian adviser Alfonso Antonini.

The Protestant army was, so we are unambiguously informed, deployed in "*battaglie*" according to the Dutch model; unfortunately however the whole reserve line, which should have been made up of alternate detachments of horse and foot, was missing and had to be replaced by the inferior light cavalry of the Hungarian *banderias*. Cannon and field defences were also lacking, but worst of all was the failure of discipline. The fact that the Bohemian forces were drawn up in the more modern Dutch fashion was of no advantage set against the doubts of the soldiers about the wisdom of giving decisive battle on the threshold of winter and with a well-fortified Prague in their rear. They were of course ignorant of their generals' conviction that no money remained for further instalments of pay, or the fact that the crown councils had already taken the decision to accept the advice of James I and pack Frederick off to Silesia where he might hope for a diplomatic resolution of the whole Bohemian adventure during the winter. There is thus no real purpose in discussing the rôle of Spaniards and Dutchmen in the engagement, for the whole significance of the White Mountain lay in the complete collapse of Frederick's position in Bohemia, Moravia, and Silesia, a collapse so sudden that all previous plans and calculations were ruined.

In the summer of 1619 an agent of the Dutch States General wrote to Buwinckhausen, the diplomat of the Union:

> Believe me that the Bohemian war will decide the fates of all of us, but especially yours, since you are the neighbours of the Czechs. For the present we shall seek out all ways of bringing you help . . . though we have many difficulties to face; the Synod has indeed decreed the aid which reflects the general feelings of our Reformed Church, but . . . some of our clergy are resisting with great obstinacy and we have been forced to banish them, and to punish their rebellion when they will not obey their authorities. . . . All this is harmful to the Bohemian cause, which we would wish to further at all times.
>
> Abroad there is nothing new, but reports of exceptional successes in the East Indies, and we are preparing to found an East India Company. If I am not mistaken it will finally take place in the month of September.

This report illustrates in a nutshell the whole situation in the United Provinces and the relation of the States General to Bohemia. Above all it makes clear that the States and their diplomats sympathized with the Czech rebellion, but that during 1618 they did practically nothing to help it, since their attention was claimed by the internal struggle between the war-party of Maurice of Orange (the Gomarists) and the more pacific spokesmen of the upper bourgeoisie (the Arminians). Before the summer of 1618 it was impossible even to consider sending help to the Bohemians, and it was no direct achievement of the Dutch that their subsidies allowed the raising of Mansfeld's regiment which was soon to wrest Pilsen from the Imperialists. At the same time however the Dutch were properly aware that every soldier sent against the Habsburgs anywhere in Europe balanced a soldier who could otherwise be set under Spinola on the Rhenish frontier.

Captain Frenck was delegated from Mansfeld's regiment to become the first fully accredited Bohemian negotiator in the Hague from the end of December 1618.

By the spring of 1619 Frenck had been joined in his appeals for assistance by the Palatine diplomat Christoph von Dohna and the Czech agent Elias Rosin of Javorník. But it was only after the execution of Oldenbarneveldt that the States General decreed a monthly grant of 50,000 Dutch florins. The money was enough to send to Bohemia a regiment of infantry under Frenck. The details of the transaction brought Philibert du Bois to the Hague, while Dutch interests in Prague were represented by the painter Jakob Hoefnagel: both these men belonged to the small Dutch colony in Prague and were in contact with the President of the Directorate Wenzel Ruppa and his colleague Peter Milner. Ruppa used Dutch subsidies, real and projected, as prime arguments when in August 1619 he recommended to the Bohemian Diet the election of the Palsgrave as King. Milner on the other hand was close to the group of "republicans" described in a despatch by the English resident in Prague, Sir Dudley Carleton:

I have heard some speake of a middle way, that is to undertake the protection of the Bohemians, but not the soveranitie, by example of Q. Elizabeth in the businesse of these provinces . . . But in this case it is to be doubted the Bohemians with theyr confederats will rather follow the example of these provinces, or the Swisse, in cantoning themselves, than that of Swede by subjecting themselfs to a sovveraigne when they have once tasted of freedome; and this I have the more reason to believe because by lettres I have seen from some of the Directors of the Bohemians, not long before the election of the Prince Palatine, I finde there was not onely such conceit in some of theyr brests, but that they were already thincking how to confederate themselfs with this state and the Hans towns. Now they have chosen a King they must chiefly addresse themselfs to Kings and absolute Princes.

Carleton was a convinced Monarchist and supported the choice of Frederick and Elizabeth Stuart. The letters of Mylner, the only man besides the now-deceased Smiřický who corresponded with the Netherlands, have unfortunately not survived. But the republican mood of the Bohemian town intelligentsia was not displayed openly at the August Diet of 1619, and the position of the burgher Estate worsened rather than improved after the election of Frederick. Mylner indeed protested that "we Bohemians will always work to uphold and strengthen our bonds with the States General of the United Provinces", and expressed his personal desire to do everything in his power for "our common cause" (*nostre commun party*) – the elimination of the threat from Spain. Yet all the entreaties during the winter of 1619–20 for the Dutch to hasten their aid and to agree with England on a common approach, all the efforts to gain support from Venice and the Hansa, Switzerland and Nuremberg, remained barren and without reward.

Frederick's career could only satisfy the confirmed Orangists, and the other members of the Council of State at the Hague realistically saw in the Bohemian war mainly a "great opportunity" to threaten the position of the Habsburgs. Since the Bohemian theatre of war was thus considered a side-issue, the detachments sent to serve in central Europe were not the best. Frenck's batallions were noted for their indiscipline and two companies of cavalry were belaboured by peasants near Žatec in September 1619. In this way too the overcautious gentlemen of the States General missed their "great opportunity".

In the circumstances the new mission of Dr. F. Rossell, Abraham Sixt, and Buwinckhausen at the beginning of 1620 brought the Czechs little comfort. They finally achieved further payment of the agreed monthly subsidies, which allowed the regiments of Stirum and the Duke of Saxe-Weimar, together with the two battalions of Seton to be sent to the front. But Frenck's "evil Netherlanders" provoked a full-scale peasant rising during the spring, and the newcomers were soon in trouble too. Stirum's cavalry fought the local population round Unhošt and Saxe-Weimar's infantry imposed heavily on the locality of Slaný. The Dutch aid was quite simply inadequate, and what there was of it came so slowly that from the spring of 1620 not a single new soldier arrived from Holland. The military observer, Jan van Mario drew attention in vain to the growing threat of the Imperialists' numerical superiority.

Why could not more help have been made available to the Czechs? One obstacle was the tension over fisheries between England and Holland. Sir Dudley Carleton reported the attitude of the Estates General on this issue in a letter to Secretary Naunton in February 1620:

Withal they said, that they were here much amused with the affairs of Germany and Bohemia; where employing all their thoughts and endeavours in assisting a prince so near his majesty, their hope was, his majesty would not at this time press them to a thing so unwillingly heard of by all the people of these provinces. I replied unto them, that I could very well witness that to be true . . . the world would never be without affairs; but for those of Germany and Bohemia, I saw no community they had with the fishing upon the coasts of England, Scotland and Ireland.

In fact Carleton knew very well. The friction between England and Holland meant that it would not be possible to realize their "grand design" of a concerted attack on the Spanish Netherlands before the termination of the truce. And this in turn signified that the decision of Madrid on 9 May 1620 to approve the plan of Archduke Albert for a simultaneous offensive by Spinola on the Palatinate and Maximilian of Bavaria on Bohemia left the Czech revolt with meagre prospects indeed. Meanwhile Anglo-French diplomacy achieved the neutralization of the Protestant Union by the Treaty of Ulm. Thus from July the road into Bohemia lay wide open to the Habsburg armies.

Bohemia's demand that the Dutch Estates should grant higher subsidies had been rejected by reference to the attitude of England, whose King James was actually negotiating with the Spanish ambassador Gondomar for his son-in-law to pacify the Czechs, while England and Spain jointly invaded Holland and divided it between them. This remarkable triumph would then be crowned by realizing James's beloved project of a Spanish marriage for the Prince of Wales. It was ultimately Anglo-Dutch rivalry which frustrated the Bohemian Estates in their attempt to create a great "anti-Habsburg coalition". The leaders of the revolt were not blind to the international situation: they appreciated that their struggle must not be localized and a few of them at least realized that their cause was part of a great new conflict between Spain and Holland which was just taking shape. But the tension between English and Dutch defeated all their best efforts.

The politicians of Bohemia saw that the country's other great liability was its lack of supplies, but here too their hour of need brought little response. They captured the interest of the Danish King, Christian IV, and profited from Swedish concern for events in central Europe to seek the help, both military, financial and diplomatic of Gustavus Adolphus. But nothing came of this in the end except the dispatch of a few cannon which became bogged down on the way to their destination. Silesia was the area most important to Sweden, and the policy-makers in Stockholm knew well enough that Poland could be held in check by pressure exerted from the side of Muscovite Russia. It was however unrealistic to expect any Swedish offensive against the Habsburgs, at least before the end of the 1620s. The Czech Estates anyway sought with relative success to neutralize Poland by sending a deputation to the *Sejm*, establishing contact with the noble opposition and entering into negotiations with the Turks. Ironically, the envoys sent from Prague through Hungary to Constantinople in the summer of 1620 were instructed specifically to follow the example of the English-Dutch agents there; but the treaty with the Porte was not even signed until after the defeat on the White Mountain and it had no practical significance.

The Turks themselves had plenty to do at home and were moreover being threatened on the flank by Persia. In Venice internal squabbles had brought to power a group which favoured neutrality and nothing was sent from there to Bohemia except a single military observer. The same dreary story was repeated in the cities of the Empire and the towns of the Hanseatic League. Only Nuremberg seriously discussed the fate of the Czechs and the question of positive assistance to them; it became a focus for the organization of funds and supplies.

Thus the "great coalition" proved ephemeral. English observers who concluded that the Czechs "fought badly for a good cause" might at least have added that they were forced to fight unaided. The only faithful support came from the Protestant Estates of Upper and Lower Austria, with whom the rebels had signed the memorable confederation in the spring of 1619: an isolated attempt to reorganize Central Europe without the Habsburgs, indeed in opposition to them. This bond with Austria lasted until the middle of 1620 and some Austrian detachments fought bravely before the gates of Prague. The last allies were the Estates of Hungary and the Prince of Transylvania, Bethlen Gabor, but their chances were as limited as those of the Czechs themselves. With the agreement of the Sultan, Bethlen occupied a large part of Hungary, had himself elected King and joined the Bohemian army in the march on Vienna, while the Turks attacked and defeated the Poles at Jassy. But Bethlen had neither money, infantry, nor artillery, and he could only wage campaigns which finished at the time of the harvest so that his soldiers could return to work in the fields. His light cavalry was cheap and numerous but no substitute for trained professional troops. The Sultan was bound by his Mesopotamian border, and in June 1620, at the worst possible moment, Bethlen proceeded to conclude a truce with the Emperor. When he re-entered the lists in the autumn it was already too late.

Simply, it proved quite impossible to imitate on Bohemian soil the example of the Dutch Estates' successful resistance to Spain. That resistance had become, during the last third of the sixteenth century, an affair of European politics, since neither England nor France could allow the United Provinces to fail. Now in 1620 circumstances were different: France was privately on the side of the Habsburgs, and the secretive activities of King James, for whom the affairs of the monarchy were an *arcanum imperii* where his subjects had no right to interfere, brought more harm than good to Bohemian interests.

The Dutch resistance could not be repeated. An analysis of those members of the Estates who played the largest part in the rebellion (based on the resolutions of the Diets from 1618–20 and the subsequent indictments by the state prosecutor Přibík Jeníšek of Újezd) shows that the backbone of the military staff was formed by the lower nobility, and the administration by the town intelligentsia. Within these groups we find also the men who displayed the most clearsightedness over foreign policy. Yet the burgher Estate, which had raised itself to a certain position in the land by 1618, lost out irretrievably and, led by the patriciate of Prague, it became in the end wholly inimical to the government of Frederick. Instead of broadening its scope, the rebel cause was further restricted in its social foundations and a hegemony of the bourgeoisie became unthinkable.

The "battle before Prague" and the fall of the capital were thus a logical culmination of the crisis of Palatine rule. The first round of the "Bohemian question" was decided against the wishes of the majority of the country's inhabitants, and the defeat on the White Mountain was the beginning of an inexorable economic, social, national and cultural regression. But the triumph of Spanish divisions in Bohemia and the Palatinate was no solution to the crisis in Castile – while so far as England was concerned the year 1621 revealed the existence of another new source of tension. The nature of the Bohemian war is now known to have been quite different from what we still read of it in the textbooks. Its consequences were to provide a whole new chapter of European history.

Five

THE DUTCH PERIOD OF THE
WAR, 1621–5

THE BREAKING OF THE BOHEMIAN ESTATES

ALTHOUGH the chief leaders of the Imperialist army, Maximilian of Bavaria and John George of Saxony, had given personal guarantees that the defeated Estates would not be punished, provided they recognized Ferdinand II as king, many refused to believe these safeguards and swarms of people, especially those who had played an active rôle in the uprising, fled the country immediately after the White Mountain. It was above all Pirna and Zittau (in southern Saxony) which became centres for noble and burgher emigrants; they found there a first refuge, and in some cases a second home. On the eastern side of Bohemia the shortest way of escape was to Silesia which avoided the horrors of re-catholicization, while most of the Moravian fugitives crossed clandestinely into Slovak areas. The following years were to show how little the Bavarian or Saxon pardons were really worth: their holders were treated just as severely by the confiscation commissions as the other rebels.

The crushing of the Bohemian Estates by military force placed Vienna suddenly in an exceptionally favourable position. The milder faction at court, among them the leading Czech Catholic politicians, sought to restrict punishment to the leading opposition figures, but they were soon pushed aside by the Spanish party whose influence over the bigoted Ferdinand II was paramount and whose vengefulness could not be restrained by any powers within Bohemia. In Moravia however Cardinal Dietrichstein managed to induce some moderation, and Silesia and the Lusatias, protected by the treaty between Saxony and the Emperor, avoided any retribution. Thus the whole weight of the victors' ambitions fell on Bohemia, on its leaders among the nobility and in the towns, as on the broad mass of the peasantry.

The first steps of the Imperialist government were limited: in the immediate aftermath of the White Mountain it was necessary to pay some lip-service to Maximilian's guarantees and the earliest confiscations affected only the estates of those who had actively furthered the rebellion and fled abroad or died before the end of the fighting. Regional commissions were set up from the end of November under the direction of Slavata and Liechtenstein to establish the Emperor's rights to goods and chattels of known enemies of the dynasty. From the spring of 1621 these activities were extended to include the property of rebels in hiding on Saxon or Brandenburg soil. The second wave of confiscation which embraced the estates and belongings of the ringleaders executed on 21 June 1621 brought a wider circle of individuals and families into the net.

This major catalogue of punishments was still not enough for the vindictive Ferdinand and his advisers, many of whom wished to recoup from the conquered land the loans with which they had financed the Imperialist military operations. Thus the general pardon of 3 February 1622 brought in its wake a third and yet more forcible onslaught which affected all members of the Estates who had remained in the country during the revolt and had not actively resisted the government of the Directorate. The vicious and arbitrary behaviour of this confiscatory commission, which in the space of 18 months destroyed the material foundations of 680 noble families (with a further 250 in Moravia) and innumerable burghers, was so unprecedented and aroused such a storm of protest abroad that the nobility were removed from its competence in October 1623, though the terror in the towns continued apace. The principle underlying the decrees of confiscation paved the way for an unrestricted assault on all traditional rights and the hard hand of Liechtenstein's régime in Bohemia extended its scope to many individuals and groups who even in abnormal circumstances would have expected their persons and possessions to be secure. According to an Exchequer decree of 18 August 1623 holders of estates which had been left in the hands of their owners as an act of grace were forced to sell them off if they were not of the Catholic religion. The arm of the commission reached also into the financial world of credit operations. The many informers working for the promise of high reward are typical of the "administrative" methods by which Liechtenstein and his officials liquidated all trace of the rebellion.

The confiscation of estates struck primarily the lords and knights of Bohemia, and with them we shall deal in a moment. In the towns it was also the richer patricians who suffered worst, but wider sections of their population were not spared. In February 1624 Liechtenstein imposed a heavy penalty on all the burghers of Prague, taking special account of those who had occupied public office in the town administration or had otherwise shown active sympathy for the revolt. The urban householders, weighed down by heavy contributions and hard hit by the decline of trades and commerce, could not pay this within the exceptionally short period of one year, and thus as late as 1628 in the Old Town alone 265 citizens were still in arrears of 43,523 florins, a sum which represented the tax liability of a whole province in a peaceful year. These fines showed very clearly the wilfulness of the government: of 265 Praguers 55 per cent were Catholics who were glibly accused of having taken part in the rising. The same happened in the New Town and its inhabitants were forced to pay an indemnity of 60,000 marks, of which 13,484 was still outstanding in 1625. To a lesser extent the burghers of the Kleinseite were similarly obligated.

Those burghers who by paying fines escaped the danger of further punishment were the most fortunate group, since their houses and workshops remained untouched. A far worse fate awaited the ones who had actively participated at higher or lower levels in military and political opposition: the confiscation of their real estate, financial exactions, and searches for articles of value like jewels and furniture turned them into beggars, and often emigrants too. The extensive properties they left behind: fields, vineyards and hopyards, passed into the hands of the urban authorities. But the sudden acquisition of so many houses and lands together with the lack of financial means and the prevailing commercial uncertainty brought wholesale economic decline: a heavy fall in the value of real estate, and a decline in trade and exchange. The taxes and other liabilities on the new property were often higher than the return it could give, while efficient use of it was hindered by administrative problems. Where military commanders or new officials took over as house-owners the gaps in the trading community were not filled; the newcomers usually played no part in productive or commercial activities and their privileges as members of the Estates often weakened the financial position of the town. These complex and powerful economic hindrances held the towns in their grip until the second half of the century.

Houses in Prague which were confiscated or abandoned were eagerly sought by the soldiers and bureaucrats of the victorious Habsburg régime. It was worse in the free and domain towns of the provinces: here the authorities could not find buyers in the neighbourhood for the large number of empty houses, and thus property values fell drastically, in some cases by nine-tenths (Hradec Králové, Kadaň, Kolín etc.). Crippled by military contributions, the councils let them go to ruin and in the tax register *berní rula*) of 1654 we find throughout the country dozens of deserted dwellings or simply mentions of places where formerly they stood. The rare cases when numerous Protestant residents remained despite the massive programme of re-catholicization (as at Ústí on the Elbe) do not affect the general picture of urban decline.

The confiscation commissions deserve close attention as evidence of how the triumphant Emperor broke down the established and tried mechanism of state administration in Bohemia. The system which became regularized in the sixteenth century and lasted until the White Mountain had separated the departments of government, providing for processes of law independent of the legislative assemblies, a Bohemian Chancery as the central director of public administration (with perhaps a lieutenancy in the country), and a Bohemian Exchequer to handle all economic matters except taxes, the latter falling to organs of the Diet. This system was certainly a constitutional compromise between the prerogatives of the ruler and Estates, and not unitary in conception, but it performed its functions well and struck deep roots, which helped its efficiency and won it the trust of all sections of the population. At the same time it was flexible enough to adapt itself to new needs as they arose. The exceptional circumstances of 1620–2 were its death-blow. The very wide powers of the commissions allowed them to decide matters of vital importance to every member of the Bohemian Estates in the interests of the reckless and determined Viennese court which was entirely unconcerned about proven methods of public administration. The Imperial *ukaze*, embodying as it did an uncompromising resolve to eliminate the Estates as far as possible from political, legislative, and judicial control, decided the fate of the Czech nation.

The consequences of the White Mountain thus penetrated

deeply into the whole social composition of the Estates and transformed the existing relation of the individual to the state. While before the White Mountain all members of the public could deal with organs of government in the knowledge that fixed forms of procedure and defined standards of conduct would be observed, a great change set in from 1621. The provincial sheriffs (*hejtman*) who formed the lowest echelon of the administration and were permanently linked to the local population by ties of blood and common interest, were replaced first by extraordinary commissioners and then by nominated officials; the latter carried out their duties according to the orders of governors (*Statthalter*) from Vienna and ceased to be any more representative of the Estates than the governors themselves were. Thus the better aspects of self-government by the Estates were abolished for ever and the trust of the people in a fair-minded civil service destroyed. Vienna used its exceptional position to protract the rule of its plenipotentiary commissioners who remained subject to Liechtenstein until his death in 1627. The whole vital question of state taxation was decided by the government without consulting the Bohemian Estates; it simply allowed them to ratify its decisions, and even the Czechs in Vienna were pushed more and more into the background.

The powers in Vienna who had financed a large part of their campaign in Bohemia by loans at home and abroad were determined to absolve their large indebtedness at the expense of the conquered country. Their first hope, that the confiscations themselves would prove a quick and effective source of revenue, showed itself to be false as early as 1621, since the looting of the *soldatesca* and the general economic collapse brought such a sharp fall in land prices that the sequestered estates fetched very little. In this crisis of the state treasury the government accepted on 18 February 1622 Liechtenstein's suggestion that a consortium be formed to lend the crown six million gulden in return for a year's profits from the Bohemian mint. The consortium, whose Catholic leaders Liechtenstein, Waldstein and Michna had no hesitation in co-opting the Dutch Protestant De Witte and the Prague Jew Bassevi, managed by hectically minting debased coins for a year to amass huge sums for itself, thus so debauching the national economy and the citizen's private purse that the *Patent* of 28 December 1623 left the currency worth only one tenth of its nominal value. These disreputable machinations destroyed thousands of families at all levels of the population, but they broadened and strengthened the economic position of the great Catholic magnates (Liechtenstein, Waldstein, Lobkovic, Slavata). The 1623 *Patent*, which at a stroke raised the main collaborators in the De Witte consortium into the highest stratum of society, was far less advantageous for the treasury than the Emperor had expected. On the contrary it brought such utter confusion into the economic life of the land that all sense of security and confidence was lost, and thus the conditions necessary for any financial regeneration and commercial recovery were pushed into a remote future.

In 1621 and the years which followed, Bohemia staggered from one calamity to the next. 1621 was especially catastrophic, as the terrifying confiscations and economic chaos were crowned by the pillaging and ever-greater financial extortions of the mercenary Imperialist troops. Immediately after the White Mountain the Emperor's generals were given free rein to plunder the estates and town houses of their defeated opponents. Their heedless destruction struck everywhere: in the east Rychnov on the Kněžná, in the west Falkenau, Doupov and Tachov; large areas of the south were laid waste, many houses in Prague and other towns were pillaged as soon as the battle was decided in November 1620. The troops of the Bavarian Duke Maximilian were set loose in Prague leaving houses without windows or doors, and the soldiers of John George of Saxony were no better. The garrisons of the two German Princes which were left in Bohemia during 1621–2 ravaged the land by extorting large sums of money and massive payments in kind. In south Bohemia Buquoy and Marradas settled permanently, and both used these methods to make their fortunes, as well as to cover the costs of their military activities and their loans to the Emperor. Marradas especially, who laid three provinces (Bechyně, Prácheň and Pilsen) under contribution without even consulting the authorities in Prague, became notorious for his exactions. In places where such demands went with increasing confiscations of land, both the workers on the estates and the peasantry at large had to endure bitter days under their new lords (many of them were foreign soldiers of fortune) whose sole concern was to enrich themselves by every means possible.

All these irregular measures brought the administration of taxes into chaos during the years 1621 and 1622, especially in the towns and villages which were forced to house garrisons; there the local authorities were driven to desperation as the reduced and exhausted population was unable to raise the high contribution and it became necessary to mortgage municipal property. The established system of taxation, which in the years before 1620 had been an independent and efficient branch of the state executive, was entirely destroyed by these uncontrolled impositions. Neither the government in Vienna nor Liechtenstein was prepared to revive it, since that would have meant bringing back the provincial tax official elected by the Estates. The profound and disastrous consequences of this economic dictatorship by the military were well-known to Vienna and Prague, but their attempts at reorganization during 1621-22 were only half-hearted. Not until the end of 1622 was military expenditure placed in the hands of a paymaster-general (*Rentmeister*) in Prague, and a *Patent* of 14 February 1623 laid the basis for a unitary system of taxes to be collected by an independent civilian administration in the provinces.

The army commanders too knew that their methods of victualling the forces of occupation were vicious, and could be made to rest less heavily on the very foundations of the national economy, but with most of them, Liechtenstein included, selfish interests prevailed over the needs of the country as a whole. Waldstein alone sought from the spring of 1622 to regularize the situation, but his suggestions were overruled by pressure from the military clique. His attempt to place foreign troops under the direction of the authorities in Prague in matters of provisioning and pay had no more positive success; instead it brought on him the enmity of the Duke of Bavaria, whose soldiers were in possession of western Bohemia. Even after the new regulation of February 1623 ways were still open for powerful generals to continue their uncontrolled extortions. The privilege gained by Marradas at the so-called *Pledge* of Vodňany in June 1623 that no troops should be billeted on his estates showed the other new landowners how to evade similar obligations.

It was not only the contribution for a local garrison which proved a burden both to noble proprietors and urban communities and grew worse from year to year. With the arrangements for tax collecting now more stable it became possible to calculate quotas and introduce order into the assessment of the individual taxpayer. A far greater and unforeseeable trouble was the quartering and feeding of soldiers on the march. One example of many is the statement of the town of Kouřím that between 10 December 1620 and 16 October 1626, a period of less than six years, it paid out 181,833 florins for the maintenance of 25 divisions of soldiers which passed through. This sum is vast enough in itself, and its crippling weight is clear if we reflect that the annual tax contribution of all Silesia before the White Mountain was only twice as much (360,000 florins), yet it does not include the sums exacted by the troops from individual citizens. The years 1622 and 1623 especially, when bad harvests aggravated the turmoil of confiscations and financial confusion, put the towns in a desperate position and left them with debt obligations which remained a burden for decades.

A large number of precise records have survived for these years between 1621–6, an interlude when no warfare took place on Bohemian soil, to show the extent of the enslavement of towns, both royal and domain, by the military commanders. The reports from Hradec Králové, Tábor and Tachov are stark and staggering: Hradec had to pay out 421,989 florins in less than a year and a half, the smaller Tábor 214,694 between 1621–3, and both were brought to the edge of ruin, like Tachov which was forced to find 164,720 florins in a year and a quarter and then a further 30,299 from 1623–5. While some other free boroughs paid lower amounts (Čáslav gave 75,970 florins up to 1628. Rakovník came off best of all in the years 1621–7 with a bill of 24,103 florins) it is generally evident that such obligations were exceptionally harsh on communities which numbered an average of 250–300 homes and proved a lasting adverse influence on both the urban economy and the private commercial sector.

At the same time as the liquidation of the rebellious nobility and burgher classes, their economic position and social influence, the government in Vienna launched a broad offensive against that religious freedom in which the Jesuits saw the chief cause of the Estates' contumacy. The Emperor's Jesuit upbringing was a valuable lever for the Catholic ultras at court, led by the extreme Papal nuncio Carafa, who aimed at the utter extirpation of all non-Catholic confessions. While the confiscation commissions and the troops in occupation were still wreaking their havoc, a start was made with the expulsion of Calvinist preachers in 1621; in the following year the same fate struck Lutheran and Utraquist preachers, and the elimination of positive religious opposition was completed by the banishing of all Protestant clergy from Bohemia and Moravia in 1624. Having thus removed the leaders of any non-Catholic culture Vienna began a programme of severe recatholicization against the whole Bohemian population. In

1624 Protestants were forbidden all activity in the free towns and in 1627–8 the downfall of the Evangelical Estates was decided by a decree forcing them to accept the Catholic faith within six months or leave the country. This measure made it impossible too for the peasantry to hold to the old creed, and counter-reforming commissions, working with the assistance of the military authorities, pressed the Catholic dogmas pitilessly on all levels of society.

It was against the nobility and towns, the political and cultural leaders of the nation, that the work of confiscation and conversion was primarily directed. The peasantry, the largest section of the population, were less immediately affected, though they had new landlords foisted upon them and a serious decline in their living standards set in. But they felt the full force of all the economic and military calamities which struck the land from the beginning of the Imperialists' offensive in 1618. The endless plundering by the *soldatesca* and the cruel exactions in tribute were often an unbearable weight around the neck of the peasant farmer: his buildings were destroyed, his fields, livestock and belongings dispersed. Many had to leave the land, and even when the arbitrary power of the garrisons was reduced (during 1621 and 1622 their will was law) the return of a civil administration brought no lightening of the load. The taxes levied by the *Patent* of 14 February 1623 were a foretaste of lasting pressure on the simple husbandry of the individual peasant and they showed too a sharpening of class considerations: the obligations of the peasantry were set at twice those of their masters and the high payments in kind undermined their position to the extent of threatening their whole livelihood. When these are added to the immoderate demands of new lords and the violent methods of the Jesuit missionaries, it comes as no surprise that many places in the east and in Moravia saw armed risings of the peasantry. The revolts of 1621 and 1622 were put down with much cruelty, but the spirits of the masses were not subdued. The further access of recatholicization in the spring of 1624, when Jesuit bigotry was enforced at the point of the sword, brought a full-scale rebellion throughout Bohemia and in eastern Moravia, which despite its lack of experienced leadership resisted the force of the government soldiery through sheer resolve and strength of numbers: a proof that the spirit of religious freedom and inherited rights had not disappeared in this lowest layer of society. Throughout the mass of the peasantry Counter-Reformation doctrines gained ground only slowly; the Swedish invasions of subsequent years interrupted the process, and for many years it remained superficial. Only with the end of the war was resistance in the country systematically overcome, while it took the rest of the century and its ever-increasing exploitation of the peasants by their feudal lords before Bohemia could be called a Catholic country. The results of the confiscations which we have been describing were far-reaching in all directions. The feudal structure of society was indeed left untouched, but both the division of property among the three Estates and their national composition were profoundly changed. At the same time the pressure of landed authority on subject peasants became ever more intense. The sale of land in debased currency (the so-called "*long coinage*") brought untold damage to traditional owners and threw all economic relations into chaos. The division of spoils which went on between 1621–8 represented a revolution within the ruling classes of Bohemia. The knights' Estate which had possessed almost a third of the soil at the beginning of the sixteenth century (in Moravia a fifth) was reduced to a bare one tenth after the confiscations; its whole material base and its social positions were destroyed. The lords and the clergy on the other hand now held almost 80 per cent of the surface of the country and this limited group of aristocrats could dictate its economic, political and cultural life. The clergy was especially well rewarded: high prelates, monasteries and Jesuit colleges gained richly in sequestered manors and valuable town houses.

It was the magnates who benefited most of all. Besides Karl von Liechtenstein, Jaroslav Martinic and Vilém Slavata, others who founded fortunes were Pavel Michna of Vacinov, Polyxena, widow of Zdeněk Lobkovic, the two Waldsteins Adam and Albrecht, Heřman Černín of Chudenice and Magdalena Trčka of Lípa. Their ranks were swelled by some successful foreigners, among them Baltazar Marradas, Christoph von Thurn and Ulrich Eggenberg. While the main lordly houses of old Bohemia managed to survive in some form, the elimination of most families of knights was a high priority for the confiscatory commissions, since Vienna saw in them the prime source of oppositional contagions. Thus there disappeared a class which in earlier centuries had given a stream of public administrators at provincial and national level, names like the Beřkovskýs of Sebířov, the Homuts of Harasov, the Kapouns of Svojkov, the Klusáks of Kostelec. When we consider the rôle still to be played in their national history by the lesser nobility of Poland, Hungary, Germany, France or England, we can see the loss which Bohemian life suffered by being deprived of its initiative and skills. Through the events of the 1620's the traditional patchwork of broad-based interrelated noble families was dislocated never to revive, and with this dislocation went a weakening of the old and accepted social network, tinged with patriarchal sentiments, whose rôle in the period before 1620 had been to mitigate the tensions of class and nationality. In this way too the Viennese government and the Catholic party in Bohemia broke down one of the moral properties of the old Estates' order and forced acceptance of its alien views and ideas. The legal guarantees of property which had early been founded on the incontrovertible nature of the national registers were now cast to the winds by the practices of the confiscators. And this took place not only through direct sequestration, but also by converting estates considered forfeit into fiefs of the crown, a procedure which was favoured by the government for smaller properties and which turned the remnants of the knightage after centuries of free operation into dependant retainers of the monarch.

The full extent of this transfer of ownership can be illustrated by a brief table of the number of estates which passed into new hands through the activities of the commissions of 1621–34. (See table following.)

These general figures show what profound personal changes the society of the Bohemian estates passed through in the third and fourth decades of the seventeenth century. When we consider in addition that it was precisely the largest domains (Rožmberk, Smiřický, Waldstein, Trčka) which were turned over to owners from abroad, it becomes clear that the nationality position, as well as the material one, within the ruling class became entirely altered in the years after 1620. In this context the collapse of the knights who had possessed both economic initiative and national consciousness was an especially severe blow; by the middle of the century they had lost all political or social significance.

Province	No. of estates	Confiscated	% Confiscated
Rakovník	56	17	30%
Žatec (Saaz)	62	45	73%
Litoměřice (Leitmeritz)	52	43	69%
Boleslav (Bunzlau)	57	46	81%
Bydžov	39	32	82%

Province	No. of estates	Confiscated	% Confiscated
Hradec (Königgrätz)	43	24	56%
Chrudim	27	14	52%
Čáslav	75	54	72%
Kouřim	87	40	46%
Beroun	74	24	32%
Tábor	60	31	52%
Budějovice (Budweis)	29	12	41%
Prácheň	79	29	37%
Klatovy (Klattau)	51	22	43%
Plzeň (Pilsen)	54	26	48%
Loket (Elbogen)	66	27	41%
Total:	911	486	53%

Of the 435 patrimonies which were not confiscated, 253 came in the smallest category, 35 were of medium size and only 147 could be designated as *latifundia*. Whereas the proportion of large units was thus here only 34 per cent, against 8 per cent middling and 58 per cent small estates (those possessing not more than two or three peasant villages), the same dry statistics reveal a very different picture for the lands which were forfeited. Here there were 275 *latifundia*, a full 57 per cent of the total, while the other estates formed 43 per cent, against 66 per cent for the unconfiscated group. The effects of this policy of deliberate robbery by Vienna and its agents are evident both in the concentration of economic activity into large agrarian units and in the harshening of the social position of the peasantry. The Habsburg régime began from 1621 to pursue a different direction, replacing advanced and proven economic methods by a heedless exploitation of the unpaid labour force of the countryside, and placing restrictions on the individual peasant producer.

Similar destruction shook the citizens of the free boroughs, those of them at least who had not fled immediately after the White Mountain defeat to avoid the full rigours of military imposition and political persecution. A superficial glance at the confiscation registers show that more than 60 burghers of the New Town of Prague, 46 of the Old Town and 29 from the Kleinseite were severely punished, most of them losing their property and livelihood. In all about 1,300 people left the capital between 1620–48 and their place in its economic life remained unfilled. Among the sequestered properties were some which even at the low valuation of the commission were worth as much

as a small or middling knight's estate (5,000–6,000 marks), while
the owners of a number of houses with vineyards and gardens
suffered more severely still. The nineteen wealthiest men of all
were merchants who each possessed more than 50,000 marks, and
their departure crippled the whole financial life of the city.
Elsewhere there had never been any comparable group of money
barons, but the chief magistrate of Žatec with his 20,000 marks
and the patrician Kořalka of Klatovy with 26,000 represented
riches equivalent to those of a very prosperous aristocrat.

The economies of many towns were thus ruined before ever
the new and higher levels of state taxation were promulgated.
These new obligations were the last straw and could often simply
not be paid, even under the threat of military execution; town
councils were forced to make good the arrears out of communal
funds or, more likely, by contracting loans which were then a
burden on the urban population at large. Such public debts
assumed unbelievable proportions in the years after 1621. While
the figure already quoted for Hradec Králové (421,999 florins for
the two years 1622–3) was extreme even in these conditions, the
average of 60,000, as at Čáslav, Český Brod, Domažlice, Kuttenberg etc., proved a near chronic burden for decades to come.

Taxes, war levies, and religious persecution were the most
brutal enduring interferences in the daily life of every town and
village in Bohemia. But further oppression awaited the citizen
through the new system of administration. Imperial magistrates
were nominated as the first representatives of the Viennese
government, and they became the lowest instance to which the
town population had to turn in matters of personal and family
concern, as well as in cases affecting the whole community.
While the behaviour of these magistrates was not always as
ruthless as the burghers of Mělník complained of, there is nevertheless ample evidence, e.g. from Tachov, Žatec and Vodňany,
that the old self-government of the towns with its guarantees of
civil justice was breaking down, and being replaced by tough,
official methods which stood outside all local influence. With the
new authorities came more payments and duties which weighed
down on artisans and traders alike, and further depressed living
standards.

One can only read with deep sadness the accounts of how
members of the lesser nobility and burghers who had played no
active rôle in the uprising desperately tried all possible ways of
retaining their inherited lands or house, or at least of being
allowed to stay in their native land, even where this went with

the cruel obligation to foreswear the faith of their fathers. As late as the 1640s noblemen were still buying the right to stay in their own country by paying large sums to the absolute state, while many others continued to pursue, often in vain, their claims to inheritances, gifts and legacies of which they had been unjustly deprived by the confiscation commissions.

The reply of all classes of society to these intolerable conditions within Bohemia was emigration. The flood of those who went abroad began immediately after the White Mountain and continued with greater or lesser intensity until the very end of the War and the middle of the century. Its dimensions cannot be stated precisely: among the peasantry especially this form of protest remained alive even later; among the nobility some conclusions are possible from the confiscation records, since a large proportion of the more than 1,200 individuals who were dispossessed before 1630 abandoned the country and found a new home elsewhere, frequently in the military service of Sweden. The emigration of public figures from the free towns began in 1621, reaching its peak a little later as the full extent of Habsburg revenge became evident. The mandate against all non-Catholics issued in 1627 completed the persecution of the Protestant urban intelligentsia. As a result, Comenius and the historian Stránský were forced abroad amid hundreds of other less well-remembered men.

The violent Counter-Reformation, asserting itself with military methods, brought such losses of householders to individual towns that their earlier prosperity turned into a ruinous and uncontrolled decadence even before the return of warfare to Bohemia in 1630. The Old Town of Prague lost 49 families in this period, the New Town 94 of its burghers. Worse still was the fate of many free boroughs in the provinces where the mercenary troops were allowed to rampage at will. Such towns would have had an average of 200 to 300 houses in the years before 1620, but persecution reduced these numbers drastically between 1621 and 1626. The reports of the Imperial magistrates give a powerful picture of the disastrous effects of confiscations and military extortions on this basic element in any urban economy. Žatec lost 255 householders, Domažlice 290, and elsewhere things were almost as serious: Chrudim had 160 deserted homes, Klatovy 187, Most 170 and Nymburk 150. Everywhere economic and social life was but a shadow of its former self; and in the years to come, as the armies returned to Bohemian soil, things were to become yet worse.

SOUTH-EAST MORAVIA IN THE WHIRLWIND OF PERSECUTIONS AND
REBELLIONS

Until March 1621 the Imperialist troops of Buquoy's "Spanish"
army remained largely inactive in the towns of central and south-
east Moravia. Only later did they move on into the Hungarian
border regions and beyond. Detachments of Spaniards and
Neapolitans were given the job of pacifying the restless Vlach
areas. Those lands (the estates of the Protestant Žerotíns,
Cardinal Dietrichstein of Olomouc and Lukov and Vsetín which
belonged to Albrecht Waldstein) remained at the heart of resistance to the Habsburgs in the months and years after 1620.
Jan Amos, also known as Comenius, the preacher at Fulnek and
director of the school of the Brethren there had his house burned
down by the Spaniards, losing his wife and children in the blaze.
He noted the attitude of his less longsuffering neighbours: "The
Moravians of the mountains around Vsetín, called Wallachians,
are a warlike people; even after the defeat of Frederick in 1620
they refused to accept the Habsburg yoke and for three whole
years defended their freedom with the sword."

The Spanish and Neapolitan soldiers who ravaged Zlín at the
end of January 1621 found themselves by March and the beginning of April under attack from rebel forces further east,
around the town of Valašské Meziříčí. The Imperialist troops
were confined within a number of small fortified settlements and
their attempts to force a way out into the mountains were beaten
back. The leaders of this assault were again the peasants of
Vsetín and Lukov who had now been given back their old detested overlord Waldstein. Their behaviour was just as much a
thorn in the flesh to the new Governor, Dietrichstein; and when
the main strength of Buquoy's army moved into Hungary against
Bethlen Gabor these popular warriors, incited by individuals
from the lesser nobility and the Protestant clergy, were able to
hold in check the whole of eastern Moravia. The Vlachs were
thus an important factor too in the plans of the fugitive leaders
of the insurrectionary Estates who had escaped from Moravia
into Silesia after the Winter King. When Frederick decided to
abandon the struggle and go to the Netherlands, the direction of
further resistance passed to Prince Johann Georg of Jägerndorf,
one of the junior branch of Hohenzollerns. At Neisse in Silesia,
close to the fortress of Glatz which was still holding out, he was
joined by a group of Moravian nobles led by the former *hejtman*
Ladislav Velen Žerotín. Among them was one, Jan Adam

Čejkovský of Víckov, who was soon to acquire an important rôle in the fighting on Moravian soil.

The vast majority of the Moravian nobility had of course given up the fight and put their trust in the "mercy of the Habsburgs". Dietrichstein did his best to encourage this mood, at least until May 1621 when he had the main leaders of the revolt put under arrest. One of them was Václav Mol of Modřelice. fiancé to Lady Anna Cedlar of Hof, the mistress of Zlín. Mol had been a member of the Moravian Directorate: he was carried to prison in Olomouc and his property confiscated. A commission was sent to his castle in Hranice to draw up an inventory of his belongings and among the effects removed were the jewellery and valuables of Lady Anna. The commissioner appointed by Dietrichstein for this purpose was his court magistrate (*Hofrichter*) Kryštof Karel Podstatský of Prusinovice, a man who was already in the service of the Cardinal before the revolt and had himself been arrested by the insurgents.

Now it was Václav Mol and not Podstatský who sat in confinement in Olomouc, and the history of the two of them, as of Anna Cedlar and Dietrichstein, helps to clarify the development of events throughout Moravia: the breaking of the old nobility, the rise of the new *latifundia*, the real meaning of the *clementia Austriaca*, the "moderation" of the ruling house.

Lady Anna was the sister and heiress of a noble who clearly sympathized with the rebellion. Her betrothed Mol was a well-known dissident; but at the same time he was not a particularly attractive character and his relationship with Anna was clearly not ideal. We know from his confiscated correspondence that he abused his fiancée, who was older than himself, in all kinds of ways and made a mockery of her in public. He borrowed a total of 30,000 florins from her on three different occasions, and tore the seal off one of the obligations, evidently to invalidate it. Lady Anna can never have recovered this money, and she seems to have had no illusions about Mol, who died in prison; yet she never disowned him to the day of her death, although it would have been to her advantage not to be associated with such a rebel.

Anna Cedlar sought to keep as much of her property as she could. She continued to live in Olomouc, mostly off what her estate of Paskov could yield, since the rest of her lands, including Zlín, had ceased to provide anything. She managed to protect some of the livestock of these ruined domains from marauding troops by transferring them to the monastery of Hradiště outside

Olomouc. The abbot of that ancient foundation was George Leodegarius, a much better businessman than theologian, who did not help the Lady in distress from Christian charity or abstract sympathy: he received in return a loan for 5,000 florins, which was no small sum. It was probably the advocacy of Leodegarius which gained Anna the favour of the all-powerful Dietrichstein. She was given back the articles seized at Hranice, as well as a royal "letter of entitlement" granting her the custody of her deceased brother's property: jewels, papers, clothing, and the rest, while the fate of his lands was left to be decided later, after the calculation of penalties for participation in the revolt.

Meanwhile of course destinies were still being settled by the fortunes of war. In the middle of May 1621 units of the Polish Cossacks under Colonel Strojnowski returned through the neighbourhood of Zlín, and they were followed by Imperialist troops being moved to the north-east parts of Moravia where an invasion was expected from the Margrave of Jägerndorf. It was known that Johann Georg intended to link up, either in Moravia or in the valley of the Vág, with the Prince of Transylvania, Bethlen, recently elected King of Hungary. The plans of Count Matthias Thurn, who was now in Bethlen's camp, were for the Moravian and Silesian rebels to combine with the Hungarians to attack Pressburg (Pozsony) and Vienna, a bold project but not a hopeless one. At the beginning of July 1621 Bethlen began an assault on Buquoy's troops in western Slovakia. During a skirmish before the fortress of Neuhäusel (Érsekújvar) Buquoy himself fell and his soldiers retreated towards Pressburg under strong Hungarian pressure. But most of Bethlen's men were cavalry units from the county militias and hajduck irregulars from beyond the Tisza; he had neither proper infantry nor artillery. His army was thus unsuited to seige warfare and an intervention by Johann Georg was the more imperative.

The Margrave left Neisse on 13 July, 1621 with about 12,000 men and set his course for eastern Moravia via Jägerndorf and Troppau. Against him stood the forces of Colonel Gauchier, deployed around the little town of Nový Jičín "that seed-bed of all heresy and rebellion". Gauchier commanded five companies of Walloon arquebusiers, light cavalry from the southern Netherlands. Besides these he had at his disposal one battalion of German foot-soldiers and 400 Neapolitans who belonged to the Italian mercenary brigade of the *condottiere*, Spinelli. Since these Neapolitans were armed and trained after the Spanish fashion, and paid for with Spanish money they were regularly spoken of as "Spaniards"; they were in fact almost certainly the same men who had earlier taken the town of Zlín.

Gauchier tried to prevent Johann Georg from reaching Vsetín or Jablunkov which was the only route into Hungary. In a limited engagement at Raduň near Troppau he had a measure of success, but early on 25 July he became encircled in Nový Jičín by Jägerndorf and the emigrant forces. The town was set on fire and while Gauchier managed to escape with a handful of horsemen the German infantry surrendered and the Neapolitans were routed. A "Spanish" chapel was later raised up over their mass graves, a monument to the régime of Madrid and the poverty of the *Mezzogiorno*.

By defeating Gauchier, Johann Georg and his troops had opened the way to Hungary, but not all of them reached it. While Jägerndorfer advanced from Vsetín to Nagyszombat (Tyrnau) his Moravian and Silesian allies remained behind. They were not strong enough to threaten Imperialist control of the most important towns: Olomouc, Brno, Kremsier, where there were garrisons under Marshall Montenegro and Colonel Albrecht Waldstein, but the latter had withdrawn to the west bank of the Moravia river and thus the whole of the east of the country was easily overrun by the Protestants.

The emigrants' forces were led by noblemen who anyway belonged to that region: Václov Bítovský the Lord of Bystřice, Jan Adam Víckov of Vsetín, Beneš Pražma of Bílkov and others. They were joined not only by colleagues of their own estate, but by the inhabitants of many towns and settlements, and by the Vlachs. Waldstein wrote anxiously of the situation:

> I have already informed Your Princely Grace that in my opinion we may expect a general uprising of the people in this land. To calm such a storm will need an army, but I am receiving no support, not even enough to hold the passes or to mount a separate campaign against the Wallachians.

It is not surprising that Waldstein had no stomach in his position for a "separate campaign against the Wallachians" although groups of these tribesmen were by August and the beginning of September streaming across to the right bank of the Morava, particularly in the mountainous area of Chřiby. But the enemies of the Habsburgs failed to exploit this favourable situation. Bethlen and Johann Georg besieged Pressburg for a month, but the town did not fall and it was only "when the grapes were already soft and the fruit full ripe", in other words about the beginning of September, that the "armies of Jägerndorf" and the Hungarians appeared on the south-east borders of Moravia. Even now Bethlen wasted more time by investing fortified towns like Strážnice and Veselí. When he failed to take Hradiště, whose surrender was already being arranged by the commander of the garrison Jan Blekta of Outěchovice, the fate of the 1621 campaign was decided. Bethlen began to treat secretly with the Emperor, and it made no difference that his allies had now completed the occupation of the eastern half of Moravia.

Among the returned émigrés the one who had greatest success was Víckov, the acknowledged chief of the Vlach hordes. On 22 September he lay siege to Hranice, then on 3 October, helped by Hungarians, he invested Holešov. He received the backing of the local petty nobility and Protestant burghers. Holešov, where Ladislav Lobkovic had instigated a Counter-Reformation in 1615, now belonged to his brother, the Supreme Chancellor Zdeněk Vojtech, and an attack on the property of a leading member of the Viennese government was a logical step with overt political colouring. One of those who took part in it was the local smallholder Peter Kopřic of Kopřice whom we have met in the affair of the deacon of Holešov, Sarkander.

On 16 October the garrison of the fortress of Helfstein surrendered to Víckov, and it was followed two days later by the town of Lipník. Throughout the whole of eastern Moravia only Bishop Dietrichstein's stronghold of Hukvaldy now held out against the troops of the allies. At the end of the month the Jägerndorf army separated from the Hungarians and moved in a north-easterly direction through Uherský Brod, Holešov and Valašské Meziříčí. Then in the early days of November it turned abruptly west as Johann Georg and Ladislav Velen Žerotín resolved on a surprise march against Olomouc. But on 12 November this attack was repulsed and with it the destiny of the whole campaign was sealed. Bethlen made a truce with the Emperor on 6 January 1622 at the Dietrichstein castle of Mikulov (Nikolsburg) in the extreme south of the country, undertaking to withdraw from Moravia and the valley of the Vág.

The soldiers of Jägerndorf and the other rebels remained in Moravia until the end of January. Then part of them under Franz Bernhard von Thurn made their way back northwards into the county of Glatz while others under Víckov retreated into Hungary. The rest dispersed. Johann Georg himself did not return to Silesia but followed Bethlen to Kassa. Neither he nor any of the dissident Moravian leaders had been mentioned in the Mikulov agreement and it was they who thus suffered the greatest defeat, since hopes and expectations had been raised within the country by their invasion which were now cruelly disappointed. Through 1622 it was only the Vlachs who held aloft the banner of revolt. The Imperial commissioners still complained that "the people are inclined more to the enemy and the Wallachians"; but these commissioners succeeded in restoring all the detested landed authorities whom the Vlachs and the peasantry had chased out during the previous year.

Among those who now returned were Waldstein and Jetřich Žerotín of Meziříčí. The latter, a Protestant, had won Imperial favour by catching and handing over 32 "troublemakers", while Waldstein detained some of the captured Vlachs of Vsetín and had two of their leaders executed as a warning. His justice was mild in comparison with that accorded to the 18 Vlachs who were hanged in Olomouc at the end of February 1623. Even this was not enough for Cardinal Dietrichstein who ordered a repeat performance in April at which a further 13 rebels were cruelly put to death.

The Lady of Zlín however, Anna Cedlar of Hof, did not return. She died in September 1622 in Olomouc and her lands and little town were now without a master. Dietrichstein, who always had an eye for the main chance, commanded a detailed inventory to be drawn up of the whole domain, since it had belonged during the rebellion to the dissident Kryštof Cedlar and was thus forfeit to the crown. The Cardinal managed these things to perfection: as a reward for the timely treaty with Bethlen he had acquired for his relatives the confiscated estates of Hranice (formerly the property of Václav Mol of Modřelice) and Lipník. Thus the lands of the Dietrichsteins began to spread out across the map of Moravia, but even so they could not match those of the Liechtenstein family whose head, Karl, the Imperial Governor in Bohemia and beneficiary of the devious financial transactions of 1622–3, was assembling for himself and his descendants an empire embracing nearly a fourth of the whole country.

The fate of the Cedlar properties is a good example of this method of quick and easy acquisition of wealth. According to the inventory the now deceased Anna had owned the devastated domains of Zlín and Otrokovice, the estate of Paskov (which was in better condition), two manors – one of them, on the outskirts of Olomouc, was entirely destroyed – two town houses in Olomouc, jewellery, bills and other belongings. Cardinal Dietrichstein immediately seized the best item from this collection: Peskov, which had once been a fief of the Bishop of Olomouc. The rest was valued and catalogued. It now emerged that the whole inheritance was heavily in debt. Against obligations totalling 140,000 florins there were claims to only 73,000 florins, plus the two lordships which remained. The once rich Lady Anna had been in financial difficulties towards the end of her life. She was indebted everywhere: to her acquaintances among the nobility, to traders, officials, servants, even to her maids, who were owed 200 florins, presumably in wages. She had borrowed 4,000 florins from the orphans' fund of the Zlín municipality, and this was money the orphans were not to see again.

Anna's two houses in Olomouc and the lands of Zlín and Otrokovice had to be used to satisfy creditors, at least the Catholics among them. The claims of Jan Adam Víckov and other rebels were immediately disallowed and taken over by the state treasury. But there were powerful supporters of the Habsburgs who could not be dismissed so easily, notably Zeněk Žampach of Potenstein. The episcopal commissioner Kryštof Karel Podstatský of Prusinovice followed the example of his employer Dietrichstein and hastened to take his portion of the Cedlar properties. This was a house on the Česká in Olomouc which was valued at more than 2,000 florins, a large item especially when reckoned as a proportion of the whole confiscated inheritance, but we know too that it was only a small part of what the zealous Podstatský eventually acquired.

This inventory of the Cedlar legacy made in September 1622 gives us a picture of the town and lordship of Zlín, and it is a sombre one. The castle was burnt out and pillaged. Neither in it, nor in the nearby farm, brewery and barns was there anything left to record. The damage inflicted during the winter of 1621–2 had prevented any spring sowing and all the fields were lying fallow. The rest of the Lord's barns contained only what had been collected from gutted peasant farms and from those who had planted crops without permission. Things were a little better in Trávník where there remained five horses, some carts and a herd of swine.

Some of the livestock had been taken by Wilhelm Ulersdorfer, the Lobkovic bailiff at Holešov. Ulersdorfer was full of ambition; after playing an active part in the rebellion he had become a convert to Catholicism and quickly gained advancement. In the rest of Zlín the commissioners could only find a little wool and fruit, a small supply of hops in the brewery and some grain in the mill of Želechovice.

Despite all the confusion the town records continued to be kept regularly and they bear eloquent witness to the travails of those Zlíners who were resolved to struggle for existence on their own soil and not, as many did, to flee elsewhere. Life was scarcely any easier in 1623, though they managed in the spring to sow at least part of the arable land. By now only about 10,000 Imperialist soldiers remained in Moravia and Dietrichstein felt so confident of the situation that he set off for Rome. But the beginning of the year had already seen signs of discontent among the Vlachs, and Dietrichstein warned his underlings before he left to keep an eye on them since, "a great fire may be kindled by a very small spark".

The episcopal lands in eastern Moravia were again the first target of the Vlach raids, with Waldstein's estates of Lukov and Vsetín coming next in line. On 28 January the Vlach "freemen" swept down on Fryšták, seized all its livestock and burned down the buildings of the newly instituted Catholic bailiffs. This action so terrified the nobility of the neighbourhood that they called in Imperialist garrisons to defend them, with the burden as usual falling largely on the peasantry. It was the more severe coming at a time of harvest failure and precipitate debasement of the currency, while the notorious Polish auxiliaries, the "Cossacks", were also subjecting Moravia to their characteristic harassment. The mood of the population was growing ever more tempestuous and Waldstein well-informed as ever, seized this moment to sell off his troubled Moravian lands (June 1623). By this time he was already *Oberstwachmeister* and commander of the army in Bohemia; his only serious rival being now the similarly ranking Marradas who represented the remains of the old "Spanish party" in Prague. On 24 April 1623 Waldstein acquired by treaty for 430,564 marks the extensive domains of the family of Smiřický around Jičín (Gitschin) in northern Bohemia, and thus laid the foundations of his later Duchy of Friedland. Zdeněk Žampach of Potenstein became the new lord of the Vlachs of Vsetín, but Waldstein soon returned to Moravia in a purely military function when it became clear that the country was still assigned a leading rôle in the plans of the exiled Estates. What was now at stake was nothing less than a project elaborated at the court of the Palsgrave Frederick in the Hague for a concerted simultaneous attack on Vienna in the autumn of 1623 from the west and east.

Both Bethlen Gabor and the Turks were to have major parts in this enterprise. Johann Georg of Jägerndorf and the Moravian emigrants were still privy to Bethlen's councils, and they were joined by Thurn who had just spent long months in Constantinople seeking, with the aid of Dutch and English diplomats, the Sultan's promise to help an anti-Habsburg coalition. But any coalition was henceforth to be directed from the Hague and neither Thurn nor any of the other Bohemian Protestants had any influence on the actual conduct of the war. In August 1623 Bethlen marched westwards from Transylvania towards Hungary with an army of 20,000 men. The harvest was already gathered in and so it was not difficult for him to amass a numerically strong though badly disciplined body of soldiers. It included a detachment of 3,000 Turkish infantrymen and was later joined by some Turkish and Tartar cavalry. By waiting for these Ottoman reinforcements Bethlen was now, as in 1621, delayed, and Ferdinand II had time to recall the Marquis of Montenegro from Germany through Bohemia by forced marches to defend his capital. Not until the middle of October did the Hungarians reach the Moravian border at Skalice and Strážnice. Near Skalice they forced their way across the frontier and on 28 October surrounded the forces of *Oberstwachmeister* Albrecht Waldstein, who was occupying the neighbourhood of Hodonín for Montenegro. Thence the mixed Hungarian-Tartar-Turkish contingents made a series of raids as far as Brno, Olomouc and Nový Jičín.

One of these raids had Zlín as its goal. Sometime during 1623 the creditors of the Cedlars had installed as bailiff there a man already encountered more than once in these pages: Peter Kopřic of Kopřice. Although the majority of the creditors were Protestants: the Martinkovskýs of Rozseč, the Žerotíns and Kunovices; there were nevertheless important Catholics among them. Krystof Karel Podstatský had claims of 2,000 florins against the Cedlars, less than those of the rebel Víckov, the burghers Karel Hirsch of Olomouc and Jan Omasta of Meziříčí or the Jew Kolman from Uherský Brod, but as commissioner for the all-powerful Cardinal Dietrichstein he possessed great influence. It is therefore surprising that he should have turned a blind eye to the appointment in Zlín of a sworn opponent of the Habsburgs.

We first encounter Peter Kopřic long before the rebellion when as the owner of a manor at Martinovice he took to court the vicar of Holešov Jan Sarkander for refusing to bury his wife in the church there. Then in 1620 Kopřic was present at Sarkander's treason trial in Olomouc and the following year he was stripped of all his possessions as a dissident. In the autumn of 1621 he joined Jan Adam Víckov in leading the attack of the Vlachs and Hungarians on Holešov. Yet by the summer of 1623 he was generally regarded as the man most likely to maintain authority in Zlín in the event of further unrest and even perhaps to prevent any more damage. While Kopřic fulfilled the first of these hopes, the second proved beyond his powers.

The court books of the town recount drily that "in the year 1623, on the Monday after All Saints, the Turks fell on this town of Zlín and took away all the things which were in the base of the tower by the Church". The town must thus have been plundered by some marauding Ottoman and Tartar soldiers, who seized not only what was being hidden in the strong Church tower, but also the belongings from several houses and farms and even the inhabitants themselves. We read of an "Anna Zuk, who was taken in 1623 into Turkish captivity" and never returned. It is impossible to calculate how many people, especially children, girls and women were dragged off from Zlín, but contemporary estimates reckoned the number at 10,000 for the whole of Moravia.

This raid left in its wake new devastation, ruin, and destruction by fire. Pillaging soldiery continued their havoc in the area until the winter season set in, when Bethlen as usual lost patience and began to seek peace terms with the Emperor. He did not realize how close the Imperialists were to exhaustion; Waldstein was already writing to Vienna that he had no more supplies, could only hold out for another fortnight at the most, and that a truce was vital. Just a few more days and the Emperor's army around Hodonín would have been in a desperate plight. The Moravian emigrants and Thurn could only hope that Bethlen would renew the struggle in the spring.

The unhappy outcome of this Hungarian invasion of Moravia in the autumn of 1623 was another grave blow for the plans to renew a full-scale war against the Habsburgs. Who could see an ally in this wretched horde of Turks, Tartars and Magyars? Neither the petty nobility, nor the burghers, nor even the Vlachs joined Bethlen in 1623. Ladislav Velen Žerotín who had hastened back to Moravia from Berlin on hearing the news of the offensive, was forced to the realization that any calculations involving Bethlen were built on sand. But he, Thurn and the rest had to try to keep the Transylvanian prince in the framework of their grand coalition and therefore the Vlach *generalissimo* Víckov was sent to the Hague in the winter of 1623–4 to plead Bethlen's case.

Bethlen however had no faith either in the Palsgrave or the States General and on 8 May 1624 he concluded a definite peace with the Emperor which guaranteed the gains he had made in Hungary under the Treaty of Mikulov. Thus Víckov's mission was doomed to failure, as was that of Thurn who had reached the same destination after crossing Germany in disguise. His friend the Margrave of Jägerndorf did not have to face this latest disaster: he died far from home at Lócse in March.

It is therefore all the more remarkable that resistance to the Habsburgs and their *soldatesca* continued in Moravia even when the Hungarians and the emigrants from the estates had once again left the country. Of course the end of the war did not mean an end to suffering; it was followed by plague, some kind of infectious disease which took a heavy toll of the population. Between Kremsier, Holešov, and Hranice Polish Cossacks took up station, preparing for reprisals against the Vlachs. At the beginning of March 1624 the troops under Colonel Strojnowski, between 700 and 1,000 men, were sent into the mountains of Vsetín. But the attack miscarried; almost half of them seem to have been killed by the Vlachs, who then descended to the nearby towns and drove out the garrisons.

About 10 March 1624 Vlachs attacked the Poles quartered in Zlín. No contemporary chronicle records the event, but it appears in later legal documents from the years 1629 and 1630 when some neighbours in the town accused each other of having stolen hidden property in 1624 and others were said to have joined the Vlachs in their raid on the local garrison. Some Zlíners had "slain the Poles and divided the spoils among them", but the elders of the town decided to annul these claims and counterclaims by binding all those concerned to rake up the past no more.

The troops seem to have returned since it is reported that "half a year long the neighbours could not enter the town for Poles". When they finally left sometime after the end of May there were many houses "that had been set in flames by the Polish soldiers". Only towards the end of 1624 did the situation in eastern Moravia calm down sufficiently for the old landlords to return and the traditional cycle of rural life to be renewed. Peter Kopřic remained in Zlín during this time and his name was a guarantee that the town would not yet be subjected to recatholicization. But the threat to the Protestant majority of loss of livelihood and exclusion from trading was now a very real one. An Imperial Patent of 12 October 1624 banished all non-Catholic priests from Moravia. They were soon followed by the Protestant lesser nobility, whose financial ruin Dietrichstein had encompassed by confiscations and fines, by reclaiming ecclesiastical fiefs and dismissing them from the episcopal service. His example was followed by others, among them Kryštof Karel Podstatský; thus it came about that the unreliable rebel Peter Kopřic was forced to quit Zlín early in 1625.

Only the Vlachs continued to fight their lords, lay and spiritual. The Lobkovic's chaplain Rudolf Petrocinius complained that they were interfering with the success of his missions and Zdeněk Žampach of Potenstein called out the army against them in November 1624. What the fugitive superintendent of the Czech brethren in Fulnek, Jan Amos Comenius wrote in his *History of the Bitter Persecutions of the Bohemian Church* was abundantly true. In the chapter on "the fate of the common man" we read:

> The inhabitants of the lordship of Vsetín and the mountains thereabouts (who are called Wallachians) continued to resist with arms and could not be brought to deny their faith or offer submission although several times the Germans, Italians and the Polish Cossacks, falling upon them through the narrow defiles in those mountains, sought to destroy them. Thus it was that these Moravian mountains served as refuge for many men.

THE UNITED NETHERLANDS, ORGANIZER AND BANKER OF THE WAR AGAINST THE HABSBURGS

In the history books the years 1621–5 are often called the "War for the Palatinate". But even if this expression is modified to that of "Bohemian-Palatine War", as in some recent work (S. H. Steinberg), it is not adequate. We have already seen that Czech resistance was not yet at an end by the summer of 1621, when the twelve-year truce between Spain and Holland expired; Marradas was still besieging Tábor, Mansfeld had retreated in good order from western Bohemia into the nearby Upper Palatinate, Třeboň and Zvíkov were holding out in the south, and Glatz in the north, not to speak of Johann Georg of Jägerndorf in Neisse. For a full two years after the White Mountain some defiance continued: Tábor, defended by Dutch soldiers and the local militia, surrendered on 18 November 1621; Třeboň, helped by Seton's Scottish regiment, endured until 23 February 1622; then Zvíkov capitulated in May and Glatz on 28 October. Moravia too remained a centre of military activity in 1621-2 and again in 1623-4. But whereas the first of these periods was primarily an epilogue to the alliance between Bethlen Gabor and the Winter King, the second was a classic broad-based anti-Habsburg coalition, turning on an axis from the Hague through Kolozsvár to Constantinople. Its focus was clearly the Netherlands and ample evidence of the rôle now falling upon Holland is provided by the documents of the *Rijksarchiv* in the Hague and the correspondence of the agents from German princes who were active there between 1621-5.

The situation was only superficially different in another area which was as sensitive as Bohemia to the fundamental antagonism between Spain and Holland. This was the Swiss Grisons (Graubünden), or more precisely the Valtellina, where a pro-Habsburg party led by the family of Planta stood against another, that of the Salis, which favoured the Bohemian and Dutch Estates, Venice and France. Between August 1618 and January 1619 pressure from the Spanish governor in Milan called forth a wave of terror against the Catholics. The new régime, associated with the Protestant preacher Jörg Jenatsch, drew nearer to the Bohemians who were themselves seeking an alliance with the Grisons. Between 18-23 July 1620 a reaction set in with the massacre of nearly 600 Protestants which brought the occupation of the Valtellina by Spanish and Austrian troops. In January 1622 the Duke of Feria, governor of the Milanese, and Archduke Leopold forced the Grisons to surrender and accept the so-called Articles of Milan. The rebellion led by Rudolph von Salis was cruelly put down and the peace signed at Lindau (on Lake Constance) on 30 September 1622 confirmed this at least temporary Spanish success: Madrid controlled the Alpine passes and neither France, nor Savoy, nor Venice nor the Pope could for the moment interfere.

Besides Bohemia and the Valtellina the Spaniards were pressing their advantage elsewhere: in the Rhineland and Alsace, and they had soldiers throughout central Europe from Germany and the

Alps to Moravia and Hungary, though this dispersal reduced the chance of a decisive strike against the United Provinces. The Dutch too were busy: between the end of November 1620, when the Hague and Amsterdam heard of the "general disaster of the King of Bohemia", and the beginning of the New Year the States General six times debated the fate of Bohemia and the Palsgrave. They were concerned to engage as many Spanish troops as possible far from their own frontiers and were thus not willing to abandon the Lower (Rhenish) Palatinate. Maurice of Orange assured Mansfeld and his officers in the winter of 1620–1 that he would guarantee their pay. The Elector Frederick was welcomed to the Hague by the States at a ceremonial audience in April 1621, and the representatives of the Bohemian Estates were similarly received in June. All were assured, "that everything would be for the best and that Their Graces wished to retain the visitors' favour to this common end".

At the same time however the Dutch were treating with Brussels about a renewal of the truce. They were clearly seeking to gain time in a situation fraught with complexities. The Palsgrave was still their only ally, and his territories were gravely threatened: the Upper Palatinate, defended by Mansfeld, was under attack from the forces of the League, while half the towns in the Lower Palatinate were held by Spinola's soldiers. The leaders of the army of the Protestant Union had concluded a truce with Spinola to expire on 14 May 1621, but that same day their representatives meeting in Heilbronn decided on the Union's dissolution. Despite this basic isolation of Holland, Maurice broke off his negotiations with the Spaniards and resolved to recommence the war.

Philip III did not live to see hostilities renewed: he died on 31 March 1621 and was followed into the grave on 13 July by Archduke Albert. The southern Netherlands thus reverted to Spain and Albert's widow the Infanta Isabella continued merely as governor and representative of Philip IV. The First Minister of the new King, Gaspar de Guzmán, Conde-Duque of Olivares, was the nephew of Baltazar Zuñiga, the former envoy of Prague; Olivares' initial task was to eliminate the dualism within Spanish policies and to reassert the control of the Madrid government against the influence of generals and ambassadors. Faced with a profound economic crisis, his problem was how to acquire the means of implementing any ambitious policy abroad. The Spain of Philip IV and Olivares had inherited so many obligations that in 1621, wittingly or unwittingly, it necessarily appeared as the logical opponent and anti-pole to the United Provinces, the representative of a different type of social and political organization. In these circumstances the twelve-year truce could not possibly have been extended.

The rivalry between Spain and Holland could equally not be restricted to the fortified frontier between the southern and northern Netherlands. Dutch capitalism, particularly the finance of Amsterdam, was developing on all sides: reclaiming the *Haarlemmermeer* at home and expanding into America, Asia and Africa. The West India Company, founded in 1621, was a direct challenge to the Spanish colonial *Imperium* and Dutch trade with Scandinavia and the Baltic was creating a whole dependent region, a lifeline for the mother country. Abraham Cabelliau and William Usselinc, the De Geers and Marselis, seafarers like Jan Pieterszoon Coen and the founders of the New Netherlands were not only builders of Holland's "Golden Age", but also sworn enemies of Spain. However the cautious gentlemen regents might view the fact, the United Provinces were by 1621 a great power, the striking model of a civilization which by its very existence became the ideal of tens of thousands of thinking people throughout Europe.

The eventual outcome of this duel between Spain and Holland could not of course be known in 1621. But the Orangists, led by the *Stadholder* Maurice, could not ignore the fact that the Dutch were largely isolated against the Habsburg monolith. It was a matter of desperate importance to them to gain the support of England: without it they had been unable to help the Czechs in 1618-20, and without it they could not guarantee even the hereditary lands of the Palsgrave in 1621, let alone restore him to the Bohemian throne.

England received tidings of the defeat of Frederick on the White Mountain at the beginning of December 1620. In the middle of the same month there were anti-Spanish riots in London which the Chancellor Francis Bacon could suppress only by calling in troops. Besides the Spanish ambassador Count Gondomar the most hated man of the moment was King James, who became the chief target of a flood of pamphlets produced during the winter of 1620-1. Perhaps the most brazen was one called *Vox populi*, written by Thomas Scott, a member of Peterhouse College, Cambridge and rector of Norwich. Scott was imprisoned by royal command but managed to escape. At this James became further irritated and expelled from court Frederick's envoy Achaz von Dohna; he began an attempt to strip of office and influence all the representatives of the "Bohemian" or, as it was now more often called, "Palatine" party.

In the spring of 1621 necessity compelled James to recall Parliament which had not sat since 1614. The King tried to impose his condition that it should not discuss foreign policy which he regarded as a royal secret, an *arcanum imperii*. But in June the Lower Chamber presented a list of its grievances, and these included the miserable *débâcle* of English policy in Bohemia, the Palatinate and the Valtellina, as well as the decline of trade and shipping. The debates between king and Parliament dragged on into the autumn since James desperately needed taxes. In November he was informed of the conditions under which the Commons would grant them: they wished to consider the Bohemian question and would only vote money if he openly intervened in favour of Frederick in the Palatinate. John Pym, twenty years later the uncrowned head of the opposition, spoke of the "religion which is being martyred in Bohemia". James would have nothing to do with these demands and rebuked Parliament for speaking ill of "our dear brother the King of Spain". But the Commons protested and pressed for England to stand out openly against Spain and the Papacy, as in the days of Elizabeth. Enraged the King dismissed them and had several opposition members imprisoned. Thus the winter of 1621–2 saw England once more without Parliament, and the English king once again short of money. The "Bohemian question" had given the Commons one of its first opportunities to essay a distinctive programme, one diametrically opposed to the policy of the Stuart monarch. This event was of deep significance for the history of the conflict between Parliament and the dynasty.

But at the end of 1621 hopes of united action by England and Holland were no greater. Frederick was not a strong character and could only waver between the rival influences of his relatives at the Hague and at the court of St James. As long as the King of England sought to persuade his son-in-law that he must abandon the Bohemian lands and his former subjects there, as well as any further struggle against the Habsburgs, all cooperation between the Dutch and Frederick's supporters in central Europe remained half-hearted. There was in fact no coordination of policy in the heart of the Continent at all. During the autumn of 1621 the armies of the League forced Mansfeld out of the Upper Palatinate, and its governor Christian of Anhalt promptly began secret peace negotiations with the Habsburgs through the intermediary of his son, who had been a prisoner since the White Mountain. Mansfeld retreated to the Rhenish Palatinate, but at almost the same time Spinola and his Spanish-Walloon troops took the important strategic fortress of Jülich in the Lower Rhineland, the same Jülich which had almost unleashed a European conflict a decade earlier. At the beginning of 1622 Spinola's forces and the soldiers of the League under Tilly moved to attack the remainder of Frederick's lands, the as yet unoccupied half of the Lower Palatinate which was now being reinforced by units from England.

James had only agreed to this move when he became convinced that the Spaniards would not leave Frederick's electorate unmolested. The Palsgrave set off secretly from the Hague with his retinue, among them nobles from Bohemia and Moravia, and crossed French territory to reach the Palatinate where he found Mansfeld's troops together with the armies of the Margrave of Baden-Durlach and Christian of Brunswick, all raised on the money of the Dutch States General. In April Mansfeld even gained a limited success over Tilly, but soon the tables were turned: Tilly defeated Baden-Durlach at Wimpfen and Christian of Brunswick at Höchst. He now linked with the Spaniards and the soldiers of Archduke Leopold, Bishop of Strassburg and Ferdinand's brother, in an attempt to encircle Mansfeld. The latter retaliated, and with the Margrave seized a strip of Alsace-Lorraine. But at the crucial moment English diplomacy again intervened, persuading the Palsgrave to rely on negotiations with Spain while James took up once more the wearisome barter over the marriage of his son Charles to the Infanta. Frederick duly retired to Sedan in France and the weakened defences of the Palatinate could not prevent the loss of the whole country.

Bavarian policies in the Rhineland were potentially in conflict with those of Philip, since Maximilian's brother was Prince-Archbishop of Cologne and Liège and his brother-in-law was the ruler of Jülich and Berg. Tilly therefore did not utilize Mansfeld's disarray to move into Lower Saxony and unite with the Spaniards in their planned attack on the United Provinces from the east. Instead, he captured Heidelberg on 16 September 1622 and the commander of the English forces, Sir Horace Vere, delivered up Mannheim early in November. With this the Palatinate was totally subjugated; in a very short time the celebrated library of the Electors was on its way from Heidelberg to Rome, where as the *Palatina* it remains to this day one of the most important constituent parts of the Vatican collection.

Having seen the fate of his patrimony sealed, Frederick returned in desolation to the Hague with the remnants of his entourage. The situation of Holland was now acute; Spinola's armies were threatening the border fortress of Bergen-op-Zoom which was only reinforced after a bold march by Mansfeld and his men. This direct confrontation led the Dutch diplomats in the winter of 1622–3 to seek on the one hand support from France, on the other a firmer anti-Habsburg coalition which could tie down the enemy in Central Europe rather than leave Spanish forces free for a campaign in the Rhineland. It was in this interest that Dutch agents, together with Thurn, were pressing the Porte in Constantinople from the autumn of 1622. Bethlen Gabor's partners in the west were to be Mansfeld, who was already recruiting an army in Frisia with Dutch money, and Christian of Brunswick, who was engaged on the same task in the Lower Saxon circle.

The Elector Palatine too was planning revenge from his exile in a palace on the Lange Voorhout of the Hague, at least until he was again restrained by his father-in-law, who in 1623 resolved on the desperate expedient of forcing the issue of the Spanish marriage through the cavalier journey of Buckingham and the Prince of Wales to Madrid.

On 23 February 1623, at an Imperial Diet called by Ferdinand II in Ratisbon, Frederick was deprived of his electoral dignity. It was transferred together with the Upper Palatinate to Maximilian of Bavaria as recompense for his past services and to win him for future ones. Maximilian had in fact by no means abandoned the idea of a more independent policy, to be directed against Spain and invoke the cooperation of France. James I was prepared to accept the *diktat* of Ratisbon, provided only that his son-in-law could be reinstated in his Rhenish lands. But the Spaniards would not promise even this, especially after the whole affair of Prince Charles's marriage with the Infanta had ended with a fiasco in Madrid. The definitive breach between England and Spain occurred only in the autumn of 1623; until then the Palsgrave was still hindered in his plans for action and could not summon the courage for an independent military enterprise. Thus valuable time was lost on the western front and the necessary coordination with the campaign in Hungary and Moravia was frustrated. Christian of Brunswick, who was supposed to join Bethlen, was instead hounded by Tilly in full retreat towards the Dutch border and his forces annihilated at Stadtlohn in August. Mansfeld too was chased from the theatre of war. He disbanded his army and made for northern Italy where he entered the service of Venice, which was preparing with Savoy and France to resist the spectre of Spanish hegemony in the Apennine peninsula. There he was joined in the spring of 1624 by Thurn, fresh from the wreckage of the aspirations he had set in Bethlen Gabor.

The diplomacy of the Dutch was not deterred by this reverse. In an effort to forestall the expected great assault on the southern frontier of the country, the United Provinces negotiated feverishly both with England and France and on 20 June 1624 were able to conclude an alliance. They were helped in part by the growing opposition to Spain of Maximilian of Bavaria, the head of the League, and the new Pope, Urban VIII, a Barberini who had been elected in August 1623. But the Dutch could not entirely ward off the attack launched in the spring of 1625. At the end of April, before the campaign was full mounted, the *Stadholder* Maurice died; his brother and successor Prince Frederick Henry, although personally concerned for the fate of the Palsgrave's family, could not prevent the fall of Breda. The delivery of the fortress, on 5 June 1625, is celebrated in Velasquez's great canvas, the painting more commonly called *Las Lanzas*.

But the Spaniards advanced no further, and thus another project gained in importance with the passing months. This was Olivares' so-called *almirantazgo*, which planned that the Spanish fleet should occupy the decaying ports of the Hanseatic League and cut off Holland's trade with the Baltic lands. Spain and the southern Netherlands, the League and the Emperor, the Hansa and Poland were to combine in depriving the United Provinces of their supplies of essential raw materials. It was an attractive scheme, lacking only the necessary practical backing from the Imperialist camp.

Against this feudal-Catholic Habsburg power block which sought to extend its influence from the Atlantic into the North Sea and the Baltic, the Dutch conceived an equally grandiose opposing front. It was to stretch from "maritime" Europe, the lands of the north-west seaboard, across the Continent as far as the Sea of Marmora. The Ottoman alliance however was known to be an insignificant factor and in 1623 it had failed completely, while without the Turks Bethlen Gabor could not venture any more decisive action. The Swedish King, Gustavus Adolphus, was willing to intervene, and his ultimate desire now, as in 1620, was to penetrate as far as Silesia whence he hoped to be able to deal a conclusive blow against the Polish Vasas. But his plans for a campaign between the Elbe and the Weser conflicted with the interests of Christian IV, King of Denmark and Norway. Hence the United Provinces and England abandoned their projected agreement with Sweden and turned to Denmark. The coalition established at the end of 1625 in the Hague included, besides England and Denmark, the Lower Saxon circle of the Empire and counted on the sympathies of Frederick, Transylvania and the Porte.

The Protestant allies prepared a grand strategy for the confrontation of 1626. Four separate armies were to march against the Habsburgs: Christian IV was to conquer north-west Germany, Christian of Brunswick to engage Maximilian's relatives in the Rhineland, Mansfeld to advance upstream along the Elbe into Bohemia and Moravia with his English and Dutch reservists, Bethlen to join with him for the capture of Vienna. Such plans needed the assistance of Frederick's partisans in Central Europe, however fickle that help might prove to be.

The coalition of the Hague was the most significant grouping of anti-Habsburg political and social forces since the beginning of the war; it seemed to bring to an end the period of localized struggles and to herald the realization of the designs of both Czech and Dutch diplomats in 1618–20. For the present, however, all the schemes were still on the drawing-board.

Six

THE DANISH WAR AND THE
RISE OF WALLENSTEIN

THE FIRST AND LAST "GRAND COALITION" AGAINST THE HABSBURGS
THE new power grouping on the threshold of the campaigns of
1626 seemed to make possible a real escape from the previous
limited conflicts where all advantages had lain with the Habsburgs. But the "grand coalition" created in the Hague brought
together some very diverse partners, and it therefore lacked inner
unity. Its policy-makers faced a difficult task, and their problems
included some of a purely technical nature.

It was also important that interest was again focused on the
lands of central Europe, despite the fact that the "Bohemian
question" was in English eyes at least now visibly subordinated
to the affair of the Palatinate, the restoration to ex-Elector
Frederick of his hereditary domains. The English ambassador in
Copenhagen, Sir Robert Anstruther, sought to gain King
Christian IV for this cause by stressing the growing threat to
north-west Germany from Spain and the League. The reports of
Abraham Richter, the agent of Saxe-Weimar in the Hague, to
his Duke Johann Ernst show however that the agreement reached
between England and Denmark during the winter of 1625–6 was a
much more restricted one than Frederick and his miniature court
on the Lange Voorhout had hoped for.

The attitude of Christian to the fate of the Czech lands had
been thoroughly realistic since the time of the Bohemian war.
His Danish-Norwegian kingdom was more interested in Hungary than in Bohemia. Vital supplies of copper passed from the
regions of present-day Slovakia through the Kattegat to Hamburg
and Amsterdam, and although this trade was, so far as can be

observed, weakening during the seventeenth century, Czech and Silesian fabrics and glass exported down the Elbe had not yet developed sufficiently to rival it. It is true that the Jesuits in the *Collegium Nordicum* of Olomouc were trying to educate missionaries for the recovery to Catholicism of northern Europe, but in half a century only 43 were sent to Denmark. Their propaganda was hardly more worrying to Christian than tendencies towards Calvinism and crypto-Calvinism.

The Danish king had thus shown no great readiness in 1618–19 to lend the support which the Directorate in Prague was entreating from him. When the Bohemian Estates elected his relation Frederick of the Palatinate to their throne, Christian only provided a trifling sum of 20,000 thalers, part of the dowry of the late Anne of Denmark, his own sister and mother of Elizabeth the Winter Queen. Until 1624 he maintained a position of reserve towards the Palsgrave and his former subjects, and it was only when the spectre of an Imperialist presence in north Germany and an Anglo-Dutch alliance with rival Sweden came to loom larger on the horizon that Christian's attitude changed. In the spring of 1625 he began to use money from Holland for recruiting cavalry, and large numbers of Bohemian and Moravian exiles joined his standard. These troops were placed under the command of Johann Ernst of Saxe-Weimar, who had already fought in the 1620 campaign; they took the field during the summer of that year against Tilly's army in Lower Saxony and later played a part in the capture of Hanover. This limited involvement was calculated to strengthen Christian's position in an area where his material interests were also those of the Dutch, the real instigators of all the projects for a grand alliance. But Christian certainly did not regard any such coalition as forming that *Corpus Evangelicorum* which years before, in 1620, even his own Danish council of state had been discussing.

Nevertheless the Hague coalition joined together the most progressive polities of the Protestant camp. Its combined army was to be sent into central Europe under the command of Mansfeld, who was made answerable to the States General of the United Provinces and to the Palsgrave. Dutch "information" was meanwhile also being passed on to the Duke of Saxe-Weimar, although he was formally in Danish service. The troops were to march upstream along the Elbe in the spring of 1626, threatening the Leaguers under Tilly and the Imperialists under Wallenstein; then they were to unite with the men of Christian of Brunswick operating farther to the west. Their coordination with the activities of Bethlen Gabor was entrusted to the latter's *aide-de-camp* Quadt, and it was Quadt who observed that advantage might profitably be taken of the major peasant rising which broke out in Upper Austria during May and engaged many of the enemy's resources.

The campaign did not develop as the Hague, London, and Copenhagen had expected. The joint army easily penetrated the Old Mark of Brandenburg but on 25 April it was halted by Wallenstein at Dessau and defeated. When Christian of Brunswick died on 16 June it seemed that the fate of the whole enterprise might be sealed. But Quadt managed to organize a diversionary movement to pass through Silesia and Moravia and join Bethlen in Hungary. At the end of June Saxe-Weimar's Danish troops set out from Stendal, crossed the Elbe, skirted Berlin (since the Protestant Electors of Saxony and Brandenburg remained aloof) and reached the river Oder in the middle of July. There they were met by Mansfeld. The two commanders split up again on leaving Frankfurt, avoided the town of Breslau, and by the middle of August already stood on the confines of Moravia at Bohumín and Teschen. As in 1621 and 1623 Moravia was for the most part prompt to desert the Habsburgs for their enemies, and Mansfeld and Johann Ernst were free by the end of the month to consider their next step. Their real wish was for part of the troops to stay in Moravia, the rest to advance towards Bethlen who was as usual delayed by having to secure the approval of Constantinople. They then planned to invade Bohemia, foregoing the chance of a direct attack on Vienna since Wallenstein's soldiers were already hot in pursuit through Silesia.

At the beginning of September the two armies left the majority of the Danish infantry in the region of Troppau and moved on into Upper Hungary. Both in Silesia and Moravia active recruiting was carried out by members of the old Estates who had returned to their homes. Helped by the inhabitants of several towns and the Vlachs from the mountains, the Protestants occupied the whole eastern half of Moravia during the autumn without difficulty. Mansfeld and Saxe-Weimar had meanwhile progressed to the valleys of central Slovakia, but here they received the news that in Germany the main Danish army had been routed by Tilly at Lutter on 27 August. Even now they were not prepared for action: at the end of September Bethlen was in Fülek and his Turkish reinforcements still only in Nógrád.

Mansfeld and Saxe-Weimar now withdrew northwards under pressure from Wallenstein who was installed in Nyitra and the two commanders met the Hungarian leader in the mountains neár Právno. Their negotiations were not easy, since the sides held different views about what should be done. Bethlen wanted all the forces to be concentrated in Hungary, but Johann Ernst wished rather to regroup in Silesia and then advance into Bohemia and the Upper Palatinate. Eventually it was decided that all the troops should first be united to face the Imperialists.

All this time Wallenstein had been moving his reduced army from Neuhäusel towards the river Ipoly where Bethlen and his Turkish allies were encamped. On 30 September 1626 the two sides stood face-to-face by the fortress of Drégely Palánk. But neither felt confident: lacking the support of the Danes and Mansfeld, Bethlen retreated stealthily in the night of 1 October, while Wallenstein withdrew back to Neuhäusel. Not until a fortnight later did all the anti-Habsburg troops join forces and at the beginning of November they were still debating how to proceed. Bethlen now regarded the year's campaign as closed; Mansfeld hoped for Venetian aid and a renewal of the war in northern Italy. He resolved to try his fortune there but it proved a last and uncompleted journey: he only reached the neighbourhood of Sarajevo in Bosnia, where he died in the last days of November. The Duke of Saxe-Weimar took over Mansfeld's command and tried to deal with Bethlen in the interests of continuing the conflict, then extending it the next spring to Bohemia and broadening its social base by appealing to the peasants of Bohemia, Moravia and Upper Austria. Amidst this bargaining, on 14 December 1626, he too died in Turóczszentmárton. His military chancery and the remnants of his army were brought back to Troppau by the Danish commissar Joachim Mitzlaff.

Something of this large-scale plan was actually realized in Silesia and Moravia during the winter by Mitzlaff and his colleague Ladislav Velen Žerotín, the former *hejtman*. They managed to recruit new Danish infantry and cavalry regiments and to stir up peasant discontent. But by spring 1627 Wallenstein too had a larger and stronger army: he used it to suppress without mercy all signs of insurrection in central and north-east Bohemia, and since Bethlen, despite his promises, failed to invade Moravia (he was now looking for fresh allies as far afield as Muscovite Russia), the Danish troops were eventually forced to retreat. Wallenstein now appeared to block their escape route into Germany, so that only a part of the cavalry was able to find its way back to Pomerania and the shores of the Baltic. It included a number of Czech officers, whom we shall shortly meet again in yet another guise – as servants of the king of Sweden.

The episode of Danish intervention in central Europe was thus at an end. Christian IV, after his complete supineness during the Estates' revolt of 1618–20, had at last sent his generals into Moravia, where circumstances forced them to rely seriously not only on the noble insurrectionists against the Emperor, but on the Vlachs and peasants and the solid burghers of Bohemia. The whole affair had an epilogue: the attempt to translate into Danish a work of the exile Comenius, his *Truchlivý* (the Mourner). Comenius, busy publishing in Amsterdam a new map of Moravia which he dedicated to Ladislav Velen Žerotín with the wish for a speedy return to their native land, can scarcely have realized that Simon Ydsted, a teacher in Bergen, was devoting his August evenings in 1627 to a manuscript called *Bedrøffuelse offuer Bedrøffuelse og Trøst offuer Trøst*.

By that time Wallenstein's troops had already moved much further north into Lower Saxony and were joining with Tilly to chase the Danes out of Germany altogether onto the Jutland peninsula. Wallenstein, who had managed the critical situation in Hungary during the autumn of 1626 just as consummately as he had managed that in Moravia during 1623, now saw his power in full ascendancy. The success was rooted in his organizational talents, since his army was now stronger than it had ever been before. It was reflected in the passing of the earlier superiority of Tilly and the League. While Tilly was now allotted subordinate tasks in the Lower Saxon Circle, Wallenstein took over the vastly important strategic region of Mecklenburg and Pomerania. These two provinces, together with the Hansa towns, played a key rôle in Spain's plans for a naval blockade of the United Provinces and their economic livelihood – the *almirantazgo*, which was being freely discussed in Madrid and Vienna from the autumn of 1624. The first step was to transfer the theatre of war to the Baltic by the united action of Spain, the southern Netherlands, the Hanseatic League and Poland. Then the Emperor would grant monopoly rights to a shipping concern intended to wrest from Holland and Denmark the control of trade with eastern Europe through the Sound. To this end Gabriel de Roy, described as "Commissioner-General for the Atlantic and Baltic Seas", was sent from Spain to cooperate with Wallenstein in Wismar. In January 1628 Wallenstein was invested with Mecklenburg as a fief of the Empire and on April 21 of the same year he received the title: "General of the whole Imperial Fleet and Lord of the Atlantic and Baltic". On the same day his patent as military *generalissimo* was extended to give its holder decisive influence wherever the might of the Habsburgs held sway.

A study of Wallenstein's military chancery throws new light on his whole policy in Mecklenburg and north Germany from his arrival there at the end of 1627 until the first termination of his command three years later. We can follow clearly how Wallenstein, whose notions of sea-faring were at the outset highly primitive, soon came to be able to make a more realistic appraisal of the situation than the Spaniards and their Commissioner General. It becomes quite evident that Spanish interests were upheld not by Wallenstein, but by the Imperial diplomat Schwarzenberg. The *generalissimo* was far more concerned to finish the war with Christian IV of Denmark who, although defeated on land, was still master of the sea.

In the spring of 1628 Wallenstein, having failed to acquire by purchase the ships of the Hansa, resolved instead to build an Imperial fleet. As Duke of Mecklenburg he was ruler of Wismar and Rostock: the former had fallen to him late in 1627, Rostock he captured the following October. With characteristic energy Wallenstein threw himself into the task of attracting the experts, finance and materials necessary to construct a fleet, while effective Danish raids on the Baltic shore underlined the urgency of the task. During the course of 1628 he managed to acquire enough money, as well as a good organizer in Count F. Mansfeld. The new ships were intended to defend the German shore and then to attack the Danish positions across the water. To this end Wallenstein requested the Emperor to send over from Dalmatia some Uskoks trained and proven in the wars against Venice.

Wallenstein's views on maritime policy and Baltic trade were however gradually changing. The Hansa towns, which he earlier regarded simply as a source of finance and supplies, began to take on the character of allies. Whereas he had supported the piracy of the first Imperialist naval captains, at the end of 1628 Wallenstein forbade any interference with merchant shipping, domestic or foreign. But this did not mean that the Hanseatic League had thrown in its lot with the Emperor – Ferdinand's power was still too weak for that, and Spanish policy too clumsy.

The best witness was the continuing resistance of the town of

Stralsund in Pomerania, which was under siege from Wallenstein's deputy, Field Marshal Arnim. A Danish attempt to land there was frustrated, but Wallenstein could not prevent both the Danes and Swedes from bringing provisions and reinforcements. In August 1628 he had to call off the siege. This was a grave blow to the newly-won Imperial prestige, almost as devastating as the disaster suffered by Spain at the same time in the Atlantic. There the whole of the silver fleet for 1628 was captured by the Dutch admiral Piet Heyn off the Cuban coast near Matanzas. Eleven million florins in booty meant almost as much to the ready imaginations of contemporary Europe as they did to the regents in the Netherlands, who were well aware that their destiny was being settled not only in north Germany but in America, off Cuba and in Brasil, in Ceylon, Malaya and Indonesia. Their *Stadholder*, Frederick Henry, was not idle at home. He chased the Spaniards from their positions in the eastern provinces, then in 1629 forced the surrender of the fortified stronghold of s'Hertogenbosch, although its Spanish garrison had been strengthened with Imperialist units.

Since there was no prospect of cooperation with Sweden, Wallenstein made increasing attempts to win to his side the Hanseatic towns and Denmark. He offered his help to devastated Wismar and guaranteed the safety of the Hansa fleet. He introduced unified weights and measures, an important step towards the development of internal commerce, and considered a canal to link Wismar with the Elbe. He granted Rostock and Wismar freedom to trade with Denmark, Sweden and even Dutch towns, restricting only the transit of arms and military provisions. A private company was to be formed for trading with Spain, directed by an Imperial admiralty in Wismar, though thanks to the unreliability of De Roy there were at most six to eight sizeable ships available. In order to woo Denmark, Wallenstein sought to convince the Emperor that he must offer mild peace terms to Christian. The treaty concluded in Lübeck on 22 May 1629 therefore restored the king in all his territories, on condition that he should not intervene again in the affairs of the Reich. Gabriel de Roy moved from Wismar to the Danish port of Glückstadt at the mouth of the Elbe. On the basis of a further agreement reached in October 1630 Glückstadt was to become the focus for Spanish trade with the lands around the North Sea and Baltic. The Peace of Lübeck of course involved Denmark's withdrawal from the coalition of the Hague, and soon afterwards

England also seceded; Charles I had anyway long ceased to make any contributton, while Buckingham's attack on France had already undermined the common anti-Habsburg front.

In the months which followed, Wallenstein was no longer seeking to control the Hansa but to neutralize it. His political vision now extended beyond North Germany, since his primary concern was henceforth to conciliate both Denmark and Holland. Wallenstein's negotiations with the Dutch envoy Foppius Aizema led to the promise, given by the *generalissimo* to the States General, that he would not allow the Spaniards to use Wismar against the United Provinces, nor let the Imperial fleet threaten the free movement of Dutch trade. After a victory over the Swedes in September 1629 he managed to break the blockade of the southern Baltic shores, and his first aim was that the naval flotilla should protect the commerce of his own "private" towns Rostock and Wismar. Only when Wallenstein withdrew from northern Germany early in 1630 was Spanish policy able to re-assert itself; and that was the beginning of the end for the Imperialist navy and the "Hansa project".

Before his departure Wallenstein sent off a part of his troops to two new battle areas: Prussia and north Italy. The war was spreading still further. Dutch involvement in Sweden was even greater than in Denmark: Gothenburg and other towns were just outposts of Holland on Swedish soil while its copper and steel had become commodities controlled by mixed Dutch-Swedish entrepreneurship as represented by families like the Trips and De Geer. Amsterdam was the goal of most Swedish exports, as it was of goods from the Baltic provinces which, since the Treaty of Stolbova (1617), had helped the Swedes to control trade between Russia and Europe. Gustavus Adolphus aimed at perfecting a system which would turn the Baltic into a "Swedish sea", and for this he still lacked the ports ruled by King Sigismund of Poland-Lithuania. In 1621 the Swedish army captured Livonia and Riga; in 1626 Gustavus began his advance into east Prussia against the Poles and their vassal, the Elector of Brandenburg. By 1629 the invaders had conquered Elbing, Memel and Pillau, and the magistracy of the city of Danzig had come to terms with them. Everywhere there were active groups of Dutch merchants, sometimes English and Scottish traders as well. With the help of Holland and France this part of the Baltic was pacified by the truce concluded at Altmark on 25 September 1629 between Poland and Sweden. The former ceded Livonia to Gustavus

Adolphus, together with the administration of the Prussian customs: thus the state of Poland-Lithuania was now, like Muscovite Russia, cut off from the sea, and the king of Sweden was free to intervene in the German military arena.

The other field of conflict was north Italy, and here too the Spanish and Austrian Habsburgs suffered a serious reverse. At the end of 1627 the last member of the house of Gonzaga died and the fiefs of Mantua and Montferrat reverted to the Empire. Ferdinand II had promised them to Spain and was not disposed to recognize the claims of the nearest heir, the French Duc Charles de Nevers-Gonzaga, who had been Wallenstein's comrade-in-arms during the wars against the Turks in Hungary. Nevers nevertheless assumed the government in Mantua, while the Spaniards, impelled by their dislike of this French infiltration and spurred on by the militant governor of Milan, Don Gonzalo de Cordoba, seized Montferrat. The Spanish intervention, carried out with the support of Savoy, immediately created a situation of great delicacy in north Italy. During the years 1628–31 most of Europe was concerned with it, from the immediate protagonists through Venice and the Emperor to England, Holland and Denmark.

Wallenstein regarded Ferdinand's promise to help Spain in the struggle for Mantua as a serious political error. Here, as in his attitude to the Hispano-Dutch conflict, the *generalissimo* was pursuing his own course, and one which did not coincide with Spanish notions. He foresaw that the actions of Madrid would lead to a war with France and that Cardinal Richelieu would hasten to take counter-measures. And indeed France soon pressed Savoy to join her own alliance with Venice and the Duc de Nevers. In the field the Habsburg armies still possessed a clear superiority, and the dispatches of Wallenstein's generals Gallas, Collalto, Colloredo, Piccolomini and Aldringen throw light on the conquest of Mantua, which eventually fell on 18 July 1630 (Ambrogio Spinola had died at the head of his troops during the siege of Casale). Yet from the standpoint of Spanish interests the Mantuan war was the greatest mistake which the Conde-Duque Olivares could have made. His intervention led to a reconciliation between France and England, who had so recently been fighting each other over the Huguenot stronghold of La Rochelle, while French diplomacy also organized the princes of the Empire against Ferdinand. Faced by this threat and the presence on German soil of Gustavus Adolphus, Ferdinand was forced to conclude the Peace of Cherasco (19 June 1631) by which he gave Mantua and Montferrat to Nevers and undertook to evacuate his troops from the Grisons, which was promptly occupied by French soldiers under the Huguenot leader the Duc de Rohan. Savoy surrendered the fortress of Pignerol (Pinerolo) in exchange for part of Montferrat, and even the *pontifex maximus* danced to Richelieu's tune. Urban VIII took advantage of the Habsburg disorder to annexe another Imperial fief, the Dukedom of Urbino, made vacant by the death of the last Della Rovere.

At the same time the Emperor's position in Germany, built up by the armies of Wallenstein, came under attack. On 6 May 1629 Ferdinand II issued the so-called *Edict of Restitution*, which gave back to the Catholic Church in the Empire all the property which had belonged to it in 1552. The decision affected two archbishoprics, twelve bishoprics and a large number of monasteries. In addition, the Calvinists were to be deprived of all the rights enjoyed by members of the Lutheran Augsburg confession. This was not of course just a religious affair, but a vast financial operation and an unprecedented assault on the political structure of the Reich. The Edict gave the Emperor *de facto* those dictatorial powers which the princes had been resisting for centuries. At a stroke it united Lutherans, Calvinists and even patriotic Catholics in a common front against Ferdinand.

Direct counter-attack was not their best form of dissent. Wallenstein, who with Tilly and Pappenheim had made possible the Imperialist triumph, presented a more suitable target. The way in which Mecklenburg had been confiscated from its reigning dukes and handed over to Wallenstein could be a precedent for similar usurpations in the future. Wallenstein's new methods of logistics, his principle that his troops must be maintained not only by conquered lands but also by those which they claimed to protect, had been under fire since the beginning of 1627 from all the Imperial estates without distinction of confession. These grievances became a central theme of the negotiations between Emperor and Electors in Ratisbon from June to August 1630. Ferdinand II was anxious to see the election of his son Ferdinand, monarch-elect of Bohemia and Hungary, as King of the Romans, and hence his successor in the Empire; he also sought positive assistance for Spain in the war against the Dutch. His influential confessor, the Jesuit Lamormain, had long approved the sacrifice of Wallenstein to the wishes of the Electors, and the *generalis-*

simo's other arch-enemy, Maximilian of Bavaria, had been gained by the first *éminence grise* of French politics, Père Joseph du Tremblay, for an alliance with Paris which was to last almost two centuries. Under the threat of openly siding with the French, the bench of Electors extorted the dismissal of Wallenstein, the decimation of the Imperialist army which was now to be placed under Tilly's command, and the referring of the Edict of Restitution to the decision of a Reichstag. In return Ferdinand received nothing at all. The electors refused to confirm the Archduke Ferdinand and declared themselves unable to give either soldiers or money for Spain's campaign in the Netherlands. Thus the Emperor had suddenly lost both his dominance in Germany and the only instrument which offered any chance of reasserting it. His army ceased to function just two months after the Swedes made their landfall on the north German shore.

Much changed in the whole character of the European conflict during the single lustrum of 1625–30. It revealed the continuing importance of the old crisis points, Bohemia and the Netherlands, as well as the growing tensions of the new: north Italy and the Baltic; it saw the extension of the war to the Atlantic and the coasts of Africa and Asia. The plans for a "grand coalition" in 1625 foundered on the dialectical contradictions among its members, and on a shortage of means and manpower. England withdrew, since she was entirely absorbed with her own pre-revolutionary crisis. The United Provinces sustained the weight of the anti-Habsburg offensive and now found in Sweden compensation for the failure of Denmark. But on the horizon, besides Sweden, there stood ever more clearly the shadow of France, which was gradually assuming for the future the leading rôle hitherto borne by the Dutch.

BOHEMIA AND THE EMPIRE, WALLENSTEIN AND EUROPE

Amid the unprecedented economic collapse and the vicious social pressures within Bohemia, 1626 dawned fairer for the hopes of the domestic population as of the exiles. It seemed to promise a new and effective continuation of the fight against the Habsburgs. The broad coalition of Holland, England, Denmark and Lower Saxony, joined by Frederick of the Palatinate, was calculated to renew the struggle on all fronts against both branches of the dynasty, while the alliance reached at the end of the year with Bethlen Gabor recalled to life the eastern offensive which had played such a significant part during the revolt of 1618–20. The opening of the Danish war showed that the conflict had finally outgrown its central European dimensions and was becoming a confrontation to involve the whole continent; it now directly embraced the two great powers of the Atlantic seaboard as the latter extended their traditional opposition to Habsburg universalism into the German military theatre.

Many Czech emigrants had been employed in the Danish army since early 1625, and even after Wallenstein's victory at Dessau Bridge in April 1626 halted Mansfeld's advance into central Germany, Bethlen's campaign continued to offer the hope of an occupation of the Bohemian lands and a new threat to Vienna. This expectation was strengthened by reports from Upper Austria where the peasant rising was diverting a major portion of the Imperialist troops and preventing the Viennese government from mounting a full-scale campaign. In September Bethlen's horde joined with the Danes in west Slovakia and the stage was set for a determined attack on Wallenstein's positions. But as we have seen the Hungarian front proved a failure and Bethlen played his usual double game. The Danish army was able to maintain itself for a time on the borders of Moravia, backed by the local émigrés under Žerotín, and even briefly to occupy a considerable portion of the country. But its defeat was turned into a rout after Bethlen's truce with the Emperor and, lacking either territorial base or links with its home country, it was destroyed during July 1627 by Wallenstein.

Although the course of military operations during 1626 demonstrated that the Protestants had little prospect of success, the very renewal of war was not without its effect on the Bohemian peasantry. It provoked active opposition to the landlords and the government in parts of the province of Boleslav (Bunzlau), and around Trutnov and Chrudim, while Čáslav and Kouřim rose in organized revolt. All these manifestations of consistent discontent were suppressed by soldiery; the Vlachs of Moravia being first isolated and then cruelly put down by Wallenstein at the end of 1627. Despite their failures another insurrection broke out around Hradec (Königgrätz) early in 1628, and this prospered well at first. Its firm organization in the hands of village magistrates and lesser nobles and its broad appeal showed that the roots of opposition to Habsburg pressure were still very much alive among all sections of the population. The danger of a common cause with the dissident Austrian peasantry, especially great when rebel orators began to appear in the neighbouring provinces of south Bohemia, forced the authorities in Vienna to redouble their security measures. The events of 1618–9 were still strongly impressed on the minds of both sides. With the conclusion of the Danish war at the Peace of Lübeck in 1629 and the major confiscations which followed in Germany, the Bohemian emigrants settled abroad or serving in foreign armies found their hopes again dashed. At home the unrest of the subject masses which had flared up in many more areas despite unfavourable circumstances was everywhere stifled by military means, and thousands more left the country.

During the years immediately following the executions of 1621 all expression of political opinion by the Bohemian Estates was silenced; even the loyal Catholic supporters of the Emperor dare not press their traditional rights or assert their rôle as joint decision-makers in state policy. Only after the far-reaching economic collapse caused by the subversion of the currency and the ravages of the soldiery, and a return to some administrative stability during 1624 could mild claims be heard from the newly-appointed officials for greater participation in the workings of government. But the Emperor still left all executive power in the hands of Karl von Liechtenstein, and when the revised Bohemian constitution was to be discussed he invited, beside his tried henchmen Liechtenstein, Slavata, Lobkovic and Martinic, only Albrecht Wallenstein. These politicians were themselves not united about how to reform the old order and therefore had no decisive force in the new arrangement: it was ultimately the court circles in Vienna which drew up the revised Form of Government (*Verneuerte Landesordnung*) which was proclaimed for Bohemia on 10 May 1627 and for Moravia on 1 July 1628. Under it the nobility and clergy remained the leading class in society and the Diet still possessed the formal right to approve taxation, but legislation and executive control were placed firmly in the hands of the monarch, while the king's exclusive prerogative to grant patents of nobility made his absolute power henceforth inviolate. The *Verneuerte Landesordnung* became the greatest prop to dynastic rule in Bohemia for more than two centuries.

It was during these uneasy twenties of the seventeenth century that the political and military career of Albrecht von Wallenstein first reached its zenith. Around his personality more than any other was centred the destiny of Bohemia and central Europe; on him was concentrated the attention and hatred of his con-contemporaries, just as it is he who has most captivated the minds of posterity. It is therefore appropriate to consider him more closely now.

The twenty-year-old Wallenstein had gained his first experience of battle and military organization in the Hungarian wars against the Turks from 1604 onwards. There too, under General Basta, he was given a good grounding in tactics and came to know many Bohemian, Italian and French noblemen in Habsburg service. In 1608 he entered the retinue of Matthias and was able to observe the various groups and interests which were vying for influence in Bohemian domestic politics. During the agitation of 1619 he callously deserted the Moravian Estates, placed himself entirely at the Emperor's disposal and intervened with his own troops against Mansfeld and the Hungarians. The part played by his regiment in the battle of the White Mountain and the pacification of the country assured Wallenstein a place in leading Catholic circles, and from December 1621 when, as military commander in Bohemia, he was able to intervene directly in the fate of the defeated Estates, he began to build his fortunes on a firm economic foundation. By an agreement with the government dated November 1622 he took full possession of the lands of the Smiřický family, and this large complex of estates formed the base around which he assembled, mainly by confiscation, the territories in his later Duchy of Friedland. These early stages of Wallenstein's public career already show clearly the two quite contradictory aspects of his activity. His unique success was due to brutal and pitiless confiscations, yet he used his exceptional economic power differently from the many rich *parvenus* who simply oppressed and crushed the local population. On the Smiřický lands he not only retained the whole existing administrative organization under the chief steward Jeroným Bukovský of Neudorf, but upheld its Bohemian traditions of enlightened management, confirmed his peasant subjects in their mild patrimonial obligations, and protected them against the ravages of the *soldatesca*. In this, as in the maintenance of severe military discipline among his troops (in Germany no less than elsewhere), Wallenstein compares favourably with the horde of *condottieri* who descended like vultures on Bohemia after the White Mountain.

De Witte's consortium gave Wallenstein an exceptional opportunity to assert himself as one of the greatest landed proprietors in Bohemia, and by 1623 his possessions numbered some sixty manors and domains. Jičín, the old centre of the Smiřický administration, became the capital of his territories, the largest feudal complex in the country. His Duchy of Friedland took on increasingly the attributes of a sovereign political entity, with its system of fiefs, its right to mint coins etc. It thus provoked the attention and envy not only of the Bohemian nobility but of many foreigners, especially the magnates and princes in nearby Germany. Members of the lordly families of old Bohemia recognized Wallenstein's services to the Emperor and the Catholic religion, but they gradually took exception to his arrogant, often tactless behaviour and in time the Duke of Friedland was on good terms only with the Trčkas and the Kinskys. The holders of court office like Slavata and Schlick were drawn by the Viennese *camarilla* into the ranks of his adversaries.

The system of reliable economic management and the firm organization of military service were two pillars of Wallenstein's rise to pre-eminence in Bohemian society; he never neglected them and he raised them far above the general feudal standards of his time. Above all he laid weight on the principle that a prosperous peasantry was the main basis for any thriving economy. To this end he was prepared to subordinate the fervent counter-reformationary strivings of the commissions, and the Duchy of Friedland remained throughout his life a *terra felix* for the peasantry where the cycle of rural life continued to follow its accepted peaceful course. In the matter of providing for his army Wallenstein was more systematic than the normal military commander who left things largely to the arbitrary exactions of mercenaries. His demands were severe, especially in enemy territory, but they did not destroy the foundations of economic life for the local population. Strong and efficient management in Friedland yielded the major part of the necessary victuals and equipment. Wallenstein's qualities as a military leader have also been much discussed. He was trained in the Hispano-Italian school which recommended a vigorous attack on the strongest part of the front, but he could also apply the methods of the Dutch and Swedes with their stress on mobility within the army and taking advantage of weakness in the opponent's camp. He always insisted on powerful artillery, and was as well able to use the techniques of the defensive fortress and trench warfare as to manoeuvre his men with the latest show of flexibility. He laid great emphasis on the quality of his generals and here, as with his economic appointments, he took no account of the religious convictions or social background of his lieutenants. As early as the beginning of the 1620s the severe discipline of Wallenstein's troops contrasted sharply with the haphazard and uncontrolled arrangements of many of his colleagues.

Wallenstein's economic and political interests extended, like his military involvement, far beyond the frontiers of Bohemia, despite the hatred for him of German cities, princes and estates. The foundations of financial commitment at home and abroad had been laid by the Smiřickýs (among their major debtors was the Elector of Saxony), but Wallenstein's transactions far exceeded the bounds of credit operations before the revolt and became an important part of international commercial relations in central Europe. They could not but strengthen too the opposition to Wallenstein among the German high nobility and his competitors in trading communities there.

A self-confident and haughty aristocrat, politician and soldier, Wallenstein created for himself an inviolate domain where even the highest dignitaries from Vienna held no sway. This was a further source of enmity and led to the formation of a strongly prejudiced front among the most influential civil, military and ecclesiastical circles. As a Bohemian nobleman he did not conceal his distaste for Hungarians, Italians and Poles, and although he often used German in the administration of his estates, with his troops and for personal correspondence, his adversaries among the princes of the Empire considered him a Czech; that in itself was another cause of the jealousy and hatred which foreigners always displayed towards him.

On the conclusion of the war with Denmark and the breaking of the great alliance which had threatened to unite all Europe against the Habsburgs Wallenstein stood at the summit of his power and fame. Here however lay the weakness behind his remarkable rise: for he could not join the established order of German politics as an equal partner, but was inevitably cast as a formidable rival to the leading Electors and the dangerous exponent of a policy which had brought the Habsburgs to a position of long-coveted hegemony. At the *Reichstag* of Ratisbon in 1630 French and Bavarian diplomacy seized the first suitable opportunity to insist on his deposition before considering the election of Ferdinand's son as King of the Romans.

With Wallenstein stood or fell the Prague banker Jan de Witte, a co-religionist and countryman of the Swedish Dutchmen Louis de Geer and the Trips and the Danish Dutchman Marselis. De Witte was involved in Wallenstein's business enterprises, among them the iron works at Raspenau, but he was above all a source of credit for the *generalissimo*. He lent vast sums, risking personal indebtedness in the hope of subsequent compensation in the Empire. When Wallenstein was deprived of his command on 13 August 1630 his banker endured the catastrophe for less than a month. On September 11 De Witte, who was now discredited on the markets of Frankfurt and Hamburg, committed suicide in his house on the Mostecká in Prague's Kleinseite. His sons were later to occupy various ecclesiastical offices but his business vanished with him. The De Geers too were bankers and suppliers of arms, yet at the same time they were laying the foundations of Swedish iron production, and more indirectly of textile and machine manufacturing as well. De Witte, by contrast, resembled his master in staking all on military operations and his wealth was dissipated by the fortunes of armies. We must be cautious about assessing the character of Wallenstein's enterprise in the economic sphere: he and De Witte were more the preservers of established practices than pioneers of new capitalist initiative.

ZLÍN DURING THE DANISH WAR AND THE VLACH UPRISINGS

In the years 1625–30 Moravia was repeatedly crossed by Imperialist and Danish armies, its emigrants made vigorous efforts to regain power, and its Vlachs rejoined the opposition to the Habsburgs. All this was reflected in the small area we have selected as a microcosm of the whole: the town of Zlín and the lands which surrounded it. In the middle of the 1620s Zlín had about 150 resident families. This was a quarter less than had lived there before 1618. But its economic life still pursued a normal course, as far as one can speak of normality in a country so regularly occupied by foreign soldiers. The carefully kept town records, a legacy of former times, show that the administration of the town was still running in its old channels.

In 1625, when the threat from Hungary seemed definitely over and the landlords were able to return, there were important changes in the government of Zlín. The domain had no new lord yet; all the property which had belonged to the family of Cedlar before the rebellion, i.e. the lands of Zlín and Otrokovice, had been placed in the hands of seven executors at the Lenten sitting of the high court. There is no trace among them of the major creditors whose names appeared in the list drawn up only three years before. Most of these men had disappeared, many had gone abroad and their rights had lapsed. We now find among the executors important provincial officials and former servants of the Governor, Cardinal Dietrichstein. Only one of them was a Protestant and he soon became converted to the Catholic faith. The most substantial claim, but not a conclusive one, now belonged to two members of the knightly family, Podstatský of Prusinovice. Kryštof Karel Podstatský, the more important of them, had already displayed his loyalty to Dietrichstein, the Habsburgs, and the Catholic Church during the course of the rebellion and had been rewarded with the title of Imperial counsellor and the post of Chief Justice (*Obersthofrichter*) of the Margravate of Moravia. He and some of the other executors had belonged to the local confiscation commissions, cooperating with the court in Vienna to destroy the opposition of the Estates.

The first act of the executors was to dismiss the existing domain officials, above all Peter Kopřic, whose past behaviour made him unsuitable. In his place they appointed a relative of Podstatský's, George Adam Falkenhon of Glošek, another member of the petty knightage who had likewise been implicated in the rebellion and had suffered the forfeiture of his lands. Unlike Kopřic however, Falkenhon had quickly adapted himself to changed circumstances, utilizing his ties of blood with the Catholic Podstatský, and by the middle of the 1620s he once again held a number of small estates in southern and eastern Moravia. Besides Zlín and Otrokovice he also managed the lands of Vsetín, formerly the property of Wallenstein and now of his colleague Zdeněk Žampach of Potenstein, another firm supporter of the Habsburgs who had nevertheless protested against the confiscations by referring to the compact of 1609 and the text of the royal coronation oath.

Falkenhon's was no easy task. All these domains had suffered in recent years. Zlín's situation after the latest invasion was so serious that he had to permit the citizens to forgo their payments on purchases of real estate. He selected from among the inhabitants a new mayor and magistrates who were to remain in office just as long as the bailiff himself. Soon after Falkenhon had taken up his duties it became clear that another storm was imminent. The harvest of 1626 was gathered in under the shadow cast by the approaching soldiers of Mansfeld and the Danes. After them came the Imperialist troops in pursuit from the north, first the divisions of Colonel Pechmann and at length the whole army of Wallenstein. Noble families and wealthy burghers fled through Zlín to the fortified cities of Hradiště and Brno. The chronicler of nearby Holešov has left a colourful description of these two armies pressing from Přerov and Olomouc through Hulín, Kremsier and Uherský Brod into Hungary in the early September days of 1626. The main line of march did not touch Zlín and the passage of the troops was so swift that no serious damage seems to have been done there. At least there is no trace of it in the town records.

The departure of the main military forces did not bring peace. The end of September saw the return to Moravia of Jan Adam of Víckov, the old lord of Vsetín, who soon secured once again the allegiance of his former subjects and the inhabitants of the other "Vlach" lands: Vizovice, Lukov and Zlín. On the last day of the month the castle of Lukov, a short distance from Zlín, which then belonged to the Protestant financial expert Stephan Schmidt von Freyhofen, opened its gates to the rebel leader. Shortly afterwards (October 21) the Danes and their allies among the peasantry seized the town of Hranice. Sydnam Pointz, an English participant in Mansfeld's campaign, attributed the fall of Hranice to the bravery of his companion, the Scot Sandilands, but in fact it is known that the town was surrendered without a fight, and its citizens were later punished for their perfidy. Mansfeld and the Danes now took Meziříčí and Nový Jičín, while the Vlachs occupied a series of similar settlements. The whole of eastern Moravia on the left bank of the Morava was either in their hands or controlled by leading representatives of the Estates like Víckov. Zlín could not avoid a visitation from the Vlach "freemen" and the worst sufferer from their incursion was the newly-appointed magistrate Elias Bystřický whose house was pillaged from top to bottom. He was regarded as an enemy by his fellow citizens as well, since they were involved in the attack and some of them were later found to have part of the magistrate's property in their possession. On his own admission Bystřický had buried his belongings in a pit somewhere beneath the house or its garden; it is therefore clear that he had been expecting an extended intrusion from his unwelcome guests.

The Vlachs, Víckov and the Danes held the environs of Zlín until April 1627, while skirmishes continued between the Imperialists in Kremsier and the insurgent peasants in Holešov. During the whole of this time Falkenhon the bailiff was almost powerless. It was not until August 1627, long after the Danish retreat northwards, that the Imperialist forces under Don Baltazar de Marradas ventured an attack against the Vlachs. On

August 13 they recovered Holešov and by the middle of October they were in possession of Lukov. Sometime between these two dates Marradas' Spanish troops appeared in Zlín, bringing with them yet more destruction and suffering.

The autumn of 1627 saw continual irregular fighting in the Beskyd mountains and at some stage Jan Adam of Víckov disappears for ever from the stage. This luckless kinsman and rival of the Imperialist *generalissimo* was also a neighbour of his fellow-Protestant Falkenhon, though we do not know how close was the connection between the two men. What is certain is that Falkenhon was replaced in Zlín and Otrokovice as soon as stability had been restored after the withdrawal of the Danes and the suppression of the Vlach rebellion. He was evidently not trusted. His successor was George Albrecht Křen of Lhodce, a member of an impoverished landed family who possessed only a few freeholds around some of the little towns of central Moravia, among them perhaps one or two episcopal fiefs. He was installed by the will of the "guardian and administrator of the lordship of Zlín", a title which by 1628 concealed the single person of Kryštof Karel Podstatský. The other six executors mentioned by the high court three years earlier were already nowhere to be seen.

Podstatský and his bailiff owed their presence in Zlín to the will of the Imperial government operating through its representative, Cardinal Dietrichstein. Like the Bishop of Olomouc, they too were pillars of the Catholic religion, and it is therefore no surprise that the town witnessed from the end of 1628 a wave of counter-reformationary oppression and an intensified exploitation of the peasantry. Late that year we find the Zlíners humbly entreating their Lord Cardinal to send them a Catholic priest. At a time when Italian missionaries were complaining that their pastoral work in east Moravia was abortive, that all the inhabitants were Wallachians and hence utterly refractory, this was a request to warm Dietrichstein's heart. There was however a shortage of priests and thus the re-catholicizing could not be expected to proceed quickly. The old literary circle was changed into a "Brotherhood of the Virgin Mary and the saintly Virgin Barbara" and the Cardinal promised to send at least a teacher to Zlín. The privations of recent years and the disappointment of their last hopes in 1626–7 had evidently broken the resistance of the Protestant Zlíners, or at least weakened it. They anyway refused to regard themselves as "Wallachians", since the solid burgherdom of the town looked askance at those shepherds and poor farmers of the mountains; it thus even proved possible a little later to employ the citizens of Zlín as a tool of oppression against the more obstinate peasants of the surrounding domain.

These were the inhabitants of the village of Kudlov which lay on the crest of the Vizov hills to the south-east of Zlín and belonged at the beginning of the seventeenth century to the Cedlar family. In November 1629 "all the people in the patrimony of Kudlov in the Margravate of Moravia" turned to the Emperor Ferdinand II with a written supplication that he defend them against their master Kryštof Karel Podstatský of Zlín. Among their grievances they assert that the new overlord does not recognize the privileges which they have been granted by the Cedlars: "Since this patrimony or village of ours called Kudlov has only recently been settled and is situated in an upland valley amongst the mountains, rocks and forests, in a place not very suitable for the sowing of seed", they beg to be granted the help they need as new tenants. "Since we, like our ancestors before us, are working in such a stubborn place, in a stony, flinty and rocky district impossible to plough and cultivate, full of hillocks and rough pasture and surrounded by mountains, we must labour hard for our daily bread." They are only able to maintain themselves through the right to graze their cattle for a small charge (presumably in the lord's forests), to collect wood, and above all to pay a prescribed sum of money instead of doing *robot*. Podstatský however would not recognize the "freemen" of Kudlov, and had begun to demand from them "excessive and unheard-of *robot* obligations". When the villagers refused to perform these, an official from Zlín accompanied by townsmen came three times to Kudlov, arresting the men, beating the women, seizing their cattle and imposing the will of his master.

This bold letter reached the Bohemian Court Chancery in Vienna and was forwarded by it for an opinion to the Moravian governor Dietrichstein, who of course promptly informed Podstatský of its contents. The latter replied to the supplication with an extensive disclaimer, stressing that he was only one of the poor executors who were forced to take care of a devastated sequestered domain which none of them wanted. This smacked of rank hypocrisy since Podstatský was really very much concerned about those "estates in a corner of the mountains among the Wallachians which have frequently been attacked by rebels and lie dangerously close to Hungary". In his view the resistance of the men of Kudlov should be broken by force. Even during the time of Karel Žerotín's *hejtmanship* the peasants of Vilímov in northern Moravia had been punished for much less defiance. According to Podstatský the villagers were not paupers: not one of their mountain homes had been burned by the soldiery and they themselves had taken advantage of the situation "to remain in a state of disobedience ever since the start of the insurrection". And if Kudlov wished to vaunt its privileges of old, then Podstatský recalled the existence of a document which his subjects would readily have overlooked. According to the agreement with Kryštof Cedlar concluded in 1608 they were required to provide every week one day of manual *robot* and one day with a team of horses on the farm at Zbožensko. Since Zbožensko had been gutted by the enemy Podstatský now intended to transfer its *robot* quota to the manor of Zlín itself.

Podstatský's account, dated 28 December 1629, reached Vienna in the following February and was soon followed by a new complaint from Kudlov which alleged that the bailiff Křen had locked up one of the nearby farmers and misappropriated 17 head of cattle. In addition he was compelling the villagers to buy fish and wine from the authorities, a requirement which had never existed before. At length Vienna issued an Imperial resolution of 28 February 1630 by which Dietrichstein was to order Podstatský to return the "cattle and other possessions and property" of the men of Kudlov, and cease his monopoly on the sale of fish and wine. The disputes about *robot* and forest rights were to be decided by the high court. But here the matter became submerged in a sea of similar suits and we can conclude that Dietrichstein's faithful servant had little trouble.

Podstatský behaved superficially like an executor of the old Cedlar estates, but only when it suited him to do so. It was growing clear that he had come to stay in Zlín as overlord in his own right. He had before him the shining example of his Eminence the Cardinal who made no bones about seizing the far more important domains of Lipník and Hranice by a *coup de main* and using them, with sublime disregard for the miseries of the impoverished heirs, as the economic foundation of his family's fortunes. The guarantors and creditors of the Cedlars do not seem to have had much of a return for their money from Zlín and Otrokovice during the 1620s and they probably preferred that these lands should pass into the hands of someone who could make more of them than mere executors.

At the end of the decade the state of the Zlín domains was no better than before. Most of the villages were burnt-out shells and many of the houses in the town had suffered some degree of damage. In 1630 payments on purchases of real estate had again to be suspended and subjects were relieved of money dues and Imperial taxation for three years. At the same time we find Podstatský being named as landlord and "our gracious master". He proceeded to install another new bailiff, Václav Čerňák, who was – after the Dietrichstein custom – a commoner. Čerňák came from a family whose members had risen in the services of the Kaunitzes (Kounic) and other landowners in the vicinity of Uherský Brod.

The changing times showed themselves in further ways. The first Catholic priest appeared in Zlín, though not yet as a resident. George Nigrinus was pastor in the distant parishes of Slavičín and Lideč. The Zlíners unanimously regarded him as a "sound and proper minister to the faith", but it is highly doubtful whether the return of the citizens to the Catholic religion was really serious. The descendants of Protestant clergy were still living in the town and the marriage of the daughter of the "late lamented priest Matouš Jarna" was attended by all burghers of any standing.

We have seen that the Zlíners allowed themselves to be used by the authorities against the rebellious villagers of Kudlov, and the vanity of "civic" status may have played a part in this. But we must also recognize the virtues of the town community during these years: the upkeep of the school and the literary circle, the legacies to the poor and orphaned. The municipal court refused to employ informers, even when they might prove advantageous to the magistrates, and resolutely declined to try a certain Marina whom popular rumour accused of sorcery. Ten years after the beginning of the great war Zlín was in a ravaged condition, with a reduced population, a new and acquisitive landlord and a puppet, intimidated council. But the will to live was unbroken and it was soon to be shown that the Zlíners' attitude to the new régime was still overwhelmingly negative. The great Vlach rebellion of ten years later was to throw them once more, rich and poor alike, into the camp of the opposition.

Seven

THE SWEDISH WAR AND THE
FALL OF WALLENSTEIN, 1631–5

"THE BOHEMIAN QUESTION" AND THE ROLE OF WALLENSTEIN

LESS than a year after Ratisbon the entry of Sweden into the war and the first great successes of Gustavus Adolphus wrought a decisive change in that balance of forces which Wallenstein's arms had created. They involved the Bohemian lands directly in the fighting once again and were the immediate cause of Wallenstein's second fateful generalship. The victory of the Swedes at Breitenfeld in September 1631 brought the theatre of war to the borders of Bohemia; the Czech emigrants were filled with new hope – to which Comenius's reform plans bore witness – and even the subjected population at home gained revived strength.

In November 1631, eleven years after the White Mountain, the Saxon army advanced into Bohemia, bringing in its train large numbers of noble and burgher *émigrés* with Matthias Thurn at their head and groups of Protestant clergy, among them the celebrated Samuel Martinius of Dražov. They promptly set about the recovery of estates confiscated in the intervening years and either entered military service or reorganized the administration and taxation system throughout the country. The invasion also raised the hopes of some Catholic converts for a return of old times. But there were cautious and mistrustful exiles who had left Bohemia immediately after the White Mountain and now used the Saxon occupation to dispose of their former property for good.

The hopes of wide sections of the population that the arrival of Saxon troops would bring not only religious liberty and the restoration of property but also immediate relief from high taxation and other burdensome obligations were soon set at nought. This army too had to be financed from public revenues, and ten commissioners of the new government of Directors sought individual loans from wealthy nobles and burghers. The Saxon presence was an especially heavy burden for the towns which had to find billets, food and fuel for the soldiers. When we consider that the citizens of the New Town of Prague paid out 666,202 florins within six and a half months from 15 November 1631 to 25 May 1632) it becomes clear that the occupation, although short, could ruin not only the civic exchequer and municipal credit but also do extensive damage to the economic position of the private burgher.

It was not simply the old Estates, decimated by confiscations and emigration, which drew strength from the Saxon campaign in Bohemia. Many of the peasantry, who had felt the full brunt of misery and destruction since 1621, found an active enthusiasm to take part in the war against the Emperor. Kryštof Čabelický of Soutice and David Chlumčanský of Přestavlky gathered together major contingents from the countryside and brought them to the assistance of the Saxon divisions. But these and other attempts to create an anti-Habsburg front within the country were largely frustrated by the duplicity of the Elector John George who hindered both the recruitment of troops for the *émigré* Czechs and the international recognition of the new Directorate in Prague.

Wallenstein, hurriedly recalled by an anxious Emperor, spent the winter months of 1631–2 organizing a new army which as early as May 1632 was strong enough to drive the Saxons out of Bohemia. The consequences of their brief occupation were severest for those who had supported the invading army in any way, above all from an official position. New confiscation commissions were set up to judge offenders; they were ordered to defray Wallenstein's military expenses, and proceeded to dispossess any person who had taken part in Arnim's campaign or served in the Swedish army. Among these were many who had lost part of their property by sequestration during the twenties and were now reduced almost to nothing. A brief glance at the figures is revealing: Wallenstein's commissions involved property worth nearly three million florins and 330 individuals: 16 lords, 126 knights and about 190 burghers. They dealt a new blow to an economic and social system which was anyway still suffering from the profound dislocation and recession since 1621.

The Saxon episode could not awake any real sympathy, either in Bohemia or among the exiles, for the selfish and cunning Elector John George. Aspirations were now becoming centred on the dynamic figure of Sweden's king and war-leader, Gustavus Adolphus. The latter's death in the battle of Lützen (November 1632) was a severe loss to the Czech emigrants both of the earlier and the new diaspora, many of whom perished with him on the field, but the military and political prestige of the Swedish army continued undimmed. For the Protestants of Bohemia it was the one guarantee of a fight to the finish with the Habsburgs: large numbers of nobles and townsmen were prepared to sacrifice their lives in its service. Some Czechs reached high rank: the Quartermaster-General Linhart of Štampach for example, and the famous Commander Zdenek Hodický of Hodice, and it was these military circles which held most resolutely to the belief that their own personal involvement could help crown with success the struggle against Habsburg absolutism.

As a result of Lützen, the revived power of Wallenstein reached its apogee in 1633. He did not intend to see it snatched away again by his own passivity. Through the tangled international situation and the tense domestic conditions within the Habsburg lands he perceived a line of action which could bring a decisive turn in European politics. From January 1633 he renewed his secret negotiations with the Saxons and the Bohemian *émigrés* but added to them new, wider contacts with Sweden and France; in August of the same year Richelieu's ambassador in Dresden passed on concrete French proposals to the *generalissimo* via Vilém Kinsky and Adam Trčka. By September a powerful anti-Habsburg alliance between Sweden, France and Saxony had been negotiated and waited upon Wallenstein's decision. At this crucial moment however, when a clear resolution was needed, either for the Emperor or against him, Wallenstein proved unable to take the final step. His hesitancy strengthened both the extreme suspicion of him in Vienna, where, as we have seen, he had numerous influential enemies, and the mistrust of his potential allies. Only in December 1633 was Wallenstein willing to come to terms with Saxony, England, Sweden and France, but now it was the suspicions of Dresden and Stockholm which delayed an outcome. By this time the grievously threatened Emperor had already set in motion his counter-attack; the destiny of the Duke of Friedland was moving to its tragic conclusion.

The murder of Wallenstein at Eger (Cheb) in February 1634

ended the life of a man who for all his less attractive characteristics and brutal thoroughness left a unique personal mark on the political, economic and military developments of his time. Wallenstein had collected around him a group of leading Bohemian magnates and created a territory, embracing almost half of Bohemia proper, whose style and economic methods became the model for many other estates throughout the country. This politico-economic block stretched from the Kinsky domains in the north through the extensive Duchy of Friedland itself to the lands of the Trčkas which occupied large areas of eastern Bohemia as far as the border with Moravia. It is understandable that the vast possessions of Wallenstein and his collaborators were a very tempting, though apparently unattainable prize for all the *condottieri* of those acquisitive times who relished the prospect of quick material gain. While the Duke of Friedland and his lieutenants lived, their whole broad expanse of order and social equilibrium remained forbidden fruit, protected from the depredations of war and plunder. But in a period which recognized no binding moral obligations and prided itself on disrespect for rights and traditions it was natural for covetous minds, both in Vienna and near at hand, to seize on any chance of eliminating the creator of this enclave, since Wallenstein was anyway the rival of the court and the all-powerful Jesuits, as of the ambitious and deceitful princes of Germany. The sharp, sometimes distinctly coarse judgments of the *generalissimo* on his opponents, from Maximilian of Bavaria and Cardinal Dietrichstein down to lesser officials and commanders, could only add fuel to the smouldering resentment.

These psychological motives however, deeply rooted as they were in the thinking of Wallenstein's enemies, were not the only driving force behind their actions. In the last analysis it was more than personal hatreds and a mere transfer of land between individuals which encompassed Wallenstein's downfall: the fundamental issue was his economic system *versus* the extreme advocates of feudal absolutism. The old and tried methods of Bohemian estate management which had brought prosperity in the years before the White Mountain were being challenged by the ideology and material interests of a new world of foreign soldiers and civil careerists, bent on greater extortions from the great mass of the peasantry. Neither Wallenstein nor his friends wished to increase the lucrativeness of their lands along these lines, and their resolute maintenance of established traditions brought both an efficiency and an inherent social stability (clearest of all in the mild forms of *robot* demanded from their subjects) which were the envy of all central Europe. The other, more brutal tendency, founded on far more extensive exactions in labour and money payments, was already being introduced into Bohemia during Wallenstein's lifetime by the régime, the army and some nobles, but until his fall it remained rather a threat; the existence of the Duchy of Friedland was the last guarantee of tolerable living conditions for the peasantry. The grudging recognition of Wallenstein's great organizational abilities and economic vision is a common undertone in the coarse invective of his enemies, scattered through Bohemia, Austria and Germany.

Wallenstein's links with the Bohemian *émigrés* in the Swedish army, above all the still influential Matthias Thurn, provided him with some support for his domestic policies, while at the same time raising a series of problems of which the greatest was restitution of confiscated estates. The latter was certainly a factor in Wallenstein's hesitation about offering definite terms to his allies, and yet it cannot have been decisive. There were enough crown and ecclesiastical lands in Bohemia as well as domains in pawn to satisfy most of the emigrants' needs, and the *generalissimo* had no time for the new upstart landlords from abroad. His distaste for them he never concealed.

The problem of Wallenstein's indecisiveness and delays during the last months of his life is a crucial one for any interpretation of the causes of his downfall. It must be stressed that they were not just the result of character failings or poor health, but stemmed also from the diplomatic methods of the time (politicians great and small would rarely follow a simple course with no mental reservations) and the realities of the situation at the end of 1633. Wallenstein could not rely unreservedly on the Swedes, whose main army was now led by Bernard of Saxe-Weimar, or the distant French, who were still not directly involved in the war, still less on the wavering Elector of Saxony. And in Vienna the atmosphere of mistrust, aggravated by the tactics of Maximilian of Bavaria, was sufficient to convince the court that any rumour directed against Wallenstein was true. The defensive tactics of the *generalissimo* late in 1633 were abundantly justified in the terms of his appointment, but the news of Swedish success during that winter gave his enemies a welcome opportunity to interpret his diplomacy as treason. The Emperor resolved to break the tension and deep suspicion by a preventive measure: the elimination of a dangerous figure who, since the death of Gustavus Adolphus, once again occupied an unrivalled military and political eminence in Germany. The brutality of the Eger murders of February 1634 followed partly from the intentional ambiguity of Ferdinand's instructions, partly from the acquisitive greed of *condottieri* like Piccolomini and Gallas.

Let us consider finally the specifically Bohemian context of Wallenstein's death. The Duchy of Friedland, which lay for the most part in a very fertile part of the country, had been raised by the care of its owner into a position where its administrative methods outshone not only the estates of the richest magnate families, but also those of the crown. It was therefore necessarily seen as a competitor both by the greatest landed aristocrats and by the most powerful property owner of all, the sovereign. Even where Wallenstein was using his economic strength in the interests of Imperial and state policy, it was easy to persuade the morbidly suspicious Ferdinand that this overmighty subject was an unwelcome economic rival, and from there it was only a step to the fear that the Duke was a political opponent of the newly-acquired absolutism of the monarch. Such anxieties were increased by Wallenstein's success in building up institutions which carried all the panoply of sovereignty for his Duchy – his system of fiefs, his mint and special coinage, his "capital" of Jičín. The notion of the King's absolute power, which together with the Catholic Church was the chief bearer of the theory of state as reflected in the *Landesordnung* of 1627, stopped short at the boundaries of Wallenstein's domains. The jealousies and suspicions of Vienna on this score thus came together with the strains caused by Wallenstein's position within the Bohemian nobility. His material resources and military success now guaranteed him first place among that group of aristocrats whose older members had been active at a time, not long past, when the voice of a few leading magnates had largely decided the course of domestic and foreign policy. In them the haughty self-assurance of the Czech noble lived on, a pride whose traces were evident even among the loyal Catholics who debated with the Emperor over the *Verneuerte Landesordnung*. There was a permanent danger that Wallenstein's attitude might spread to wider sections of the nobility and threaten the Habsburg edifice at its weakest point. Here again appeared the central and most potent argument which finally weighed with the vacillating Emperor, the bond which held together all the links in the chain of enmity. The very repercussions of Wallenstein's fall, the revelation that some of his lieutenants (Schaffgotsch and others) had been active in Troppau and parts of Silesia, demonstrated that public opinion still looked to Sweden and in lesser degree Saxony for release from the Habsburgs; an important element throughout Bohemian society was still ready to resort to arms against the dynasty.

Only the confiscation of the estates of Albrecht von Wallenstein, Jan Rudolf and Adam Erdman Trčka of Lípa and Vilém Kinský of Vchynice completed the revolution within the Bohemian landed order, and set a seal upon it. Whole territories in the north, east and centre of the country passed into the hands of foreigners sublimely indifferent to the traditions of Czech politics and economic management, in all things the willing tools of successive Habsburg Emperors. Those confines which had earned the epithet of *terra felix* now shared the bitter fate of the rest of Bohemia and became a *terra deserta*. Among Wallenstein's 24 estates the old Smiřický patrimony of Kumburk had maintained pride of place, and its capital Jičín was also the Duke's favourite residence; it was now valued at 500,000 florins, while several others (Friedland, Nový Zámek, Hořice Kost etc.) were estimated at between 150–300,000. The vassal domains, fiefs of the Duchy, showed by their number (there were 55 of them) and value (almost 1,800,000 florins) how systematically and extensively Wallenstein had made himself the protector of a class of country knights; their significance as skilled commanders of his armies and administrators of his properties we have already observed.

The valuation of the Wallenstein estates was fixed at the enormous sum of 9,280,000 florins; the possessions of his faithful colleagues, the Trčkas and Kinsky, were worth almost half as much. The lands of Jan Rudolf Trčka, among whose 21 domains the most important were Ledeč, Světlá and Smiřice, brought the Emperor over three million gulden through confiscation and sale. Those of his son Adam Erdman, valued at 870,000 florins, were sufficient to found the fortunes of the Piccolomini family in Náchod and the Colloredos in Opočno. A similar destiny awaited the patrimony of Vilém Kinsky around Teplitz and Česká Kamenice which was estimated at more than 600,000 florins.

From the Bohemian point of view the downfall of Wallenstein meant above all the interruption of those progressive economic tendencies which he had represented as Duke of Friedland and successor to the Smiřickýs. But with him there disappeared other features of Bohemian "civilization" as it had existed before 1620: rationality, religious tolerance and the habits of mind which had made the Prague court of Rudolph II a pioneer in many fields from alchemical speculation to the politics of equilibrium, and the reconciliation of opposites. In all this the tragic course of the "Bohemian question" was set by the events of 1620; the personal drama of Albrecht Wallenstein was just the most spectacular of its manifestations.

Wallenstein was gone, but his former comrades-in-arms remained. Those who had come to terms with the court in time, and made common cause with the Spanish party headed by the Viennese ambassador Oñate and the *generalissimo's* old rival Marradas, were rewarded with parts of the patrimony of Friedland. Neither Marradas himself on his south Bohemian estate of Hluboká, nor the other Spaniards like Verdugo at Doupov or the Huertas, were to found permanent magnate dynasties. Most of Wallenstein's murderers were similarly short-lived: Butler died soon after his master, the Leslies were extinguished during the eighteenth century at Nové Mesto on the Metuje, the old Trčka preserve. But the families of Gallas around Friedland, Aldringen at Teplitz, Colloredo at Opočno and Dobříš, Piccolomini at Náchod survived for centuries, in some cases until after the Second World War, like the Dietrichsteins and Liechtensteins. Surprisingly the remaining Waldsteins never made any attempt to rehabilitate their famous kinsman, nor to reverse the judgment of the confiscation commission (Wallenstein himself had anyway not contested the dispossessing of his countrymen in the 1620s). Josef Pekař, who quite properly saw the fate of Wallenstein as a tragedy for Bohemia, nevertheless exaggerated the "Czech" character of his political programme, just as the Austrian scholar Heinrich von Srbik laid too much weight on its "German" aspects.

Part of his programme was to survive in some of the young men who had grown up around Wallenstein. It was not realized in his nephew and heir Maximilian Waldstein who managed to retain for himself a few of the family estates centred on Münchengrätz (Mnichovo Hradiště) and Třebíč. But it can be seen in the son of the High Chancellor Zdenek Lobkovic, Václav Eusebius, who later became chief minister at the court of Leopold I. Lobkovic, like Wallenstein, fell at length into Imperial displeasure and learned, if only in exile on his domain of Roudnice, the fickleness of Habsburg favour. He too could comprehend problems in their full breadth and the realism of his vision was then passed on to others like the Kinskys and Kaunitzes. Maria Theresa's great Chancellor ranks with his boundless sphere of interests, his chill calculating rationality, and his idiosyncracies as the last great *condottiere* of the seventeenth century.

The economic developments which were so brutally cut short in 1620 and 1634 were later to be pursued by the sons and grandsons of Wallenstein's very murderers. On the Friedland estates the Gallases instigated such terrors of exploitation that the area was one of the centres of the great peasant revolt in 1680, but ten years later we find a quite different situation. It was the encouragement of cottage industry and the export of cloth and other manufactures which provided Johann Wenzel Gallas with the basis for his political career as ambassador to Rome, the Hague and London, and as Viceroy to Naples.

In 1634 Wallenstein was in his grave. Gone too were Frederick the Palsgrave, who had died at the same time as Gustavus Adolphus, and many of his Bohemian lieutenants. Others, among them Frederick's Chancellor Wilhelm Ruppa, had been broken by the failure of the Saxon invasion. The traditional order of Bohemia was in its last throes.

THE PETTY WALLENSTEINS OF MORAVIA

Although Moravia and Silesia treasured very few favourable memories of Wallenstein, it was there that the last repercussions of his death were felt. In Silesia the Viennese court hurriedly moved against the second great concentration of the *generalissimo's* supporters and their troops. Wallenstein's intimate colleague General Schaffgotsch was seized at Troppau in the middle of February 1634 and later executed. The new commander of the Imperialist armies, Götz, dispatched his military commissar Samuel Schneider of Lilienfeld to imprison the leader of Schaffgotch's regiment, Lieutenant-Colonel Freiberger, and hand him over to Wallenstein's old foe Count Schlick.

Schneider however was evidently privy to the conspiracy and warned Freiberger, who could not yet have known of Wallenstein's death, that his arrest was imminent. Freiberger acted quickly, and on 2 March, a week after the *generalissimo's* murder, he made his troops swear an oath of loyalty to the Duke of Friedland and his "allies" the Electors of Saxony and Brandenburg. He managed to bring most of the citizens of Troppau and some of the local gentry onto the side of the rebellion. A Czech preacher appeared in the town and tried to restore the Protestant religion. With the help of authorizations bearing the Troppau municipal seal and signed by Estates' representatives from the Principalities of Troppau, Jägerndorf and Ratibor, Freiberger now sought to organize military opposition among the nobles, towns and garrisons of Upper Silesia. His infantry was joined by dragoons from Czech regiments and it was expected that the insurrection would be supported by soldiers quartered in nearby Moravia. Proclamations called for a fight against the Emperor, the destroyer of the *Reich* and the exterminator of the true faith, and for the conclusion of peace with the assistance of the Saxons and Swedes. Their author was probably the commissar Schneider.

Of the towns, only Jägerndorf and Hlubčice joined the rebels. Then the news was received of Wallenstein's death and an Imperialist army appeared before Troppau. Freiberger surrendered on 20 March and was sent to Vienna for punishment. Schneider, two burghers and one rustic who had served as courier were beheaded in Troppau at the end of March and the town was laid under indemnity. The "Troppau rebellion", however short-lived, is proof that in 1634 there were still many in Silesia who opposed the Habsburgs: townsmen, Czech Protestant clergymen, sections of the nobility and peasantry. It may be presumed that this would have been the social composition of any rising against the dynasty.

Meanwhile the "Moravian regiment", on which the conspirators of Troppau were counting, seems to have remained inactive. Wallenstein had few friends in Moravia. His subjects on the lands of Lukov and Vsetín had preferred Jan Adam of Víckov and been glad to be rid of his presence. The town chroniclers have little good to report of his armies, most of his fellow-nobles had long been estranged, and the head of the Habsburg régime in the country, Cardinal Dietrichstein, was one of his bitterest enemies. But there were dozens of people in Moravia who could look back on long years of collaboration with Wallenstein and among the nobility were some of his relatives and old colleagues. The sons of the High Burgrave Adam Waldstein were settled at Třebíč, and the *generalissimo's* brother-in-law Karel Žerotín was living temporarily in Přerov. Žerotín heard of the murder through Count Jiří of Náchod who with Žampach of Potenstein had once stood very close to Wallenstein. Žerotín knew nothing of the negotiations with Protestant Europe and his relations with

Wallenstein were fairly lukewarm. His reactions appear from a letter written to Náchod on 6 March 1634: "As the tree, so is the fruit; as the labour, so the recompense; as the service, so the reward."

Within the small Catholic party in Moravia there were several lesser epigones of Wallenstein, and a comparison of their careers with his allows us to form a sober judgment of the *generalissimo's* remarkable qualities. One of them was Kryštof Karel Podstatský, whom we have already encountered as lord of Zlín from 1630. Podstatský never became a great entrepreneur or leader of men, but the course of his life ran parallel in some ways to that of Wallenstein. Both came from the same kind of social background: noble families which were not unimportant, but possessed no extensive landed estates – Kryštof Karel's father owned three small domains in central Moravia and was related by marriage to the Silesian Falkenhons of Glošek, members of the local *noblesse de robe*. Both were orphans early in life, though this was nothing extraordinary in an age when expectation of life was only about 40 years. Podstatský and his three brothers, coming from a family whose religious allegiance was divided, received a Catholic education, perhaps at the Jesuit College in Olomouc – certainly Kryštof Karel later sent his own sons there and was regarded by the Society as a benefactor. Wallenstein was of course brought up a Protestant, but it was probably the Olomouc Jesuits who arranged his first marriage with Lucrezia Neksech of Landeck and thus set him on his way into the ranks of the Moravian Catholic nobility. Both Wallenstein and Podstatský gained their first public office during the 1610s with the backing of the local Catholic hierarchy. Wallenstein improved his material position by making an advantageous marriage, while Podstatský too showed ambition in this direction: his first bride was Marie Magdalena Bruntálský of Vrbna whose kith and kin were the greatest families in the land, among them the Žerotíns and hence, indirectly, Wallenstein himself, for Wallenstein's second wife was a Žerotín.

After this their paths separated. Wallenstein went off to seek advancement on the battlefields of Hungary and Friuli; Podstatský occupied until 1619 the post of chief episcopal justice in Kremsier and steward of the civil code of Olomouc. When Colonel Waldstein vanished from Olomouc with the Estates' war-chest, Kryštof Karel was seized and imprisoned for six months in the town hall. But his brother Tas Václav Podstatský, although a Catholic, joined the rebellion and, according to tradition, fought against the Emperor at the White Mountain with a rosary in his hand. Their cousin Jan Štastný Podstatský, lord of Podštat and Bartošovice, a man of learning and by far the richest of the three, was a Protestant and therefore automatically on the side of revolt.

Kryštof Karel was soon rewarded for his loyalty. He became commissioner to Cardinal Dietrichstein when the latter returned to Moravia as governor, and was responsible for drawing up inventories of confiscated property. His services soon earned him first the episcopal fief of Stará Ves, then Zborovice, and through his second wife, the Austrian Anna Salomena von Poisbrunn, he inherited Uhřice. He naturally took steps to protect his new property against marauding soldiers. When in 1622 he requested Dietrichstein to guarantee the defence of Uhřice, the Cardinal ordered "that he should draw up his complaints against the army in German", since not even the governor himself could understand Czech, let alone the military commanders. Potstatský replied in Czech again, with the apology that he could "express himself tolerably in spoken German, but less well in the written form". He continued to write to the Cardinal in his vernacular, at least until 1629, but by 1625 we find him laboriously recording important family details in a miserable broken German.

In 1623, while Wallenstein was defending Hodonín against the Hungarians, Podstatský was hurriedly sent to Uničov to "disarm the town" and then to Uherské Hradiště as the "senior commissar for national defence". Neither Wallenstein nor Podstatský particularly distinguished himself at this time, but the former of course far outstripped the latter in his gains from confiscated property. Podstatský's brother, Tas Václav, had been turned into a pauper by the commissions, his cousin Jan Štastný seems to have saved himself with the help of his relatives by becoming a Catholic. Kryštof Karel announced that he had lost large sums through the default of noble debtors, among them the Cedlars of Zlín – and for this reason he was appointed one of their executors in 1625.

It was the same story with worldly honours. At a time when Wallenstein was already *generalissimo* and Duke of Friedland, Mecklenburg and Sagan (1627), Podstatský was raised into the lords' Estate with the title of baron, and his arms, a pair of silver horns on a red ground, augmented with a Bohemian lion set somewhat crestfallenly against a black background. The royal lion was anyway being granted to so many new nobles that it had lost its cachet, and the sable ground could please nobody.

From 1630 Podstatský took over Zlín permanently and became in practice the unchallenged lord of the manor. A legal transfer to him of the property seems never to have taken place (there is certainly no record of it in the national land registers) but it was evidently not regarded as a matter of great importance. Dietrichstein continued to call Podstatský the "executor of the domain of Zlín". From the time when he assumed his cousin Jan Šťastný's claims on the Cedlars, Kryštof Karel was the leading creditor, and he presumably satisfied the rest with annuities. Otrokovice and Zlín made up for Uhřice which he had been forced to sell. He lived mostly near his bishop in Olomouc, occupying the Cedlars' house there which had likewise fallen to him. Podstatský's situation took a distinct turn for the better in 1634, Wallenstein's fateful year. His cousin Jan Šťastný, chief scribe of the Margravate of Moravia, died and left him the estates of Bartošovice near Příbor and Liptáň near Moravský Beroun. But the Imperial service was no unfailing source of profit, and a further sign of the sovereign's favour, permission to change the black colour of his blazon to blue, was not able to settle Kryštof Karel's mounting debts. Despite a dowry of 10,000 gulden from his third wife Elizabeth Maria Pražma of Bílkov, the daughter of a rebel who had been condemned but later converted, pardoned and reinstated, Podstatský was at length forced to sell both Liptáň and Otrokovice. The loss of Otrokovice, which bordered on Zlín and was intimately linked with it, is clear testimony to the reduced circumstances of the provincial *hejtman* of Olomouc.

While Podstatský was engaged on official business his wife would stay at Zlín with his two eldest sons, George Valerian and Sigismund Andrew. Podstatský too liked to visit the town, since he was concerned to put his estate on its feet again as soon as possible. He therefore tried to force the municipal council to take in hand the rebuilding and reoccupying of deserted and burnt-out buildings. He had a new terrier made of his peasants' lands and incorporated any unclaimed plots within his own dominical portion.

Podstatský's will was carried out by his officials, who were no more fastidious in their methods than those of Dietrichstein. There were scarcely any noblemen among them; only one member of the local gentry was employed in Zlín: Andrew Bavorovský of Pingelt. His successor Bernard Minikator had once been with

Podstatský in the service of Dietrichstein and his life had been threatened in 1626 by the peasantry. After him came Václav and Jan Čerňák and Lorenz Handacz, son of a burgher from Olomouc. This "manager and book-keeper for all My Lord's estates" then settled in Zlín. But later (1641) Podstatský seized all his possessions in the town, just as ten years earlier Wallenstein had confiscated the property of the *hejtman* of the Duchy of Friedland, Gerhard Taxis.

We do not know the reasons for Podstatský's disagreement with Handacz, though it is certain that such officials were apt to operate in their own interests as much as those of their employers. No administration was easy during these years in Moravia, and the absence of open warfare between 1627 and 1637 only made things a little less bad. The situation was most critical in 1634 when the authorities had once again to grant a moratorium on debt repayments. At the same time the period which had been allowed by Podstatský in 1631 for rebuilding houses and farms destroyed by fire came to an end, and unrestored gutted properties were claimed by the landlord. In various ways Podstatský succeeded in extending his dominical holdings; only with the manual forces necessary to work on them was he less fortunate.

Even the most unscrupulous and acquisitive authorities were not able to break the peasants entirely. Who would pay the taxes, the contribution so vital to the state in time of war? Who would till his lordship's fields and offer up feudal dues to him? Podstatský was thus forced to moderate his demands, at least, as he imagined, for a temporary period, or he was threatened with having to bear the contribution himself. There was simply no money, and therefore the creditor, "seeing such a poverty-stricken community, waived the rest of the debt". The mayor and council, in their turn, relinquished claims on the population which they had had to defer year after year. Podstatský's intervention seems anyway to have produced little effect. Both the material and personal tragedies of the 1620s remained unhealed, as is shown by repeated instances of inhabitants being carried off into Turkish captivity. By the end of the 1630s Podstatský had returned the burnt-out and abandoned plots to his subjects' ownership.

Conditions during the 1630s brought no prospect of the economic recovery for which Podstatský so dearly longed. He knew as well as anyone that in this "Wallachian-infested outpost" it was not possible to push the peasantry too far. The example of the villagers of Kudlov was catching, and the mountains of the Hungarian border were close at hand. In the hills the flame of Vlach unrest still flickered and more than one rebel against authority found haven there. Meanwhile these diehards were ceasing to be a spectre to the citizens of Zlín: the Zlíners themselves now had very little more to lose.

We do not know whether the aging Podstatský had any idea of this change in mentality. What is certain is that his wife Elizabeth Mary employed people in her retinue who were wholly unsympathetic to the behaviour of the new landlord. Among them was Jiřík Ondrů, now also known as Facalka, many-times mayor of Zlín, who had married one of Mary Elizabeth's ladies-in-waiting, Kateřina Popov. It was during Jiřík's term of office in the twenties that the attacks of burghers on Imperialist troops had taken place, and he was the man who had forbidden any further discussion of the matter. He too had been instrumental in protecting Marina Sabášková against charges of witchcraft. He must have retained tempting memories of that period of power, and Jiřík Ondrů was one of those figures who come to the fore whenever danger and disaster threaten. Such a stormcloud, which called in question the whole fragile stability of Moravia since 1620, was growing among the Vlachs in the mountains from the beginning of the 1640s.

EUROPEAN POLITICS IN THE AGE OF GUSTAVUS ADOLPHUS AND WALLENSTEIN

In his pamphlet *A Trumpet for the Year of Grace* Comenius, standing on the threshold of the Swedish invasion of Germany, welcomed the "great monarch of the North" Gustavus Adolphus as a warrior against the Babylonian Emperor. His tract is rather a mirror of the mood of the Bohemian exiles than an accurate presentation of the real aims of Swedish policy. Gustavus Adolphus set foot on the shores of Pomerania in July 1630 with quite other intentions than the freeing of the Bohemian lands from the Habsburg-Catholic yoke. Such ephemeral literature which vaunted him as a great conqueror was of course welcome. It corresponded to the portrait painted by two manifestoes which were published in five languages at the time of the King's landing and distributed by Johann Adler Salvius. In them Gustavus is depicted as the saviour of the German Estates and the freedoms which they are unable to defend unaided. To his own royal council the king soberly admitted that his concern in Germany was not to thwart Spanish or Turkish plans for European hegemony but simply "to guarantee Sweden's position for a few years to come." Of course he was unable to overlook the "Bohemian question", especially in 1620 and 1625; but in both cases his correspondence reveals that he was not interested in Bohemia proper. It was Silesia and its strategic situation which attracted him as a chance to neutralize the hostility of Poland.

Gustavus was prepared to settle Czech emigrants in the Baltic lands which he had acquired in 1617 by the Peace of Stolbova, and in 1629 he named Matthias Thurn governor of Ingria after the latter had surrendered his post as commander of the Danish armies. But no kind of "New Bohemia" was to grow up beside the Baltic. Thurn was soon ordered back to Germany to canvass support for Swedish plans. These were in essence twofold: to ensure the security of the home country (*Utilitas et securitas patriae*) and to conquer an undefined area within the Empire (*occupatio Germaniae*). In no circumstances was the impression to be created that Sweden was entering on a religious war, for that would threaten the relationship with France which had just a few months earlier mediated the five-year truce with Poland and Altmark.

The Swedes and their King were also being backed by Moscovite Russia, where French agents had successfully worked on the regent, Patriarch Filaret. During the years 1628–33 the Russian government sold Sweden large quantities of corn which were then resold on the Amsterdam exchange at a fourfold profit. As well as such indirect financial support, Muscovy granted Gustavus Adolphus priority in the supply of the saltpetre necessary for making gunpowder. This assistance can be estimated as equivalent to the French subsidies which were transmitted by the entrepreneur and banker, Louis de Geer. The Swedes had every need of it, since they were not welcomed with open arms in north Germany. Only a few princes rose to support them: the Dukes of Pomerania, Mecklenburg-Strelitz and Mecklenburg-Schwerin, who owed the recovery of their lands after Wallenstein's demission to Gustavus; the Hohenzollern administrator of the Archbishopric of Magdeburg; and the Landgrave of Hesse-Cassel. Meanwhile the Electors of Brandenburg and Saxony remained hesitant.

Things began to improve only after 31 January 1631 when a five-year agreement was signed with France at Bärwalde which provided for aid at the rate of 400,000 thalers per annum. In return for this the Swedes undertook to maintain 30,000 infantry and 6,000 cavalrymen in Germany. More important still, the terms of the pact were to be published, so that Cardinal Richelieu could be held to them before European public opinion. De Geer did not return empty-handed: he automatically gained a contract for extra armaments. Gustavus Adolphus was an expert on Dutch tactics with their flexibility, major use of artillery, and emphasis on the fire-power of smaller units deployed in line abreast; he thus saw the pressing need for many more cannon and muskets.

Since France was more and more involved in Italy and the Rhineland, the Swedes were left to bear the brunt of the contest in Germany themselves and they were scarcely fortified by the knowledge that Frederick of the Palatinate, that lacklustre nominal king of Bohemia, was on their side. The Electors of Brandenburg and Saxony struggled to retain their neutrality and the Imperialists under Tilly took full advantage of it: among other things it allowed them to invest the key to the valley of the Elbe, Magdeburg.

Gustavus Adolphus was unable to hasten to the city's defence, but he forced Brandenburg into an alliance and increased his pressure on Saxony while all the time feverishly building up the army which he had put under the command of Wallenstein's former field mershal, Arnim. The troops of the Emperor and the League besieged Magdeburg for a month before taking it on 20 May 1631, then sacking and burning it. Swedish publicists led by Adler Salvius took full advantage of the destruction of Magdeburg and the massacre of its inhabitants to launch bitter invective against Tilly and the Habsburgs, and this extensive polemical literature had its significance. Saxony was at last forced to throw in its hand with Gustavus, though the Elector John George was little pleased to be linked in alliance with the three brothers of the Saxe-Weimar line of the Wettins, kinsmen of the Johann Ernst we have already encountered. It was the youngest of them, Bernard, who best represented the Weimar military tradition.

Tilly, whose sovereign and employer Maximilian of Bavaria was secretly in league with France and had given orders that he should take part in no serious engagement, had hoped to be able to reorganize his army on Saxon soil, but by doing so he drove Dresden into the arms of the Swedes. The allied forces pressed forward to deliver battle, and on 17 September 1631 they met Tilly at Breitenfeld. Tilly's *tercios*, drawn up on the Spanish model, were able to scatter the Saxon infantry, John George being among the first to flee the field. But the Swedish foot regiments under Banér and Horn threw back the attacks of Pappenheim's cavalry while Torstenson's artillery wrought havoc among the enemy. The Swedish cavalry under Gustavus Adolphus then completed the rout of the Imperialists. The victory at Breitenfeld was however no White Mountain, as the more sanguine of the Czech emigrants had hoped. Pappenheim was driven back to the Weser and Tilly retreated on the Danube to ensure the defence of Bavaria; but it was the Saxons under Arnim who were sent into Bohemia, not the Swedish king and Frederick the Palsgrave. Gustavus proceeded to the occupation of Thuringia and Franconia, then marched forward with great speed to the Lower Palatinate. He spent the winter at Mainz surrounded by a court of princes of the Empire, while his close colleague and friend Axel Oxenstierna ruled most of Germany as governor-general in Frankfurt. It seemed as if most of the *Reich* was suddenly and completely in the hands of Sweden; Bernard of Saxe-Weimar was even granted Franconia as a personal fief.

Since the career of Gustavus Adolphus was cut short by his death at the end of the following year it is almost as difficult to guess at the real plans which animated him as it is with Wallenstein. He seems to have aimed at creating a Swedish protectorate over the greater part of Germany. His *Corpus bellicum et politicum* was certainly not to be either an "Evangelical union" or a grand coalition, but rather an effective *directorium absolutum* of Sweden as a great power. Nor was Frederick of the Palatinate, who gravitated into Gustavus' entourage from the beginning of 1632, regarded as anything more than a future vassal. Such an attitude was not of course likely to thrill the king's allies in Paris who had used the presence of Swedish troops on the Rhine to occupy the capital of Lorraine, Nancy, and drive out the fervently Leaguist and pro-Spanish Duke.

Gustavus resumed military operations in March 1632. His "armed diplomacy" was now directed primarily against Bavaria and the terrified Maximilian was forced to entreat the Emperor in favour of recalling Wallenstein, whom the Duke himself had played a leading rôle in dismissing. Tilly attempted to prevent the Swedes from crossing the Danube, but he was brushed aside and mortally wounded near Rain at the end of April while Gustavus Adolphus and Frederick marched into Munich in triumph. Nothing, it appeared, could halt the Swedish advance on Vienna, especially if the invaders appealed to the dissident Upper Austrian peasantry. But Gustavus decided instead to confront Wallenstein, who had already (May 1632) driven the Saxons out of Bohemia and was regarded by Maximilian and the courts in Madrid and Vienna as their only saviour. Elsewhere at this moment the Poles were threatened with war against Russia over Smolensk, while the Spanish Netherlands were in turmoil; the Dutch *Stadholder* Frederick Henry had captured the fortress of Maastricht, the only link between Brussels and the west of Germany, and all the efforts of Pappenheim to regain it were fruitless.

Wallenstein, compensated for his loss of Mecklenburg with the Duchy of Glogau in Silesia and granted unheard-of plenipotentiary powers, now refused to share his command with Archduke Ferdinand, the crowned King of Bohemia and Hungary (later Ferdinand III.) He left Gallas to occupy northern Bohemia and set off with his main army into the Upper Palatinate, intending to cut the Swedish supply lines with the Baltic. The Swedes reacted by withdrawing to the vicinity of Nuremberg where both sides faced one another throughout the uneasy summer of 1632. Gustavus could not shake off Wallenstein, and the latter now began to gain the initiative. At the beginning of September the two armies moved apart and Wallenstein marched through Thuringia to Saxony, planning to pitch camp for the winter around Leipzig. Importuned by the Elector John George, Gustavus also eventually turned towards Saxony, and these tactics evidently caught Wallenstein unawares, since he would otherwise not have sent part of his forces to join the campaign in the Netherlands. Now he had to recall them hurriedly, and it became clear that the Swedes were preparing for a decisive battle despite the advance of winter. This came on 16 November 1632 at Lützen, near Leipzig. As before, in the skirmishes around Nuremberg, neither one side nor the other could gain a clear advantage. Since Wallenstein abandoned the field at dusk the Swedes claimed victory; but they paid for it with the death of their king who had personally taken part in one of the cavalry charges. The Imperialists lost Pappenheim, and his place as Wallenstein's deputy and heir apparent was taken by the sinister Ottavio Piccolomini. Wallenstein's defensive tactics again proved their value at Lützen; but the more flexible attacking methods favoured by the Swedes and the Dutch were brilliantly vindicated after Gustavus's death by the rising Protestant hero Bernard of

Saxe-Weimar who captured Wallenstein's artillery. Many of the hopes of the Bohemian exiles perished with Gustavus Adolphus and with Frederick the Palsgrave who died in the same month. The Palsgrave's eldest son Frederick Henry, who was accepted in 1620 as future King of Bohemia, had predeceased his father at the end of the 1620's in Holland. Thus links between the emigrants and the Palatine dynasty were seriously weakened, although the Winter Queen, Elizabeth Stuart, continued to reside in the Hague and employed her title as Queen of Bohemia until her death in 1662.

After the battle of Lützen John George of Saxony joined with Christian IV of Denmark in seeking to come to terms with the Emperor and it seemed that a general pacification was in prospect. But Oxenstierna, who had assumed power at the head of the Swedish council of regency, managed to hold together the nucleus of the German Protestant camp in the so-called League of Heilbronn (April 1633). The resolutions taken at Heilbronn meant on the other hand that the German princes recovered part of their control over affairs, and Oxenstierna could not prevent the French from paying their subsidies in future to the new alliance rather than Sweden alone, or hinder the growing influence of French diplomacy led by the Marquis de Feuquières in the politics of the Empire.

Wallenstein, whose tendency to alternate between decisive military activity and willingness to negotiate had been prominent ever since 1631, now began to conduct indirect and secretive talks with the Swedes as well as those with the Saxon Field Marshal Arnim which the Emperor had approved. The *generalissimo* was the central factor in European politics and his doings were closely watched by France and Holland, as well as the Spaniards who were making large monthly contributions to the upkeep of his army. As the negotiations dragged on inconclusively Wallenstein's many critics found voice. Several members of the Bohemian nobility were among them, above all Slavata, and they included Archduke Ferdinand, who felt himself slighted, and the Viennese "Spanish" party led by the ambassador Oñate and Marradas. Wallenstein counted on his own indispensibility to both Austrian and Spanish Habsburgs, and perhaps to convince the court in Vienna he suddenly interrupted the talks to hasten to Silesia and force the capitulation of the Swedish army at Steinau (10 October). But by now it appeared that the Franco-Swedish coalition and even Saxony would be prepared to destroy the

Habsburgs entirely. This would satisfy Wallenstein and the Bohemian *émigrés*, and for this reason he freed the Swedish generals and Czechs captured in Silesia, including Thurn. Such inconsistencies were well calculated to inspire mistrust on all sides.

The most serious development however was Wallenstein's new disagreement with Spanish policy-makers. Madrid still reposed confidence in the *generalissimo*, but in Vienna, Milan and Brussels active members of the *partido militar* had turned against him. When the Duke of Feria sought to transfer his troops in the autumn of 1633 along the classic "Spanish road" from the Milanese through the Tyrol to Swabia, Alsace and the Rhineland, he found his way blocked by a Swedish army under Horn. Feria appealed for the assistance of some of Wallenstein's forces which were operating in south-west Germany under the command of Marshal Aldringen. Wallenstein was thoroughly opposed to this, just as he refused to take any steps against the Dutch. But Aldringen consulted with the military council (*Hofkriegsrat*) in Vienna, whose President was another of Wallenstein's personal enemies Count Schlick, once the commander of the Moravian regiments at the White Mountain, and then acceded to Feria's request. This was a warning sign that the *generalissimo's* authority might be on the wane. Feria and Aldringen forced their way into Alsace, but then in the middle of November Bernard of Saxe-Weimar captured Ratisbon and penetrated into the northern part of Bavaria. Now the Elector Maximilian in his turn called for help from Vienna and Wallenstein. The latter hurriedly left Silesia, retaining there a part of his army under Schaffgotsch, and crossed Bohemia into the Upper Palatinate. But he soon withdrew again towards Bohemia and took over Pilsen, which was to be the winter quarters for his soldiers. For all the solid reasons which could have lain behind this decision, it was easy to interpret it as treasonable at a time when the Duke of Bavaria urgently required support.

At the turn of the years 1633–4 it was Vienna and Pilsen which faced each other. Wallenstein's supporters, among them the Spanish agent Father Quiroga, were continually losing ground, and the generals who had been summoned to Pilsen to swear an oath to their leader on 11–13 January began to drift towards the Emperor. Their paths to Vienna lay through the south Bohemian estate of Hluboká where Baltazar de Marradas was beginning to

bring together all the important military figures who, like Aldringen, preferred Ferdinand II to the uncommitted Wallenstein.
About the middle of January 1634 Piccolomini was spreading
reports that Wallenstein aimed to force the Spaniards out of
Italy, and Marradas added the rumour that he wished to dispossess the German Electors. On 24 January Ferdinand issued a
decree dismissing Wallenstein and naming Gallas in his place; he
offered an amnesty to all who had taken part in the Pilsen agreement, excepting only the *generalissimo* and his closest colleagues.

There now followed four more weeks of uncertainty, explicable
from Wallenstein's side only by the apathy into which his bodily
and mental infirmity was leading him. Ferdinand finally pro-
scribed him (18 February), and Wallenstein fled from Pilsen to
Eger where he was nearer the Saxons and Swedes; but neither
Arnim nor Bernard of Saxe-Weimar lifted a finger to save him.
The Emperor prepared to march into Bohemia personally and a
campaign against Pilsen was organized from Hluboká. But all
this proved unnecessary; the "military execution" by treacherous
underlings in Eger on 25 February 1634 had already removed
from the European stage its most colourful protagonist.

From the standpoint of international politics the murder of
Wallenstein was a serious error. It could be used as a good illus-
tration of how little the Emperor and the Habsburgs as a whole
felt themselves bound by legal forms. It could be seen as the
result of Jesuit and Spanish intrigues. Richelieu and his publicists
accused Ferdinand of perpetrating an *acte sanglant* and pointed
to Oñate as the spiritual father of the deed, the more so since
even minute study of Wallenstein's correspondence revealed
nothing which could be accounted treasonable. The announced
trial of the general was now cancelled and the Emperor and the
Spanish government visibly assumed all responsibility for his
death by richly rewarding those who had deserted him in time.

The Archduke Ferdinand joined Gallas, the new lord of Friedland, as nominal commander of the Imperialist armies. Fresh
Spanish troops under the Cardinal-Infant which had been intended for the southern Netherlands united with the Austrians
in south Germany. Although Horn and Bernard of Saxe-Weimar
defeated and killed Aldringen at Landshut, Horn was then suddenly forced to withdraw to Prussia with part of the Swedish
forces since the Poles had gained the upper hand over Russia in
the war for Smolensk. Bernard was left with 20,000 men facing

twice that number of Imperialist and Spanish soldiers. In the two-day battle of Nördlingen (5–6 September 1634) the Swedes were crushingly defeated.

The immediate political consequence of this disaster was the end of the League of Heilbronn, and with it the end of Swedish dominance in Germany. Real power in the anti-Habsburg camp now passed to France, and since Sweden had shown herself unable to fight a war on two fronts, along the Baltic and in central Europe, Richelieu had to emerge from the background to take over open leadership of the struggle. At the end of April 1635 he concluded a new treaty of alliance with the Swedes, then on 19 May declared war on Spain. This automatically meant that the southern Netherlands, where the Cardinal-Infant had assumed control, ceased to be a serious danger to the United Provinces, and the shrewd, calculating regents in the Hague and Amsterdam were not slow to appreciate the changed situation. Holland could gradually withdraw from the European theatre of war and seek more advantageous use of her forces in areas like Brazil where an attack on Spain yielded most reward.

Sweden and France could now no longer keep in their camp the Protestant electors of Saxony and Brandenburg. After negotiating a temporary truce with Dresden at Pirna in November 1634, the Emperor gained even better terms by the Peace of Prague which was signed on 30 May 1635. The Saxons were confirmed in their possession of the two Lusatias (Upper and Lower), but they undertook to break all political links with foreign powers. Bohemian emigrants were excluded from the amnesty proclaimed in Prague; the Edict of Restitution was repealed for forty years; the date chosen as standard for settling disputes over property rights was fixed at 1627. The Peace of Prague was accepted by all the Electors and most of the Protestant princes and cities of the Empire. Those whom it failed to satisfy were few – among them Arnim, who resigned and left Saxony. Many Protestant powers assumed neutrality and the religious element in international politics was further weakened. But the basic anti-Habsburg coalition of France, Sweden and Holland survived, although it was now manipulated by Cardinal Richelieu, and rendered illusory all hopes of a general pacification.

At the same time as plans for a Swedish-controlled directorate in Central Europe fell to pieces, a still more ambitious venture further east also ended in failure. At the beginning of the 1630s both Sweden and France had been trying to induce a simultaneous rising against the Polish-Lithuanian state by Turkey, its Tartar vassals from the Crimea and the Ukrainian Cossacks, while Transylvania under Bethlen's successor György Rákóczi was to attack the Habsburgs in Hungary. But all the schemes for an eastern front proved vain. The Sultan was preoccupied with a protracted war against Persia (1630-8), and was unwilling to see any independent action on the part of his Transylvanian subjects. The Tartars chose to fall upon Moscovite Russia rather than Poland, and the Cossack revolt was delayed. Thus Moscovy was forced to bear the whole brunt of the campaign which began in 1632 following the accession to the Polish throne of Wladislaw IV (1632-48), the same Wladislaw who in his youth had been designated as the future tsar by the Polish party during the "Time of Troubles". The Russian armies besieging Smolensk (the whole episode has therefore been called the War of Smolensk) were to be joined by Wrangel, commander of the Swedish forces in Prussia, but the death of Gustavus Adolphus and then, a year later, of the Patriarch and regent Filaret weakened the alliance between Stockholm and Moscow. Muscovy was hampered by peasant unrest and further Swedish auxiliaries from Germany were late in arriving, so that the peace concluded with Poland in June 1634 at Poljanovec came as a needed release; by it Wladislaw gave up his claims to the Russian throne but retained Smolensk. A year later Sweden and Poland agreed on terms for a twelve-year truce at Stuhmsdorf. Thus the weakness of Sweden's great-power position was revealed also in the east of Europe; she was too poor and vulnerable to sustain such a broad-based military strategy. The years of Swedish hegemony were effectively over after Nördlingen and with the end of the Russian phase of the Thirty Years War.

Over too was the era of great personalities like Gustavus Adolphus and Wallenstein, and the age of the all-powerful *condottiere*. The rôle of major military entrepreneur now began to fall increasingly to the state, as was already the case in Holland. Such changes were of course gradual and cannot always be precisely localized. But the whole character of the anti-Habsburg coalition quite clearly altered in the middle of the 1630s, and that is in the present context the most important fact.

Eight

NEW HORIZONS AND
NEW MISERIES

THE FRENCH PERIOD OF THE THIRTY YEARS WAR

The diplomatic activity of Richelieu's agents from 1635 could leave no-one in any doubt that France was taking seriously its duel with the Spanish and Austrian Habsburgs. On 25 February 1635 an offensive and defensive alliance was concluded with the Dutch, and at the end of the same month the Peace of Compiègne propped up the failing power of Sweden. In the summer treaties were signed with Savoy, Mantua, and Parma to keep the enemy occupied in northern Italy, while the French-arranged truce of Stuhmsdorf separated Poland from the Habsburgs. Finally, at the end of October Bernard of Saxe-Weimar and his army were taken into French service.

These diplomatic successes were called for, since Spain too was ready to make a strong armed response to the French declaration of war (17 May 1635). Immediately after the battle of Nördlingen a secret compact had been signed at Ebersdorf (31 October 1634) to link Spain, the Empire, and the Catholic princes of Germany and revive the programme of the old League which had been dissolved at the beginning of the 1630s. For Madrid and Olivares this agreement at Ebersdorf was the culmination of long efforts: the Holy Roman Empire as a whole was now to assist the Catholic King through his dignity as Duke of Burgundy in the struggle against the insurgents of the United Provinces. But there was nothing in the terms about war against France, and among the signatories the name of Maximilian of Bavaria was missing. Nor was everything perfectly untroubled in the relation between Madrid and Vienna. Olivares was prepared to back the offensive against Sweden with finance, but not with military aid; he was even unwilling to let Spanish subsidies be used for recruiting troops to this end. On the contrary he put pressure on Ferdinand II to join in a decisive attack on France and to send the Imperialist army under Gallas into action on the Rhine. In the end a compromise was reached since the Emperor, unlike his hot-blooded son, was content to pursue the well-proven strategy of the localized conflict.

With the conclusion of the Peace of Prague the policy-makers in Vienna recovered their nerve, and they were now ready to play their part in the far-reaching plans of the Spaniards. The Conde-Duque Olivares, now the real ruler of his country rather than the weak Philip IV, was at once the first and the last leader of Habsburg Spain whose political programme logically looked to universal monarchy as its ultimate aim, and he threw everything possible into the endeavour. The Cardinal-Infant, together with Piccolomini and Gallas at the head of the Imperialist forces, began a campaign directed at the very heart of France. Gallas invaded Lorraine and the Franche-Comté, while in July 1636 Piccolomini penetrated almost to the outskirts of Paris. But then the situation began to change for the worse.

The Imperialist armies in the Rhineland had little concern for scruples, and their behaviour in taking prisoner Richelieu's pensioner the Archbishop of Trier combined with unfortunate Spanish lapses within Germany to place a trump card in the hands of French propaganda. The "Most Christian King" Louis XIII, that ally of Lutheran Swedes and Calvinist Dutchmen, could now be presented in the broadsheets as the defender of a prince of the Catholic Church arrested by the Spaniards, even as the defender of the faith as such. Against such arguments the publicists of Madrid found themselves at a loss. Only the quickest-witted of them, Francisco de Quevedo and Diego de Saavedra de Fajardo depicted the struggle as a contest for power whose leading spirit was not Louis XIII but Richelieu.

At the same time Swedish troops led by Banér and Torstenson were strengthening their position in central Europe, and at the battle of Wittstock (4 October 1636) they defeated the Imperialists and Saxons under Count Hatzfeld. In the course of 1637 the French and Dutch won successes on the territory of present-day Belgium and Artois. As the French began to conquer the latter, Frederick Henry retook Breda and occupied the area between the rivers Scheldt and Meuse which later came to be called the "Lands of the Generality". But gradually the Dutch and Swedish advance slowed down; both preferred to hold certain key positions rather than engage on risky large-scale military operations. The fighting power of their armies was declining as supply conditions worsened and the importance of heavy cavalry and infantry, the decisive weapon of Gustavus Adolphus, was lessened. Cuirassiers were now beginning to be superseded by dragoons, a kind of infantry on horseback like the light Polish and Hungarian cavalry which Wallenstein had taken the initiative of introducing. Artillery had now to be more mobile: this meant reducing the calibre of cannon, and capturing a town thus once more became a serious problem.

The far-reaching projects of Holland and France for the conquest of the whole of the Spanish Netherlands proved illusory. Frederick Henry could not overcome any more strategic fortresses, indeed he lost several which had been taken earlier, like Venlo and Roermond. His attack on Antwerp was repulsed, and in the end it was only sea power which protected the Dutch from a Spanish counter-offensive. The Spaniards in their turn were now concerned to provision their troops in the Netherlands from the Atlantic, since the land link with Italy was again in danger. Here in fact they were able to recover their position at least temporarily: the French had occupied the Valtellina in 1635, but their conduct produced in March 1637 a rising of the Grisons under Jörg Jenatsch. Richelieu's garrisons were forced to leave, whereupon Jenatsch was murdered by his nephew Pompejus Planta (January 1639) and an agreement was reached with the Habsburgs which provided for the independence of the canton but left the chief passes under Spanish control.

Meanwhile however the wavering Austro-Spanish dominance in Germany was dealt another blow. Gallas had been capitalizing on jealousies between the Swedish general Banér and Bernard of Saxe-Weimar, but at the beginning of 1638 the latter, backed by French supporting troops who included the later celebrated Marshal Turenne, seized the fortress of Breisach on the Upper Rhine and occupied Alsace and the Breisgau. This again broke the connection between Milan and Brussels. Bernard made strenuous efforts to obtain Alsace as a Duchy for himself, but he died suddenly of smallpox in July 1638 and his army passed into French service. Only two years later Banér died in a similarly unexpected fashion and his plans for a personal patrimony somewhere in the Empire were also rendered null. After Banér only Torstenson remained of the universally recognized Swedish military leaders and the generals in Germany were already beginning to fall out among themselves. The authority of Axel Oxenstierna was weakening: the Chancellor's son Johann showed little talent, and when his brother Gabriel died (1640) his ruling group lost its majority on the Council of Regency. It was clear that as soon as Gustavus's daughter Christina came of age (she would be 18 in 1644) Oxenstierna's influence would be reduced still further.

The same changing of the guard was taking place in the Netherlands. In October 1639 the new Spanish "armada" of Don Antonio de Oquendo was defeated in the Channel by Admiral Maarten Harpertszoon Tromp. Thus at one stroke the attempt to send reinforcements to the Cardinal-Infant was frustrated and the fleet destroyed on which the Conde-Duque had set his best hopes. On top of this another flotilla of Spanish and Portuguese ships, dispatched from Lisbon in 1638 to occupy Brazil, was annihilated off Pernambuco in January 1640 by a substantially smaller number of Dutch vessels. Holland now gained firm control over the coast of Brazil and the regents saw ever more clearly that their exploits overseas were more lucrative than indecisive warfare on the continent of Europe, despite the severe financial straits of the West India Company. But although public opinion in the Seven Provinces was becoming profoundly weary of fighting, the *Stadholder* Frederick Henry tried to continue and even extend the policies of Maurice of Orange. When his son, the later William II, married Charles I's daughter, the *Stadholder* felt himself the equal of the other members of Europe's monarchist club. This inevitably brought him into conflict with the burgher oligarchies which had been crushed but not destroyed with Oldenbarneveldt in 1618. The regents and merchants of Holland, backed by opposition groups in the less important provinces, stood out against the house of Orange over both domestic and foreign policy. They considered it the Dutch interest to protect the commercial freedom of Holland and Zealand by engaging in overseas expansion. Against this Frederick Henry sought to win the United Provinces a leading position in Europe by territorial gains nearer home. He also wished to lend support to his son's father-in-law Charles I who was just beginning his own struggle with Parliament. The solid patricians of Holland however were sympathetic to the Roundheads, and looked above all to take advantage of England's temporary incapacity for the benefit of their own trading empire.

The internal problems of the Netherlands and Sweden were however far outrun by the crisis within Spain. The Mantuan War (1628–31) meant that Spain was bound hand and foot in Italy, had made a barely concealed enemy of France and placed her finances in a hopeless predicament. The Council of Finance (*Consejo de Hacienda*) declared as early as August 1628 that it would need an extra two million ducats by the end of the year, and this a bare month before the news that Dutch pirates had seized the whole of the New World silver fleet.

Olivares resolved on a thorough reform of the administration, and in 1634 he replaced the existing *Consejo de Estado* with an executive organ, the *Junta de Ejecución*. Despite all his efforts Castile, the heart of the Spanish state, could not be made to yield any more revenues or soldiers than it was already providing, indeed the prospects were for a sharp decline. The Conde-Duque's plan to unite the individual crowns of the Iberian state in a single *Unión de Armas* thus led him logically to the conclusion that war in Italy, Germany, the Low Countries and the empire across the seas could only now be prosecuted if those regions which had previously held aloof be made to contribute. This meant above all Portugal and Catalonia, but in both these proud kingdoms the Estates regarded Olivares as the representative of an acquisitive Castile and refused to satisfy his demands, even when a princess of the blood royal, Margaret of Savoy, was sent to Lisbon as governor. In 1637 unrest broke out in Évora and elsewhere and very nearly turned into the open revolt for which Richelieu was ready with military support. As yet the noble magnates led by the Duke of Braganza wished to avoid a full-scale rising, but the commercial patriciate of the towns nursed deep hatred for a king of Spain who could not even protect Brazil.

In the event it was Catalonia, not Portugal, which provided the first breach in Olivares' policy. The beginning of the Franco-Spanish war in May 1635 had turned the principality of Catalonia (a part of the crown of Aragon) into an area of key strategic significance, since it represented a full half of the border between the two warring states. Olivares demanded that the Catalans contribute money and men for the defence of the frontier. Castile was already quite unable to balance its budget and for the year

1636-7 the Council of Finance expected outgoings of about 11½ million escudos, a sum of fantastic magnitude. That summer a French army penetrated into Catalonia and took the fortress of Salses. The Conde-Duque instructed the Viceroy, the Count of Santa Coloma, and his ministers not to spare constitutional privilege where it interfered with the needs of national defence. Thus by the beginning of 1640, when the French were driven out of Salses, Catalan opposition to Olivares was intense; led by the eloquent priest Pau Claris it threatened to remove the whole province from the clutches of the Conde-Duque just as he was celebrating a victorious campaign.

Olivares was not unaware of the gravity of the situation. He knew that he had neither men nor money, nor the kind of generals who could replace Spinola and Feria. He saw salvation in a separate peace with the United Provinces, since the costs of the war in Flanders were two-fifths of all state expenditure. But the Dutch would not relinquish Brazil, and the loss of Brazil would mean revolution in Portugal. The desperate situation forced desperate measures: Olivares turned the Castilian army which had recaptured Salses on the Catalans to compel them into submission. The Parliament (*Corts*) however, on which he had counted, never met; instead there were disturbances between the local population and the soldiery which led by May to open rebellion in Barcelona. On the feast of Corpus Christi, 7 June 1640, Santa Coloma was murdered and power passed into the hands of the Catalan *Diputació*, the city council of Barcelona and the nobility. Olivares sought to pacify the province by sending a new Viceroy, the Catalan Duke of Cardona, but the latter died before he could attempt a settlement. Things were now drifting out of control and before the eyes of the Conde-Duque the Catalans were "beginning a revolt like that of the Dutch, without rhyme or reason".

This was not all. Olivares had been trying to eliminate noble opposition in Portugal by directing its members to join the army in Catalonia. Throughout the autumn of 1640 resistance grew, fanned by Richelieu's agents, and on December 1 a *coup d'état* took place in Lisbon which banished Princess Margaret and proclaimed the Duke of Braganza as King John IV. Olivares now endeavoured once more to come to terms with Catalonia, but the popular movement there was too strong for him. On 16 January 1641 Claris declared the country a free republic under French protection, then a week later, under strong pressure from

Paris, announced that Catalonia would join France as it had done once before under the rule of Charlemagne. French and Catalan troops faced the Spanish army under the Marqués de los Vélez on the hill of Montjuich before the gates of Barcelona on January 26 and forced it to retreat. It was a clear sign that there could be no quick end to the insurrections in Catalonia and Portugal, and thus that the days of Olivares' rule were numbered. In the summer of 1641 he was still strong enough to frustrate a plot prepared by the Duke of Medina Sidonia, but the following year a disastrous inflation totally undermined his position. On 17 January 1643 Philip IV issued a decree exiling him to his country estates where he died two years later on the verge of madness.

Two months before Olivares' disgrace, Cardinal Richelieu also died, soon to be followed by his King, Louis XIII. In place of the infant Louis XIV another Cardinal, Mazarin, took over the reins of government. But these changes in personnel could not halt the catastrophic decline of Spain. During 1642 and 1643 her armies in the Netherlands suffered a series of defeats from Guébriant and Condé which culminated in the disastrous rout of the famous Spanish infantry at Rocroi (19 May, 1643). Rocroi became the symbol of the demise of a military system which had sustained Spain as a great power; meanwhile the forms of government established by Olivares were themselves being liquidated. Philip IV first declared that he would rule alone and dispense with a *privado* or chief minister, but in fact he soon handed over this responsibility to the nephew of the Conde-Duque, Don Luis de Haro, the embodiment of mediocrity, whose only concern was to conclude a peace which would not lose Spain too much territory.

Catalonia's fate was still open. For a brief period during 1640 it had spoken for the whole peninsula in opposing the hated régime of Olivares. It was a paradox that the Catalans had managed to bring together the entire population of the peninsula: nobles and peasant-farmers from Castile, the merchants of Lisbon and the Levant, the Aragonese and the Basques, against the Conde-Duque, the one man whose life-work had been to impress on the country a consciousness of its unity. At the same time Catalonia became unwillingly aware in its very act of self-defence that it was an integral part of Spain, and the Catalan rebellion symbolized the tragedy of the Spanish "Golden Age". The defeat at Rocroi was a nail in the coffin of Spanish militarism. Elsewhere too, internal dissension and sheer exhaustion had taken their toll: by 1643 the only escape was a general peace. Influential circles in Spain, Germany, Sweden and the Netherlands desired it, and serious negotiations could now begin. The generals yielded pride of place to the diplomats and their task became restricted to that of creating advantageous bargaining positions. The last lustrum of the Thirty Years War forms the epilogue to a conflict which had reached an *impasse* and whose resolution now lay only in compromise.

THE BOHEMIAN QUESTION AND THE POWER STRUGGLE

The five years after Wallenstein's death were filled for Bohemia with the economic problems of a devastated and exhausted country. The direct effects of the warfare and the strengthening of the anti-Habsburg coalition by France's entry into the lists did not touch the Czech lands; it was rather the definitive loss of Lusatia to Saxony in 1635 which was more immediately sensible – the Emperor had sacrificed Bohemian unity to buy the Elector John George out of the Franco-Swedish alliance. Political life was still limited to the Estates' routine approval of the Imperial demands, but some signs of opposition were beginning to make themselves felt, primarily through the call for a certain share in administration and the important decision-making of state, above all on economic matters. While Ferdinand II lived these endeavours, however mild, could register no success, for the old Emperor insisted on his plenitude of power and was mistrustful towards the whole nobility, even those elements within it which were utterly faithful to the dynasty. The more circumspect Ferdinand III who came to the throne in 1637, allowed a shadow of cooperation to the Estates in drawing up some amendments to the Form of Government (*Landesordnung*) in 1640, but he did not deviate in substance from his father's legacy of feudal centralized monarchy.

The situation changed again when the Swedes under Banér renewed their activities in central Europe, and from the spring of 1639 their occupation of parts of Bohemia once again allowed many noble and burgher *émigrés* to return to their native land. Zdenek of Hodice now became the leading representative of emigrant interests. The international aims of Swedish policy proclaimed the restitution of the state of affairs which had existed in 1618; they thus raised new hopes among many Czechs at home and abroad, but these stood unhappily in sharp contrast to the unbridled marauding of the advancing soldiery. Under those circumstances Banér's promise that he had come to bring peace to Bohemia could carry little conviction, either in 1639 or during his second invasion of 1641. The Swedish armies took the whole of southern Bohemia and most of Silesia; but Prague, defended by the Emperor's brother Leopold William, the pluralist Bishop of Olomouc, held out against Banér, and France was too busy with popular discontent at home to engage in anything outside her war with Spain.

The Swedish recovery raised again the problem of war goals in central Europe. During the negotiations with France at Hamburg in 1638 Oxenstierna had stood firm on a demand for the restitution of everything to the conditions of 1618, in other words the *status quo ante bellum*. Richelieu had no interest in such a radical programme, and was prepared from the start to compromise on the central European issue. Moves in this direction took place at the *Diet* of Ratisbon in the winter of 1640 and during the following year. The Habsburgs for their part proposed 1627 as a base date for settling the religious question and excluded the so-called hereditary lands – in their eyes Bohemia, Austria and Hungary – from the terms of reference. Banér, who was aware of the vast gulf which lay between the Swedish and Viennese positions, also realized the danger that France and the princes of the Empire would force through a mediated solution. He therefore sought to dissolve the Ratisbon assembly. But... Banér died in May 1641 and his successor, Lennart Torstenson, suddenly invaded Silesia during the spring of 1642, defeated the Imperialists near Schweidnitz at the end of May and pursued them into Moravia. The Emperor's army retreated down the valleys of the Oder and Bečva until on 9 June it was put to flight by Königsmarck at Holešov. The Swedes could now probably have captured Uherské Hradište, but their commanders were not interested in such restricted objectives. They wanted to strengthen their position for an attack on Vienna from the rear and they therefore turned unexpectedly on the fortified and well-provisioned Olomouc. The city soon capitulated (14 June) and henceforward it became the main pivot of Swedish power in central Europe. But Torstenson now changed his plans and for the winter of 1642–3 withdrew his army to Saxony. He left only limited forces in Moravia under Colonel Paikul, the leader of the Olomouc garrison. Most of the fortified towns and castles remained in Imperialist hands and day-to-day warfare depended once again on Sweden's allies within the country, the enduring groundswell of popular discontent.

This was still in good supply. Throughout the 1630s there had been no real peace, at least not in the eastern half of the land. To his death in 1636 governor Dietrichstein had not been able to subdue the rebel Vlachs and when, in 1638, the régime which succeeded him sent a force under Colonel Halbich to put down the menace, the dissidents surrounded his troops at Rokytnice near Vsetín and disarmed them. The government vainly tried to pay back the Vlachs in their own coin by raising a body of loyal Catholic tribesmen, but this proved no more effective. It was fruitless to capture and hang a few outlaws from the Beskyd mountains when the causes of their rebellion continued unchecked and even grew worse. The pressure of taxation was now so great that from 1640 to 1643 no local rates could be collected. Banér's campaign of 1639–40 and Zdenek of Hodice's activities in north-east Bohemia had revived all the terrors of the local feudal magnates; the occupation of Olomouc only heightened their anxieties.

Throughout the winter of 1642–3 Moravia was divided into two: the north and centre were controlled from Olomouc by the Swedes, the remainder was still held by the Imperialists based on Brno, Hradište, Kremsier, Přerov and the fortresses of Helfstein and Hukvaldy. In the spring of 1643 Habsburg reinforcements arrived from Hungary and invested Olomouc. Torstenson promptly raced southwards from Saxony; failing in his first plan to take Prague by direct attack, he avoided an engagement near Hradec Králové against the Imperialists under Gallas (who had succeeded the incompetent Leopold William) and hastened into Moravia. Pursued by the hesitant Gallas, Torstenson reached Olomouc at the beginning of June and within a few weeks, helped by the Vlachs, he again controlled most of the towns in the centre of the country. The inhabitants of Vsetín and its environs now became a vital territorial link between the Swedes and their potential allies in Hungary, above all the Transylvánian prince György Rákóczi who was himself preparing for a contest with the Emperor. Torstenson next captured Holešov and Kremsier and the former Wallenstein territory of Lukov (27 June 1643). Not until the beginning of July did Gallas's main forces reach him, and then they were not sufficiently strong to attack the Swedish positions first around Tovačov and later in the vicinity of Horní Moštenice near Přerov. By the end of the month the

Swedes, aided by the "Wallachians and Slavaks" had occupied an even larger area in the east of Moravia, but the last days of August brought a sudden change. Torstenson received news that the dispute with Denmark about control of shipping through the Sound had turned into war. The reckless moves of Christian IV against the town of Hamburg caused the *Riksråd* in Stockhölm to resort to arms and recall its army from Moravia. Within a few weeks Torstenson had marched his men through Schleswig to Holstein and entered the peninsula of Jutland. Troops under Horn invaded the Danish provinces in the south of Scandinavia proper while a fleet raised with Dutch credit through Louis de Geer occupied the offshore islands. The Imperialists under Gallas who pursued the Swedes through Germany were defeated at Jüterbog and Magdeburg and forced back into Bohemia. Christian sued for peace and signed a treaty at Brömsebro (25 August 1645) by which he lost the islands of Ösel and Gotland and three smaller territories. The port of Gothenburg was no longer isolated and Sweden had achieved a direct link with her west European allies and trading partners. In addition another Danish port, Glückstadt at the mouth of the Elbe, had to be sacrificed to its larger rival Hamburg and its Spanish resident Gabriel de Roy was forced to leave. Denmark was now clearly reduced to the rank of a second-rate power.

Yet the main cost of the war between Sweden and Denmark was borne, characteristically, by the Moravians. The departure of Torstenson's army at the beginning of September 1643 caused the evacuation of most of the towns and castles which the Swedes had occupied. The Imperialists could thus regain the upper hand. Sometime during that winter of 1643–4 they must also have recaptured Zlín, since at the end of the year, as military units were assembling to mount a decisive campaign against the Vlachs, we learn that the town council was paying for "the imprisonment of one Wallack", presumably in the city gaol of Olomouc or the Spielberg above Brno. In January 1644 an army was ready under General Buchheim and the Habsburg commissar Johann von Rottal to attack the rebel stronghold Vsetín from all four points of the compass. The Imperialists' advantage was overwhelming: against their artillery and 4–5,000 men, among them local Catholic tribesmen and some *hajducks* from nearby Hungary, stood a few hundred Vlachs, a handful of Swedish musketeers and some "Slovaks" from the Rákóczi lands along the valley of the Vág.

As they advanced, the individual columns of the attackers disarmed the local inhabitants, burned, devastated and murdered. In Zlín a senior official confiscated the peasants' weapons, but here Buchheim's men did not set fire to the villages around, evidently out of a consideration for the loyalty of Podstatský their lord. On 26 January a company of soldiers under Colonel Welisch was the first to reach Vsetín; in its wake villages lay in ashes and suspects were rounded up in droves. Before it, all the peasants from the domain and nearby Lukov were forced into a final desperate resistance. The result was inevitable: Vsetín lost a full fifth of its male population: 30 fell in the struggle, nearly 50 were executed, many others fled. Nearly 90 peasants deserted the lands of Lukov. Others were held in the prison in Zlín or apprehended on the Hungarian side of the border.

Among all the "Vlach domains" Zlín was least affected by this repression. Of 341 recorded householders, 16 were executed and 21 fled. The town itself numbered 111 householders and 24 labouring families: three of them were hanged, two more drawn and quartered. Then a register of peasants was prepared, together with a list of all those who had been in possession of firearms. Almost a third of the population handed over weapons – among those represented were three widows of men who had died in the rebellion. Elsewhere on the domain the villages of Lůžkovice and Želechovice in the valley lost one-third of their inhabitants, Jaroslavice more than one-fifth, Příluk a tenth; the hill settlements of Kudlov and Březnice each suffered one execution, but two others, Mladcová and Prštná, escaped untouched. The register was completed on 16 February 1644, probably in Zlín itself; then a decree was read to the assembled peasantry, an oath sworn, and the document sent to the government in Brno bearing the communal seal. The subjugated people undertook to repent and mend their ways. Through the person of their commissary Rottal they promised the Emperor and his administration to dispense with all evil-minded Protestant preachers, abandon their arms, pay their taxes promptly, deliver up all malefactors within six weeks and refrain from taking revenge on those who had lately supported the Imperialist side.

This was not the end of the punishment. Yet many of the obligations remained on paper: the people simply fled over the frontier into Hungary. 21 more households left Zlín and they were a very sensible loss; for the authorities it meant the disappearance of at least 100 subjects. Rebels continued to be hunted until the end of March 1644 and no real peace followed even then. Although Rákóczi's advance was checked before he could leave Upper Hungary, Imperialist troops stayed positioned in Moravia to block any Swedish march on Brno.

It was no better the following year. Torstenson's victory at Jankov in eastern Bohemia over General Götz reopened the way into Moravia where the Olomouc garrison was beleaguered. Again the plans were for a joint operation with Rákóczi which would be joined by the peasants of Upper Austria, perhaps also by the Moravian rebels, and end with an attack on Vienna. But once more they foundered on Hungarian delays. Torstenson laid siege to Brno and it was July before he was reinforced by the first units of Magyar cavalry. By August it was clear that the blockade of Brno had failed: Rákóczi had not crossed the Vág and was held back by his Ottoman overlords who were unwilling to see a further campaign against the Emperor. The same month Transylvania concluded peace at Linz and buried all the hopes of anti-Habsburg forces for a decisive victory. Shortly after this Torstenson resigned his command and military operations fell into a state of chaos which was relieved only by the abilities of his successor Karl Gustav Wrangel, already famous for his exploits on the Baltic and at Jankov. Moravia remained exposed to the depredations of both sides and each of its zones, Imperialist and Swedish, was laid under contribution. It is not surprising to hear that people were still fleeing to the mountains. At the beginning of September the plague struck: in Holešov it cut short the activity of the anonymous town chronicler, one of the most notable witnesses to the life of eastern Moravia during these years.

Another of its victims seems to have been Kryštof Karel Podstatský, councillor to the new Bishop of Olomouc, the Archduke Leopold William, that unsuccessful military leader and later governor of the Spanish Netherlands. During the Vlach uprising he had scarcely dared show his face in Zlín – he was apparently too-well known and disliked. His eldest son, George Valerian followed the pattern of his father in serving the Bishop and was appointed keeper of the two episcopal fortresses of Helfstein and Hukvaldy. In May 1643, at a ceremony in Vienna, he married Regina von Wolzogen, the widow of the lord of Lukov, Jan Friedrich von Minkwitz, who had himself been the grandson of the financier and entrepreneur Stephan Schmidt von Freyhofen, a Protestant and friend of Karel Žerotín.

It was at Lukov that the Podstatskýs hid some of their valuables when the Vlachs threatened in 1643: among them were the land registers of Zlín, whose disappearance without trace is a serious loss for our understanding of economic developments in the town. Nor do we know whether the dying Kryštof Karel realized how many empty houses still remained there, despite his efforts over a period of fifteen years. The unsettled times made it impossible to bury him in the family vault at St. Michael's in Olomouc; instead his earthly remains were laid to rest in the parish church of Zlín. He left behind him two more solid reminders, both additions to the list of economic undertakings in the region: a new brewery and distillery.

Kryštof Karel's successors continued his policy: they built new farms which required cheap manual labour and thus maintained the tendency towards increased thraldom of the peasantry and higher payments in *robot* and money. The family did not however stay long in Zlín. His widow, Lady Elizabeth Maria Pražma of Bilkov, remarried Jan Friedrich the elder of Minkwitz and soon became involved in disputes with her stepsons, especially George Valerian, who was now also her son-in-law. The latter's machinations brought an attempt in February 1646 at Uherské Hradište to break up Kryštof Karel's heavily insolvent inheritance, about half of which was formed by the domain of Zlín with its small town, its villages, its church, brewery and distillery, its forests with their game, its school, its *robot* labour force and feudal dues. Since three of Podstatský's five children were still minors Elizabeth Maria had to face the accusation that she was managing the estate badly, especially through the loss of eighty peasant families which had defected, and should be relieved of her stewardship. Prominent local nobles were called in, headed by Johann von Rottal, Gabriel Serényi and J. Jakartovský of Sudice, but they proved unable to resolve the quarrel. In 1653 a commission was set up under Jakartovský to administer the estate and in January 1655 it sold Zlín to Gabriel Serényi for 52,000 Rhenish gulden (about 45,000 thalers). Of this sum at least 25,000 gulden went on the settlement of debts. The leading creditor was now John George Sedlnický of Choltice, member of a family which later became celebrated for serving the Austrian and Prussian courts in some of their least popular functions. John George himself was notorious in Zlín as a ruthless oppressor of the peasantry who carried orphans away from the town to work on his farms throughout central Moravia.

Even though there was no more serious warfare in Moravia

THE THIRTY YEARS WAR

after 1645, conditions were still very difficult. In 1646 the later master of Zlín, Gabriel Serényi, then *hejtman* of the province of Hradište, issued a sinister patent which ordered that "the war contribution be raised for a period of three years on beer, vines, meat, fish, wool, footwear and firewood, all arrears of payment to be made good by rigid military execution". It is small wonder that people continued to flee or join the army, though whether as many left Zlín as George Valerian Podstatský asserted in evidence against his stepmother is difficult to determine. The town annals are silent on the matter, but this is presumably because economic disorder was so great that for the year 1649 there are no entries at all. In 1647 we find a series of observations like the one which records that "Nicholas Holíků has gone off to the war and there is no knowing whether he is dead or alive".

Neither 1648 nor the year which followed it brought any real peace to Moravia. It was only in July 1650 that the Swedish garrisons received orders to evacuate Olomouc, Uničov, Sovinec and Fulnek, which they had continued to occupy while their demand for overdue pay was settled. After them, Jägerndorf and the Hlubčice region were relieved; then the rest of Silesia together with Friedland in Bohemia. On 24 July, as the chronicler F. M. Kernerius relates: "was held in Olomouc a great ceremony and solemn procession in honour of the glorious peace, with the firing of cannon and muskets amid a vast concourse from all the lands of His Majesty the Emperor." At the same time the commissar Jan Jakartovský was writing to Ferdinand III in Vienna about the state of things in the town:

> There were in Olomouc before the coming of the Swedes 700 houses of burghers, noblemen and priests. Now however of the 77 which belonged to the nobility and clergy only 23 are habitable, 18 are completely destroyed and 36 in a devastated condition; while of the 623 burgher dwellings only 145 are lived in, 242 being utterly ruined and the rest ravaged. Besides this there used to be 656 houses in the suburbs tributary to the city, but of these not one is still standing. Even in 1640 the population of this place was 30,000 souls, now there are not more than 1,675.

It was calculated that throughout Moravia 63 castles, 22 towns and 330 villages had been annihilated. Not only Olomouc, but the other royal boroughs Brno, Znojmo and Jihlava had entirely lost all trace of their suburbs. Zlín too was full of deserted houses and its situation was not helped by the Imperialist garrison which stayed there until the summer of 1650. Even in 1652 instalments on recently purchased property were not being honoured and new owners were promising to pay "when the others pay". If Moravia was not turned into a complete wilderness, and even the sorely-tried Zlín was able to lend assistance to still worse-hit areas, it was due to the merits not of the authorities, but of their officials. Thirty years of war, poverty and suffering had drained Zlín of all intensive economic and social life. This is revealed by the town records, always a good guide to the evolution of an urban community, which in the middle of the seventeenth century ceased to be kept regularly and thus to be a reliable historical source. Such a situation was fortunately only transitory, and two men remained in Zlín: the long-serving town clerk and schoolmaster Jiřík Přerovský and the chief magistrate Jan Mezuláník, who soon took it upon themselves to rebuild cultural life. The neglected and unfashionable small town began before long to play its role again in the weakened fabric of the Moravian body politic. The heroes of this new period were to be, not the noble lords but far rather the rebels of 1621, 1624 and 1644, and the common people who had borne the brunt of a terrible conflict and were still strong enough to endure the trials which followed it.

The difficulties facing any reconstruction of normal civilized existence weighed equally heavily on Bohemia proper. The latest operations of Imperialist and Swedish troops had brought it also to the last stages of collapse, and we can gauge from some precise sources the full extent of the plight of its free boroughs towards the end of the war. Indebtedness was now a heavy and uniform burden on all classes of society. The state itself was in debt to the tune of 10,500,000 florins by 1637; so were the great landowners and the smaller proprietors, the free and domain towns, and the peasantry. The many Diets and government commissions which considered this problem, beginning during the course of the war (1636, 1640, 1642, 1643, 1644), could at best grant only temporary relief; further loans, themselves often unfunded, postponed the reckoning without averting it, and while providing relief to the debtor both worsened his chances of extra finance in the future and hindered the activities of his creditors. It is not surprising that the conditions brought dissatisfaction at all levels of the economy.

We have already noted the weight of public debt in the 1620s, and the exceptional load which military expenses placed on the exchequer; by the end of the war this had reached crisis proportions. An inventory drawn up in 1651 by the Vice-Chamberlain Oldřich Sezima Skuhrovský of Skuhrov reveals that nineteen free boroughs (Prague is not included) owed the enormous sum of 11,603,435 florins. Pride of place in this figure belonged to the cost of the army, which proved itself to have been just as destructive of the urban economies of Bohemia as the troops of the Swedes and other belligerents. Purely military expenses amounted to 10,376,809 florins which were primarily made up of direct contributions to the Imperialist forces (5,016,849) and another large composite sum (4,179,477) from those towns which had lumped together the cost of both home and enemy armies. The obligations and damage imposed by the Swedes and their allies thus formed only a certain proportion of the latter figure, plus a known sum of 1,180,883. In addition to these frightening unproductive expenses the same nineteen boroughs had incurred debts of 1,226,626 florins guaranteed by bonds to private individuals and corporations. The repayment of all the obligations was inevitably a slow business and it is not until the end of the century that it begins to disappear as an item in the average urban budget. Some towns were in a truly catastrophic situation: Most owed over $2\frac{1}{4}$ million florins, and the debts of Litoměřice (864,438), Mladá Boleslav (810,718) and Písek (661,724) were all far beyond the normal capacities of these boroughs. The Old Town of Prague with its figure of 393,141 florins represented an approximate average.

When the Swedes eventually handed over Wallenstein's old town of Friedland their commander, Benjamin Magnus Nortman, left behind an inscription on the wall of the castle with the date 1 September 1647: *Pax Bello Potior – Sequor Trahentia Fata*. Peace is stronger than war; but I must follow the fates wherever they drag me. Nortman had been incapacitated by a war-wound, but at least the fates were kinder to him than to many he left behind in central Europe. He was ennobled with the title of Croneborg, and his grandson was to be the celebrated Swedish natural historian of the eighteenth century, Linnaeus.

Nine

THE COMPROMISE AND THE PEACE

WARFARE AND DIPLOMACY

IN the correspondence of Imperialist generals and diplomats the first discussion of possible peace overtures appears during the year 1640. A letter from Johann Adolf Schwarzenberg in Ratisbon to Ottavio Piccolomini, written early in October, argues that Ferdinand III must not allow himself to be anticipated by mediation from the Papal Curia; nor dare he leave the field open to a Swedish claim that the Habsburgs do not desire any negotiations. Schwarzenberg stresses the great desire of the Dutch to conclude hostilities and the general willingness of Germany's princes to follow an Imperial lead.

By 1641 the peacemakers-to-be were all provided with instructions, and the Swedish directions of the same October contain a set of thoroughly realistic political claims. But as yet there was nothing specific about Bohemia. Only in June 1645 do we find among the Swedish proposals a demand that "the Kingdom of Bohemia be restored in matters ecclesiastical and secular to that flourishing situation where it stood in 1618". This wording was not unequivocal: it indirectly recognized Habsburg government in the Czech lands. From the very beginning of the protracted negotiations which were at last set in train during 1644 in the two Westphalian cities of Münster and Osnabrück the true "Bohemian question", i.e. the struggle for the Bohemian state as it existed prior to 1618, was always a peripheral issue. In Münster sat the representatives of the Catholic powers, in Osnabrück those of the Protestants, while at the same time bargaining went on in all the capitals of Europe; only Prague was missing from the list. On one hand stood the spokesmen of Brussels, Madrid and Vienna, on the other those of France, Sweden and Holland; between them the less dramatic mediation of Venice and the Papal nuncio Chigi.

The Spanish Habsburgs, desperately weakened both in the Iberian peninsula and on their French front, were now understandably on the defensive, as were their Austrian cousins, deserted by the Electors of Saxony, Brandenburg and intermittently Bavaria too. But the other camp was also enfeebled. France lost a valuable ally in 1644 with the death of Pope Urban VIII and his replacement by Innocent X (1644–50), who had known Spanish proclivities. The same year Gustavus Adolphus's daughter Christina reached her majority and this of itself damaged the position of the Oxenstierna clique of aristocrats and financiers. Christina was more sympathetic to France than to the Dutch, and in Adler Salvius she found an adroit exponent of her policies.

The most serious changes were however taking place in the Netherlands. In 1645 the Dutch fleet for the first time gained control of the Sound and the trade routes of the Baltic. The merchant patriciate of the province of Holland and the city of Amsterdam could now see no reason for continuing a war with Spain from which only France could be the gainer. *Gallus amicus sed non vicinus* ran their proverb and they were thoroughly of opinion that a duly neutralized Spanish Netherlands would represent a much more suitable Southern neighbour than the great power of France. Spanish diplomats were, like Schwarzenberg, well- informed about their adversaries' attitudes and their representative at the Westphalian talks, De Brun, utilized them to the full. Madrid showed great readiness to make sweeping concessions to the Dutch, provided only that they would detach themselves from the anti-Habsburg coalition. When the *Stadholder* Frederick Henry died in 1647, in the midst of the negotiations, the oligarchy of Holland took control. Despite the objections of Zealand, Friesland, and Utrecht and against the wishes of the new Orange claimant William II, Holland persuaded a majority of the States General in favour of a settlement with Spain; a separate peace was signed in Münster during January 1648. This agreement recognized the existing frontier between both halves of the Netherlands: the United Provinces thus kept the Northern parts of Flanders and Brabant and the town of Maastricht, as well as their possessions in the East and West

Indies. They also received a guarantee that the river Scheldt would be blocked to navigation. Official recognition of the independence of the Republic was now a mere formality, as was the Spaniards' promise that they would seek the approval of the Emperor (who gave it) and the Imperial Diet (which did not). These trifles affected the real situation not a whit.

The separate peace was at once a triumph of the Republic over Spain and of Holland over the Prince of Orange and the rest of the Netherlands. It can equally be seen as an outright victory of Amsterdam over all other Dutch interests and the ending of the war confirmed the privileges of that same urban oligarchy which Maurice of Orange had brought low thirty years earlier. This was a situation intolerable to the young and ambitious *Stadholder* William II. In his view the Republic should be joining with its allies the King of England and the court of France to combat their foes: the English Parliament and the Spaniards. For this programme he was prepared to fight openly, and thus he not only supported the attempts of English and Irish royalists at violent intervention in Britain, but also sought to destroy by military means the opposition of the Dutch Estates, above all the regents of Amsterdam. He laid siege to the city and seemed for a moment to have success within his grasp, but the material resources of his enemy were too great and William's sudden death in 1650 prevented another trial of strength. The position of the bourgeois patricians was now unassailable and in the future the Republic resolved to appoint no more *Stadholders* from the house of Orange. Thus the "Eighty Years War", the outcome of an initial revolutionary situation in the 1560s, resulted in victory for a class which had made the Netherlands, especially the province of Holland, the most advanced region of contemporary Europe. This "Golden Age" of the Dutch was of course paid for with the lives and work of a steadily growing mass of urban poor, while the very narrowing of the Republic's social base (by the increased exclusiveness of the regent oligarchy) already heralded the beginnings of decline. The Netherlands were indeed soon to be overtaken by Cromwell's England, itself an economy and society born of revolution.

While the United Provinces had never officially committed themselves to a resolution of the "Bohemian question", the relation of England to the heirs of Frederick the Palsgrave now living in the Hague was more complex. Around 1640 the issue of the Palatinate at least had come under discussion in connection

237

with general criticism of Stuart foreign policy. The sympathies of the Parliamentary opposition went out to the family of the Winter Queen and certain leading figures among the Czech exiles, above all Comenius, who was called to England by some of the Commons under John Pym in 1641. At that point of time the Parliaments in London and Edinburgh had enjoined their government to "put right all that has been lost through the fault of evil counsel" and there seemed to be the chance of a positive change of mind in favour of the Czech Protestants. But in the winter of 1641–2, during the months of Comenius's stay, a group of his friends were implicated in Charles I's plot for a royalist *coup d'état*. This abortive plan, due to have been put into operation early in January 1642, was also supported by the new Palsgrave, Karl Ludwig, Frederick's eldest son, while a younger son, Prince Rupert "of Lusatia", born at Christmastide 1619 in the Hradschin overlooking Prague, offered his services to the king when the war against Parliament began in earnest from the spring of 1642. In June Comenius left England and travelled through Holland to Sweden; he had seen the first portents of the coming revolution and could only lament it as a conflict which would finally eliminate England from the coalition against the Habsburgs.

With the fall of the Stuart dynasty the question of the Palatinate lost its relevance and the *émigrés* from Bohemia, having again failed to raise Dutch circles in their favour, could now only turn to Sweden and, with less sanguine hopes, to Saxony. Worse than that: English, Irish and Scottish mercenaries were increasingly attracted during the last stage of the War to Spanish and Imperialist service. By this time the Habsburgs were still less able than the Swedes to put "national" regiments into the field, even by drawing heavily on their local peasantry. The English Civil War and the rising in Ireland cut across a direct recruiting drive which had recently been undertaken by Ottavio Piccolomini to raise troops in Britain for the Emperor. In the spring of 1644 Piccolomini himself arrived in the south of England from the Spanish Netherlands and was greeted by the Cavaliers with the slogan that "Emperors and Kings must help each other against their treacherous vassals". It is not known whether this view was shared by Prince Rupert, who was defeated at Marston Moor in July of the same year: his own father, after all, had been equally treacherous from the Imperialist point of view. With the winter of 1644–5 the royalist position grew precipitately worse, and more and more noble volunteers crossed the seas to the southern Netherlands and France. In the spring of 1647 the conclusion of the first Civil War left so many Cavaliers "without king or country" that they flocked into Spanish service. Piccolomini and the Brussels court of Leopold William used such English royalists as go-betweens with the "Dutch rebels", the circles around Frederick Henry of Orange. Charles I from his prison in the castle of Holmby was supposed to have approved the entry of his supporters into the Spanish army of Flanders, at least until his "new war" should break out.

This duly took place at the beginning of 1648, when many royalists as if by prearrangement quit the Spanish colours and set sail again for south-west England or Scotland in ships provided by the *Stadholder* William. But in the summer Fairfax forced one Cavalier army to capitulate at Colchester and Cromwell annihilated another at Preston. By the end of the year the incarcerated king awaited his imminent trial and the execution which horrified monarchist Europe (30 January 1649). What remained of the royalist faction prepared to re-enter the service of Spain; its last attempt to revolt in England was to end in the shattering defeat of Worcester (3 September 1651).

At the time of the Hispano-Dutch peace in January 1648 England's rôle in the European conflict was thus already reduced to that of potential supplier of war materials – and of course revolutionary example. Neither the Spaniards, nor Leopold William in Brussels, nor Mazarin's government seem to have been burning with the desire to assist Charles Stuart in his grim struggle and prolong the bloodbath in England; all were themselves near the end of their strength. The greatest willingness to intervene still came from Charles's son-in-law, William II. But there was never any serious threat of a legitimist crusade against the Parliamentarians on the part of the monarchs of Europe: even William II's intentions were, as we have seen, entirely blocked by the new aggressive neutrality of commercial interests in his country.

By the end of the 1640s the "grand coalition" of 20 years earlier had become just a nostalgic reminiscence, above all for Protestant Bohemia. With the departure of England and Holland the anti-Habsburg camp came to demonstrate more and more its essentially feudal character. Since the Czech exiles were represented largely, with the exception of a group in Saxony, by spokesmen of bourgeois background, this meant that their hopes of a proper hearing were now still further reduced. The twelve-point programme which they put before the Congress of Westphalia at the beginning of April 1646 was easily rejected by the Imperialist delegate Trautmannsdorf as unacceptable. The French in particular, despite all the assertions of German historians to the contrary, were much more concerned at Münster with prosecuting their war against Spain than with Machiavellian schemes for dominance in the Holy Roman Empire.

It was with the help of French diplomacy that Christina was able to undermine the position of the Oxenstiernas, father and son. To eliminate the great Chancellor entirely while the war was still on was out of the question, but the Queen used Adler Salvius to maintain a more conciliatory course at the peace-table, while Oxenstierna's belligerent party still pressed for the maximum of military success. This latter was in itself no easy matter. The spring and summer of 1645 had seen one more failure in the series of abortive joint campaigns involving Sweden and her Transylvanian ally: henceforth the theatre of war was transferred back to Germany. Here too stalemate was approaching. In May 1645 the Imperialists and Bavarians had scattered a French army under Turenne at Mergentheim in Franconia, only to lose their advantage three months later at Allerheim in Swabia. In 1646 Turenne together with the Swedes under Wrangel penetrated into Bavaria, and Wrangel in his march south even took the town of Bregenz in Vorarlberg. But he achieved no more. Maximilian of Bavaria first signed a truce with the invaders, then, as soon as they had quit his territory, succumbed to pressure from the Imperialist army and reverted to the Habsburg side. In August 1647 Wrangel's army advanced again, this time through Eger into western Bohemia; but at Třebel (Triebel) he was again halted. By now Sweden's chances of imposing her earlier demands at Westphalia had quite faded: at the end of 1647 the secret instructions to her delegates contained no precise conditions of claims to be made on behalf of Czech emigrants or non-Catholics within Bohemia. The only notable exception remained Silesia whose strategic importance as a counter against a hostile Poland was still evident in Stockholm.

After the Dutch withdrawal from the conflict Sweden's negotiators found their position further weakened by the desertion of the German Protestant princes. For them peace was now a desperate necessity, to be bought at any price. "This war has lasted so long", wrote one contemporary, "that they have left it

more out of exhaustion than from a sense of right behaviour . . .
Now it is at last coming to its close, but without bringing anything
to its proper conclusion". The Imperial Estates were no longer
interested in any justice for the Czechs and this was even truer of
Mazarin in France, threatened by a wave of peasant and urban
risings, and by growing resistance from the nobility which announced the *Fronde* to come. Although the final major campaign
of Turenne and Wrangel into south-west Germany destroyed the
Imperialists at Zusmarshausen, and a little later the very last
troops Ferdinand III could spare to send to the Spanish Netherlands were scattered by the Prince de Condé at Lens, no steps
were taken by Paris to capitalize on the situation.

Spain's position was desperate in the extreme, despite the
ending of hostilities with the Dutch. On top of the paralyzing
separatist struggles in Catalonia and Portugal there had now
come a revolutionary crisis in the Viceroyalty of the Two Sicilies.
This southern Italian territory, known more familiarly as Naples,
had borne with Milan a large part of the cost of Spanish military
commitment, and had also, at least until a serious outbreak of
plague in the 1630s, provided many recruits for both Spanish
and Imperialist armies. In return some of its noble families had
found new opportunities to further their ambitions, especially by
way of the confiscations in Bohemia: examples of this were
Ottavio Piccolomini and Matthias Gallas, the Dukes of Amalfi
and Lucera, the Carettos, Collaltos, Colloredos and others.

At the end of 1646 the Spanish Viceroy in Naples d'Arcos
imposed new taxes on consumption to cover war expenses. But
early in July the following year there were clashes in the capital
between the populace and the tax-collectors, in the centre of
which stood a young fishmonger's assistant called Tommaso
Aniello or Masaniello. By the 7 July the whole city was effectively
in the hands of the insurgents, who claimed that they had no
grievance with Spain itself. Masaniello's group was soon joined
by the Neapolitian burgher intelligentsia who brought to the
rising a new element of hatred for the Viceroy's Spanish advisers
and the local barons. On 10 July the mediation of the Archbishop
of Naples, Cardinal Filomarino, even seemed to have produced a
settlement between the Viceroy and the rebels, but this the
aristocracy, led by Don Giuseppe Caraffa, were determined to
frustrate. Their attempt on the life of Masaniello was a failure;
instead it was Caraffa who was killed with several of his lieutenants. Masaniello was now declared leader of the loyal Nea-

politans (he was styled *Capitano generale del fedelissimo Popolo*) but his position was insecure. First he was placed in durance as a "madman"; then, having succeeded in escaping, he was assassinated by conspirators in Spanish pay (16 July). With the death of Masaniello the "seven days" of popular rule in Naples were at an end, but the anti-Spanish movement continued. Resistance was taken up by his rival Genoino, and after him by the Prince of Massa. In October 1647 Gennaro Annese proclaimed Naples a republic, with as its first "Duke" the French-supported candidate Henri de Lorraine, Duke of Guise. By the beginning of 1648 it was no longer a popular but an Estates-dominated régime which hindered the activities of the Spanish monarchy. Soon the tables were again turned: Count Oñate, once the Spanish ambassador in Vienna, was sent to Naples as Viceroy and in April 1648 he came to terms with Gennaro Annese, drove the French out of the country and renewed Spanish government there. The Two Sicilies now returned to their apathetic rôle as a part of Madrid's system of hegemony in Italy, and this second short "Italian period" of the Thirty Years War was over even more swiftly than the first.

The whole situation in Europe was clearly ripe for a compromise. On 8 March 1648 an accord was reached in the Westphalian cities on the fundamental question of confessional relations in the Empire: it was agreed that the state of things on 1 January 1624 was to be re-established. Further lengthy negotiations over the so-called *satisfaction* (the settlement of the claims of the Swedish army) resulted in a decree issued on 17 July regulating economic issues and including an Imperial amnesty, which was however limited to Catholics. The skilful diplomatic isolation of Spain by France eliminated the final remaining obstacle, and by early August the proposal for a peace settlement had been approved; it was signed in Münster and Osnabrück on 24 October 1648. All this time the last important military episode in the war was running its parallel course, and fittingly its scene was Prague where hostilities had begun exactly thirty years earlier. In the summer of 1648 the Swedish general Königsmarck suddenly invaded Bohemia and on 26 August he seized that part of its capital which lies to the west of the Vltava: the Kleinseite and the Hradschin. But instead of now striking directly for the right bank of the river, the attackers gave themselves over to plundering. The other Swedish armies were not yet at hand and Prague had the opportunity to organize its defences. When the main strength of the enemy under its commander, the Count Palatine Karl Gustav, later King Charles X and a relative of Frederick the Palsgrave, reached the gates of the city it was ready to resist, and it prolonged this defiance until the final deliverance in November.

The failure before Prague was a consequence of the whole acquisitive character of the Swedish war-effort. It could no longer count on the fighting spirit of the Upper Austrian peasantry, nor was there in Bohemia the prospect of any further widespread movement against the Habsburgs. In Prague a majority of the people could not now remember how things had been before the war, and there were many citizens who stood rather to lose by the advent of Swedish government. Contemporary observers are agreed that the population of Bohemia was by this time equally badly disposed towards the soldiery of both sides. It seems anyway that the Swedes had not conceived their action as anything other than a chance to strengthen their hand at the conference table, though even the capture of all Prague would scarcely have had a significant effect on negotiations already so far advanced. Thus the "Bohemian question" was at length disposed of, in the second clause of the fifth article of the Peace ratified in Osnabrück, which laid down 1 January 1624 as base date for all the affairs of central Europe. This was of course a point in time by which the power of the Habsburgs was unassailable, and hence it meant automatic international recognition for the rule of the dynasty in the Bohemian lands. The Czech exiles were reduced to seeking some recompense through *satisfaction*; only as Catholics could they ever return home.

Besides a few Dutch radicals and Pope Innocent X, the spokesmen of the Bohemian emigrants were the only group in European public opinion which condemned the Peace of Westphalia. At the end of 1649 their leader, Comenius, wrote a letter to Axel Oxenstierna in which he bewailed the fate of his countrymen and his native land in a tone of deep remorseful pessimism:

Our God has till now been strong in showing our neighbours that in deserting our cause they have also deserted their own . . . To accuse others in misfortune is the way of an ill-bred man. It would therefore be unworthy of us to rail at others in our own distress and complain of their behaviour. Rather it is the beginning of wisdom to look within ourselves and search our own omissions and want of humanity . . . For we must admit that we have not taken enough thought for ourselves, but always besought others to carry the fight on our behalf.

THE AFTERMATH: BOHEMIA AND MORAVIA

The long struggle of 1618–48 showed conclusively how vital were advanced economic conditions for the political power of states. The crucial international position of the Netherlands and France in western Europe and the rôle of Wallenstein in the battle for the centre of the continent turned the attention of governments in increasing degree to the problem of strengthening their economies. Questions of technology and industrial development came to the fore in the plans of territories both great and small.

The Bohemian lands, the prime support of Habsburg power in central Europe, had remained throughout the course of the conflict a leading object of the attentions of both sides, and by its end they were merely the plaything of material ambitions. For all that their decimated population had paid the greatest price in property and human life, had now lost all chance of acting out any distinctive part in future developments. 1648 signified the beginning of the most tragic chapter in Bohemian history and for three centuries to come the nation was to be exploited by foreigners in the interests of outsiders. On top of the loss of political independence came the cruel blows of cultural and spiritual oppression. In contrast to the comparative liberty of religion in Germany, albeit regularly dictated by individual states, Bohemia remained under the exclusive control of the Catholic Church and felt the full burden of its intolerance in all fields of expression. While the major lands of the Empire could now recover from their economic exhaustion and build a greater autonomy for the future, Bohemia, which had been their senior, declined into provincial obscurity.

The fullest consequences of the Thirty Years War were felt throughout the framework of Czech life, public and private. The War was the first serious rent in the fabric of the Bohemian state, and the separation from it of Lusatia the first step in a more modern *Drang nach Osten* on the part of the princes of Germany. Internally, although the feudal nexus was structurally unchanged, fundamental shifts took place in the relation of the leaders of the Estates to government and to the king; a new line was drawn between the rights of the state on one hand and the obligations of its inhabitants on the other. There was a profound break in the concept of politics: mutual recognition between monarch and Estates as independent and equal partners was replaced by the unilateral *diktat* of the ruler. The prescriptive rights of the peasantry which had been recognized before the White Mountain at all levels of government were now sacrificed to the interests of a domineering nobility, while a foreign ideology and foreign influences widened the gulf between social classes.

The economy of Bohemia was ruined for many long years by the calamitous population decline during the War: from about 1,700,000 to less than one million. This loss in manpower was aggravated by the exceptional damage to dwellings, cultivated land and all kinds of equipment and resources. At the same time the reduced human and material potential was exposed to ever-growing military and other demands from the state and its leading magnates. The most basic change in economic relations, and the one which was to have most far-reaching consequences, was the creation of a largely deprived peasantry, entirely dependent both materially and spiritually on the authority of the lord. The victorious Habsburg régime sold out the people to the mercenary forces on which it relied for its own power. The *robot* came to demand up to half the peasant farmer's working time; feudal payments, taxes and tithes could eat up two-thirds of the gross return on his husbandry. Within another thirty years of West-phalia, by the March *Patent* of 1680, the government took a final step in the process of entirely overturning the conditions which had obtained in 1618: its policy ushered in the period of "bloody revolt" in the Bohemian countryside.

Thus the peasant sector, which had represented a powerful, autonomous economic force and had played a basic rôle in the well-developed domestic market before the White Mountain, was now pressed into the position of mere supplier of labour to its proprietors, deprived of almost all rights. Its earlier lively part in agricultural production and cottage manufacturing was effectively eliminated. Among the landlords many of the smaller operators, especially among the knights, fell by the wayside, and the strong initiatives which had come from this class, the fresh techniques they had brought to small rural communities, were submerged amid the great concentrated *latifundia*. The towns too had lost their self-government and were crippled for decades by ac-cumulated debt and the capital destruction of the War. Clear evidence of the new absolute predominance of a small group of magnates and Catholic prelates is given by the figures for land ownership: almost three-quarters of the whole of Bohemia now belonged to the lords and the Church (60 per cent and 12 per cent respectively), as against 13 per cent to the effete boroughs and 10 per cent to the knights, whose proportion had earlier been almost one-third.

The culture of Bohemia before the White Mountain had been among the freest and most flexible in Europe. Now the pressure of war and an inimical ideology sapped the creative powers of its people and material conditions demanded their whole attention. Most of its intellectual leaders were in exile, men like Jan Amos Comenius, Pavel Stránský, Pavel Skála of Zhore, and the counter-reforming régime hindered even the feeble strivings of a Bohuslav Balbín or Tomáš Pešina in favour of the Czech nation. The native language was forced into obscurity for almost two centuries and Czech inspiration could find no public outlet. The only healthy foundation for future evolution was the sturdy insistence of the rural population on maintaining its maternal tongue, its religious toleration and its inborn independence of mind.

The tragedy of the White Mountain has a wider European relevance. Czech philosophers and sociologists, among them J. L. Fischer, have shown keen interest in the history of the Czech democratic tradition and located its roots precisely in these lowest strata of society during the years after 1620. At the same time the German Protestant thinker Bolewski, the director of the Evangelical Academy in Loccum, has pointed to the significance of that tradition for the development of German political attitudes He sees it in the context of the age-old opposition between German and Czech as the key to understanding the "decadence" of both German and Bohemian history during the seventeenth century. The Prussian conception of state and nation, which from the eighteenth century came to dominate German public life and has left its profound imprint on the whole of recent German history, was able to grow precisely because it was left with no democratic counterweight. The weakness of Bolewski's humane view of political life is itself intimately linked with the capitulation of the democratic impulses in the German Reformation of the sixteenth and seventeenth centuries. And the beginning of that chapter in the development of modern Europe is inseparable from the character of Bohemian society on the eve of the Thirty Years War and its tragic eclipse on the battlefield of the White Mountain.

Let us now return to the microcosm of the small Moravian town whose fate we have been following through a period of over thirty years. In the mid-1650s a register of taxable rustical land (the so-called *Acreage Book*) was prepared for the whole of the country as a guide to fiscal obligations. In it the domain town of Zlín, under its new owners the lords of Serényi, is depicted in sombre colours. At the end of the previous century Zlín had contained almost 200 householding families. In the 1620s there were about 150, by 1644 only 125; now in 1656 the commissioners found only 84. Of these, 7 possessed houses on the market square, 3 were peasant proprietors, 47 owners of individual peasant holdings, 2 free-farmers or occupiers of former freeholds, 21 artisans and three cottagers. The *Acreage Book* makes no mention of landless labourers or retainers, but there were clearly not many of these. Several who had been listed as "retainers" in 1644, when there were 24, now appear as householders. Between the beginning and the end of the war the population of Zlín was thus reduced by approximately one-half.

The estate of Zlín was by no means the worst hit in Moravia. Historians of an older generation spilled much ink arguing whether the catastrophic worsening of the peasant's situation in seventeenth century Bohemia was caused by the Habsburg state and its tax impositions or by the local lords of the manor and their officials. Concrete analysis of the situation in Zlín and elsewhere shows however that these are secondary considerations, since the peasantry was weighed down by a uniform burden of demands whose totality was the sum of all feudal obligations. Everything belonged to it in equal measure: the contribution, tithes and dues, the *robot* and the payments in kind. The rôle of individual factors was relatively less significant than their combined weight as the material reality of the dominance of a single feudal ruling class.

Consider again the example of Zlín. Its new lord of 1656, Gabriel Serényi, was certainly far better than his predecessor Kryštof Karel Podstatský of Prusinovice. Podstatský had been a pure rapacious careerist, a man who, as we saw, extorted new labour services while the war was still on and extended the area of his demesne land by claiming possession of fields which were left fallow since the peasants had no seed to sow them with and no cattle to graze on them. Taking much trouble to establish his own exclusive distillery and brewery and forcing the Zlíners to buy his supplies of fish, Podstatský was the perfect example of the ruthless landowner. Serényi immediately showed himself very different from Podstatský and his sons in that, although his family was of Hungarian origin, he wrote in Czech, his father was a Protestant who had supported the rebellion in 1619, and his wife, Elizabeth Zahrádecký, had belonged to the Bohemian Brethren. When old Lady Zahrádecký had asked Karel Žerotín whether she should permit the marriage of her daughter to a Catholic, Žerotín had replied, in the spirit of that already doomed Moravian tradition of tolerance, that if Elizabeth herself was decided then she could not oppose it "for religion's sake, which is outside the power of Your Grace". During the long war Gabriel Serényi owned the two estates of Svetlov and Vasilsko, and proved fair-minded towards the inhabitants of his little town of Bojkovice, even granting them some additional privileges. From the 1640s he was provincial *hejtman* and rose into the lords' Estate; he now acquired, besides Zlín, the lands of Bojanovice, near Hustopeč and Lomnice near Tišnov. At the beginning of the 1660s his career reached its climax when he was appointed *hejtman* of the whole Margravate of Moravia. In this capacity he called up the national militia against the Turks in 1663, before dying the following year.

Serényi did not live at Zlín. He delegated the administration of the domain to his burgrave, Nicholas Bavorský, who came from a local burgher family and henceforth ran the estate for a full forty years from 1654, both for Gabriel and his son František Gabriel. The latter also followed an official career, eventually becoming Chief Justice and *hejtman* of the province of Brno, where he still possessed the lands of Lomnice. František Gabriel differed from his father in his artistic and cultural interests: under him the modest family library was expanded and he created a splendid new Baroque ensemble at Lomnice with castle, church and a notable funeral chapel. He had a new townhall built and saw to the completion of the restyled main square. He granted plots of land to the town and cancelled its debts, confirmed its old privileges and provided for the modernizing of its school.

At first sight he seems a characteristic Baroque cavalier, patron of the fine arts and music, and altruistic supporter of his peasantry. But if we compare the Serényi's concern for their lands (the elder in Zlín and Bojkovice, the younger in Lomnice) it becomes clear that the main interest of both was the highest possible rate of economic return. The recovery of Lomnice from its destruction was accomplished less by the privy purse of František Gabriel than by the sweat of the peasantry of Zlín.

Gabriel Serényi knew that the decayed agrarian sector was an unreliable economic base (he realized more than crude profit-seekers like Podstatský or Rottal), and he was therefore eager to stimulate the production of manufactures. During the years 1651-2 he established or renewed guild regulations for the most important trades in Zlín and added new corporations to those already existing. This was the path of tradition, and Comenius for one – whose father was probably born in Serényi's village of Nový Svetlov – had grave doubts about it:

> Although it gives an appearance of order in the affairs of state and church, even of education, nevertheless it contains the seeds of tyranny, and therefore they have done well in the Netherlands to reject the guild system. Let everything be open to all men, so that within the bounds of reason they may undertake what they please, and this will redound to the public good.

Such economic liberalism was inconceivable in the unprepared Moravia of Serényi. Yet these very years of the 1650s and 1660s saw two projects, each prepared by a local mercantilist *avant la lettre*, for curing the manufacturing ills of the Margravate which themselves recommended the abolition of the guilds. Hynek Morgenthaler, a magistrate from Brno, and the advocate Sebastian Malivský saw that the level of production in the old guilds was a guide to the kind of market available for a given craft, but they emphasized that the route to economic growth lay through higher artisan standards rather than inflexible regimentation.

Ten years later František Gabriel Serényi established or renewed the guild charters and registers of Lomnice. Of course it was one thing formally to constitute such associations, quite another actually to raise a town from stagnation. František Gabriel took a direct course: between 1667–71 he simply transferred from Zlín to Lomnice at least 32 families – 160 or more persons. The stereotyped entry in the town records: "resettled in Lomnice through the will and by order of the authorities" demonstrates that the Zlíners did not move of their own volition. In only one case do we read that a family was acting on its private initiative. In the period before 1620 movement of peasants on this scale purely by the *fiat* of the landlord was quite unheard-of. The first instance of it in Moravia was the transfer after 1644 of many recalcitrant Vlachs to the estate of Kvasice, which lay in the centre of the country and belonged to the Imperial commissioner Jan von Rottal. Investigation if its earliest registers reveals that a majority of the inhabitants of one village there (Nová Dedina) were bearers of names which are familiar from the lists of Vlachs in Vsetín and Lukov drawn up during 1644. The Zlín case was thus not the first, and certainly not the last of its kind.

What did this emigration of Zlíners to Lomnice mean for the little town they were deserting? According to a visitation of 1670 there were then 98 householders in Zlín, which meant (including a certain number of casual labourers) between 500 and 600 people. The town had therefore lost at least one-fifth of its inhabitants, the majority able craftsmen. So many weavers had left that the guild registers, begun in 1657, were simply transferred with them to Lomnice. Besides this, some who departed had played an important part in the cultural life of Zlín. The traditional family of Klabík is an example: Jan Klabík was cantor at the nearby school of Želechovice in the 1660s. There he wrote and illustrated a beautiful hymn-book in which he perpetuated his own allegiance to Zlín. This hymn-book was, it seems, inherited by his brother Nicholas, and then became transferred with the latter to Lomnice. Thus an important product of the spiritual life of a community which possessed an 80-year-old literary fellowship passed into an environment where all Church music was under the control of the authorities. There were no Klabíks in this new home, and only their hymn-book remained. In Zlín the fellowship still survived to uphold standards of singing and as late as 1681 Václav Svorec compiled and painted for it a new hymn-book. Its links with earlier non-Catholic traditions are beyond dispute: a whole series of its hymns was modelled on examples in the printed work of the exile Jiří Třanovský (Tranoscius) called *Cithara Sanctorum*. Protestant contacts must therefore still have been alive, even at this date.

But how was it possible for the number of householders in Zlín actually to increase between 1656 and 1670 when a fifth of the population had emigrated? And how could eleven new farms have been created when the authority was appropriating all untilled soil? Part of the answer seems to emerge from the text of the last urban privilege granted to the community of Zlín by František Gabriel Serényi at the end of 1672. According to it the lord first and foremost wrote off the debt contributions both of corporation and individual citizens, and further bound himself to pay the rector of the school and the organist. He waived the demands for *robot*, dues, *escheat* and payments in kind, all of which the town had anyway long ago commuted with previous authorities, provided that Zlín would abandon its right to control the sale of beer and the levying of excise. Thus the Zlíners gained temporary relief, but the cost to them of confirming their old privileges and being released from debts was a high one. Serényi strengthened the peasant character of the town, and the sum effect of his measures was as detrimental to it as those of an overtly maleficent landlord like Podstatský.

Besides, the consequences of war were far from eliminated by 1670 or 1672. If we carry ourselves forward to the year 1700 and imagine a journey from Zlín to Uherský Brod on that same map of Moravia which Comenius had drawn in 1626 we shall find some very noticeable changes. Whereas around 1600 the traveller on this road would have passed through nine estates great and small, by 1700 only four remained, and as far as the Kaunitzes of Brod all were in the hands of foreigners. The petty nobility had almost disappeared and the whole of Eastern Moravia under the shadow of the Carpathians belonged to magnates: the Rottals, Liechtensteins, Castelcornos, Magnises and Serényis, all families whose rise dated from the time of the great War.

Zlín itself covered the same ground area in 1700 as a century before. But the boundaries of the town itself had changed: the once flourishing settlement around the church had vanished completely and with it three whole streets. Elsewhere the place was still full of "burnt-out, deserted and demolished houses". The separate township of Trávník had disappeared and all that remained of it was a single peasants' street "outside the borough". Only the "Long Lane" had been extended, and it by the addition of some workers' cottages where *robot* obligations were worse than elsewhere. Thus in 1700 Zlín was smaller and more like a peasant community than it had been a hundred years earlier. Even in 1731, when it is again possible to construct a list of the inhabitants of the town, we still find them fewer than at the end of the sixteenth century. The figures for 1731 are 124 householders and 68 tenants, a total of 192 families, whereas in 1592 there had been (excluding Trávník) 153 holdings and 198 families in all. Thus it took over 80 years to heal the wounds which war had inflicted, and a full three generations felt these direct effects. And by 1731 the town was wholly in the power of its territorial lord:

he had acquired the brewery and the malthouse, the tavern on the square and the brickworks, he controlled both the urban mills. The baths at Dřevnice had vanished, the washhouse and shambles fallen on bad times, the manorial distillery passed to a new Jewish tenant. Craft manufactures had declined and the annual fairs retained only a little of their former importance; most artisans had now to work on the land for part of their livelihood.

Where, finally, could this extra agrarian activity find enough soil? Although the population was smaller it must have produced more, since revenues increased. In Zlín as elsewhere during the seventeenth century the authority appropriated extensive stretches of the most fertile country land and its subjects were forced to seek compensation further afield. The Zlíners found it on the cold north-facing slopes of the local hills: and although their numbers were few, the way there an inhospitable walk across the mountainside, and the area itself a wilderness of bushes and undergrowth, their back-breaking labour brought results. Most of these assarts were cut during the lengthy service of Nicholas Bavorský; it was he who thus benefited from the special feudal due payable to the bailiff on such occasions and popularly known as the butter levy, since it was often rendered in pints of butter.

Zlín's greatest wealth therefore lay in the skill and endeavour of its people. Their numbers, as we have seen, recovered slowly, under the pressure of the new serfdom and the progressive decline into rustic obscurity. But there were major changes in their composition. During the War many old families fell by the wayside and after 1644 there were few left of any standing. A different patriciate only began to develop through the second half of the century, and the process culminated in mass migrations from other nearby Serényi domains along the borders of Moravia and Hungary. Whereas the population of the town in 1670 was still three-quarters made up of the descendants of families known to have been there at the beginning of the century, the next decades brought an influx from the south-east which helped to stamp the area with a linguistic character it still possesses. By 1700 only 14 families remained of the 198 listed in the register for 1592; 127 of the 189 names are entirely new.

The picture of Zlín after the Thirty Years War is thus a sombre one, and more gloomy than many of the conclusions drawn for other parts of Bohemia, though we must not forget that some localities suffered still worse privations. Whereas Zlín was encountering certain economic difficulties before the outbreak of hostilities, they did not amount to any kind of crisis and it was only the war which brought dislocation of the labour force, a decline in production, trade and civil autonomy. The subjects of the Zlín estate were dragged progressively into a state of real bondage as their lord gained powers to hold or move them at will. But the picture has rays of light: however much traditions might be threatened and even existence hang in the balance, the town never became just the passive plaything of authority. Through all its sufferings it carried an essential resolve which drove its farmers to recover new ploughlands when time allowed, and its textile-workers, weavers, and cobblers to pursue the established crafts of the place until an era of fresh opportunities dawned a century later. A concern for school and hospital, the Church and its music, these are likewise pointers to the enduring but sorely-tried virtues of one small but typical settlement in Moravia.

Ten

THE PEACE AND ITS CONSEQUENCES

THE long-awaited settlement was signed at the headquarters of the Imperial delegation in Münster on 24 October 1648. The so-called "Hall of Peace" in the town's *Rathaus* with its inscription *Pax Rerum Optima* over the portal was in fact the venue only for the preliminary agreement between Spain and the Netherlands, proclaimed on 15 May and perpetuated on canvas by the official Dutch painter, Gerald Terborch. Not until 18 February 1649 were documents ratifying the whole "Peace of Westphalia" exchanged, and on 21 February the congress dispersed after a great celebration and shouts of *Vivat Pax* – only to reassemble the following April in Nuremberg for a discussion of the practical realization of the pacification terms. This lasted until June 1651 and ended in a decisive diplomatic success for the Imperialists, ably represented by Ottavio Piccolomini.

There were a number of problems which the Westphalian agreements left entirely unresolved. One was the war between France and Spain which dragged on through the first and second *Frondes* (1648–51, 1652–4) until in November 1659 the French, backed by Cromwellian England and a new alliance of princes of the Empire (the *Rheinbund*), could dictate terms on a tiny island (the Isle of Pheasants) in the frontier river Bidassoa. This too was a compromise solution: France evacuated Catalonia and Portugal and returned the Franche-Comté, while Spain agreed to the marriage of the Infanta with Louis XIV, conceded Rousillon, Artois and some smaller territories on the southern borders of Germany, abandoned its claims to Alsace and removed its garrison from the fortress of Jülich in Westphalia. Worst hit by this arrangement was Spain's faithful ally the Duke of Lorraine. The Peace of the Pyrenees, the conventional name given to this treaty, was a typical agreement between two feudal states, exhausting itself in bickering over territory and matrimonial bargains. Yet at a deeper level it sealed the future of Spain as a monarchy of the second rank and confirmed the France of Louis xiv as dominant power over a large tract of Europe.

Nor did Westphalia touch the long-standing rivalry between Sweden and the state of Poland-Lithuania. The new Vasa king of Poland, Jan Kazimir (1648–68), began his reign with an attack on the Cossacks of the Ukraine and their powerful protector, Moscovite Russia. In 1654 Sweden, under Charles x Gustav, the besieger of Prague, joined his enemies, perceiving a splendid opportunity to disarm unrest at home through a triumphant foreign campaign. Charles's successes were however too great to hold together a precarious alliance which had early lost its Eastern protagonist and attracted instead Brandenburg and France. The Swedish victory after a three-day struggle at Warsaw (1656) brought the Emperor and Spain openly onto the Polish side, a momentary resurrection of the old alliance, and Charles's involvement in the subsequent civil war within Poland lost him the support of Brandenburg, which concluded a separate peace (1657). In May 1657 Frederick iii of Denmark (1648–70), inheriting the short-sighted policies of Christian iv, declared war on Sweden, and again Charles's vigorous response both on land and sea brought him more success than was diplomatically sound. The dictated peace at Roskilde (1658) gave him Scånia, Bornholm, Trondhjem and a share in the Sound tolls, but left him politically isolated. An anti-Swedish coalition was formed by the Emperor, Poland, Brandenburg and the Dutch; this took control of the situation and used French mediation to impose compromise agreements at Copenhagen (between Sweden and Denmark) and Oliva (between Sweden and Poland), both in 1660. Meanwhile the Russo-Polish hostilities lingered on until mutual exhaustion forced peace in 1667 with recognition of the *status quo ad* 1654. The latest stage of the Northern war brought most gain to Brandenburg and indirectly to France, whose influence now began to replace that of the Dutch in Sweden and the Habsburgs in Poland.

The clearest result of Westphalia was its territorial changes, and in this sense it remained formally valid until the dissolution of the Holy Roman Empire early in the nineteenth century. Two

new sovereign entities were created from what had previously
been parts of the *Reich*: the Netherlands and Switzerland. Of the
Swiss cantons only the Grisons (Graubünden) had been directly
involved in the war, but the decision at Münster to release them
all from Imperial obligations was the reward of the Protestant
cantons as a whole, and above all of the mayor of Basle, Johann
Rudolf Wettstein. It was the Empire which had to pay for the
Habsburg determination to preserve intact the *Erblande* of the
House; and thus Vienna's success in retaining Silesia and giving
no liberties to the Protestants of Bohemia and Austria had to be
balanced by the cession to Sweden of a part of Pomerania, a
series of bishoprics, among them Bremen and Verden, and
practical control over the rivers Oder, Elbe and Weser. In addition the Austrian Habsburgs handed over the fortress of
Breisach, thereby opening up for France the door to Alsace and
Lorraine, and beyond that the whole of south Germany. Here
the guarantee of continuing French influence was still Maximilian
of Bavaria, who was recompensed with the retention of his
electoral dignity granted in 1623 and the acquisition of the Upper
Palatinate; the successors of Frederick the Palsgrave were
allowed to return to their Rhenish lands only, and were given a
new, inferior electoral title. But the gains of the Bavarian Wittelsbachs were overshadowed by those of the Hohenzollerns of
Brandenburg: now the Church lands of Magdeburg, Halberstadt
and Minden linked the territory of the old Electorate with their
Cleves-Jülich inheritance in the Rhineland. Saxony, whose
diplomacy had more than once rescued the Habsburgs from dire
peril, received only Lusatia, which had already been assigned to
it at the Peace of Prague in 1635. The devoted clients of Sweden
in Germany gained even less.

Besides these new geo-political arrangements the Congress of
Westphalia settled two basic problems which affected the Ger-
manic core of the Holy Roman Empire: the ecclesiastical and the
constitutional issues. It decided them by a compromise which
pleased no-one and which drew vain protests from the Papal
nuncio Cardinal Chigi, later Pope Alexander VII. Chigi was
forced to bow to the fact that the powers had rejected Curial
intervention and the peace document was forearmed against the
expected fulminations of Rome. The inglorious response to the
Papal Bull *Zelo Domus Dei*, which was dated December 1648
but proclaimed only in January 1651, underlined the declining
international effectiveness of the sanctions of the Curia. The

Edict of Restitution and the provisions of the Peace of Prague were revoked, the princes and Estates of the Empire received full sovereignty, the Electors lost their dominant position, and henceforth the Emperor would need the approval of the Reichstag for decisions of foreign policy – the *jus pacis et belli* was in future to be shared. Disputes over religion were no longer to be resolved either by the Emperor or by the majority, but through the amicable agreement of both sides. The squabble over a base date to which everything could now return ended with rejection both of the radical Protestant claim for 1618 and of the Catholic demand for 1630. The compromise of 1 January 1624 brought an irony of fate: for the area which had traditionally enjoyed most confessional tolerance, the Habsburgs lands, and especially the kingdom of Bohemia, found that the old authoritarian principle of *Cuius regio eius religio* was now reapplied in full measure. But the men of 1648 were not interested in religious issues as such, and ever since 1618 these had always, as we have seen, been inseparably linked with political and social problems, merely lending a certain "ideological" content to the struggle for power. The thesis of the Swedish historian Göransson that the religious aspects of the War were in continual decline thus seems to be misplaced.

For the future development of European society, however, the most important consequences of the long War lay in forces unmentioned by the clauses of Münster, the Pyrenees, Oliva and the rest. The treaties did not and could not give expression to a truth which only the passage of time has revealed: that the Thirty Years War meant the completion of one stage in the process of world history, and that Westphalia inaugurated an era where this history becomes effectively a unitary one involving the whole continent of Europe and the overseas dependencies of the maritime powers.

In what ways did this come about? It did so primarily because the War changed the structure of European society, a society which under the pressure of events during the conflict for the first time became aware of its existence and its essential unity. The War embraced all the states of Europe for greater or lesser periods of time, with the single possible exception of the Ottoman dominions in the south-east, which nevertheless themselves exerted a not insignificant influence on its course. The entire continent was divided into two warring camps, for all that both coalitions were unstable and some countries wavered between them or passed from one to the other. And this fact is rendered no less valid because a fully European strategy is evident more in propaganda and planning than in reality, or because the idea of an anti-Habsburg front with western and eastern wings remained a dream from 1619 to 1645. There are scholars who have doubted whether the War was in fact important enough to stand as a distinct subject of historical study (S. H. Steinberg is the most recent); there are others who see it as the first step towards world conflict. The truth is surely that the traditional view of the War as a struggle which began at a local level and turned into something "general" is false. Already during the years of the "Bohemian War" people were reflecting on the sort of complex interaction which meant that the Czechs' demand for help from Holland and England could not be satisfied, since these two "natural allies" were in contention about fishing rights in the seas between Scotland and Greenland and the division of former Portuguese territories in the East Indies.

There were other ways in which the Thirty Years War differed from its sixteenth century predecessors. It was the first conflict where active diplomacy played an important rôle, and thus it meant a new stage in the evolution of international relations. Without subsidies from Spain Vienna could not have held out in 1618–20 – and subsidies were unthinkable without the influx of silver from America. The same was still true in succeeding decades, and Austrian diplomacy was therefore vitally concerned over all developments in the southern Netherlands, Catalonia, Naples and Milan. Without Dutch subsidies and Dutch organizational strength anti-Habsburg resistance during 1621–5 could not have maintained itself; there would have been no coalition of the Hague, no Swedish invasion of central Europe after 1630. Without France and her backing neither Sweden nor Transylvania nor Catalonia could have prospered. Thus we can say that a precondition for the generalizing of the conflict was the presence in early seventeenth century Europe, if not of an economic unity, at least of a framework for exchange and the first signs of a world market, whose centre of gravity was the whole area between Baltic, Atlantic and Mediterranean.

The War was such a protracted and intensive undertaking that it demanded entirely new methods of military organization and the maintenance of armies. In other words fighting could no longer be left to private entrepreneurs on land and sea. *Condottieri* of the Wallenstein type could not compete with the state as military employers. The English were forced in the end to construct a new kind of fleet under the guidance of Republican generals, while even the Netherlands had to put a national navy in the place of ships loaned from trading companies. As the size, composition and equipment of armies changed, the financial sources which supported them became the instruments of power politics. In some cases these sources were clearly defined and ultimately inadequate: Spain continued to live basically off Old Castile, the Austrian Habsburgs off the credit of their cousins in Madrid and nebulous hopes of solvency through confiscations or military plunder. During the time when Wallenstein was still regarded as a devoted servant of Habsburg power he was growing aware that those methods were not enough and therefore sought to establish a more solid economic base through control of the commerce of his "subject" towns and a share in their revenue. The Danes financed their policies from the profits of their customs; the Swedes counted on securing their status as a great power by a monopoly on the carrying trade between Russian and western Europe, domination of the Prussian ports and the Sound, subsidies from Holland and later France, and finally a substantial *satisfaction* in Germany. Ultimately however Sweden did not manage to find any complete solution to the problem, still less was this possible for more retarded states like Poland.

There is one further relevant fact which rendered the Thirty Years War quite different from what had gone before: it openly displayed the very clear links between economics and politics. This was not just a question of debits and credits – if indeed we can speak of credits at all amid such destruction of human life. Losses on the field of battle were, by comparison with later conflicts, limited, although the rising standards of medical care were not yet able to prevent many times that number of deaths among the wounded, especially as a result of plague outbreaks among the soldiery. There were certainly incomparably more victims in the civilian population. If in Germany some districts lost up to one-third of their inhabitants, central Europe and the Bohemian lands contained more than a few places where the decline reached 50 per cent. Yet it was ultimately less the depredations of the fighting itself which affected demographic trends than the dispersal of productive resources and the undiminished claims of the ruling classes.

The War acted as a catalyst to accelerate certain socio-economic changes which were already in progress before it broke out. We can indeed say (in the spirit of Lenin) that the economic realities remained in essence unaltered by war and that their basic evolutionary tendencies existed quite separately from it. But it is also a fact that the conflict had different contexts, here contributing to the economic rise of the Netherlands, there creating the preconditions for a revolutionary shift of productive relations in England, elsewhere perhaps encouraging boom conditions in neutral countries. Against this it meant the destruction of the middling classes in central Europe, the temporary elimination of the nobility from private initiative in places as far apart as Bohemia and Holstein, the liquidation of Johan Skytte's land reform in Sweden's Baltic territories and the exaggeration of the move towards a new serfdom over a large part of Europe. In time this last point was to prove most vital of all: the West now gained a series of advantages which the East lacked, and a further step was taken towards the artificial separation of the two; a foundation was growing for the myth that the Eastern half of the continent was a natural source of food and raw materials, and a ready market for cheap finished goods. This of course was a long-term process, still uncompleted in 1648 or 1660, but the three decades of the "Great War" proved an important stage in its development.

It is evident too that the picture was not totally or uniformly sombre. Western regions of Germany recovered more easily than Eastern ones, and some Imperial cities had more working capital at the end of the fighting than earlier. The war brought a boom in agriculture, and production on the land was therefore placed in difficulties rather by its conclusion than its outbreak. Trade in corn was never interrupted, exports of textiles from West to East increased sharply (even though it is difficult to believe that the amount passing from England to Russia really rose by 300 per cent between 1620 and 1640), the cooperation of Swedes and Dutch laid the foundations for the rapid expansion of copper and iron mining in Scandinavia, not to speak of new armaments and engineering needs. A comparison between the fate of the undertakings of De Geer and Trip in Sweden and those of Jan de Witte in Bohemia is instructive: it shows that production which served exclusively military demands stood on feet of clay and collapsed as soon as the conditions which had favoured it were past.

Thus the Thirty Years War underlined an already existing inequality of economic development. It did not alter the basic direction of trade routes or the intensity of commercial contacts. It was only temporarily, for instance, that Denmark was able to act in place of the Netherlands as intermediary between the Baltic and the Iberian peninsula. The long-term rise of the Dutch was not halted and Holland lost its lucrative trade with the enemy (*Handel op de vijand*) only in the latter half of the century as England took over the Spanish market permanently.

With this we come to a final point: the War, which was a power-political and diplomatic struggle underpinned by a transition in the evolution of economies, changed the order of European politics and directed it into new channels. Of the two organizational models which the men of 1618 had seen as the focus of the two belligerent camps, the United Provinces and Spain, the latter had by 1648 vanished irretrievably from the perspectives of a succeeding generation. Olivares' dream of world monarchy, so suggestively formulated in the middle of the 1620s, was taken over after 1648 by the publicists of the *Roi Soleil*. For the second half of the seventeenth century another opposition became the axis on which European politics turned: that between the United Provinces and France. How and why England later replaced Holland, which ultimately sank into the rôle of junior partner in an amalgamated firm and to some extent became just a banking and commercial filial to it is one of history's most fascinating questions, but one outside the scope of the present book. It is however a fact that Great Britain and France were to be competing models for the rest of Europe until at least the end of the eighteenth century.

In the great transformations of the period we have been considering, the place of religion as a dominant ideological factor became as it were relativized. Although it was precisely the France of Louis XIV which made a last attempt to mobilize it for political purposes, this is only a further proof that the Bourbons after the death of Colbert had become the spiritual heirs of Habsburg Spain. There is only limited value in the approach of some modern historians who see in the Thirty Years War a struggle between absolute and Estates monarchies. They are in fact compelled to employ a single concept of absolute monarchy for a number of very different polities. If we use instead the Marxist definition of *feudal* absolutism, then we can point to a certain balance between feudal and bourgeois factors in the France of the *ancien régime*, but not in Spain or Austria, and it is not of much consequence simply to prove that absolutism manifested itself in different parts of Europe in various forms and with various social functions. The same is true of "Estates feudalism", within which must be counted Poland as well as the Netherlands.

Another obscure aspect of the historiography of the War lies in the relation postulated between political developments and the superstructure of ideas – the notions of Baroque and Classicism. Several French historians, led by V.-L. Tapié, have temptingly depicted the Baroque as a mood which grew out of its Spanish background and turned into the artistic expression of a society of lords and peasants, grouped around castle and church, the society of a new feudal age. Against this Tapié (and after him Roger Portal, P. Chaunu, P. Francastel and R. Mandrou to a lesser extent) see in Classicism the mirror of a society basically bourgeois but living under an absolute monarch. Here again the historian lacks the right kind of material for comparative study. But an analysis of the origins of the Bohemian Baroque demonstrates that this theory of Tapié's is oversimplified. What we call Bohemian visual, musical and literary Baroque has its roots in the period *before* the White Mountain. Nor can it be seen as exclusively the ideological weapon of a dominant feudalist Catholicism, for if so, how can we explain that the first Baroque church in Bohemia was built on the Kleinseite by Lutherans with the help of fellow-believers throughout western Europe? Baroque in the plastic arts came into its own from the middle of the century, when the old tradition of Prague Mannerism, strongly realistic in character, became influenced by a naturalistic form of north-Italian Baroque, and when there were generous patrons of the style among ecclesiastical dignitaries and institutions and representatives of a neophyte aristocracy. But its creators did not work exclusively for castle, palace or cathedral; they were equally at home in the urban environment and found many commissions there.

All this is easier to ascertain in the visual arts than in the field of social and historical thought. Just as the figure of Michelangelo evades simple definition, so does that of Comenius, in whose work are combined elements of Protestant Humanism, Mannerist emblematics and symbolism, and Baroque forms of expression. It would be wrong to classify Comenius: his writings and personality reflect all the major problems with which he wrestled through his long life (he only died in 1670, in Amsterdam). His greatness is intimately linked with the struggle for everyday existence and inseparable from the iron laws of temporal limitation.

The achievements of Comenius and Grimmelshausen, Opitz and Gryphius, Descartes and Huyghens, Grotius and Quevedo were all reactions to basic issues of the time. The eternal interplay of literature and politics takes on its own forms in any period of history and it is very easy to generalize about them meaninglessly. Yet at least it is clear to us today that the work of the literary figures of the seventeenth century belongs to study of the Thirty Years War, as do the learned circles which grew up around the *Fruchtbringende Gesellschaft* in Weimar, or the Dutch and Swedish patrons of Descartes and Comenius, around the English *Royal Society* and the French *Académie des Sciences*. *Inter arma silent musae*: the proverb made sense against a background like that of the last century, when men distinguished pedantically between disciplines. But Clio, the muse of history, was born of the tragedy and comedy of epic and lyric poetry, and although neither Comenius's *Orbit Pictus* nor Grimmelshausen's *Simplicissimus* is in any sense a treatise on economics or politics, nevertheless both must belong in any final assessment of the period. For all the suffering, bloodshed, and sheer exhaustion which the Thirty Years War indubitably brought, it created the conditions from which, through the crises and revolutions of the mid-seventeenth century, modern Europe was born.

What, in conclusion, has our analysis of the three "levels" of the War demonstrated? The history of the little town of Zlín can help to disperse one attractive myth: that the War was not really so destructive after all. Throughout much of central Europe it was in fact incalculably deleterious, setting back the development of communities by nearly a century and burdening them with a shortsighted, incompetent, upstart nobility which could only prosper at the expense of the peasantry.

The history of the "Bohemian question" is a tragedy equally stark. The flourishing and advanced society of the Czech lands before 1620 was by no means doomed or anachronistic, but its adherents "fought badly for their good cause" (as the English observer had it), and the subsequent refeudalization was a step backward which delayed any further development and fettered all economic initiative. It also changed the whole character of the state. Henceforth the Czech-German opposition grew in intensity, not only in that German settlers spread inwards from the over-populated borderhills, but that the frontier remained a chronically discontented region, easily persuaded into witch-hunts during the seventeenth century and more serious demagogies nearer our own day. Henceforth too the Habsburg Monarchy was fated to be an institution resting on archaic social foundations, where whole sectors of administration were in the hands of the new "Austrian" nobility which had made its fortune through the confiscations. Yet even in the period we have been considering there are signs that the Austrian people were already conceived of separately from their rulers. Various plans emerged for popular anti-Habsburg confederations embracing several provinces, and the years of "darkness" in Bohemia after 1648 – the *temno* – are largely so called because we know as yet all too little about them.

The general history of the War is that of a clash between two power blocks which links the early bourgeois revolution in the Netherlands during the sixteenth century with that in England during the seventeenth century. It grew out of a crisis in central Europe which was primarily political, but where, as recent study of inflation in Italy and Germany during 1619–23 has shown, economic factors were barely concealed beneath the surface. Their rôle appears clearest of all in the "six contemporary revolutions" of the 1640s which gave Karl Marx food for thought when he encountered them in the pages of Schlosser's *Weltgeschichte*. By the end of the struggle one "model" – the Spanish – was eliminated, and one "problem" – the Netherlandish – resolved. Much of this process needs further clarification, particularly from the point of view of domestic developments in Spain and Holland.

What is beyond dispute is the thesis, first sustained by Soviet historiography in the 1940s (especially by O. L. Vajnshtejn) that the Thirty Years War belongs intimately with the story of the Dutch revolution and the movement for liberation from Spain. It is remarkable how little Dutch historians, with the exception of I. Schöffer, E. H. Kossmann and J. Presser, have considered the relations between the United Provinces and the rest of Europe during the "Golden Age" of the Netherlands. There is no lack of work on agrarian and industrial advance, on the financial rôle of Amsterdam and the profits of Dutch entrepreneurship. But we need to know precisely how an internal, bourgeois-led revolution could become a bogy for its adversaries throughout Europe. Some enemies spoke of a "new Holland" in Bohemia during 1618–19, even in the Hansa towns a decade later. Dutch intrigues were imagined in places where they were demonstrably not involved: in Catalonia, Italy, Transylvania. Everywhere rebellions of the Estates were confused with class conflicts, and in much traditional writing are still so confused today. The end of the War coincided with a major crisis within the Netherlands: the beginning of the unrestricted rule of the regent patriciate and the first signs of the contest with England. Both the apotheosis of peace and the apotheosis of Dutch power contained within them the seeds of dissolution.

The Thirty Years War has so frequently been interpreted as a milestone in the history of Europe, as a warning and an appeal to a more contemporary world, that it would be banal to repeat such formulations here, or to engage in the pamphleteering endeavour of seeking in the past something which appears to justify a political decision already taken. In the light of the events of 1968 we cannot recall 1618 without also remembering 1648, just as it is not convincing for a Czech to consider the revolutionary March of 1848 while ignoring the Whitsun reaction in the same year, or 1918 and not 1938. But one thing is born out by all these dates and by the whole history of the Thirty Years War: that the part of the European continent which since the beginning of recorded history has been the home of the Czechs and Slovaks has always reacted very sensitively to world events. The period we have been studying belongs very notably among those during which the national past of Bohemia became closely linked to the whole international situation, and this is a fact of which Czechs have been aware from Comenius and Andreas Habernfeld through Jan Jeník of Bratřice to František Palacký and Anton Gindely. It may be argued, as a modest corollary, that the rest of Europe would do well to pay just attention to the Bohemian standpoint in its interpretation of those events.

Notes on Literature
and Sources

CHAPTER ONE AND GENERAL

IN recent years a series of new works has shown that the interest
both of historians and the reading public in the Thirty Years War
is on the increase. Just before and after the Second World War a
number of authors (George Pagès, C. V. Wedgwood, O. L.
Vajnshtein, Günther Franz) attempted to provide a general
interpretation of the conflict; we are now seeing the amendment
of some of their conclusions and new contributions to an overall
picture.

One of these is the book by the Soviet historian V. M. Alekseev:
Tridtsatiletnyaya Vojna, Leningrad, 1961, which is written in a
non-specialized way on the basis of the latest Russian research.
More recently S. H. Steinberg: *The "Thirty Years War" and the
Struggle for European Hegemony 1600–1660*, London, 1966, has
produced a *compterendu* with a distinctive approach and incorporating the work of some East European historians. Far
from accepting the thesis that the War was all-destructive, Steinberg so underestimates the concrete results of the struggle that
he even doubts the justice of calling it a Thirty Years War at all
(hence the inverted commas in his title). This view is not shared
by T. K. Rabb in a sober analysis of the economic consequences
of the War ("The Effects of the Thirty Years War on the German
Economy", *Journal of Modern History*, xxxv, 1962). Rabb is also
the editor of an interesting anthology, prepared for the university
student, which presents the opinions of a varied selection of
historians – among them Czechs – on the conflict and its protagonists (*The Thirty Years War. Problems of Motive, Extent and
Effect*, Problems in European Civilization, Boston, 1964).

Another, more significant collection of works has examined the War as a historical category in the development of society through the sixteenth and seventeenth centuries. A series of papers on the "general crisis of the seventeenth century" which appeared in the pages of the journal *Past and Present* between 1954 and 1962 has now been edited in book form by Trevor Aston: *Crisis in Europe, 1560–1660*, London, 1965. Most of the contributors take the view that the Thirty Years War acted as a catalyst in hastening divisive tendencies already existing before it. Further support for this position has come from H. Kamen: "The Economic and Social Consequences of the Thirty Years War", *Past and Present*, 39, 1968, who examines the relation between the War and the crisis, and concludes that Germany saw the sudden worsening of an economic malaise but not a complete shift in development. Kamen's argument is weakened by the fact that he analyses only areas within Germany, and then compares them with the evolution in Eastern Europe. That the situation in Central Europe was different again has been demonstrated by the present author ("The Thirty Years War and the Crises and Revolutions of Seventeenth Century Europe", *ibid.*).

Besides these writings, all more or less influenced by Marxism, there exists another way of viewing the crisis which is well represented in contemporary French historiography. Its most traditional exponent is Roland Mousnier: "Les xvie et xviie siècles. Les progrès de la civilisation européenne", *Histoire générale des civilisations*, iv, Paris, 1954, but it receives far more challenging expression in works by R. Mandrou: *Classes et Luttes de Classes en France au début du* xviie *siècle*, Florence, 1965; Pierre Vilar: "Le Temps des Hidalgos", in the attractive volume entitled: *L'Espagne au temps de Phillippe* ii, Collection Âges d'or et Réalités, Paris, 1965, and Pierre Chaunu: *La Civilisation de l'Europe Classique*, Paris, 1966.

If we consider the Thirty Years War as the reflection of some kind of crisis or series of crises, then it follows that we must examine its role in relation, on the one hand, to the Eighty Years struggle between Spain and the United Provinces, and on the other, to the revolutions in England and elsewhere during the 1640s. The character of the Spanish monarchy in the sixteenth and seventeenth centuries has attracted an extensive literature over recent years and this is not the place to rehearse it. For a Central European viewpoint the reader may be referred to this writer's: "Současnýstav bádání o 'Španělské odchylce' či

'Úpadku Spanelska' v 16.–17. století, *Československý Časopis Historický*, XI, 1963, pp. 341–52, and a number of works by the Hungarian historian T. Wittman: "España en la 'Monarquía Española' de Campanella", *Acta Historica*, xv, 1964, Szeged, pp. 3–17; "A spanyol abszolutizmus néhány vonása a xvi. században", *ibid.*, pp. 19–20; "Apuntos sobre los métodos de investigacíon de la decadencia castellana", *Nouvelles Études Historiques*, Budapest, 1965; "Sobre el presunto caracter 'Turco' del absolutismo español del 'siglo de oro' ", *Anuario*, 7, Rosario, 1964, pp. 309–20; "Vitoriától Suárezig. A xvi századi spanyol államelmélet mérlege", *Filologiai Közlöny*, 1966, pp. 53–66. Wittman concludes that the Mediterranean absolutism of the Spanish type differed from other absolutisms in both Western and Eastern Europe. His thesis was critically received by A. N. Chistozvonov: "Nekotorie aspekty problemy genezisa absolutizma", *Voprosy Istorii*, I, 1968, pp. 46–62, who held the opinion that two models of feudal absolute monarchy are sufficient, the one associated with serfdom, the other incorporating capitalist forms and evidently inapplicable to Spain.

A different position is adopted by the French Marxist historian and literary sociologist Noel Salomon in his study of the structure of the Castilian countryside: *La Campagne de Nouvelle Castille à la fin du xvie siècle d'après les Relaciones topográficas*, Paris, 1964. According to Salomon the Spanish monarchy lived off the productive forces of peasant farmers and shepherds and the exploitation of all kinds of land taxation. At the end of the sixteenth century it is impossible to speak in Castile of a balance of power between aristocracy and bourgeoisie, and therefore of any "absolute monarchy". A similar viewpoint emerges from the latest general account of Spanish history, prepared by members of the "school of Barcelona" under the influence of their revered master J. Vicens Vives: *Introducción a la Historia de España*, by A. Ubieto *et al.*, Barcelona, 1967. J. Reglá recognizes a "Golden Age" only in the realm of the spirit, and regards intervention in Central Europe as a catastrophe both for Bohemia and Spain. On the battlefields the representatives of a "modern order" – a Europe of modern states – met those of a "traditional order", the hierarchical polity of feudalism. The Spanish historian thus reaches a conclusion quite opposite to that proclaimed by Bohdan Chudoba.

Chudoba's eulogy of the Catholic Church and the spirit of the Baroque (*Španelé na Bílé Hoře*, Prague, 1945; *Spain and the*

Empire 1519–1643, Chicago, 1952) is not even cited in two new publications which deal directly or indirectly with the relations between Bohemia and Spain at the time of the Thirty Years War. The first of these, by E. Beladiez, studies Wallenstein and his attitudes to the Holy Roman Empire and Spain (*España y el Sacro Imperio Romano Germanico. Wallenstein 1583–1634*, Madrid, 1967). The other, the work of joint authors, is the latest biography of a leading Spanish diplomat during the reigns of Philip III and Philip IV, Count Gondomar (J. M. Castroviejo and F. de P. Fernández de Córdoba: *El Conde de Gondomar, Un azor entre ocasos*, Madrid, 1967). Both books assign a central rôle to Czech events, but they are at the same time contributions to traditional diplomatic and military history, and therefore ask no new questions about the deeper significance of the conflict or its Bohemian roots.

It is surprising that Dutch historians have devoted so little attention in the last few decades to the real importance of the Eighty Years War and the revolutionary aspects of the revolt against Spain. This is true of the influential brief history of the War by J. Presser *et al.*: *De Tachtigjarige Oorlog*, Amsterdam, reissued 1964, and the relevant chapters of the great history of the Netherlands begun under the direction of J. M. Romein: *Algemene Geschiedenis der Nedarlanden*, vols. 4 and 5, Utrecht, 1952. The character of the Dutch revolution received some discussion between 1954 and 1956 in the columns of the magazine *Bijdragen voor de Geschiedenis der Nederlanden*, IX, 1954, pp. 324–8; x, 1955–6, pp. 58–67, 239–48; XI, 1956, pp. 103–6. It was interpreted in a conservative way by Geyl and Rogier, and in a non-conservative way by B. A. Enno van Gelder. A Marxist approach was developed by E. Kuttner: *Het Hongerjaar 1566*, Amsterdam, 1949, and by Wittman and Chistozvonov in the works cited above; I have considered the whole question in my own monograph: *Nizozemska Politika a Bila Hora*, Prague, 1958, Introduction. Since then a further radical interpretation by the American historian G. Griffiths: "The Revolutionary Character of the Revolt of the Netherlands", *Comparative Studies in Society and History*, II, 1959–60, pp. 452–72, has provoked an answer from the Dutchman I. Schöffer: *ibid.*, III, 1961–2, pp. 470–77. Schöffer has contributed the latest brief account of the revolution in the Netherlands ("De Nederlande Revolutie" in *Zeven revoluties, Amsterdam*, n.d., pp. 9–28) and a stimulating study of the relationship between the Dutch "Golden Age" and the European crisis ("Did Holland's Golden Age Coincide with period of crisis?", *Acta Historiae Neerlandica*, I, Leiden,1966, pp. 82–107). The problem of the English revolution in the seventeenth century has also been summarily treated by Schöffer: "De Engelse revolutie" in: *Zeven revoluties*, 29–50, but the standard modern accounts are above all the writings of Christopher Hill, most recently: *The Century of Revolution, 1603–1714* (History of England), vol. 5, Edinburgh, 1961, and: *Reformation to Industrial Revolution. A social and economic history of Britain 1530–1780*, London, 1967. By contrast the essays of the radical conservative H. R. Trevor-Roper (some are collected in the book: *Religion, the Reformation and Social Change*, London, 1967) show a distinctly polemical character.

The revolutionary wave in the middle of the seventeenth century has repeatedly engaged the attention of the Soviet historian B. F. Porshnev, who in 1964 published an expanded version of his previous work on the relation of the masses to the feudal régime and the rise of the bourgeoisie (*Feodalizm a narodnie massy*, Moscow, 1964). The situation in Europe before the conclusion of the Peace of Westphalia and the outbreak of the Fronde in France is the subject of Porshnev's best monograph, carefully edited by R. Mandrou as: *Les Soulèvements populaires en France de 1623 à 1648*, Paris, 1963. Mandrou is himself the author of two stimulating books on the French *ancien régime: Introduction à la France moderne, 1500–1640*, Paris, 1961; and *La France aux* XVIIe *et* XVIIIe *siècles*, Paris, 1967.

Besides the more general products of present-day historiography, the years since the war have seen a flood of specialized works. Any study of the broad problems of the Thirty Years War must of course lean heavily on such sources, and in these observations about further reading it is impossible for me to do more than mention the ones which have proved most useful for this book. The same is true of the references to archival material which are appended to individual chapters. Evidently there are some documents relating to the War in most of the major European archives and libraries. The present writer is preparing a survey of the sources which, thanks to the peculiar ordering of society in the Habsburg Monarchy, are now preserved on Czechoslovak territory, and this will appear as accompaniment to a seven-volume edition of selections from them now being prepared by the Czechoslovak Academy of Siences: *Documenta Bohemo-Slovaca, Bellum Tricennale Illustrantia*, from 1971. These materials are so extensive and fundamental that no new interpretation of the War can be valid which does not draw on them. But the contents of other archives are likewise indispensable, even for domestic Czech questions, and I have collected evidence for this book from a number of them. My sincere thanks are due to archivists and librarians in Leipzig, Berlin, Rostock, Schwerin, Merseburg, Dresden, Heidelberg, Erlangen, Wroclaw, Poznaú, Gdańsk, and Budapest, in the City Archives of Amsterdam, the Rijksarchiev of the Hague and the Riksarkivet of Stockholm, in the Public Records Office, the British Museum and several other English libraries, and in the Bibliothèque nationale of Paris. In other cases I have been helped by the work of colleagues – especially those in Rome – and by the century-old photographic collections of the State Central Archives in Prague, where I have examined documents from Simancas, Madrid, Brussels, Copenhagen, the Vatican and elsewhere.

CHAPTER TWO

The beginning of the crisis in Central Europe has received diligent study from German and Austrian historians. A conservative, pro-Habsburg view is given in the general work by H. Hantsch: *Die Geschichte Österreichs*, 1–11, Graz 1953, 1959, while E. Zöllner's: *Geschichte Österreichs*, Vienna, 1961 gives a more liberal and balanced account. The same is true of the important and constructive writings by the Upper Austrian historian Hans Sturmberger: *Georg Erasmus Tschernembl. Religion, Libertät und Widerstand*, Linz, 1953; "Die Anfäange des Bruderzwistes in Habsburg", *Mitteilungen das Oberösterreichischen Landesarchivs*, 5, 1957; *Kaiser Ferdinand* II *und des Problem des Absolutismus*, Vienna, 1957. Sturmberger too doubts whether either the Austrian or the Spanish Habsburgs ever attempted to introduce absolutism during the seventeenth century. His approach, with its sympathies for Austrian Protestantism and the community of the Estates, is parellelled by that of Grete Mecenseffy in her: *Geschichte des Protestantismus in Österreich*, Vienna, 1956.

V.–L. Tapié has devoted a major part of his scholarly career to the history of Central Europe in the seventeenth century, most recently in a contribution on problems of methodology: *Méthodes et Problèmes de l'histoire de l'Europe Centrale*, *Extrait des Études d'Histoire des Relations Internationales*, *Mélanges Pierre Renouvin*, Paris, 1966. The rôle of the Habsburgs is considered in general by A. Wandruszka: *Das Haus Habsburg*, Vienna, 1956, English translation, London 1964; and in its diplomatic extensions by R. Belvederi: *Dell'elezione di un Ré dei Romani nelcarteggio inedito del Cardinale Guido Bentivoglio, 1609–1614*, Rome, 1951; "Un Nunzio Pontifico di fronte alle tensioni delle potenze europee nei primi decenni del secolo XVII", *Humanitas*, X, 1955, pp. 561ff. Two articles by R. F. Schmiedt in new histories of Germany cover this period: "Vorgeschichte, Verlauf und Wirkungen des Dreissigjährigen Krieges", in Max Steinmetz, *Deutchsland 1476–1648*, Berlin, 1965, pp. 271–383; "Deutschland von 1608 bis 1648", in *Deutsche Geschicte*, Band 1, Berlin, 1965, pp. 593–628.

On the subject of Rudolf II the monograph by J. B. Novák: *Rudolf II a jeho pád*, Prague, 1935 is still unsurpassed. Gertrude von Schwarzenfeld's biography: *Rudolf II, Der Saturnische Kaiser*, Munich, 1961 is more a belletristic essay, evidently influenced by the work of G. R. Hocke on Rudolfine Prague as an international centre of European Mannerist culture (*Die Welt als Labyrinth*, Hamburg, 1957). There is a useful study by T. Wittman which complements the conclusions of Belvederi and Sturmberger on the crisis of the Austrian Habsburgs: "Az osztrák Habsburg-hatalom válságos éveinek történetéhez, 1606–1618", *Acta Universitatis Szegedinensis, Sectio Historica*, 1959.

Czech and Slovak historiography has made important advances in its approach to the problems of Bohemia on the eve of the White Mountain. There is a useful summary for the postwar decades in the *compte-rendu* prepared for the Stockholm conference of 1960 (*20 ans d'historiographie tchécoslovaque 1936–1960*, Prague, 1960). Since the older works which dealt with administrative questions (V. Pešák: *Začátky organizace české komory za Ferdinanda I*, Prague, 1930; K. Stloukal: *Česká Kancelář Dvorská*, Prague, 1931) attention has shifted to economic and social relations. Research into taxation, begun by A. Gindely and O. Placht, has been continued by M. Volf: *Nástin správy českých berní v dobe předbelohorské*, Prague, 1941; V. Pešák: *Berní Rejstříky z roku 1b44 a 1620*, Prague, 1953 and J. Kolman: *Berní Rejstříky a berne roku 1567*, Prague, 1963. The burden of taxes was obviously connected with changes in the value of money, and several authors have considered the effects on the region of the "price revolution" of the sixteenth and seventeenth centuries. After the study by J. Janáček: *Rudolfinské drahotní řády*, Prague, 1957 there appeared a stimulating article from the Cracow historian S. Hoszowski on the movement of prices in Central Europe: "L'Europe centrale devant la révolution des prix. XVIe et XVIIe siècles", *Annales E.S.C.*, 3, 1961, pp. 441–56. Hungarian conditions have been sketched into the European economic framework by T. Wittman: "'Revolyuciya cen' i yeye vliyanie na Vengriyu vo vtoroi polovine XVI v", *Srednie Veka*, XX, 1961, pp. 166–88. Hoszowski's approach has been taken up again by J. Petráň: "K problémům tzv. 'cenové revoluce' ve střední Evrope", *Numismatický Sborník*, VIII, 1964, pp. 47–74, while there is useful material in a volume which contains discussions about prices and wages held in Prague in 1962 (*Kolokvium o dejinách cen a mezd v 16. a 17. století*. Zápisky katedry čs. dejin a arch. studia KU, Prague, 1962). To this M. Hroch and J. Petráň have added two contributions, already mentioned in the text, on the nature of the regression in Central Europe: "K characteristice krise feudalismu v XVI–XVII století", *Československý Časopis Historický*, XII, 1964, pp. 347–64; "Europejska gospodarka i politika XVI i XVII wieku: Kryzys czy regres?" *Przegląd Historyczny*, LV, 1964, pp. 1–21.

Greatest interest logically attaches to the study of economic relations on the estates of the nobility before the White Mountain and the condition òf the peasantry. Since the pioneering work of J. Pešák on the management of the Smiřický lands, this research has been continued by J. Křivka, J. Jirásek and A. Míka. Two monographs deserve special mention: J. Válka: *Hospodářská politika feudálniho velkostatku na předbelohorské Morave*, Prague, 1962; and J. Petráň: *Zemedelská výroba v Čechéch v druhé polovine 16. a počátkem 17. století*, Prague, 1963. The state of things in Silesia is outlined by F. Matejek: "Gospodarka szlachecka i chlopska na Środkowym Śląsku w XVI wieku", *Studia a materiały z dziejów Śląska*, IV, pp. 423–52. What is still lacking is an analysis of the landed estates of the middle and lower nobility and the towns, whose combined property holdings formed two-thirds of the total before 1620. Here fundamental issues remain unresolved, although there is abundant matter in published series of records (especially the Snemy Český and Archiv Český) and the rich survivals of archival documentation. An extensive discussion about the so-called "second serfdom", carried on by A. Míka, J. Petráň, J. Válka, A. Matejek and others, has thrown much light on the general economic situation but without as yet yielding overall definite conclusions. There is much methodological value in an article by Petráň on the class struggle and its function in the context of Bohemian society before and after the White Mountain: *Pozdnefeudální lidová hnutí. Úvahy o problémech a metodách*, Prague, 1967, pp. 107–50.

Many gaps exist too in our knowledge of the state of Bohemian and Moravian towns. J. Janáček is almost the only recent scholar to have considered, besides the three cities of Prague, other centres of population like Jihlava. Janáček is the author of the relevant chapters in the collective history of Prague: *Dejiny Prahy*, Prague, 1964. There are valuable books on urban society by F. Kavka: *Majetková, sociální a třídní struktura českých mest v první polovine 16. století*, Prague, 1959, and J. Marek: *Společenská struktura moravských královských mest v 15. a 16. století*, *Prague, 1965*. The numerous domain towns and their important place in the national economy of Bohemia still await systematic examination. About the typical domain town of Zlín no detailed work has ever been published and the parts of the present work which deal with it are therefore based entirely on archival sources. These are firstly municipal registers, begun in the sixteenth century, then the records of the Moravian state administration (now in the State Archives (*SA*) at Brno) and fragments of various family archives (*FA*) like the *FA* Podstatský-Liechtenstein-Castelcorn in *SA* Brno and Janovice, the *FA* Serényi in *SA* Brno, etc. An example of the information which they provide is given in an article devoted to the most famous product of the neighbourhood, Comenius, and his family background: J. V. Polišenský: "Nové poznatky o Komenského rodišti a rode", *Listy Filologické*, 90, 1967, pp. 404–10.

The extensive documentation which covers economic and social changes around the turn of the sixteenth and seventeenth centuries is widely scattered, and some is still stored in the Haus-Hof- und Staatsarchiv in Vienna. Most of the records left by the central organs of the Bohemian state were returned to Prague after 1918 and can now be found there in various deposits of the first section, Central State Archives (*SCA*). This contains too the records of the Estates administration for Bohemia; its Moravian counterparts are dispersed through different parts of *SA* Brno, while those for Silesia survive only fragmentarily in *SA* Opava (Troppau). The proceedings of the central offices of old Hungary have come down to us in incomplete form, mostly in various Viennese archives and partly in the Országos Levéltár in Budapest. Slovakia, however, retains some exceedingly important county (*comitat*) records (many of later than seventeenth century date) and magnate archives whose Publico-Politica sections often include official material (e.g. the *FA* Thurzó in *SA* Bytča, *FA* Illésházy in *SA* Bratislava, parts of *FA* Pálffy and Eszterházy in the Slovak State Central Archives (*SSCA*) in Bratislava). A similar position in the public life of sixteenth-century Bohemia was occupied by the Rožmberks (*FA* Rožmberk in *SA* Třeboň), Pernsteins and later Lobkovices (both *FA*s in *SA* Žitenice) and in Moravia by the Žerotíns (most of whose archive is now in *SA* Brno, though parts are in *SA* Janovice).

The thorny topic of political thinking in Bohemia before the Wàr can be examined on the one hand by reference to contemporary literature, on the other by considering the manuscripts and printed books in old libraries which already existed during the period we are reviewing. The most priceless survivals are those in Prague: the University Library which includes the collections of the Lobkovices (both the main family library and the so-called "Roudnice library"), and the National Museum which also manages the former Nostitz and Kinsky libraries. A major part of the book treasures of old Bohemia was carried off to Sweden at the close of the Thirty Years War. The fortunes of one such library, that of the Rožmberks, have been described by Emil Schieche: "Die Rosenbergische Bibliothek vor und nach Juli 1648", *Stifter Jahrbuch*, v, 1957, pp. 102–40. It is anyway rarely easy to establish when individual volumes were acquired, and whether they were read. One exception is the collection – or what remains of it – made by Johann von Eggenberg in his castle library at Český Krumlov, since the owner regularly supplemented his ex libris with an inscription noting when and where he had come by his books, and added a comment to signify his impressions or his mood of the moment. Only in such cases can firm conclusions be drawn. For the Bohemian lands no major town libraries have survived from this period, but Slovakia preserves intact some significant examples: Levoča, Bardejov and Kežmark.

CHAPTER THREE

Basic works for these years are the already-cited study by J. B. Novák: *Rudolf* II *a jeho pád* and two monographs by K. Stloukal: *Papežská politika a císařský dvůr pražský na předelu* XVI a XVII *století*, Prague, 1925; *Počátky nunciatury v Praze*, Prague, 1928. One portion of Rudolf's eastern policy is analyzed by J. Matoušek *Turecká Válka v evropské politice v letech 1592–1594*, Prague,

1935, while the interactions between Poland and the Habsburgs have received attention from W. Konopczyński: *Dzieje Polski nowozytnej*, I, 1506–1648, Warsaw, 1936, W. Czapliński and – most recently – F. Hejl. Relations between the Austrian and Spanish branches of the Habsburgs are covered by Chudoba, and more objectively by G. Mecenseffy: "Habsburger im 17. Jahrhundert; die Beziehungen der Höfe von Wien und Madrid während des Dreissigjährigen Krieges", *Archiv für Österreichische Geschichte*, 121, 1955. There is an account of the diplomacy of Madrid – especially in its secretive aspects – by C. H. Carter: *The Secret Diplomacy of the Habsburgs, 1598–1625*, Columbia, 1964, but a far more modern approach can be found in the stimulating synthesis of sixteenth and seventeenth century Spanish history by J. H. Elliott: *Imperial Spain, 1469–1716*, London, 1963.

A series of studies by J. Janáček have pointed the international importance of Prague before the White Mountain in the political, economic and cultural life of Europe, and there is valuable material in Kamil Krofta's apology for old Bohemia, issued on the eve of the Second World War: *Nesmrtelný Národ*, Prague, 1940. Printed sources likewise provide evidence of the positive merits of this Bohemian society in the years before 1618: among older publications are A. Rezek's edition of the memoirs (*Pameti*) of Mukuláš Dačický of Heslov (1880), K. Tieftrunk's: *Pavla Skály ze Zhoře Historie Česká od r. 1602 do 1623* (1867), the volumes of the *Archiv Český* and the *Snemy České*, records of the national Diet, and Pavel Stránský's: *Respublica Bohema* (original Latin edition 1634). More recently there have appeared the proceedings of the State Council for the years 1602–1610 (*Protokoly české státní rady z let 1602–1610*, Prague, 1952) and this author's edition of the historical writings of Pavel Skála and Andreas Habernfeld: *Historie o válce české 1618–1620*, Prague, 1964.

A closer analysis of the power struggle along the lines suggested here may be found in J. V. Polišenský: *Viléma Slavaty relace o jednáni v příčine knížetství Opavského 1614–1615*, Slezský Sborník, 1953, pp. 488–498; "Slezsko a Válka Třicetiletá" *Česko-polský Sborník vedeckých prací*, I, Prague, 1955, pp. 311–328; "Turecké války, Uherská povstání a veřejné mínení předbelohorských Čech, *Historický Časopis*, VII, 1959, pp. 74–103; (the latter in conjunction with J. Hrubeš). The sources for the invasion of Bocskai and his troops were edited in 1894 by F.

Kameníček, who the same year also published an article in the *Časopis Českého Muzea*: "Vpády Bočkajovců". A selection of them was used by the present writer for his series of contemporary popular texts: *Kniha o Bolesti a Smutku, Výbor z moravských kronik* XVII *století*, Prague, 1948. The most recent account in Hungarian is by K. Benda: *A Bocskai Szabadságharc*, Budapest, 1955, which should be studied together with the already-mentioned work of T. Wittman. The history of Zlín in this period is illustrated above all by the town registers (now in the District Archives (*DA*) of Gottwaldov) and local chronicles, especially the memoirs of Jan Urban of Domanín (MSS. in the castle library at Mnichovo Hradište) and Jiřík (George) Hovorius, the anonymous *Lamentations and Mournful Complaint of the Land of Moravia* (*Lamentací, pláč a naříkání zeme Moravské*) and the notebooks of Josef Securius.

The political crisis which led to the Defenestration of 1618 is illuminated by a number of studies dealing on the one hand with the leaders of the "old" Czech nobility, on the other with the new radicals of the Spanish party. The biographies of the last two Rožmberks which were compiled by their servant Václav Březan have been published several times, the latest edition being by J. Dostál: *Poslední Rožmberkové*, Prague, 1941. The anti-Habsburg activity of Peter Vok Rožmberk receives attention in O. Hulec: "Konspirační charakter předbelohorské protihabsburské opozice, *Jihočeský Sborník Historický*, XXX, 1961. The demise of the related family of Hradec (Neuhaus) – their inheritance passed to Vilém Slavata – is described by K. Stloukal: "Konec rodu Pánů z Hradce", *ibid.*, XXXIII, 1964, a scholar whose first research, half a century ago, was dedicated to the early years of Cardinal Dietrichstein. Two typical representatives of Estates society in Moravia have received serious attention in monographs by F. Hrubý: *Ladislav Velen ze Žerotína*, Prague, 1930, and O. Odložilík: *Karel st. ze Žerotína, 1564–1636*, Prague, 1936. Earlier work by J. Glücklich and V. Kybal had already demonstrated the connections between the domestic Bohemian crisis and wider European power struggles (*cf.* especially Kybal's book on Henri IV: *Jindřich* IV *a Europa v letech 1609–1610*, Prague, 1911).

A manifold abundance of archival materials exists for the years preceding the Thirty Years War in Bohemia and any account of it would demand a volume in itself. As an example we may quote some sources relating to the rise of the so-called "Spanish" court party. The radical and "Roman" programme drawn up by its first adherents in 1584 is preserved in the archives of the Olomouc chapter (*SA* Olomouc) and the Archbishopric of Prague (now administered by the *SCA*). Most of the Dietrichstein papers are brought together in *SA* Brno (*FA*; Historica), but the correspondence of the Cardinal is also to be found among the episcopal records of Kroměříž/Kremsier (now *SA* Olomouc) and in a series of Czech archives. The correspondence of the Pernsteins and Lobkovices is now mostly in *SA* Žitenice (north of Prague), together with the papers of the families: Hurtado de Mendoza, Cardona and Manriquez de Lara. There are Spanish MSS. and printed matter scattered through the Lobkovic libraries (now administered by the Prague University Library), the Eggenberg collection in Český Krumlov, the castle library in Kroměříž and what remains of that of the Dietrichsteins (transferred to Brno). More may be found among the University and Chapter Libraries in Olomouc, the Nostitz collection in Prague (now renamed "Dobrovský Library" and supervised by the National Museum), and the Bohemica of Jan Jeník of Bratřice.

CHAPTER FOUR

Recent decades have seen much attention paid to the period of the Bohemian War, both within Czechoslovakia and beyond its borders, though the basic factual account by Anton Gindely: *History of the Thirty Years War* I–III: *History of the Bohemian Revolt*, New York, 1884, has yet to be surpassed. The culmination of two traditional approaches to the problem is to be found in studies by J. Pekař: *Bílá Hora*, Prague, 1921, and K. Krofta: *Bílá Hora*, Prague, 1913, the one sympathetic, the other violently opposed, to the pretensions of the Counter-Reformation, while the state of research at the beginning of the 1930s is well revealed by the articles in the commemorative Wallenstein volume (*Doba belohorská a Albrecht z Valdštejna*, Prague, 1934) with contributions from O. Odložilík, K. Stloukal and J. Prokeš. The latter at the same time undertook a partial edition of the correspondence books of the Bohemian Directors: J. Prokeš: *Protokol vyšlé korespondence kanceláře českých direktorů z let 1618 a 1619*, Prague, 1934.

New and pioneer work was then begun by V.-L. Tapié and Josef Macůrek. The former's interest in Franco-Czech relations gave rise to an important book: *La politique étrangère de la France et le début de la Guerre de Trente Ans, 1616–1621*, Paris, 1934, edited for a subsequent Czech edition by Z. Kalista.

Macůrek has thrown new light on Czech–Polish interconnections (*České povstání 1618 az 1620 a Polsko*, Brno, 1937), as well as producing a series of articles – published in the magazine *Sobótka* (Wroclaw) between 1947 and 1951 – on the Silesian question at the beginning of the War. Silesia has also naturally attracted the attention of Polish historians, especially W. Czapliński: "Ślsk i Polska w pierwszych latach wojny trzydziestoletniej", *Sobótka*, III, 1948, pp. 141–181. A co-operative study by Macůrek and M. Rejnuš collects together evidence of contact between the Bohemian lands and Upper Hungary (*České zeme a Slovensko ve století pred Bílou Horou*, Prague, 1958, especially pp. 130–147) from the archives of the Thurzós and Pálffys, the towns of Skalica, Žilina, and Trnava, etc.

The present author has devoted two monographs to the problem of relations between the rebellious Bohemian Estates and the advanced lands of Western Europe: *Anglie a Bílá Hora*, Prague, 1949; *Nizozemská politika a Bílá Hora*, Prague, 1958. A similar analysis of links with Spain at this time has still to find a publisher. On Swedish attitudes to the revolt there is J. V. Polišenský and M. Hroch: "Švédská politika a české stavovské povstání 1618–1620", *Historický Sborník*, VII, 1960, pp. 157–90; on the question of the Valtellina: B. Baďura: "Zápas o Valtellinu a český odboj protihabsburský (1618–1620)", *ibid.*, pp. 123–56; on the interest shown by Charles Emmanuel of Savoy a dissertation has been written by Z. Šolle. More narrowly military history is illuminated by V. Líva's edition of the registers of the *Militare* from the *CSA* in Prague: *Prameny k dejinám Třicetileté Války*, III, 1618–25, Prague, 1951. There is also specialized work like that of J. Dobiáš on the campaigns of 1618 (*Dejiny Pelhřimova*, II, Pelhřimov 1936; *Zrádné proudy v českém povstání roku 1618*, Prague, 1939); Z. Kalista on Buquoy's march towards Prague: "Buquoyův itinerář z konce českého tažení", *Vojensko-historický Sborník*, n.p.n.d. 5–158; and F. Hrubý on a Swiss observer of the White Mountain: "Švýcarský svedek Bílé Hory", *Český Časopis Historický*, 37, 1931, pp. 42–78. The progress of the fighting in south Bohemia has been described by J. Volf in a series of articles based on the Buquoy archive, now in *SA* Třeboň (*Jihočeský Sborník Historický*, XXIX–XXXIII, 1960–64); compare the same author's study of the town of Budweis: "Pokus budejovického patriciátu připojit se k českému povstání r. 1618", *Časopis Společnosti Přátel Starožitnosti*, LXIX, 1961. The most detailed account of the actual defenestration is still that by F.

Macháček: "Defenestrace Pražská 1618", *Český Časopis His-torický*, XIV, 1908.

The most original contribution to the history of the Bohemian War from a non-Czech is a short but worthy book by the Austrian historian H. Sturmberger: *Aufstand in Böhmen*, Munich–Vienna, 1959. Much still lies forgotten in German archives which could illuminate the policies of Bohemia's German allies: the Palatinate correspondence now in the Geheimes Staatsarchiv in Munich; that of Christian of Anhalt in Oranienbaum–Magdeburg, of Johann Ernst in Weimar. The most important sources for Habsburg activities are those of the Haus-, Hof- und Staatsarchiv in Vienna, the Bavarian documents in Munich – which were drawn upon by D. Albrecht for his analysis of the policies of Duke Maximilian (*Die auswärtige Politik Maximilians von Bayern, 1618–1635*, Göttingen, 1962), and the archives of Simancas and Brussels. The latter contains, for example, the correspondence of Diego de Zeelandre from Vienna.

The proceedings of the Diets and other Estates' assemblies between 1618 and 1620 are recorded in the History of Pavel Skála (original MS. in the Library of the Czech National Museum) and in the printed dietal resolutions, of which the largest collection is in the *SCA*. On the confederations of 1619 there is a study by R. Stanka; *Die böhmischen Conföderationsakte von 1619*, Berlin, 1932, and a new analysis by V. Vaneček is in progress. The rôle of the petty nobility in the rebellion is illustrated by the indictments of the public prosecutor, Přibík Jeníšek of Újezd, mentioned in the text (*DA* Jindřichův Hradec). The policy of the Palsgrave is described by Helmut Weigel: *Franken, Kurpfalz und der böhmische Aufstand*, 1, Erlangen, 1932, and I. G. Weise: "Beiträge zur Beurteilung des Kurfürsten Friedrich V aus der Pfalz", *Zeitschrift für Geschichte des Oberrheins*, 85, 1932, pp. 385–422, while Adam Wandruszka has presented a number of small contributions from Italian sources to the history of the White Mountain.

The second volume of the projected collection of texts entitled *Documenta Bohemo–Slovaca* will be devoted to the years 1618–20. It will contain especially materials from Buquoy's military chancery (*SA* Třeboň), together with the correspondence of some pro-Habsburg magnates: Lobkovic (*SA* Žitenice), Slavata (*ibid.*, above all the letters written from Passau, and *SA* Jindřichův Hradec), Cardinal Dietrichstein (*SA* Brno and Olomouc) and others, and some valuable writings by neutrals like

Adam Waldstein (mainly in *SA* Mnichovo Hradište). It is much more difficult to follow the activities of the Directorate and the Palatine government, since too many people were at pains to obscure their traces in the years after the White Mountain. Fragments have survived in the documents of the Imperial confiscatory and prosecutory commissions which bear witness to the opposition of the humbled Estates (the writings of Jeníšek mentioned above, or the Bohemica of Jan Jeník of Bratřice in the National Museum). There is also material in the *Prolegomena* to Skála's *History of the Church* (National Museum in Prague and castle library in Mnichovo Hradište). Wallenstein's chancery has preserved a fraction of the military correspondence of the estates' government (*SA* Mnichovo Hradište, especially in the sections *Historica* and *Autographs*). This fundamental source is augmented by smaller archival collections: the correspondence of the Upper Hungarian magnates Thurzó (*SA* Bytča), the papers of Verdugo and Nostitz (*SA* Klášterec nad Ohří), Martini (National Museum in Prague) and Aldringen (*SA* Děčín). More documents have survived in Moravia, mainly in *SA* Brno, since there the administration was not destroyed at one stroke. Beyond this there are less extensive records in many other archives and libraries: we may cite the *SA* Český Krumlov and Zámrsk, the *DA* České Budejovice (Budweis), the *SCA* and University Library in Prague and the episcopal library in Litoměřice. Valuable evidence is scattered through the letters of the Thurns and Teuffenbachs, Collalto, Colloredo and Zdenek Lev Kolowrat-Libsteinský. All these writings are of course limited by the social background of their authors – burgher diplomats and politicians were rarely to the fore – and come overwhelmingly from the victorious Habsburg camp; indeed they were often suitably arranged in order to back some claim for recognition of services rendered to the dynasty.

CHAPTER FIVE

The years after 1620, which used to be known as the War for the Palatinate, were studied by the indefatigable Gindely: *History of the Thirty Years War*, IV: *Geschichte der Gegenreformation in Böhmen*, Prague, 1894, and by J. Goll: *Die französische Heirat*, Prague, 1876. Since then new perspectives have been opened up by two more Czech historians: O. Odložilík with his work on the Bohemian émigrés: *Ze zápasů pobelohorské emigrace*, Brno, 1933; *Z korespondence pobelohorské emigrace z let 1621–1624*,

Prague, 1933; *Povstalec a emigrant* – a biography of J. M. Thurn –
London, 1944; and the Moravian F. Hrubý, who first described
the collapse of the rebellion on his native province "Pád českeho
povstání na Morave", *Ceský Časposi Historický*, 29, 1923, then
wrote the important biography of Ladislav Velen Žerotín mentioned under Chapter Three above, and edited a major set of
documents: *Moravské korespondence a akta z let 1620–1636*, I,
Brno, 1634. There is information about the state of the Czech
lands after 1620 in the Wallenstein anthology: *Doba belohorska
. . .*, and a specialized study of the currency question in these
critical years by E. Nohejlová–Prátová: *Dlouhá mince v Čechách
v letech 1621–3*, Prague, 1946. The new taxation burdens are
analyzed in V. Pešák: *Vojenské vlivy na správu kontribuce v
Čechách 1621–1623*, Prague, 1946, and valuable material on the
confiscations is provided in two books by T. V. Bílek: *Dejiny
konfiskací v Čechách r. 1618*, Prague, 1882; *Jmení jesuitských
kolejí*, Prague, 1888.

The present writer has expanded his account of the diplomatic
situation in a number of articles: the policies of the Dukes of
Saxe-Weimar in: "Die Universität Jena und der Aufstand der
böhmischen Stände in den Jahren 1618–1620", *Wissenschaftliche
Zeitschrift der Universität Jena*, 7, 1957/8, pp. 441–7; the rôle of
Spanish troops during the campaigns against Bethlen Gábor,
Mansfeld and the rebels in: "Od Bílé Hory k Masaniellovu
povstání r. 1647", *Historický Sborník*, III, 1955, pp. 146ff; the
Dutch attempts at a grand anti-Habsburg coalition headed either
by the Danes or the Swedes in: "Anglická a jiná svedectví o bitve
na Bíle Hoře, *CSPSC*, LXVIII, pp. 203–8; "Denmark–Norway
and the Bohemian cause in the early part of the Thirty Years
War", *Festgabe für L. L. Hammerich*, Copenhagen, 1962. For a
more general account of the "Bohemian question" in the early
years of the War, see J. V. Polišenský and M. Hroch: "Die
böhmische Frage und die politischen Beziehungen zwischen dem
europäischen Westen und Osten zur Zeit des Dreissigjährigen
Krieges" in *Probleme der Oekonomie und Politik*, Berlin, 1960,
pp. 23–55 (also in Russian in *Srednije Veka*, 24, Moscow, 1963,
pp. 240–58). The lasting hostilities in Moravia can be followed in
V. Fialová: *Jan Adam z Víckova, moravský emigrant a vůdge
Valachů 1620–1628*, Brno, 1935, and the same authoress's exem-
plary edition of the important *Chronicle* of Holešov (*Kronika
Holešovská 1615–1645*, Holešov, 1967). Details of the Vlach risings may be found in F. Dostál: *Valašské povstání za Třicetileté*

Války, Prague, 1956, and a series of articles by Dostál in the periodical *Válašsko*.

The activities of the Palsgrave and his government in exile in Holland have been studied most thoroughly in F. H. Schubert: "Die pfälzische Exilregierung im Dreissigjährigen Krieg", *Zeitschrift für Geschichte des Oberrheins*, 102, 1954, pp. 575–680, who also provided a biography of the Palatine diplomat Camerarius: *Ludwig Camerarius (1573–1651)*, Kallmünz, 1955. On the rôle played by the Valtellina and the beginnings of French involvement in northern Italy there is valuable work by Romolo Quazza: *Storia politica d'Italia, Preponderanza Spagnuola 1559–1700*, Milan, 1950; *Politica europea nella questione Valtellinica, la lega franco–veneta–savoiarda e la pace di Monçon*, Venice, 1921, and a life of one of the protagonists by G. Pfistner: *Georg Jenatsch, sein Leben und seine Zeit*, Basel, 1939. The links between the war for the Valtellina and the Bohemian question are considered by B. Baďura in his article cited above. On the prospects for intervention by Denmark see T. Christiansen: *Die Stellung König Christians IV von Dänemark zu den Kriegsereignissen im Deutschen Reich und zu den Plänen einer evangelischen Allianz 1618–1625*, Kiel, 1937.

The core of the third volume in the series *Documenta Bohemo-Slovaca* will consist of the extensive papers of Cardinal Dietrichstein (*SA* Olomouc and Brno) and the military leader R. Collalto (*SA* Brno). The diplomatic missions of G. L. Schwarzenberg to England, the United Provinces and Spain are documented in *SA* Český Krumlov. 1621 sees the beginning of the military correspondence of Heinrich Schlick, later President of the *Hofkriegsrat* in Vienna (*SA* Zámrsk) and the secret exchange of letters between the young Prince of Anhalt and Verdugo (*SA* Klášterec and Ohří). Developments in Hungary can be followed through the correspondence of the Illésházys and other families whose archives have remained in modern Slovakia, while some of the writings of the Eggenbergs and Khevenhüllers have found their way into the collection of *Autographs* in Mnichovo Hradište. Other useful materials survive from the Nostitzes (*SA* Klášterec n/O.) and Rudolph Thun (*SA* Dečín).

The bases for any modern biography of Wallenstein are the sources in the Valdštejn archive at Mnichovo Hradište which illuminate the details of the generalissimo's economic and political ascendancy. The *SCA* in Prague has been utilized by K. Vít for his Czech-language dissertation on Jan de Witte, Wallenstein's banker, and by A. Ernstberger, for a book on the same subject (*Hans de Witte, Finanzmann Wallensteins*, Wiesbaden, 1954). But a mass of documentation on Wallenstein remains completely untouched.

CHAPTER SIX

The years 1625–30 saw the destruction of old Bohemia by the constitutional revolution embodied in the *Verneurte Landesordnung*, a process hastened by Albrecht Wallenstein who with his organisation, rather than his prowess on the battlefield, helped to avert the perils which threatened the Habsburb dynasty. The interest of modern historiography has therefore quite legitimately concentrated on the problem of the invasion of Central Europe by the Danish coalition in 1626–7, the Spanish "maritime" plans for the North German coast, and finally the "Italian period" of the Thirty Years War – the struggle for Mantua.

The Wallenstein question itself was stirred up in the 1930s by a duel between two distinguished historians: Josef Pekař, who regarded the generalissimo as an "indecisive traitor and stupid intriguer" (*Valdštejn. Dejiny Valdštejnského Spiknutí*, Prague, 1934; and in German translation: *Wallenstein*, Berlin, 1937), and Heinrich von Srbik who saw in him an idealistic fighter for a unified Germany (*Wallensteins Ende*, Salzburg, 1932). Wallenstein's greatness as an entrepreneur was underlined by A. Ernstberger: *Wallenstein als Volkswirt im Herzogtum Friedland*, Reichenberg, 1929. There is an attempt to draw together the present state of the debate in J. V. Polišenský: *Zur Problematik des Dreissigjährigen Krieges und der Wallensteifrage, Aus 500 Jahren deutsch-tschechoslowakischer Geschichte*, Berlin, 1958, pp. 99–136. Wallenstein's rule in Mecklenburg is examined by M. Hroch: "Valdštejnova politika v severním Nemečku v letech 1629–30", *Sborník Historický*, v, 1957, pp. 203–28; and *Waldstein und die norddeutschen Hansestädte 1627–30*, the latter reviewed by B. F. Porshnev and A. S. Kan in *Voprsoy Istorii*, 1962/4. Hroch's article on more general economic affairs at this time is also available: "Der Dreissigjährige Krieg und die europäischen Handelsbeziehungen", *Wissenschaftliche Zeitschrift der Universität Griefswald*, XII, 1963, pp. 533–43. Important correctives to the accepted picture of Wallenstein as an economic manager are presented in two as yet unpublished Prague dissertations: K. Vít on Jan de Witte, and A. Stanka on the mining and industrial enterprise at Raspenua.

The present writer's study: "Morava a vztahy mezi evropským východem a západem 1626–7", *Macůrkův Sborník*, Brno, 1961 is based on local sources and uses in addition the correspondence of Johann Ernst of Saxe-Weimar (Sig. H 18 of the archives in Weimar) and the relation of Mitzlaff (in the Rigsarkivet Copenhagen). It draws too on an earlier article by F. Roubík: "Valdštejnovo tažení na Slovensko roku 1626", *Sborník Archivu Ministerstva Vnitra*, VIII, Prague, 1935 which made use of Wallensteiniana from the *SCA* in Prague. Moravia in these years is covered by the second volume of F. Hrubý's collection of sources: *Moravské korespondence a akta, 1625–1636*, Brno, 1937, and the already-cited works by V. Fialová and F. Dostál. For the Vlachs there is B. Indra: "Odboj mesta Hranic 1620–1627 a jeho potrestání", *Časopis Vlasteneckého Muzeálního Spolku v Olomouci*, 55, 1940. The peasant rebellion in Upper Austria was described in two old-fashioned but solid volumes by F. Stieve: *Der oberösterreichische Bauernaufstand des Jahres 1626*, Vienna, 1904–5; they are now augmented by Mecenseffy: *Geschichte des Protestantismus in Österreich*, pp. 149ff., and F. R. Schmiedt's dissertation: *Der Bauernkrieg in Oberösterreich vom Jahre 1626 als Teilerscheinung des Dreissigjährigen Krieges* (Diss. Halle, 1963). There is an extensive literature on Christian IV of Denmark. The most useful contributions in this context are H. D. Loose: *Hamburg und Christian* IV *von Dänemark*, Hamburg, 1963, and P. Vilar: "Un gran proyecto anti-holandès", *Hispania*, 88, 1962. On the *Landesordnung* the most recent study is that of H. Sturmberger: *Kaiser Ferdinand* II . . . The latest work on the Bohemian emigrants is the book by E. Winter: *Die tschechische und slowakische Emigration in Deutschland im 17. und 18. Jahrundert*, Berlin, 1955. The state of knowledge about the greatest of them is reviewed by J. Patočka: "L'état présent des études coméniennes", *Historica*, I, Prague, 1959, pp. 197ff. The reader may also be referred to the major new biography of Comenius by M. Blekastad, Oslo, 1969.

Volume Four of the *Documenta* will include a rich selection of Wallenstein materials from his military chancery (*CSA* Prague) and from Mnichovo Hradiště). Their only rival as a source for the events of these years is the chancery of Collalto (*SA* Brno) which is especially valuable for the war of Mantua. Further documentation is to be found among the papers of Matthias Gallas and Aldringen in *SA* Dečín, and the correspondence of Schlick and Piccolomini in Zámrsk, the latter containing also a few letters of

Trčka. Spain's maritime enterprise on the Baltic and Wallenstein's two-edged response to it are illuminated by the remains of the chancery in Prague, and especially by the important correspondence of G. L. Schwarzenberg and the Imperial ambassador J. C. Khevenhüller in Český Krumlov.

The activities of Wallenstein's opponents are better known. The writings of Slavata are in *SA* Jindřichův Hradec; those of Michna and Martinic in the autograph collection at Mnichovo Hradiště and the archives of Klášterec nad Ohří and Klatovy. The correspondence of Marradas is more scattered. The papers of R. Thun are still in *SA* Děčín, while those of Humprecht Černín, Wallenstein's quartermaster-general, are in Jindřichův Hradec. Silesian documents about the crushing of the rebellion are in *SA* Opava (Troppau), and some of the military archives in Slovakia offer rich pickings. The Waldstein autograph series I-IV in Mnichovo Hradiště have already been mentioned more than once, and are a vast store of letters from the whole continent. They include, for example, some of the correspondence of Olivares and Oñate.

CHAPTER SEVEN

The newest contributions to the period 1630–35 are by Dieter Albrecht: the short monograph: *Richelieu, Gustav Adolf und das Reich*, Munich/Vienna, 1959, and the last part of the book: *Die auswärtige Politik Maximilians von Bayern*. Spanish policy is further illuminated by G. Marañon's biography of Olivares: *El Conde-Duque de Olivares. La pasión de mandar*, Madrid, 1952, and other recent work on the nature and functioning of power in Madrid (A. Domínguez Ortiz: *Política y Hacienda de Felipe IV*, Madrid, 1960; F. Tomás Valiente: *Los validos en la monarquía española dei siglo XVII*, Madrid, 1963). The standard interpretation of the war for Mantua is R. Quazza: *La guerra per la successione di Mantova e del Monferrato, 1628–1631*, Mantua, 1926. On the vagaries of Papal politics there is useful work by D. Albrecht: "Die deutsche Politik Papst Gregors XV", *Schriftenreihe zur Bayerischen Landesgeschichte*, 53, Munich, 1956, and A. Leman: *Urbain VIII et la rivalité de la France et de la Maison d'Autriche de 1631 à 1635*, Lille, 1920. The literature on Wallenstein has been cited in the previous section. To it may be added the standard military history of the Thirty Years War: E. von Frauenholz: *Entwicklungsgeschichte des deutschen Heerwesens*, III, 1–2, Munich, 1935–41.

The relevant essentials of Swedish development in these years may be derived from English translations of two sound and fundamental handbooks: I. Andersson: *History of Sweden*, London, 1956; and E. Heckscher: *Economic History of Sweden*, Harvard 1954. Gustavus Adolphus himself has been the subject of a classic of Swedish historiography: Nils Ahnlund: *Gustav Adolf the Great*, English translation Princeton, 1940, and an outstanding modern biography in two volumes by Michael Roberts: *Gustavus Adolphus: A History of Sweden, 1611–32*, London, 1953–8, which combines a general approach with close analysis of particular problems. The same author has also devoted attention to the rise of Sweden under its immediately preceding monarchs (*The Early Vasas: a History of Sweden 1523–1611*, London, 1968), and edited an important anthology of texts from the Swedish seventeenth century: *Sweden as a Great Power 1611–1697*, London, 1968.

For the "War of Smolensk" a convenient bibliography of Soviet work may be found in V. M. Alekseev: *Tridsatiletnyaya Vojna*, pp. 171–82. Whereas B. F. Porshnev sees this episode as one aspect of a contemporary power struggle between Sweden and Russia on the one hand and Habsburg-influenced Poland on the other, O. L. Vajnshtein regards Muscovy as still adhering to its traditional political notions. A. S. Kan has also shown himself critical of Porshnev's thesis, which can be found outlined in a *compte-rendu*: "Les rapports politique de l'Europe occidentale et de l'Europe orientale a l'époque de la Guerre de Trente Ans, xiᵉ Congres International des Sciences Historiques, *Rapports*, iv, Stockholm, 1960, pp. 136–63.

The progressive withdrawal of the United Provinces from the conflict is described by P. Geyl in his general account: *The Netherlands in the Seventeenth Century*, i, 1609–1648, New York, 1961, and in an essay on the stadholder Frederick Henry: *History of the Low Countries*, London, 1964, pp. 43–78. There is an extensive bibliography in J. Presser's: *De tachtigjarige Oorlog, Van het bestand tot de Vrede van Munster*, Leiden, 1963, pp. 381ff. France is dealt with briefly by V.–L. Tapié: *La France de Louis* xvIII *et Richelieu*, Paris, 1952, and R. Mandrou: *La France aux* xvIIᵉ *et* xvIIIᵉ *siecles*, Paris, 1967. Relations between Spain and Austria have yet to be studied thoroughly, but there is material in Mecenseffy's: *Habsburger im 17, Jahrhundert*. The Spanish historian J. M. Jover has written a remarkable monograph on the international reactions to the Peace of Prague: *1635: Historia de una polémica y semblanza de una generación*, Madrid, 1949, while broader perspectives are revealed by J. A. Maravall's book: *La philosophie politique espagnole au* XVIIe *siècle*, Paris, 1955.

For this period too the documents in Czechoslovak archives which will be drawn upon by the fifth volume of *Documenta Bohemo–Slovaca* provide the material base for a fresh approach to Wallenstein and his European importance. The Prague portion of the generalissimo's military chancery (1631–4) is now less complete than the Viennese one, and we must always reckon with the fact that the most vital negotiations either went unrecorded or are only represented by incomplete evidence. Yet the Bohemian Wallensteiniana – both in Prague and in Mnichovo Hradiště – are still uncommonly rich, and their scope has been extended by many subsequent acquisitions, especially in the *Autograph* section, which includes for example the correspondence of the Dutch diplomat Aizema in 1634. Since Wallenstein's estates mostly passed into the hands of his treacherous generals, it is necessary to refer again to the archives of Ottavio Piccolomini (*SA* Zámrsk), Heinrich Schlick (*Ibid.*), Slavata (*SA* Jindřichův Hradec), Gallas and Rudolph Thun (*SA* Děčín), Colloredo and Morzin (*SA* Zámrsk) and the papers of Dietrichstein.

Among the scattered literary survivals from the protagonists of the final tragedy the most important is the *Diarium et Itinerarium* of Putz von Adlersthurm (MS. in *SA* Mnichovo Hradiště). There are interesting details of the reaction to Wallenstein's fall and the so-called "Troppau rebellion" in *SA* Brno (Cerroni MSS., etc.). The problem of Wallenstein had a vast influence on contemporary pamphleteering and even artistic work: this can be seen in all the larger Czech collections, especially in the section *Bellum Tricennale* at Mnichovo Hradiště, the town museums of Prague and Cheb (Eger), and among the drawings which belong to the castle library in Český Šternberk. There is more illustrative material in the former Waldstein gallery at the castle of Duchcov, great hall of the Waldstein palace in Prague, and the castles of Náchod, Frýdlant and Opočno.

CHAPTER EIGHT

Historians of recent decades who have investigated the years from 1635 to 1643 have shown a clear tendency to concentrate on France and Spain. The best introduction to Spanish problems is the book by J. H. Elliott (*Imperial Spain*) already mentioned under Chapter Three. Another volume by Elliott, on the Catalan revolt of the 1640s (*The Revolt of the Catalans*, Cambridge, 1963), is perhaps the most significant of all contributions to the understanding of Spain's rôle in the European politics of the period. It may be supplemented by P. Vilar: *La Catalogne dans l'Espagne moderne*, I, and on the question of French intervention – J. Sanabre: *La acciòn de Francia en Cataluña*, Barcelona, 1956. There is as yet no good survey of the revolution in Portugal, but F. Mauro has written a study of the contemporary Portuguese economy: *Le Portugal et l'Atlantique au XVIIe siècle, Paris*, 1960. Economic relations between Spain and Northern Europe are examined by H. Kellenbenz: *Unternehmerkräfte im Hamburger Portugal-und Spanienhandel 1590–1625*, Hamburg, 1954, and the same author has thrown light on some material aspects of the alliance between France and Sweden: "Hamburg und die französisch–schwedische Zusammenarbeit im Dreissigjährigen Krieg", *Zeitschrift des Vereins für Hamburgische Geschichte*, 49–50, 1964.

The France of Richelieu is the subject of books by V.-L. Tapié and R. Mandrou, both cited in the previous section. The Cardinal's extensive policies in the Netherlands are described in the early chapters of H. Lonchay: *La rivalité de la France et de l'Espagne aux Pays-Bas, 1635–1700*, which can be read in conjunction with volume four of Henri Pirenne's standard work: *Histoire de Belgique*, and A. Leman: *Richelieu et Olivares*, Lille, 1938. The important study of the Cardinal-Infant and Spanish policy by H. van der Essen: *Le Cardinal-Infant et la politique européene de l'Espagne, 1609–1641*, Louvain, 1944, unfortunately only takes us up to the year 1634.

It is equally regrettable that N. Ahnlund's biography of another major protagonist of these years, Chancellor Oxenstierna, could not be continued beyond 1632. There is however a useful new account of Swedish ambitions in a monograph on that country's rise to the status of great power: W. Than: *Den svenska utrikenpolitikens historia 1560–1648*, Stockholm, 1960. Interesting work on the Baltic states has been accomplished by the German historian Walther Hubatsch in a series of books: *Im Bannkreis der Ostsee*, Marburg, 1948; *Skandinavien und Deutschland im Wandel der Zeiten* (together with M. Gerhardt, 1950); *Unruhe des Nordens* Göttingen, 1956. It is also worth noting the response to Hubatsch from J. Peters in the pages of the *Zeitschrift für Geschichtswissenschaft*. An attempt to grasp wider dimensions of Baltic politics has been made, with mixed success, by J. Paul: *Europa im Osteeraum*, Göttingen, 1961.

Swedish activities in Bohemia and Moravia have a historiography reaching back to the pioneering studies of B. Dudík: *Schweden in Böhmen und Mähren 1640–1650*, Vienna, 1879; B. Bretholz: "Neue Aktenstücke zur Geschichte des Schwedenkrieges in Böhmen und Mähren", *Zeitschrift des Vereines für Geschichte Mährens und Schlesiens*, VIII, b. 12ff and J. Loserth: "Zur Geschichte der Stadt Olmütz in der Zeit der schwedischen Okupation", *Ibid.*, II, 1898. More recent work from the Swedish side is to be found in P. M. Hebbe: *Svenskarna i Böhmen och Mähren*, Uppsala, 1932, and – on the campaigns of Banér and Torstenson – L. Tingsten: *Fältmarskalkarna J. Banér och Lenart Torstenson säsom härforare*, Stockholm, 1932. There is an important analysis of the Bohemian question as a part of Swedish foreign policy in the introductory chapters of S. Göransson: *Den europeiska konfessionspolitikens upplösning 1654–1660*, Uppsala–Wiesbaden, 1956.

The basic factual account of developments within the Bohemian lands during the last years of the War is still that by A. Rezek: *Deje Čech a Moravy za Ferdinanda III az do konce třicetilleté valky*, Prague, 1890. This, together with volume I of E. Denis *La Bohême depuis la Montagne Blanche*, Paris, 1903, and the short summaries by O. Odložilík in *Československa Vlastiveda* IV, Prague, 1934, and J. V. Polišenský in *Přehled*, *Československých Dejin*, I, Prague, 1958, are the only sources of general information for this critical period in the history of the Czech nation. There are details of the Vlach revolt and its punishment in F. Dostál: "Historie Valachů ve velkém díle o československých dejinách", *Valašsko*, VI,, 1958, pp. 131ff.

After the fall of Wallenstein Bohemia and Moravia remained the material base which underpinned the activities of the Habsburgs and their diplomats and generals. It is therefore logical that so much significant correspondence has survived in Czech archives. The sixth volume of the *Documenta* will contain, in the first place, military and diplomatic documents left by Ottavio Piccolomini and Heinrich Schlick which deal primarily with Habsburg plans for involvement in Western Europe. The Piccolomini papers, formerly in the family castle at Náchod, suffered extensive damage in the last century, though this was partially redressed through the reacquisition of papers sold off earlier. They cover England, the Southern Netherlands, Spain and the Spanish provinces in Italy, and are augumented by the contents of the library which is still *in situ* at Náchod. The Schlick materials, on the other hand, give a wealth of information about the processes of central government in Vienna.

A second group of documents, as yet entirely unconsidered, is that relating to Wenzel Eusebius von Lobkowitz, later minister of Leopold I, who laid the foundations of his subsequent career while a junior associate of the generalissimo (*SA* Žitenice). Here too there is additional information in the Lobkovic libraries (University Library, Prague). The third major source is the military chancery of Matthias Gallas, that less than radiantly success-ful Imperial commander in the fight against the Swedes, covering the years 1633–47 (*SA* Děčín). Beyond these there are interesting collections already mentioned for previous periods: the Kolowrat and Colloredo papers in *SA* Zámrsk (the latter containing a series of copies of documents from Vienna); the *Autographs* of the Waldstein family archive in Mnichovo Hradiště, a surprisingly varied and useful anthology; the Schwarzenberg correspondence in Český Krumlov; the writings of the High Chancellor Slavata, dating from the first half of the 1640s (*SA* Jindřichův Hradec); some of the surviving records of the Silesian provincial adminis-tration (*SA* Opava).

The letters of Rudolph Thun (*SA* Děčín) come to an end in 1636, but they are replaced by those of the brothers Magnis (*SA* Brno), which throw further light on the relations of the Habs-burgs to Poland, and Moravian attitudes to the Swedish occupa-tion after 1642. In the same archive are the papers of Jan von Rottal, the national commissar and organiser of the campaign against the Vlachs. There is more information about the Swedes in Moravia scattered through various sections of *SA* Brno and Olomouc, while the district archives in the latter city contain the still incompletely-catalogued collection made by Béla Dudík in the last century. The writings of the Jakarcovskýs of Sudice are in the Černín family archive at Jindřichův Hradec.

CHAPTERS NINE AND TEN

The basic threads of the years 1643–50 are several: the final de-cline of Spain, mortally stricken by the wave of revolutions in 1640; the elimination of England from the European struggle by the events of 1640–42; the predominance of France over her Swedish and German allies, torn apart through their own dissen-sions; and the half-hearted attempts by Sweden to decide things on the battlefield, or at least to gain an advantageous diplomatic position, which led in the end to the inevitable peace compromise.

For Spain there are, beside works mentioned above, two sober summaries by Juan Reglá, the one in the *Introducciòn a la historia de España*, pp. 431ff., the other in the *New Cambridge Modern History*, V, 1961. On more specific aspects of the decline, see V. Palacio: *Derrota, agotamiento, decadencia en la España del siglo* XVII, Madrid, 1956; J. M. Jover: *Política mediterránea y política atlántica en la España de Feijóo*, Oviedo, 1956; M. Fraga Iribarne: *Don Diego de Sauvedra Fajardo y la diplomacia de su época*, Madrid, 1956. The latest general survey of the revolutionary seventeenth century in England is Hill's: *Reformation to Industrial Revolution*. The relation of England to Europe in the same period, especially to the United Provinces, is analyzed by J. R. Jones: *Britain and Europe in the Seventeenth Century*, London, 1966. The same subject is touched on repeatedly by C. R. Boxer: *The Dutch Seaborne Empire*, London, 1965.

In a series of articles B. F. Porshnev put forward the thesis that it was the struggle against revolutionary England and fear of an internal crisis inside France which led Mazarin to engineer a hasty and, for his allies, detrimental peace in Westphalia: "Angliiskaya respublika, frantsuzskaya fronda i Vestfalskii mir", *Sredniye Veka*, III, 1951, pp. 180–216; "Angliiskaya revolyuciya i sovremennaya jej Francia", *Angliiskaya burzhuaznaya revolyuciya*, II, pp. 71–89. This author has investigated Porshnev's views with the help of the Piccolomini correspondence (J. V. Polišenský: "Česká Otázka, habsburská politika a anglická revoluce 17. století", *Sborník Historický*, V, 1957, pp. 175–202), and comes to the conclusion that the people really contemplating action against England in 1647 and 1648 were not Spanish and French politicians but the Dutch stadholder Frederick Henry, and even more so his son William II of Orange. On this matter compare P. Geyl: *History of the Low Countries* (Frederick Henry and King Charles I, 1641–7, pp. 43–78; William II and the Stuarts 1647–50, pp. 79–109); on the Dutch withdrawal from the War see C. Smit: *Het Vredesverdrag van Münster, 30 januari 1648*, 1948; and J. J. Poelhekke: *De Vrede van Münster*, 1948.

Dutch social and economic development in the years before the conclusion of the separate peace of Münster are described by J. A. van Houtte: *Economische en sociale geschiedenis van de Lage Landen*, Zeist, 1964, pp. 136–214. There are two recent general accounts of the "Golden Age" in Dutch culture, one by H. A. Enno van Gelder: *Cultuurgeschiedenis van Nederland in vogelvlucht*, Aula–Boeken, 1965, pp. 108ff., the other by T. Wittman: *Nématalfödl Aranykora*, Budapest, 1965. Another side of this "Golden Age" appears from J. Presser's lecture on the poor in Holland: *Arm in de Gouden Eeuw*, Amsterdam, 1965. An approach (through archival sources) to the social composition of Amsterdam in these years can be found in J. V. Polišenský and S. Hart: "Praha a Amsterodam 17. a 18. století, *Československý Časopis Historický*, xv, 1967, pp. 827–846, and there is valuable material in the chapters contributed by N. Mout to the volume: *Komenský v Amsterodamu*, Prague, 1970.

Porshnev's book on popular uprisings before the Fronde has been mentioned several times. It was first published in Russian as: *Narodnye vosstanie vo Frantsii pered Frondoy*, Moscow/Leningrad, 1948, and subsequently in French translation as cited under Chapter One. There is an important reply to it by R. Mandrou: "Les soulèvements populaires et la société française du xviie siècle, *Annales*, 14, 1959, pp. 756–65, while a new edition of documents now provides further information (R. Mousnier: *Lettres et Mémoires addresés au Chancelier Séguier, 1633–49*, Paris, 1964). The latest work on the Fronde has come from a Dutch historian, E. H. Kossmann: *La Fronde*, Leiden, 1954.

The classic modern study of the Peace of Westphalia is Fritz Dickmann: *Der Westfälische Frieden*, Münster, 1959, which supersedes the more sketchy monograph by M. Braubach: *Der Westfälische Friede*, Münster, 1948. Some of the fundamental documents are made accessible in the *Axta Pacis Westphalicae* (*Instruktionen. Band I, Frankreich, Schweden, Kaiser*, Münster, 1962. From the Czech side the very substantial account by B. Šindelář: *Vestfálský Mír a Česká Otázka*, Prague, 1968, stands alone, though Šindelář's views may be found more accessible in two German articles: *Die böhmischen Exulanten in Sachsen und der Westfälische Friedenskongress*, Sborník prací FF UB, Brno, 1960, pp. 215–250; "Comenius und der Westfälische Friedenskongress, *Historica*, v, 1963, pp. 71–107.

There remain a number of books which tackle the broad question of the consequences of the War. The serious effects of protracted conflict during the period are discussed by J. U. Nef: "War and Economic Progress 1540–1640", *Economic History Review*, xii, 1942. S. H. Steinberg on the other hand, as we have seen, warns against exaggeration in this direction (*The "Thirty Years War"* ... pp. 92–122). Steinberg bases his conclusions on a work which I have not been able to see (R. Ergang: *The Myth of the all-destructive fury of the Thirty Years War*, Pocono Pines,

Pennsylvania, 1956). But two other authors whom he cites: K. F. Olechnowitz: *Handel unde Seeschiffahrt der späten Hanse*, Weimar, 1965, and J. A. van Houtte: "Onze zeventiende eeuw 'Ongelukseeuw'?" *Medelinghen Koningkije Vlaamse Academie*, 15, 1953, are dealing with very specific issues, and it is still dangerous to build overall theories on such evidence.

The closer one investigates the matter, the more difficult do generalisations appear. But the extent of the tragedy itself is clear. The economic condition of Bohemia has been analyzed by V. Pešák on the basis of the indebtedness of individual towns: *Obecní dluhy královských, venných a horných mest v Čechách, zvláš̌te Starého mesta pražského po třiceliteté válce*, Prague, 1933. For the state of the peasantry the great source is the extensive series of tax records, the *Berní Rula*. Unfortunately not all of these have yet been published (16 volumes out of 33 have appeared), but number two is of basic importance – K. Doskočil: *Popis Čech roku 1654*, Prague, 1953.

The seventh and last volume in the projected set of *Documenta Bohemo–Slovaca* will consist mainly of diplomatic documents connected with the peace negotiations in Münster and Osnabrück Most weighty among them are the papers of Ottavio Piccolomini with their Netherlandish, English, French and Italian purview (*SA* Zámrsk). Piccolomini was also involved in the subsequent talks with the Swedes which dragged on in Nuremberg until 1650. In the same archives are some important contemporary letters from Schlick and Colloredo. Gallas' chancery (*SA* Dečín) gives out in April 1647 and a more extensive source is provided by the papers of Johann Adolf von Schwarzenberg, now in Český Krumlov. They concern especially his mission to General Hatzfeld in north Germany during 1643 and 1644 and his stay at the court of Archduke Leopold Wilhelm in Brussels from 1645 to 1660, during which he was kept informed of the Westphalian talks. Schwarzenberg heard of developments in Münster and Osnabrück through the Spanish representative De Brun, while by the Imperial ambassador in Madrid, Caretto, he was fed with news from the Spanish capital. Since he was also in close contact with Vienna he is a first-class witness. The useful memoranda of Dr Vollmar are in the same collection. There are relations about the 1644 debates in Münster among the *Historica* in the Dietrichstein *FA* (*SA* Brno), and some Trautmannsdorf fragments in *SA* Klatovy and Klášterec nad Ohří. Light is thrown on the situation in Lorraine and the Franche-Comte by the family papers of the

Belrupts (*SA* Janovice). For Moravia, besides the materials quoted in previous sections, many scattered deposits survive in Kroměříž, Holešov, Olomouc and especially Brno. The latter archives contain the important Magnis collection for the years 1644–9.

The smaller-scale records, local administration and the rest, are vast, and no start can be made on listing them here. Yet they are vital for any real analysis of the full effects of the War: documents like the long series of patrimonial registers which begin in the 1640s and regularly continue into the present century. For the war years – as we have seen in the case of Zlín – they are frequently in no order at all. This in itself represents a major challenge to historians of the future.

APPENDIX

Most important variants of Central European place names

Form used	Czech	German	Hungarian
Breslau	Vratislav		
Brno		Brünn	
Budweis	Budějovice		
Čáslav		Czaslau	
Eger	Cheb		
Elbogen	Loket		
Hradec Králove		Königgratz	
Ipoly (Hung.)		Eipel	
Ivančice		Eibenschütz	
Jägerndorf	Krnov		
Jankov		Jankau	
Jičín		Gitschin	
Jihlava		Iglau	
Kassa (Hung.)	Košice	Kaschau	
Kolozsvár (Hung.)		Klausenburg	Cluj (Romanian)
Kremsier	Kroměříž		
Kuttenberg	Kutná Hora		
Litoměrice	Leitmeritz		
Locse (Hung.)	Levoča	Leutschau	
Mikulov		Nikolsburg	
Mladá Boleslav		Jungbunzlau	
Morava (river)		March	Morva
Most		Brüx	
Nagyszombat (Hung.)	Trnava	Tyrnau	
Neuhäusel	Nove Zámky		Érsekújvár
Olomouc		Olmütz	
Pilsen	Plzen		
Prague	Praha	Prag	
Pressburg	Bratislava		Pozsony
Teschen	Těšín		
Trebon		Wittingau	
Troppau	Opava		
Turóczszentmárton (Hung.)	Turčiansky Svätý Martin		
Ústí nad Labem		Aussig	
Vág (river; Hung.)	Váh	Waag	
Vltava		Moldau	
Žatec		Saaz	
Zlín	now officially called Gottwaldov		
Znojmo		Znaim	

Index

INDEX

Also available from NEL Mentor

Shaftesbury

G. F. A. Best

Shaftesbury's long career was largely devoted to relieving the condition of the destitute of Victorian England. Yet, just as his other achievements have been overshadowed by this work, so the complexity of his motives and personality have been hidden by the popular legend of the simple, pious and soft-hearted philanthropist.

Professor Best assesses this legend. He reveals that Shaftesbury's championing of reform and his share in the foundation of a public health service were no less important than his success in rescuing the poor from the intolerable living and working conditions which resulted from the industrial revolution. He also discusses those aspects of Shaftesbury's personality which the Victorians were eager to overlook – the self-righteousness, violence and suspicion present in the aristocrat who inspired so much pity and compassion for the plight of the poor.

G. F. A. Best is Professor of History at the University of Sussex.

NEW ENGLISH LIBRARY

Frederick the Great

Ludwig Reiners

Frederick the Great, even during his lifetime, became a legend. He was called 'one of the greatest soldiers ever born', 'a hero'; yet Ernst Arndt, the poet, said 'Frederick the Great made Germany small.'

This informal biography' shows Frederick himself, the man behind the myths. He is seen as an individual of outstanding interest and importance, restored to life through the author's enthusiasm and skill and his thorough research into the voluminous records available under the heading: Frederick the Great.

NEW ENGLISH LIBRARY

Luther and the Reformation

V. H. H. Green

The Reformation marked a decisive turning point between
the relatively static medieval world and the restlessness
of the present day. Politics and religion were inextricably
linked and with the Reformation the political face of
Europe was changed.

Martin Luther was at the heart of this change: whether he
was its agent or instrument is still a matter of some dispute.
In this new assessment of the man and his life Dr. Green
clarifies the background to the Reformation and the
atmosphere in which Luther's role was to develop. In the
context of Luther's life he traces the stages in the break
with the Roman church and accurately describes the
importance of this man.
Dr. Vivian Green is a doctor of divinity of Cambridge and
Oxford universities and a Fellow of the Royal Historical
Society.

NEW ENGLISH LIBRARY

The Siege of Paris

Robert Baldick

The Siege of Paris in the autumn and winter of 1870–71 was remarkable in several respects. It was the last full-scale siege of a European capital, the first occasion of the indiscriminate bombardment of a civilian population and the origin of a division in the French nation which has still not been healed. Yet for a long time it has been regarded as a heaven-sent retribution for the sins of a frivolous society or as an amusing interlude in the grim history of European conflict.

Robert Baldick has put the Siege into perspective. THE SIEGE OF PARIS is not military history, but rather an entertaining, informative and successful attempt to portray life in Paris during those dark and momentous days in her history.

NEW ENGLISH LIBRARY

Gods and Heroes of the Greeks

H. J. Rose

THE HANDBOOK OF GREEK MYTHOLOGY by
H. J. Rose is known to all students of mythology, but for
too long his simpler handbook GODS AND HEROES
OF THE GREEKS has been unavailable. In it he sets
out clearly the powerful stories of the ancient Greeks,
combining his meticulous academic skills with a readily
understandable style. This the first paperback edition of
this remarkable work.

Michael Grant, himself author of a book of myths
(MYTHS OF THE GREEKS AND ROMANS) called
Rose's work 'The most reliable general account of the
myths'.

Professor Rose was Emeritus Professor of Greek in the
University of St. Andrews.

NEW ENGLISH LIBRARY

Viking America

James Robert Enterline

VIKING AMERICA is a startling book which questions
most of the theories about the discovery and colonisation
of North America. Enterline argues that Norsemen sailed
to America and established colonies there; Nordic maps
may have reached Columbus, thus partly revealing to him
what he is thought to have discovered. He also contends
that the legendary 'Vinland' was actually located in
sub-Arctic Canada. These theories make for a thoroughly
controversial book which is at once startling and
fascinating.

NEW ENGLISH LIBRARY